STUDY GUIDE
FOR USE WITH
-
MICROECONOMICS
Second Edition

DAVID N. HYMAN

Prepared by
Donald P. Maxwell
University of Central Oklahoma

IRWIN
Homewood, IL 60430
Boston, MA 02116

Printed in the United States of America.

ISBN 0-256-09100-5

2 3 4 5 6 7 8 9 0 MG 8 7 6 5 4 3 2

CONTENTS

PART I

INTRODUCTION TO ECONOMICS

PART EXERCISE

Inside Information: *Statistical Abstract of the United States*

In chapters 1 and 2 you will learn about marginal analysis and opportunity cost. Your choice to attend a university involves an analysis of the extra benefits and costs associated with the consumption of additional years of education. In addition to the cost of tuition and books and other explicit outlays, a major cost of your education is the income that you sacrifice while being a full-time student.

Suppose the extra benefit (increased future income and other nonpecuniary benefits) from attending your university another year is $50,000. Tuition, books, and other expenses are $10,000 per year. Use the earnings and income data in the *Statistical Abstract of the United States* to get average or median annual earnings which can be used as a measure of the sacrificed income during the year. Be sure to note the demographic and industry characteristics that underlie your data (race, occupation, union, industry, sex, region, etc.). If the total cost of an additional year of education is the sum of tuition, books, other expenses, and sacrificed income, would you attend another year of college? Why?

1   ECONOMICS: WHAT IT'S ALL ABOUT

CHAPTER CONCEPTS

After studying your text, attending class, and completing this chapter, you should be able to:

1. Describe the mechanism of the economy and the discipline of economics.
2. Understand the concepts of scarcity and opportunity cost.
3. Discuss major branches of economic inquiry: microeconomics, macroeconomics, positive analysis, and normative analysis.
4. Understand the concept of an economic model and its uses.
5. Explain rational behavior and marginal analysis, a method of analyzing the way we make decisions.

THE CHAPTER IN BRIEF

Fill in the blanks to summarize chapter content.

Economics is a study concerned with the use society makes of its (1)_____ (scarce, abundant) resources in attempting to satisfy the (2)_____ (normal, unlimited) desires of its members. The economy represents the mechanism or structure that organizes scarce resources for the purpose of producing the goods and services desired by society. (3)_____ (Inflation, Scarcity) is the fundamental problem facing all economies. It is also the reason decisions or choices involve (4)_____ (opportunity costs, production costs).

The real cost or opportunity cost of any choice is the value of the sacrifice required in making that decision. That sacrifice represents the foregone opportunity to pursue the (5)_____ (next best, any) decision. A fundamental problem confronting an economy is how to best meet the desires of individuals in a world of scarcity. Economies do this by addressing several basic questions: (a) What will be produced? (b) How will goods and services be produced? (c) To whom will goods and services be distributed? An economy's answers to the first two questions reveal the (6)_____ (fairness, efficiency) with which resources are used to satisfy the desires of society. The third question requires that society make value judgments regarding the distribution of income.

The two major branches of economic analysis are macroeconomics and microeconomics. (7)_____ (Macroeconomics, Microeconomics) is concerned with the economic behavior of individual decision-making units in the economy. (8)_____ (Macroeconomics, Microeconomics) is concerned with the effects of the aggregate economic behavior of all individuals, firms, and institutions. Inflation and unemployment are two topics that are studied in (9)_____ (macroeconomics, microeconomics), whereas the determination of prices and an analysis of markets are subjects dealt with in (10)_____ (macroeconomics, microeconomics).

Positive economic analysis seeks to determine (11)_____ ("what ought to be," "what is"). (12)_____ (Positive, Normative) economic analysis emphasizes the "should" or "ought to" approach. Positive analysis tries to uncover cause-and-effect relationships that are subject to empirical observation and verification. In contrast, normative analysis depends upon the analyst's (13)_____ (value judgment, mathematical skills). Disagreements arise among practitioners in any discipline. With positive analysis, it is possible to resolve disagreements empirically. With normative analysis, disagreements stem from different value systems and must be resolved in ways other than looking at the "facts."

Economic analysis helps us understand the world around us. It helps us understand the functioning of the various sectors in the economy and the choices made by individual decision-making units. (14)_____ (Assumptions, Economic theories) simplify reality so that the underlying cause-and-effect relationships among variables can be understood. (15)_____ (Economic variables, Data) are quantities or dollar amounts that have more than one value. Theories are necessary in order to better understand the complexities of reality.

(16)_____(A bar graph, An economic model) is a simplified way of expressing a theory. It can be expressed verbally, graphically, in tables, or mathematically. Assumptions underlie a theory because theories are (17)_____(depictions of, abstractions from) reality, and it is necessary to establish the environment and motivation of people for which the theory holds. Economic models can be used to develop hypotheses. A hypothesis is a statement of relationship between two variables that can be tested by empirical verification. A good model is one that can generate accurate predictions. But even a model that does not predict perfectly can still be useful in helping us understand the causal relationships among variables and the consequence of the assumptions underlying the model. The causal relationships that we want to understand are difficult to isolate unless we make the assumption of (18)_____(*ceteris paribus*, the invisible hand). Otherwise, we cannot be sure that we have identified the exact relationship between the two variables of interest.

Economic analysis makes the assumption of rationality. Rationality means that most people behave as if they are comparing the additional gains or benefits from a choice or decision to the sacrifices or opportunity costs associated with that decision. The opportunity cost of a decision is known as its marginal (19)_____(benefit, cost). If the marginal benefits of a decision exceed the marginal costs, the individual's net gain or benefit (20)_____(increases, decreases). If the marginal cost of a decision exceeds the marginal benefits, the decision would not be undertaken because the individual would experience a net (21)_____(loss, gain). If a choice or decision is pursued to the point where marginal benefits and marginal costs are equal, the individual achieves the (22)_____(maximum, minimum) net gain.

KEY TERMS REVIEW

Write the key term from the list below next to its definition.

Key Terms

Economy
Economics
Opportunity cost
Microeconomics
Marginal analysis
Theory
Variable
Economic model
Marginal cost

Macroeconomics
Scarcity
Positive analysis
Normative analysis
Ceteris Paribus
Behavioral assumption
Rational behavior
Marginal benefit

Definitions

1. _____: the cost of choosing to use resources for one purpose measured by the sacrifice of the next best alternative for using those resources.

2. _____: economic analysis concerned with the individual choices made by participants in the economy—also called *price theory*.

3. _____: seeks to forecast the impact of changes in economic policies or conditions on observable items, such as production, sales, prices, and personal incomes. It then tries to determine who gains and who loses as a result of the changes.

4. _____: the mechanism through which the use of labor, land, structures, vehicles, equipment, and natural resources is organized to satisfy the desires of people who live in a society.

5. _____: the imbalance between the desires of people in a society and the means of satisfying those desires.

6. _____: evaluates the desirability of alternative outcomes according to underlying value judgments about what is good or bad.

7. _____: a study of society's use of scarce resources in the satisfaction of the unlimited desires of its members.

8. _____: economic analysis that considers the overall performance of the economy with respect to total national production, consumption, average prices, and employment levels.

9. _____: a quantity or dollar amount that can have more than one value.

10. _____: "other things being equal"—used to acknowledge that other influences aside from the one whose effect is being analyzed must be controlled for in testing a hypothesis.

11. _____: establishes people's motivation for the purpose of understanding cause-and-effect relationships among economic variables.

12. _____: a decision-making technique involving a systematic comparison of benefits and costs of actions.

13. _____: the additional benefit obtained when one extra unit of an item is obtained.

14. _____: the sacrifice made to obtain an additional unit of an item.

15. _____: an abstraction or simplification of actual relationships; establishes cause-and-effect relationships.

16. _____ : seeking to gain by choosing actions for which the benefit exceeds the cost.

17. _____ : a simplified way of expressing economic behavior or how some sector of the economy functions.

CONCEPT REVIEW

Concept 1: *Describe the mechanism of the economy*

1. List the three basic questions that all economies must answer:

   a. _____

   b. _____

   c. _____

Concept 2: *Opportunity cost*

2. Identify the likely opportunity costs associated with the following decisions.

   Hint: Think in terms of what would likely be sacrificed in pursuing a decision. In other words, what would have been the next best use of your time, money, or resources?

   a. You decide to attend a university full time.

   b. Your decision to purchase a new home results in a larger portion of your income committed to mortgage payments.

   c. You are having such a good time in the Caribbean, that you decide to extend your vacation by taking an additional week of vacation at no pay.

   d. As a manager, you decide to commit some of the corporation's resources to a plant expansion project.

Concept 3: *Positive and normative analysis*

3. In the blanks provided, indicate whether the following statements involve positive (P) or normative (N) analysis:

   a. _____ Fred ought to get his act together.

   b. _____ My professor arrives for class late every morning.

   c. _____ The drought in the Midwest is increasing corn prices.

   d. _____ Government is too obtrusive and therefore its power should be reduced.

   e. _____ Lower state income tax rates are always preferable to higher rates.

   f. _____ Poverty is a serious problem in the United States.

4. Monitor your own statements as you interact with friends, family members, or fellow students and try to determine if your statements are based upon fact or observation or value judgments. For one day, carry a sheet of paper divided into two columns—label one column "fact" and the other "value judgment." Record your interactions with others and think about whether positive or normative statements are being made.

Concept 4: *Economic models and uses*

5. Develop a hypothesis regarding the level of family spending on goods and services and the level of family income. Describe that hypothesized relationship by setting up two columns of data reflecting the variables in your hypothesis. Is the hypothesized relationship a positive or negative relationship? Suppose that you gathered actual data on your variables and for some

6

families your hypothesized relationship did not hold. Of what use is the *ceteris paribus* assumption in trying to isolate the relationship between family spending and income?

Family Spending on Goods   Family Income ($)
and Services ($)

6. Suppose that you want to investigate the relationship between prices of restaurant meals and the quantity of meals demanded by local area households. Economic theory implies that there is a negative relationship between price and quantity demanded but that income, tastes, preferences, and other variables also influence quantity demanded. Clearly state your hypothesis and its underlying assumptions.

Concept 5: *Marginal analysis*

7. Suppose child care legislation is enacted providing for child care payments of up to $1,000 to low-income working families and tax credits for other families with children under age 4 in which at least one parent works. Assume that you are a single parent with young children. Using marginal analysis, assess the impact of such a program on your decision to work or to work additional hours.

8. Assume that the price you are willing to pay for an additional unit of a good measures the marginal benefit received. How could you measure the marginal cost of the decision to consume that extra unit?

9. A rational decision maker comparing the extra gains and losses of a decision will _____ net gains if the decision or choice is pursued to the point where _____ equals _____. Explain the logic of this statement.

Advanced application: opportunity costs

10. Suppose that you are a farmer capable of producing corn or soybeans. Over the years you have maintained records regarding your total production of both crops. Assume that you have made full and efficient use of your resources throughout this period. Furthermore, assume that the only reason corn relative to soy production has changed is because of your desire to grow the combination of crops that produce the highest net farm income. Referring to your production data below, determine the opportunity cost of producing an additional bushel of soybeans. If the current price of a bushel of corn is $7, what is the dollar value of that opportunity cost?

Production Data *(000s of bushels)*

	Soy	Corn
1981	100	20
1982	50	40
1983	25	50
1984	0	60
1985	75	30
1986	150	0
1987	125	10

a. Opportunity cost measured in bushels of corn: _____ bushels

b. Opportunity cost measured in dollars: $ _____

Advanced application: marginal analysis

11. You are an administrator of the Environmental Protection Agency concerned with allocating cleanup funds from the agency's Superfund for the removal of toxic wastes. The following data represent the marginal benefits and costs associated with removing units of pollution from a polluted river. Your task is to decide if there is a net gain to society from cleaning the river and what level of pollution reduction would maximize that net gain.

Units of Pollution Reduction	Marginal Benefits	Marginal Costs
	(millions of dollars)	
0	$0	$0
1	10	2
2	8	4
3	6	6
4	4	8
5	2	10

   a. Is there a net gain to society from cleaning the river? Discuss.

   b. Nets gains are maximized at a level of pollution reduction of _____, where marginal benefits and marginal costs are _____.

MASTERY TEST

Select the best answer.

1. Which of the following best describes the study of economics?
   a. A study concerned with how to make money
   b. A fuzzy combination of Wall Street and insurance
   c. A study of how society uses its goods and services in determining the proper distribution of income
   d. A study of how society uses its scarce economic resources in satisfying the unlimited desires of society

2. The mechanism through which resources are organized in order to satisfy the desires of society is known as:
   a. a corporation.
   b. government.
   c. an economy.
   d. a factory.

3. Scarcity means that:
   a. resources are in finite supply.
   b. poverty takes its toll on those with limited means.
   c. choices are unnecessary.
   d. an imbalance exists between desires and the means by which those desires are satisfied.

4. The real cost of a choice or decision is its opportunity cost. Which of the following best defines opportunity cost?
   a. The actual dollar outlay required to produce a good or service
   b. The value of the forgone next best alternative
   c. The value to the resources required to implement the decision
   d. The value of the loss that occurs when a speculative investment does not meet profit expectations

5. If a state government had a limited amount of tax and other revenue but decided to substantially increase the amount of appropriations to public education, appropriations to other functions such as corrections, health, and welfare would diminish. What concept is represented by this statement?
   a. Opportunity costs
   b. Normative analysis
   c. Efficiency
   d. None of the above

6. Microeconomics is a branch of economics that:
   a. studies the impact of inflation on the unemployment rate.
   b. studies the behavior of individual decision-making units in the economy.
   c. studies the effects and consequences of the aggregate behavior of all decision-making units.
   d. is only concerned with the determination of income.

7. Macroeconomics is a branch of economics that:
   a. studies the effects and consequences of the aggregate behavior of all decision-making units in the economy.
   b. is only concerned with the determination of individual market prices.
   c. studies the behavior of individual decision-making units in the economy.
   d. studies neither inflation nor unemployment.

8. Topics such as business cycles, unemployment, and inflation are studied in _____, whereas the determination of prices and the study of individual markets are studied in

   _____.
   a. positive analysis/normative analysis
   b. normative analysis/positive analysis
   c. microeconomics/macroeconomics
   d. macroeconomics/microeconomics

9. Which of the following involves value judgments?
   a. Normative analysis
   b. Positive analysis
   c. The search for a superconducting material operable at room temperature
   d. The decision to install lifeline (discount) electric utility rates for the elderly
   e. A and d

10. _____ makes "ought to" or "should" statements, whereas _____ makes statements based upon observable events and therefore can be subjected to empirical verification.
    a. positive analysis/normative analysis
    b. normative analysis/positive analysis
    c. macroeconomics/microeconomics
    d. microeconomics/macroeconomics

11. The decision-making technique involving a systematic comparison of the benefits and costs of actions is known as:
    a. deductive reasoning.
    b. total gains analysis.
    c. marginal analysis.
    d. *ceteris paribus*.

12. A/An _____ is a simplification of reality seeking to uncover the underlying cause-and-effect relationships among economic _____.
    a. assumptions/variables
    b. economic theory/assumptions
    c. hypothesis/theories
    d. economic theory/variables

13. Which of the following is true regarding economic variables?
    a. Economic variables have more than one value.
    b. Economic variables are quantities or dollar amounts.
    c. Economic variables are necessary to economic theories and models.
    d. All of the above.

14. A/An _____ is a simplified way of expressing an economic theory.
    a. economic model
    b. assumption
    c. abstraction
    d. economic principle

15. Which of the following assumptions is necessary in order to isolate the relationship between two variables?
    a. "All things allowed to vary"
    b. "All things held constant"
    c. "*Ceteris paribus*"
    d. B and c

16. If gasoline prices rise, the quantity of gasoline demanded will fall. This statement is a/an:
    a. assumption.
    b. theory.
    c. abstraction.
    d. hypothesis.

17. If household purchases of automobiles are determined by both the level of household income and the interest rate and you want to isolate the relationship between interest rates and auto sales, you must assume:
    a. that the interest rate remains unchanged.
    b. that auto sales remain unchanged.
    c. that household income remains unchanged.
    d. none of the above because you would want to know both the effect of interest rates and income on auto sales.

18. Which of the following best defines rational behavior?
    a. Seeking to gain by choosing to undertake actions for which the marginal benefits exceed the associated marginal costs
    b. A comparison of the total gains and losses from a decision
    c. Decisions that avoid habit or impulse purchases
    d. Improving net gain by pursuing decisions in which the marginal costs of a decision exceed the marginal benefits

19. _____ can be defined as the extra benefit received from undertaking some action.
    a. Total benefit
    b. Total gain
    c. Marginal benefit
    d. Total net gain

20. _____ can be defined as the extra cost associated with some action.
    a. Total cost
    b. Marginal cost
    c. Total loss
    d. Total net loss

21. The total net gain from a decision or action reaches a _____ when a decision or action is pursued to the point where _____ equals _____.
    a. maximum, total cost, total benefit
    b. minimum, marginal benefit, marginal cost
    c. minimum, total benefit, marginal benefit
    d. maximum, marginal benefit, marginal cost

22. The sacrifice made to obtain an additional unit of an item is known as:
    a. opportunity cost.
    b. the maximum tradeoff.
    c. marginal cost.
    d. a and c.
    e. b and c.

23. You are an executive earning an annual income of $50,000. You are considering quitting your job and returning to college to complete a degree. You estimate that the cost of tuition and books will be $8,000 for the year. The total cost of completing your education:
    a. is the cost of tuition and books only.
    b. is the opportunity cost and is less than $8000.
    c. is the opportunity cost which is slightly larger than the cost of tuition and books because transportation costs need to be considered.
    d. is several times larger than your outlay on books and tuition and consists mainly of your forgone income during the year.

24. Suppose you are considering voting for a politician, in part, because the politician says that higher taxes are bad. His political opponent argues that higher taxes may or may not cause serious work disincentives.
    a. The preferred politician's position is based upon positive analysis.
    b. The political opponent's argument is based upon normative analysis.
    c. The political opponent's argument is heavily influenced by personal value judgments and is thus an example of positive analysis.
    d. Neither politician is employing normative analysis because both individuals are basing their comments on "facts."
    e. The preferred politician is expressing a value judgement and is using normative analysis.

25. As a manager for a local retailer, you collect product price and sales data to determine how sales are influenced by price changes. You expect to find that when prices rise, quantities purchased decrease and vice versa. Instead, you find the following result: higher prices are associated with more goods purchased. Which one of the following statements is correct?
    a. The manager has shown that intuition serves as an unreliable guide in analysis.
    b. The unexpected result is an indication that it is necessary to collect and analyze data before predicting outcomes.
    c. The manager did not isolate the relationship between product price and quantities purchased. He did not make the *ceteris paribus* assumption. Thus, it is uncertain whether observed changes in quantities purchased are the result of price changes or other influences.
    d. Observation should precede theory. Explanations should always be made to fit the facts.

26. Fred chooses to go on a date with Sarah, but by doing so sacrifices the opportunity to take Mary. Fred's choice reveals:
    a. that Fred is not maximizing his net gains (net benefits) because he could date both ladies.
    b. that Fred's perceived marginal benefits from his choice are greater than the opportunity costs.
    c. that Fred's sacrifice (opportunity cost) is greater than the marginal benefits realized from the date with Sarah.
    d. None of the above—People do not use marginal analysis when making personal choices.

27. The perceived value or benefit to you from a pizza is $9. The pizza's price is $11. Will you purchase the pizza?
    a. Yes, because I am a billionaire and price is no consideration.
    b. No, as a billionaire, I still nevertheless maximize my net gains or benefits by purchasing up to the point where marginal benefits no longer exceed marginal costs.
    c. No, because the price of the pizza exceeds my opportunity cost.
    d. No, the marginal benefit associated with consuming the pizza exceeds the marginal cost.

THINK IT THROUGH

1. Define economics, including its branches, microeconomics and macroeconomics. What are some topics typically addressed by each of these branches?

2. Explain why scarcity and opportunity costs are related. Give an example from your personal or business experiences of the opportunity cost of a decision.

3. As you will discover later in the text, under certain assumptions it can be shown theoretically that a perfectly competitive economy will produce a distribution of income where labor receives an income based upon its productive contribution to the enterprise. This is consistent with the protestant ethic which states that hard work and reward should go hand in hand. These statements involve both positive and normative analysis. Discuss.

4. Define the concepts of economic theory and economic models. Discuss the importance of assumptions underlying models and theories.

5. Pollution is harmful to society, and the reduction of pollution levels increase society's total benefits. But if a 50% reduction in the pollution level resulted in an equality between the marginal benefits and marginal costs associated with pollution reduction, society would be better off if pollution were not eliminated completely. Reconcile the two statements.

6. A rational person would never engage in habit or impulse buying. Discuss.

7. A hypothesis requires the use of the *ceteris paribus* assumption. Why? Give an example.

8. A theory must depict reality. Do you agree? Explain.

CHAPTER ANSWERS

The Chapter in Brief

1. Scarce 2. Unlimited 3. Scarcity 4. Opportunity cost 5. Next best 6. Efficiency 7. Microeconomics 8. Macroeconomics 9. Macroeconomics 10. Microeconomics 11. "What is" 12. Normative 13. Value judgments 14. Economic theories 15. Economic variables 16. Economic model 17. Abstractions from 18. *Ceteris paribus* 19. Cost 20. Increase 21. Loss 22. Maximum

Key Terms Review

1. Opportunity costs 2. Microeconomics 3. Positive analysis 4. Economy 5. Scarcity 6. Normative analysis 7. Economics 8. Macroeconomics 9. Variable 10. *Ceteris paribus* 11. Behavioral assumptions 12. Marginal analysis 13. Marginal benefit 14. Marginal cost 15. Theory 16. Rational behavior 17. Economic model

Concept Review

1. a. What will be produced?
   b. How will goods and services be produced?
   c. To whom will goods and services be distributed?

2. a. If you attend a university full time, there are a number of potential sacrifices all of which have value. The most obvious sacrifice is the potential income you could have earned had you been employed full time. You may have less time to spend with your family and friends, as well as less leisure time. Direct outlays on tuition, room, and board could have been invested or saved.
   b. As recently as the early 1970s it was not uncommon for homeowners to allocate only 15% of their incomes to mortgage payments. Today it is more common for families to spend as much as 25% to 35% of their incomes for housing. If you commit a much larger share of your income to housing, given scarcity (or a limited income), you must cut your spending elsewhere. The reduction in the value of goods and services consumed as a result of purchasing a more expensive home represents the opportunity cost of your decision.
   c. If you choose to take a week of vacation without pay, you obviously sacrifice the income you would have earned otherwise. That extra week, as a result, is much more costly to you than the previous week of vacation.
   d. If corporate funds are to be used for a specific project, they cannot be used for alternative investment projects. Depending on the needs of the firm, the funds could be invested in financial assets generating an interest income. The funds could be used for other investment projects yielding income. Businesses interested in achieving the highest level of profit will usually allocate funds to the projects yielding the highest return because to do otherwise would mean that the firm would be sacrificing opportunities to earn profit.

3. a. N b. P c. P d. N e. N f. N

5. *Hypothesis*: Other things held constant, family spending on goods and services is expected to be positively related to family income.

   If upon gathering data on family spending and income it is found that the relationship between spending and income is not positive, that does not mean that your hypothesis is invalid. To determine the validity of your hypothesis, you must isolate the relationship you are interested in from all other variables that might influence family spending. If you do not, you cannot be sure that an increase in family spending is the result of increases in income or some third variable.

6. *Hypothesis*: Other things being the same, the price of restaurant meals and the quantity of restaurant meals demanded are expected to be inversely (negatively) related.

   The *ceteris paribus* assumption is necessary to control for other factors that influence quantity demanded, such as income and tastes and preferences. For instance, prices could be falling but incomes could fall as well. A family might dine out less often even at lower prices if their income has fallen.

7. As a working parent and particularly a single working parent, one of the major costs associated with work is child care. If you worked full time at the minimum wage of $4.25 per hour and paid $450 per month for child care for two children, you would have $230 dollars left over to support you and your family. There is little incentive to work full time for a month just to bring home $230. But suppose that as a result of new legislation, $100 of that monthly child care bill is paid for by the government. You are now left with $330 per month. This amount, although insufficient to meet the minimum needs of a family of three, is nevertheless still very important. If you were deterred from working before the new law, publicly subsidized child care payments increase the net gain to you from work and might induce you to seek employment. If you are already working, these payments might induce you to work additional hours because now the net gains from work are higher.

   The marginal benefits from working an additional hour include among other things the value of goods and services that can be purchased with the income earned from that hour of work. The marginal cost of work involves the sacrifices incurred in order to work. These sacrifices include the loss of leisure time, the loss of time spent with family and friends, and the resources spent on such things as child care and transportation that could have otherwise been spent on goods and services.

   Child care subsidies can be viewed as reducing the marginal cost of an hour of work or as increasing the marginal benefits realized from work. A reduction in day care costs increases the amount of the hourly wage available for non-day care expenditures. In this sense, the marginal benefit of an hour of work increases. Regardless of how the problem is viewed, total net gains from work increase. This will likely increase employment among single parents.

8. The marginal cost of a decision to consume a unit of a good is the sacrificed next-preferred goods that could have been consumed. The dollar value of this forgone consumption is a measure of marginal cost.

9. Maximize, marginal costs, marginal benefits

   If marginal benefits exceed marginal costs from some action, a person can add more to his or her total benefits than total costs by undertaking the action. In other words, net benefit or gain increases. As long as marginal benefits exceed marginal costs, total net gains can be increased by pursuing an activity. When an activity has been pursued to the point where marginal benefits and costs are equal, no further increases to net benefits can be realized because the addition to total benefits would just be offset by the addition to total costs of the action.

10. a. Two fifths of a bushel of corn. Historical production data reveal that for every 10,000-bushel increase in corn production, there is a 25,000-bushel decrease in soy output. Because the farmer is fully using his or her resources and employing these resources efficiently, the only way soy production can be increased is by withdrawing resources from corn production and employing those resources in soy production. Consequently, for every bushel increase in corn production, there is a 2.5-bushel decrease in soy production. In

other words, for every additional bushel of soy produced, corn production must be reduced by two fifths of a bushel.

    b.   Two fifths of a bushel times $7 per bushel = $2.80. The opportunity cost of producing a bushel of soy measured in dollars represents the dollar value of that sacrificed output of corn.

11. a.   Yes, because marginal benefits from pollution reduction up to a point exceed the sacrifice incurred in reducing pollution.

    b.   3, equal at $6 million. At this point, society's total benefits and costs equal $24 million and $12 million, respectively. Society's net gain is therefore $12 million. No other level of pollution reduction will result in as large of a net gain.

Mastery Test

1. d 2. c 3. d 4. b 5. a 6. b 7. a 8. d 9. e 10. b 11. c 12. d 13. d 14. a 15. c 16. d 17. c 18. a 19. c 20. b 21. d 22. d 23. d 24. e 25. c 26. b 27. b

Think it Through

1. Economics is a study of how society uses its scarce resources to satisfy the unlimited wants of its members. Macroeconomics is a study of the effects of the aggregate economic behavior of all decision-making units in the economy, whereas microeconomics is concerned with an analysis of the decision making of individual firms, households, or other decision-making units. Business cycles, inflation, and unemployment are topics covered in macroeconomics. Microeconomics, also known as *price theory*, analyzes among other things individual markets and the determination of prices.

2. If there were no scarcity, the opportunity costs of decisions requiring the use of resources would be zero. There would be such a thing as a "free lunch." If resources were available everywhere and in unlimited supply, the farmer in the above example could at any time produce more soy or corn without having to sacrifice the output of the other.

3. The first statement regarding a competitive economy's ability to reward labor on the basis of labor's productive contribution is deduced from economic theory, which itself is a collection of postulates based upon empirically verifiable observations. In this sense, this statement involves positive analysis. The second statement declares that this method of income distribution is "good." But this is based upon a value system consistent with the protestant ethic, which is only one of many possible value systems. It is therefore a normative statement.

4. Economic theory is a simplification of reality seeking to establish and explain important cause-and-effect relationships in the economy. An economic model is a simplified way of expressing a theory. A model can be presented verbally, in tables, in graphs, or mathematically. Assumptions are necessary for both theories and models because they outline the environment or motivation of people for which the theory and model hold.

5. If pollution reduction were undertaken to the point where marginal benefit and marginal cost were equal and that happened to be at a 50% level of pollution reduction, then no further net gains to society could be realized by additional reductions in pollution. In fact, if additional pollution reduction beyond the 50% level resulted in marginal costs exceeding marginal benefits, society would experience a net loss and be worse off than when there was more pollution.

6. In fact it might be quite rational for a person to engage in habit or impulse buying if that person experiences psychic loss, dissatisfaction, or stress associated with certain actions or choices. A person may buy the first used car he or she sees but may be doing so in part because of a distaste for bargaining and haggling. A person may shop only locally because of an aversion to driving in traffic.

7. A hypothesis is a statement of relationship between two economic variables. To be certain that you have isolated the cause-and-effect relationship between the two variables, it is necessary to hold the effect of other influencing variables constant. Otherwise, you cannot be sure that the relationship you have hypothesized is valid or instead results from some third variable that you have not considered.

8. A good theory yields accurate predictions, but even a theory that predicts inaccurately is of value in establishing cause-and-effect relationships and determining the significance of assumptions.

APPENDIX TO CHAPTER 1:
GRAPHS: A BASIC TOOL FOR ANALYZING ECONOMIC RELATIONSHIPS

THE APPENDIX SUMMARY IN BRIEF

Fill in the blanks to summarize appendix content.

Describing data graphically requires a number of considerations. Does the variable take on positive values only or does it also take on negative values? What is the unit of measurement? For what purpose are the data to be plotted? If you want to present a cause-and-effect relationship between two variables, a plot of the variables on a (1) _____ (set of axes, bar graph) would be appropriate. If you are interested in the cause-and-effect relationship of a third variable, a (2) _____ (bar graph, set of axes) cannot be used. If you are only interested in presenting the fluctuation in a variable over time, a plot on a set of axes is usually all that is required, although a bar graph can be employed.

Because most economic variables take on positive values, a set of axes having an origin in the extreme (3) _____ (northeast, southwest) corner is required. As you read vertically upward or horizontally rightward from the origin, units of measurement become increasingly positive. Each axis is defined in terms of a unit of measurement. Units of measurement can be discrete or continuous. A (4) _____ (discrete, continuous) variable is expressed in units that are indivisible. A (5) _____ (discrete, continuous) variable is divisible into fractions of a whole.

A plot of a specific set of values or (6) _____ (coordinates, intersections) of two variables on a set of axes produces a curve when the points are connected by a line. The curve can reveal important information regarding the association among the two variables plotted. If the variable on the vertical axis increases when the variable plotted on the horizontal axis increases, there is a (7) _____ (positive, negative) relationship between the two variables. If the variable on the vertical axis decreases when the variable plotted on the horizontal axis increases, the relationship is a (8) _____ (positive, negative) one. If there is no change in the variable plotted on the vertical axis when the variable on the horizontal axis changes, there is no relationship between the variables.

The (9) _____ (intersection, slope) of a curve describes the rate of change in the variable on the vertical axis given a change in the variable on the horizontal axis. A curve describing a positive relationship between variables has a (10) _____ (positive, negative) slope. A curve describing a negative relationship has a (11) _____ (positive, negative) slope, and a curve indicating no relationship between the two variables has a slope of zero. On a bowl-shaped or inverted bowl-shaped curve, a slope of zero represents the point at which the curve (or the value of the variable plotted on the vertical axis) reaches a maximum or minimum value. Two curves that just touch each other but do not intersect have (12) _____ (unequal, equal) slopes at that point of tangency. If two curves (13) _____ (intersect, are tangent), the two slopes at that point can both be positive or negative or one can be positive and the other negative, but they cannot be equal to each other as is the case with (14) _____ (an intersection, a tangency).

19

KEY TERMS REVIEW

Write the key term from the list below next to its definition.

Key Terms

Origin
Curve
Slope
Bar graph
Intersection
Tangency

Coordinate
Positive (direct) relationship
Negative (inverse) relationship
Discrete variable
Continuous variable
Time series data

Definitions

1. _____: Measures the rate at which the Y variable, on the vertical axis, rises or falls along a curve as the X variable, on the horizontal axis, increases.

2. _____: Data that show fluctuations in a variable over time.

3. _____: On a set of axes, the point designated by 0, at which variables X and Y both take on values of zero.

4. _____: A graph that shows that value of a Y variable as the height of a bar for each corresponding value of the X variable.

5. _____: The point at which two curves cross on a set of axes.

6. _____: Depicted by a downward-sloping curve on a set of axes; it indicates that variable Y decreases whenever variable X increases.

7. _____: Depicted by an upward-sloping curve on a set of axes; it indicates that variable Y increases whenever variable X increases.

8. _____: A variable that can realistically and meaningfully take on minute fractions of values.

9. _____: A point at which two curves just touch each other but do not intersect.

10. _____: A pair of numbers that corresponds to values for variables X and Y when plotted on a set of axes.

11. _____: A variable that cannot vary by fractions of units.

12. _____: A straight or curved line drawn to connect points plotted on a set of axes.

CONCEPT REVIEW

1. a. Using the production data from question 10 in the Concept Review section in Chapter 1, construct the following bar charts:

Production Data

	Soybeans (000s of bushels)	Corn (000s of bushels)
1981	100	20
1982	50	40
1983	25	50
1984	0	60
1985	75	30
1986	150	0
1987	125	10

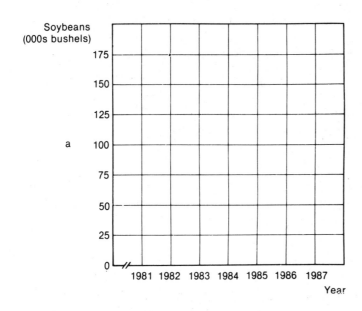

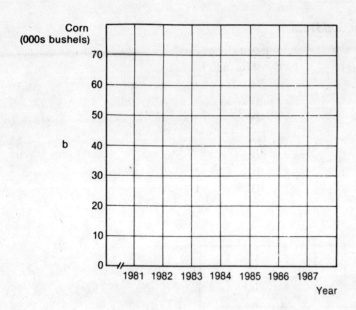

b

Corn
(000s bushels)

70
60
50
40
30
20
10
0

1981 1982 1983 1984 1985 1986 1987

Year

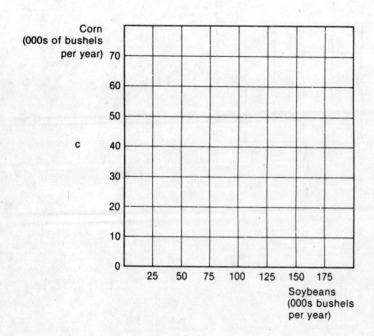

c

Corn
(000s of bushels
per year)

70
60
50
40
30
20
10
0

25 50 75 100 125 150 175

Soybeans
(000s bushels
per year)

22

b. Which of the above bar charts depict time series data and which depict a functional relationship representing the concept of opportunity costs?

    1.   Figure A _____

    2.   Figure B _____

    3.   Figure C _____

2. The following data represent quantities of tennis rackets demanded by consumers and supplied by producers at various prices:

Tennis Rackets

Price per Racket	Quantity Demanded	Quantity Supplied
	(000s per month)	
$10	75	15
20	65	20
30	55	25
40	45	30
50	35	35
60	25	40
70	15	45

a. In the figure below, plot a curve showing the relationship between price and quantity demanded by consumers. The relationship is a _____ relationship and has a _____ slope.

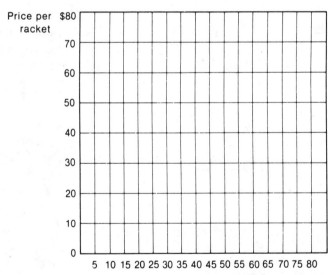

b. In the figure below, plot a curve showing the relationship between price and quantity sup-
    plied by producers. The relationship is a _____ relationship and has a
    _____ slope.

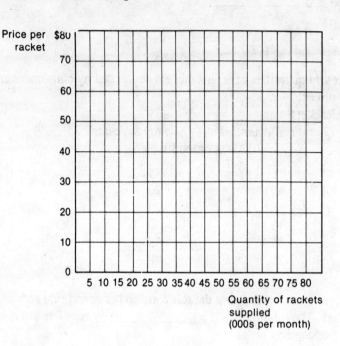

c. In the figure below, plot both curves from parts a and b above. The coordinate at which the
    two curves cross is called a/an _____. At what price and quantity supplied and
    demanded do the two curves cross? Price _____, quantity demanded
    _____, quantity supplied _____.

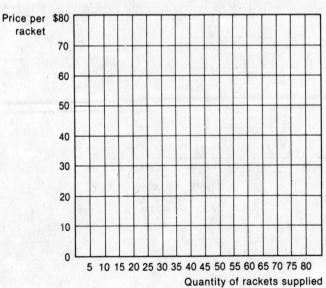

3. Suppose that you are a manager for a producer of business forms and you have noticed that over time your sales of business forms appear to increase as the rate of growth in the nation's output or GNP increases. That observed relationship is depicted in the table below:

	Rate of Growth in GNP (%)	Sales of Business Forms
Year 1	3.0	15,000
2	3.5	17,000
3	2.0	11,000
4	5.5	25,000
5	6.0	27,000

a. In the figure below, plot a time series curve describing the behavior of the rate of growth in GNP.

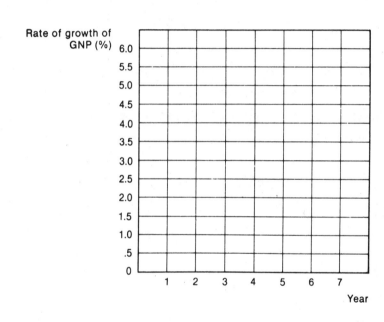

b. In the figure below, plot a time series curve describing the behavior of business forms sales.

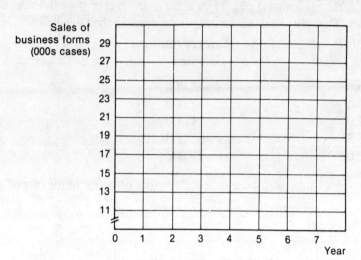

c. In the figure below, plot the functional relationship between the rate of growth in GNP and sales of business forms.

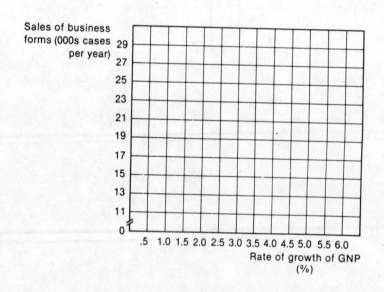

26

4. a. For the figures below, indicate whether a tangency exists or an intersection occurs at:

Point A in left figure: _____

Point B in right figure: _____

b. For the figures below, indicate whether the curves at the point of tangency or intersection have a positive or negative slope.

Curve 1 in left figure: _____

Curve 2 in left figure: _____

Curve 1 in right figure: _____

Curve 2 in right figure: _____

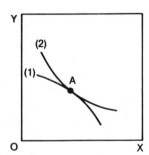
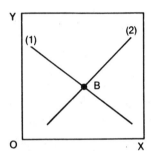

5. Referring to the figures below, indicate on the numbered spaces below whether the slope at the designated points are positive, negative, or zero.

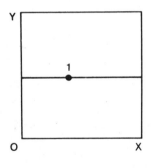
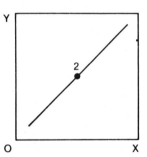

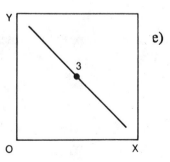

e)

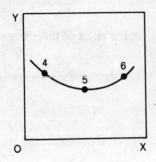

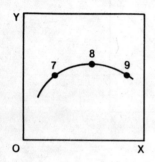

1. _____

2. _____

3. _____

4. _____

5. _____

6. _____

7. _____

8. _____

9. _____

Advanced applications

6. Using the data shown in question 3, what would you predict to happen to business form sales if the rate of growth in GNP is expected to be 4.5% in year 6?

7. Suppose two variables are related to each other by the following equation:

$Y = a + bX$, where $a = 10$ and $b = 1/2$

a. Complete the table. (Use the Y1 column for the case where a = 10.)

X	Y1	Y2
100		
200		
300		
400		
500		
600		
700		
800		

b. Plot the relationship between X and Y1 in the figure below.
  (1) The slope = _____
  (2) The intercept (value of Y1 at X = 0) = _____

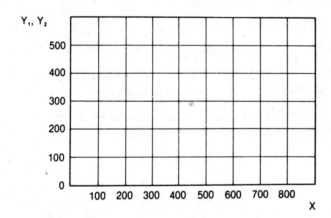

c. Assume that the constant term a in the above equation increases from 10 to 60. Complete column Y2 above and plot the new relationship in the figure in part b. The curve has shifted _____. The slope = _____ and the intercept = _____.

MASTERY TEST

Select the best answer.

1. Which of the following does not indicate a functional relationship between variables X and Y?
   a. As X increases, Y increases
   b. As X decreases, Y increases
   c. As X increases, Y remains unchanged
   d. As X decreases, Y decreases

2. When a value for X is paired with a value for Y on a set of axes, this combination of values is known as:
   a. a tangency.
   b. an intersection.
   c. a coordinate.
   d. the origin, if at least one value is zero.

3. A curve represents a set of coordinates that are connected by a line. Which of the following statements is true?
   a. A curve by definition cannot be a straight line.
   b. A curve must have either a positive or negative slope.
   c. A line of zero slope is not a function and therefore is not a curve.
   d. A curve may be a straight or a curved line. If it is a curved line, it is possible to have a positive, negative, or zero slope at different points on that curve.

4. If Y increases as X is increased, there is a _____ relationship between X and Y. If Y decreases as X is increased, the functional relationship is said to be a _____ one.
   a. adverse, positive
   b. negative, positive
   c. obtuse, negative
   d. positive, negative

5. A function exhibiting a positive relationship between X and Y has a _____ slope and a curve that is _____.
   a. positive, upsloping
   b. negative, downsloping
   c. positive, downsloping
   d. negative, upsloping

6. A function exhibiting a negative relationship between X and Y has a _____ slope and a curve which is _____.

   a. positive, upsloping

   b. negative, downsloping

   c. positive, downsloping

   d. negative, upsloping

7. Which of the following defines the origin?

   a. The origin is the beginning of a set of time series data.

   b. The origin is the coordinate on a set of axes where the value of variables X and Y are both zero.

   c. The origin is the coordinate on a set of axes where the values of variables X and Y represent the initial values of the data plotted.

   d. The origin is that point on the northeast corner of a set of positive axes.

8. The slope can be defined as the:

   a. change in Y/change in X.

   b. rate of change in Y over time.

   c. rate of change in X over time.

   d. None of the above.

9. A _____ variable is indivisible into fractions of a unit, whereas a _____ variable is divisible into fractions of a whole.

   a. continuous, discrete

   b. discrete, continuous

   c. positive, negative

   d. time series, constant

10. Which of the following variables have discrete units of measurement?

    a. Automobiles

    b. Gasoline

    c. Coffee beans

    d. The nation's money supply

11. Of the following variables, which one is a continuous variable?

    a. Computer

    b. House

    c. Basketball

    d. Natural gas

12. When two curves just touch each other, they have _____ slopes.
   a. equal
   b. unequal
   c. positive and negative
   d. only zero

13. The point at which two curves just touch each other is called:
   a. a tangency.
   b. the origin.
   c. a data point.
   d. an intersection.

14. The point at which two curve cross is called:
   a. a tangency.
   b. the origin.
   c. a data point.
   d. an intersection.

15. The values of X and Y at an intersection:
   a. will be the same on both curves.
   b. will be the same on both curves for the X variable only.
   c. will not be the same on both curves.
   d. depend upon the placement of the origin.

THINK IT THROUGH

1. Referring to the data below, plot the price and quantity demanded data on the axes below. On the same set of axes, plot the price and quantity supplied data and interpret the meaning of the intersection. Suppose a third variable changes, such as the introduction of VCRs, and as a result the quantity of movie tickets demanded at each price level declines by 20,000 tickets per week. What happens to the curve representing the demand data? What happens to the intersection?

Price per Ticket	Quantity Demanded	Quantity Supplied
	(000s per week)	
$2	80	20
3	70	30
4	60	40
5	50	50
6	40	60
7	30	70

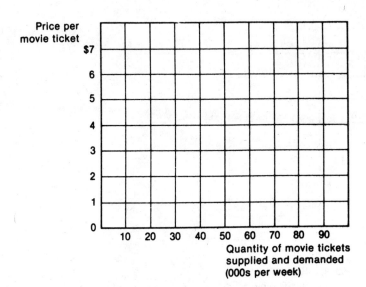

Price per movie ticket

Quantity of movie tickets supplied and demanded (000s per week)

2. The following data represent the relationship between interest rates and building permits issued for new residential construction in a local housing market. Plot the relationship on the axes below and determine if a positive or negative relationship exists. Because of a regional recession, assume that local incomes decline and outmigration of people reduce the demand for new housing and thus reduce building permits issued by 100 permits per month at each mortgage rate. Plot the new relationship on the same set of axes and compare the position and slope of the new curve to the one that you previously plotted.

Mortgage Rate %	Permits Issued per month
8.5	1050
9.0	1000
9.5	950
10.0	900
10.5	850
11.0	800
11.5	750

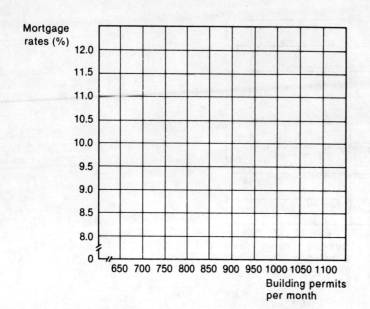

ANSWERS TO CHAPTER APPENDIX

The Appendix Summary in Brief

1. A set of axes or a bar graph 2. Bar graph 3. Southwest 4. Discrete 5. Continuous 6. Coordinates
7. Positive 8. Negative 9. Slope 10. Positive 11. Negative 12. Equal 13. Intersect 14. Tangency

Key Terms Review

1. Slope 2. Time series data 3. Origin 4. Bar graph 5. Intersection 6. Negative relationship
7. Positive relationship 8. Continuous variable 9. Tangency 10. Coordinate 11. Discrete variable
12. Curve

Concept Review

1. a.

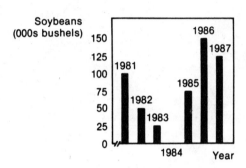

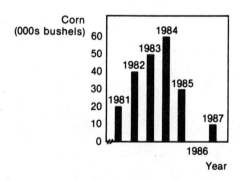

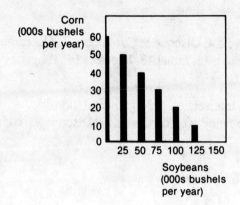

b. (1) Time series
(2) Time series
(3) Functional relationship

2. a.

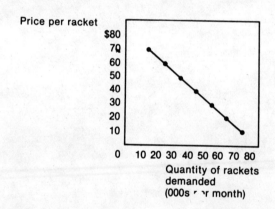

Negative, negative

b.

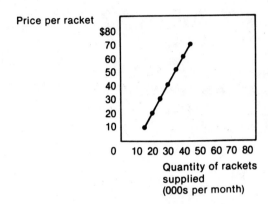

Positive, positive

c.

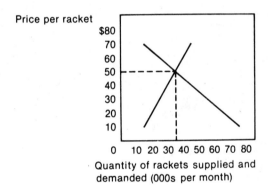

Intersection, $50, 35, 35

37

3. a.

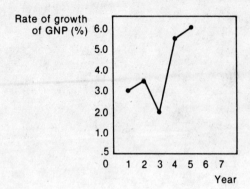

b.

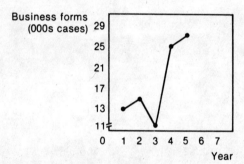

c.

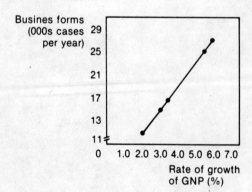

4. a. Tangency, intersection

   b. Negative, negative, negative, positive

5. 1. Zero 2. Positive 3. Negative 4. Negative 5. Zero 6. Positive 7. Positive 8. Zero 9. Negative

6. From the functional relationship shown in part c of question 3, it can be seen that a positive relationship exists between the rate of growth in GNP and sales of business forms. The slope of the curve is the change in business form sales for each percentage change in the rate of growth of GNP. Business form sales increase by 4,000 cases for each 1% increase in the GNP growth rate. If you expect that the growth rate of GNP will be 4.5% in year 6, then sales of business forms can be predicted to fall from 27,000 to 21,000 cases.

7. a.

Y1		c. Y2		Upward, 1/2, 60
60		110		
110		160		
160		210		
210		260		
260		310		
310		360		
360		410		
410		460		

   b.

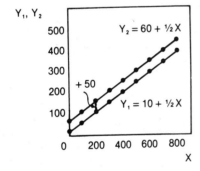

      (1) 1/2 (2) 10

Mastery Test

1. c 2. c 3. d 4. d 5. a 6. b 7. b 8. a 9. b 10. a 11. d 12. a 13. a 14. d 15. a

Think It Through

1. The two curves intersect at point A in the figure below. At that point, the values for price and quantity are the same on both curves. At a price per movie ticket of $5, the quantity demanded and quantity supplied both equal 50,000 tickets per week. A reduction of 20,000 tickets demanded at each price shifts the demand curve leftward. The new intersection shows that a price of $4 is now required to equate quantity demanded and quantity supplied at a level of 40,000 tickets per week.

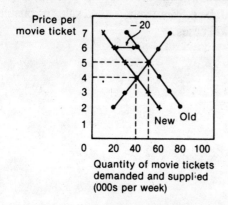

2. The relationship between mortgage rates and new building permits issued is a negative one. If building permits issued decline at each mortgage rate by 100 permits per month, the new curve lies to the left of the old curve but has the same slope.

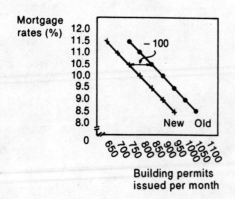

40

2 PRODUCTION POSSIBILITIES AND OPPORTUNITY COST

CHAPTER CONCEPTS

After studying your text, attending class, and completing this chapter, you should be able to:

1. Explain how limited available technology and scarce resources imply limited production possibilities over a period of time.
2. Show how the use of productive capacity to make more of one good or service available involves sacrificing the opportunity to make more of other items available.
3. Understand the concept of productive efficiency and discuss its significance.
4. Discuss the basic determinants of a nation's production possibilities and how these can expand over time.
5. Demonstrate that when you use income over a period to buy more of one item, you sacrifice the opportunity to buy more of some other item over the period.
6. Explain how international trade can allow citizens to enjoy consumption possibilities that exceed their nation's domestic production possibilities.

THE CHAPTER IN BRIEF

Fill in the blanks to summarize chapter content.

(1)_____(Economy, Production) is the process of using economic resources or inputs in order to produce output. Economic resources consist of labor, (2)_____(capital, money), natural resources, and entrepreneurship. The quantity and productivity of economic resources and the extent and efficiency with which they are employed determine the output potential of a nation during a given period of time. Constraints in the availability or use of resources represent the (3)_____ (opportunity costs, scarcity) confronting nations. (4)_____ (Technology, A larger labor force) allows us to delay the sacrifices implied by scarce resources by increasing the productivity of resources. Improvements in resource productivity mean that a nation can produce more output with a given endowment of resources.

A (5)_____(marginal benefit, production possibilities) curve is a convenient tool for showing the implications of scarce resources. Assuming (a) a given quantity and productivity of resources, as well as a given state of the art with respect to technology and (b) full and efficient employment of resources, it can be shown that a nation can produce more of one class of goods, such as environmental improvement services, only by (6)_____(sacrificing, increasing) the production of other goods. That sacrifice is a nation's (7)_____ (dollar outlay, opportunity cost) of producing more of a given good. As a nation produces more of a good, the opportunity cost (8)_____(rises, falls) because resources that are increasingly (9)_____ (less, more) productive must be transferred from the production of other goods. This implies that a given increase in the production of one good will require ever (10)_____ (smaller, larger) reductions in output of other goods. The law of increasing costs exists because resources (11)_____ (are, are not) equally adaptable to all employments.

A point on the production possibilities curve represents a combination of the two classes of goods in question where output is at a maximum. A point inside the curve implies either (12)_____ (unemployed, fully employed) resources or (13)_____(efficiently, inefficiently) employed resources. A point outside the curve represents a combination of goods that is (14)_____(attainable, unattainable) in the short run. But with an increase over time in the quantity and productivity of resources, together with improvements in technology, a point outside the curve is attainable in the long run.

Maximum production is attainable in the short run when resources are employed fully and efficiently. Productive efficiency means that a nation (15)_____(can, cannot) reallocate resources among the production of goods and services and achieve a gain in the output of one good only by causing a reduction in the output of another. Specialization and the division of labor are critical for the attainment of maximum productive efficiency.

The process of economic growth can be shown as (16)_____(inward, outward) shifts over time in the production possibilities curve. A nation can generally produce more of all goods over time as long as it experiences resource growth and an improvement in the quality of resources and technology. A nation's growth is influenced by its willingness to forgo some (17)_____ (future, current) production of consumable output so that resources can be used for the production of (18)_____(consumable outputs, capital). Production of capital today increases the production possibilities in the future not only by increasing the quantity of capital but also by increasing the productivity of other resources.

The problem of scarcity confronting nations also confronts the individual. An individual has a limited amount of income per time period with which to consume and save. Given the prices of goods and services, that limited income can purchase, at a maximum, those combinations of goods and services which require the full expenditure of income. A curve representing these various combinations of goods and services is known as a (19)_____(budget line, production possibilities curve). An increase in income over time allows the individual to consume more of all goods. This is shown by an (20)_____ (inward, outward) shift of the budget line. Holding income constant but allowing prices to fall likewise (21)_____ (increases, decreases) the quantities that can be purchased. This too shifts the budget line (22)_____(inward, outward). Rising prices or inflation will shift the budget line (23)_____ (inward, outward) if income remains constant. Finally, given a limited income and constant prices, the only way an individual can consume more of one good is by reducing consumption of other goods. The opportunity cost of consuming more of one good is the (24)_____(increase, reduction) in consumption of quantities of other goods.

KEY TERMS REVIEW

Write the key term from the list below next to its definition.

Key Terms

Economic resources	Production possibilities curve
Labor	Law of increasing costs
Capital	Productive efficiency
Natural resources	Division of labor
Entrepreneurship	Economic growth
Technology	

Definitions

1. _____: the inputs used in the process of production.

2. _____: the specialization of workers in particular tasks that are part of a larger undertaking to accomplish a given objective.

3. _____: the equipment, tools, structures, machinery, vehicles, materials, and skills created to help produce goods and services.

4. _____: a curve that show feasible combinations of two goods (or broad classes of goods) that can be produced with available resources and current technology.

5. _____: the talent to develop products and processes and to organize production of goods and services.

6. _____: the expansion in production possibilities that results from increased availability and increased productivity of economic resources.

7. _____: the knowledge of how to produce goods and services.

8. _____: the physical and mental efforts of human beings in the production of goods and services.

9. _____: attained when the maximum possible output of any one good is produced given the output of the other goods. At this point it is not possible to reallocate economic resources to increase the output of any single good or service without decreasing the output of some other good or service.

10. _____: acreage and the physical terrain used to locate structures, ports, and other facilities; also, climate and natural resources that are used in crude form in production.

11. _____: states that the opportunity cost of each additional unit of output of a good over a period increases as more of that good is produced.

CONCEPT REVIEW

Concept 1: *Scarce resources and limited production possibilities*

1. List four economic resources:

   a. _____

   b. _____

   c. _____

   d. _____

2. Which of the following uses of resources will likely increase labor productivity? (+, Increase; 0, No change.)

   a. _____ Expenditures on capital

   b. _____ Expenditures on more fashionable clothes

   c. _____ Expenditures on health care

   d. _____ Expenditures on education and training

   e. _____ Expenditures on military goods

43

Concept 2: *Production possibilities and opportunity cost*

3. The data in the table below represent the production possibilities for a nation producing two classes of goods.

Production Possibilities	Consumer Goods (millions of units)	Capital Goods
A	0	90
B	20	80
C	40	65
D	60	47
E	80	26
F	100	0

a. On the axes below, plot a production possibilities curve from the data in the table above.

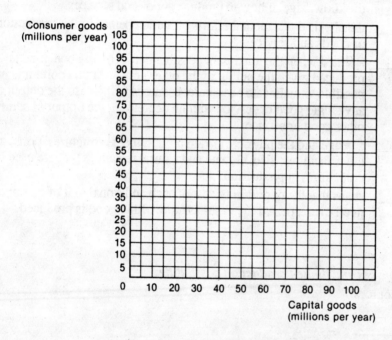

b. What is the meaning of a point <u>on</u> the production possibilities curve?

c. What is the opportunity cost associated with an increase in the production of consumer goods by 20 million units?

   (1) From point B to C? _____ units of capital

   (2) From point C to D? _____ units of capital

   (3) From point D to E? _____ units of capital

   (4) From point E to F? _____ units of capital

d. Do opportunity costs rise or fall as additional units of consumer goods are produced? Explain.

4. Referring to the figure below:
   a. Interpret the meaning of point A.
   b. Interpret the meaning of point B.

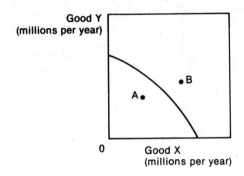

Concept 4: *Determinants of a nation's production possibilities*

5. Indicate whether the following events would cause the production possibilities curve to shift outward (O) or would leave it unchanged (U):
   a. _____ Increased production of houses at full employment
   b. _____ Increases in the quantity of resources
   c. _____ Improvements in the quality and productivity of economic resources
   d. _____ A reduction in prices
   e. _____ Increases in income
   f. _____ Improvements in technology

6. a. On the axes below, draw a production possibilities curve for a nation. Now assume that economic growth is taking place. Draw a new production possibilities curve on the same axes reflecting this growth.

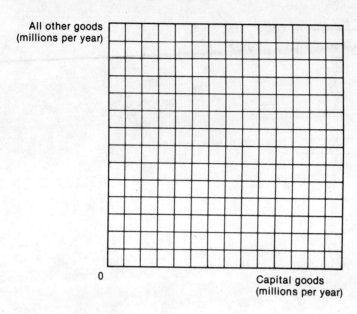

b. On the axes below, draw a production possibilities curve for a nation. Assume as above that the nation is experiencing growth, but also assume that the economy is investing more heavily in capital and technology than the economy shown above in part a. Draw a new production possibilities curve reflecting this.

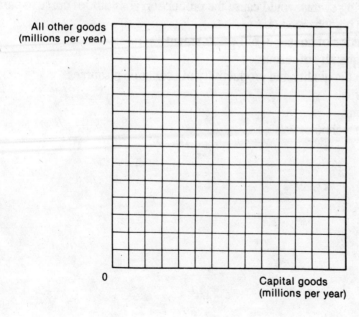

7. a. If a nation used resources for capital or technological improvements for a specific industry, such as the aircraft industry, what are the implications regarding future levels of production not only in the aircraft industry but for other industries as well?

   b. Show the shift in a nation's production possibilities curve that results from the use of resources discussed above.

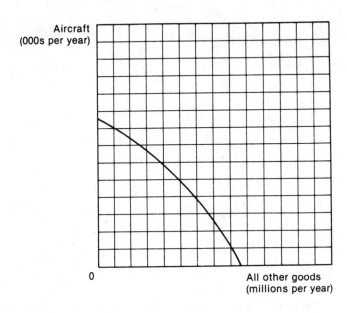

Aircraft
(000s per year)

0   All other goods
                     (millions per year)

Concept 5:   *Limited income and opportunity cost*

8. Suppose that as a university student you receive $50 per month from your parents to be used as spending money. You spend all of your money each month on beer or compact discs (CDs). Assume that the price per six-pack of beer is $2.50 and the price of a CD is $10.

   a. Determine six combinations of beer and CDs that cost a total of $50. List the combinations in the table below.

Combination	Beer (six packs)	CDs (units)
A	_____	_____
B	_____	_____
C	_____	_____
D	_____	_____
E	_____	_____
F	_____	_____

b. Plot these combinations below. The curve that you have plotted is called a
_____.

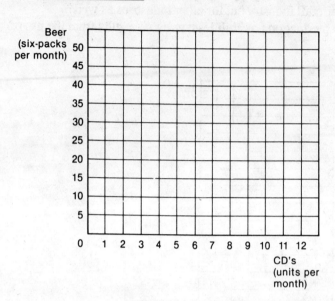

c. On the figure in part b, show what would happen to the curve if:
   (1) your parents began to send $100 per month
   (2) your total funds are still $50, but the price of beer increases to $5 and the price of CDs decreases to $5.

9. **Advanced application: budget line**
   a. Derive the equation for the budget line in Question 8, part b.
   b. In question 8, part c1 alters the equation for the budget line in what way? Part c2 alters the equation in what way?

MASTERY TEST

Select the best answer.

1. Which of the following can be defined as the process of using economic resources to produce outputs?
   a. Economics
   b. Production
   c. Economy
   d. Technology

2. Economic resources consist of:
   a. money, credit, and capital
   b. labor, capital, and money
   c. labor, capital, natural resources, and money
   d. labor, capital, natural resources, and entrepreneurship

3. Which of the following best defines capital?
   a. Money
   b. Socks and bonds
   c. Investment funds available for speculative financial outlays
   d. Goods or skills that are produced in order to produce goods and services

4. Scarcity exists in the short run because:
   a. at a given point in time technological growth increases at a constantrate.
   b. at a given point in time the quantity and quality of resources and the state of technology are fixed.
   c. resources are usually employed inefficiently.
   d. the world's resources are in finite supply.

5. A nation must sacrifice the output of some goods in order to produce other goods during a given period of time if:
   a. there is less than full employment of resources.
   b. resources are inefficiently employed.
   c. there is both full and efficient use of economic resources.
   d. a nation relies on capital goods production.

6. If a nation is currently operating at a point on its production possibilities curve, in order to increase production of one good, the production of other goods must be:
   a. held constant.
   b. increased.
   c. decreased.
   d. None of the above.

7. If a nation is currently operating at a point inside its production possibilities curve, it:
   a. has full employment.
   b. has unemployed and/or inefficiently employed resources.
   c. is operating at full potential.
   d. must reduce the output of one good in order to produce more of another good.

8. The law of increasing costs states that:
   a. opportunity costs rise as more of a good is produced.
   b. opportunity costs fall as more of a good is produced.
   c. rising resource prices are inevitable because of scarcity.
   d. economic growth is always associated with inflation.

9. The law of increasing costs is the result of the fact that:
   a. resources can be easily adapted to the production of any good.
   b. scarcity reduces supply and increases costs.
   c. resources are not equally adaptable to all employments.
   d. people reach a point of satiation at which they no longer purchase goods.

10. Economic growth is the process whereby the production possibilities curve shifts:
    a. inward.
    b. outward.
    c. either inward or outward.
    d. outward, then inward.

11. Points outside of the production possibilities curve are _____ in the _____.
    a. attainable/short run
    b. unattainable/short run
    c. attainable/long run
    d. unattainable/long run
    e. b and c

12. Production efficiency is achieved:
    a. if resources are reallocated among the production of goods and services and the output of one good can be increased without decreasing the output of other goods.
    b. if there is no waste in the production process.
    c. if resources are reallocated among the production of goods and services and the output of one good can be increased only by reducing the output of other goods.
    d. at a point within the production possibilities curve.

13. If nation A commits a larger share of its resources to capital and technological improvements than nation B, then over time _____ will realize _____ outward shifts in its production possibilities curve.
    a. nation B/larger
    b. nation A/smaller
    c. nations A and B/the same
    d. nation B/smaller

14. An individual's ability to consume goods and services depends upon:
    a. income only.
    b. the rate of inflation.
    c. the individual's income and the prices of the goods and services consumed.
    d. tastes.

15. A/An _____ is a curve indicating an individual's ability to consume various combinations of two goods or services over a period of time.
    a. production possibilities curve
    b. income curve
    c. price line
    d. budget line

16. The budget line shifts _____ when there is a/an _____ in income.
    a. inward/increase
    b. outward/decrease
    c. inward/decrease
    d. outward/decrease or increase

17. An individual's ability to increase the consumption of goods and services is _____ when the price of one or both goods _____.
    a. increased/decrease
    b. decreased/decrease
    c. increased/increase
    d. unchanged/increase unless income decreases

18. The sacrifice or opportunity cost associated with an individual's consumption of an additional good :
    a. is the reduction in other goods consumed when the individual does not spend all of his or her income.
    b. is the increase in other goods consumed when unused income is spent.
    c. is the reduction in other goods consumed when an individual has no additional income.
    d. None of the above

19. How is a nation's production possibilities curve affected in the long run by a boom in both new and existing housing sales in the present?
    a. Since housing is not productive capital, there is no impact on the nation's production possibilities curve.
    b. Housing consumption increases worker productivity, causing a move up along the production possibilities curve.
    c. Increased housing production in the present means that fewer other goods and services, including capital, are produced. The rate of economic growth will not be as great at it would have otherwise been, causing the production possibilities curve to shift outward by a smaller amount.
    d. The production possibilities curve will initially shift inward, but will eventually shift outward as labor productivity increases.

20. You received a monthly income of $1,000 which is spent on food and automobile payments. The cost per month for food is $400 and the monthly auto payment is $200. Let F represent the monthly food cost and A represent the monthly auto payment. Which of the following expressions represents your income constraint (or budget line)? Assume F is placed on the vertical axis and A on the horizontal axis.
    a. $1000 = $200 A + $400 A
    b. $400 = $400 F - $200 A
    c. $1000 = $400 F + $200 A
    d. F = 2.5 - .5 A

21. Which of the following statements best explains why a nation's consumption possibilities line lies outside of its production possibilities line?
    a. International trade requires nations to give up more than they receive, adversely affecting production and causing the production possibilities curve to shift inward away from the production possibilities curve.
    b. If nations specialize in and export goods for which they have an comparative advantage and import goods for which they have a comparative disadvantage, more goods can be obtained through domestic production and trade than from domestic production alone.
    c. The consumption possibilities line lies outside the production possibilities line because consumers are able to borrow and spend more than their domestically earned income.
    d. In order for the consumption possibilities line to lie outside of the production possibilities line, a nation must always export more than it imports.

22. Which of the following best explains a linear production possibilities curve?
    a. Beyond some level of production, worker productivity increases at an increasing rate.
    b. As more of a given class of goods is produced in a period, proportionately more of the other class of goods must be sacrificed.
    c. The opportunity cost of producing a given class of goods over a period remains constant.
    d. The opportunity cost of producing a given class of goods over a period decreases.

23. Suppose a nation produces two types of goods, capital and food. However, assume that in the capital goods industry firm A produces 2 units of capital per worker per week whereas firm B produces 5 units of capital per worker per week. If resources are fully employed, is this nation at a point on its production possibilities curve?
   a. No, a worker can be reallocated from firm B to firm A for a net gain of 4 units of capital.
   b. Yes, full employment guarantees that a economy is on its production possibilities curve.
   c. Yes, full employment means full production and allocative efficiency.
   d. No, a worker can be reallocated from firm A to firm B for a net gain of 3 units of capital. Thus, the economy must be inside of its production possibilities curve.

THINK IT THROUGH

1. Explain why a nation's endowment of economic resources necessitates choices between current and future uses of resources.

2. Explain under what conditions a nation incurs an opportunity cost as it produces more of a good. How does the law of increasing cost fit into your discussion?

3. How do technology and capital expenditures improve the quality or productivity of "other" economic resources?

4. Assume that the United States contributes disproportionately more resources to the defense of Western Europe than do the other NATO allies, and as a consequence these other countries can invest a larger share of their resources in capital and other goods and services. Use production possibility curves to show both the short- and long-run consequences regarding the economies of the United States and Western Europe.

ANALYZING THE NEWS

Using the skills derived from studying this chapter, analyze the economic facts that make up the following article and answer the questions below, using graphical analysis where possible.

1. What could be the consequences for the United States production possibilities curve if the United States is slow in moving towards robotic technology?

2. Why might other nations like Germany and Japan choose to adopt such technology?

Robots ready to march in U.S., though industry here lags

By William S. Bergstrom
Associated Press

AUBURN HILLS, Mich.—American industry is placing record orders for robots to wield its arc welders and swing its paint sprayers, but the future of U.S. robot manufacturing is far from automatic.

America invented the industrial robot, but among its largest manufacturers, GMFanuc Robotics Corp. imports most of its machinery from Japan while Cincinnati Milacron Inc. of Ohio said in February that it would sell out to Swiss-based Asea Brown Boveri AB.

The changes illustrate the head start Japan and Europe have in robot use, and the catching up the U.S. must do before its robot industry can thrive.

"There's tremendous potential, yet it's lower than our Japanese counterparts," said Eric Mittelstadt, president of GMFanuc. "They sell almost as many in a year as we have installed in the history of robotics."

Robotics got its start in the U.S., said Joseph Engleberger, who founded the world's first industrial robot manufacturer, Unimation of Danbury, Conn., 30 years ago.

"We originated all the technology," said Engleberger, whose pioneer robot ran for 100,000 hours in a General Motors Corp. factory before it was enshrined in the Smithsonian Institution in Washington, D.C.

But the idea of robots caught on faster in countries such as Japan and Germany because labor there was harder to find and more expensive, said Patrick McGibbon, robots analyst with the U.S. Commerce Department's International Trade Administration.

Now Japan has 176,000 industrial robots to the United States' 37,000. In robots per production worker, the U.S. trails Japan, Sweden, Germany and Italy, according to the Robotic Industries Association.

"Our key competitors, Japan and Germany, are increasing their usage at a faster rate than we are, not a good sign for the competitiveness of American industry," spokesman Jeffrey Burnstein said.

Yet orders for U.S. robots are growing, the Ann Arbor, Mich.-based trade group said. Manufacturers placed a record $517.4 million in robot orders with U.S. firms last year, up 33 percent from $388 million in 1985.

Robots usually conjure up images of science fiction characters such as R2D2 in "Star Wars," or devoted servants without such human drawbacks as boredom, independent thinking, inattentiveness or the need for health and retirement benefits.

Robotmakers usually focus on more vital roles, such as helping hospital patients, exploring the ocean floor, handling hazardous waste or defusing bombs.

"I pushed the use of personal robots in health care," said Walter Weisel, president of Prab Robots Inc. in Kalamazoo until 1989, when he resigned and became an industry consultant.

"That market is so big that whenever it gets rolling, it's going to dwarf whatever happens in industrial robots," Weisel said.

On the GMFanuc plant floor, yellow and black robot arms whirl, bob and turn like long-necked birds as the $30,000 to $100,000 systems go through the programmed motions they will carry out in customers' factories.

Robot welders trace the patterns of seams they'll join. Spray-gun robots move over and under car bodies and other shapes they'll paint.

Robots with suction-cup arms pluck panes of glass from stacks, tilt them back and position them in the window openings of car and truck frames.

Plant workers are inured to the idea that automation has its place. "We've been dealing with robots for 20 years now," said United Auto Workers spokesman Reg McGee.

When robots are brought in, the union often is involved from the start, with its own people installing them, McGee said.

GMFanuc, a joint venture of General Motors Corp. and Fanuc Ltd., Japan's largest robotics company, occupies a glass-walled building on 56 acres 20 miles north of Detroit. Gravel and dirt still occupy the part of the building that remains to be finished as sales rebound from a low of $103 million in 1987.

The dip came after GMFanuc lost $90 million in orders from automakers, who pleaded slow sales and a shortage of cash, said company President Mittelstadt. Since then, GMFanuc has increased its percentage of non-automotive business to 40 from 10 to 15 percent.

It also has cut its dependence on GM, selling robots to Ford, Chrysler, Nissan, Toyota, Peugeot, Saab and Volkswagen.

The company uses every marketing tactic available, from working with state development agencies to making telephone pitches to machine shops and small manufacturers.

Sales last year totaled a record $223 million, Mittelstadt said.

The U.S. Commerce Department's 1991 U.S. Industrial Outlook described the robotics market as promising, but said 1990 shipments grew too slowly.

"Unless the pace of shipments picks up, domestic customers will seek systems integration from foreign sources and/or cancel orders with U.S. integrators," the publication said.

The Council on Competitiveness, a non-profit group of business, labor and education leaders studying global technological competition, placed the U.S. in the "losing badly or lost" category, the lowest of four ratings, in robotics and automated equipment.

Industry-government coordination would help, the council said in a March report. Six government agencies spent about $150 million exploring robotics in 1990, but most of it was to develop a robotic arm for NASA's space station.

Engleberger blamed short-term, profit-oriented thinking for holding back the use of robots in U.S. industry.

He said he predicted correctly 17 years ago that by 1990 industrial robots would be a $3 billion business.

"It was exactly that, or maybe more. The only thing I missed on was where it would be," he said. "About 65 percent of it is in Japan, with the balance split between Europe and the United States."

Source: "Robots Ready to March in U.S., though Industry Here Lags," *The Chicago Tribune*, August 4, 1991, Section 7, p.9B.

CHAPTER ANSWERS

The Chapter in Brief

1. Production 2. Capital 3. Scarcity 4. Technology 5. Production possibilities curve 6. Sacrificing
7. Opportunity cost 8. Rises 9. Less 10. Larger 11. Are not 12. Unemployed 13. Inefficiently
14. Unattainable 15. Can 16. Outward 17. Current 18. Capital 19. Budget line 20. Outward
21. Increases 22. Outward 23. Inward 24. Reduction

Key Terms Review

1. Economic resources 2. Division of labor 3. Capital 4. Production possibilities curve
5. Entrepreneurship 6. Economic growth 7. Technology 8. Labor 9. Productive efficiency
10. Natural resources 11. Law of increasing costs

Concept Review

1. a.   Labor b. Capital c. Natural resources d. Entrepreneurship
2. a.   + b. 0 c. + d. + e. 0
3. a.

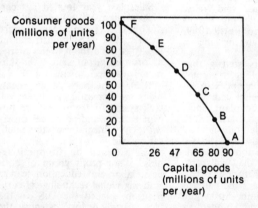

   b.   A point on the production possibilities curve represents a maximum level of production
        over a period of time for consumer and capital goods. At this level of production, resources
        are fully and efficiently employed.
   c.   (1) 15 (2) 18 (3) 21 (4) 26
   d.   Rise. Opportunity costs rise because in order to produce more and more consumer goods,
        increasing quantities of resources have to be reallocated from the capital goods industry to
        the consumer goods industry, and these resources are increasingly less adaptable to con-
        sumer goods production.
4. a.   A point inside the curve represents a level of production involving unemployed resources
        or inefficient production or both.
   b.   A point outside the curve is unattainable in the short run because of resource constraints.
        In the long run, however, it is possible to reach point B if the productivity and quantity of
        resources increase.

5. a. U b. O c. O d. U e. U f. O

6. a.

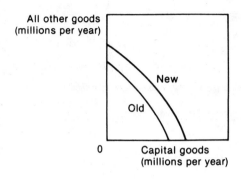

b.

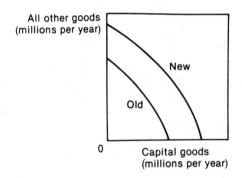

7. a. Even if capital or technological improvements were made only in the aircraft industry, the levels of production in other industries would likely increase. The capacity to produce in the aircraft industry has increased, which means that more aircraft <u>can</u> be produced than before. Since capital increases the productivity of other resources, more aircraft could be produced with the same quantity of resources previously employed in the aircraft industry, or the same number of aircraft could be produced as before but now with fewer resources. These resources, therefore, could be used elsewhere in producing other goods and services.

b.

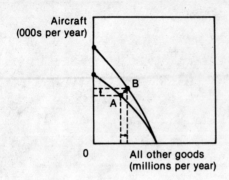

8. a.

Combination	Beer	CDs
A	20	0
B	16	1
C	12	2
D	8	3
E	4	4
F	0	5

b. Budget line

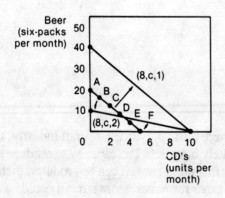

c. (1) (on figure above)
(2) (on figure above)

9. a.   As me that the student's income (I) is spent in its entirety on beer(B) and compact discs (CDs). Furthermore, assume the price of beer(PB) and the price of a CD (PCD) are $2.50 and $10, respectively.

I = (PB)(B) + (PCD)(CD)

Solve the above equation for (B).

B = I/PB - (PCD/PB)(CD)

Notice that the vertical intercept of the budget line is the level of income divided by the price of beer. Also notice that the slope of the budget line is negative and equals the ratio of prices of the two goods.
   b.
   (1)   An increase in income will increase the intercept term or constant term in the above equation. The budget line will shift upward.
   (2)   A decrease in the price of CDs and an increase in the price of beer will make the slope less negative and will decrease the intercept term. The budget line becomes flatter, with the vertical intercept decreasing.

Mastery Test

1. b 2. d 3. d 4. b 5. c 6. c 7. b 8. a 9. c 10. b 11. e 12. c 13. d 14. c 15. d 16. c 17. a 18. c 19. c 20. d 21. b 22. c 23. d

Think it Through

1. A nation's endowment of resources, whether plentiful or limited, is a constraint to future growth. With full and efficient use of resources, a nation can produce only so much over a given period of time. Using resources today for capital means giving up the consumption of other goods today. But capital increases the future capacity to produce and also increases the productivity of economic resources. Because of this, a nation that forgoes consumption today and invests in capital will be able to consume more tomorrow.

2. A nation incurs a sacrifice or opportunity cost associated with the use of resources when (a) there is full employment of resources and (b) efficient production of output. If this were not the case, a nation could produce more of one good without necessarily reducing the consumption of other goods by either employing its resources more fully or by more efficiently producing its output.

At full employment and efficient production, a nation incurs rising opportunity costs if it produces more and more of a given good because of the law of increasing costs. Because resources are not completely adaptable to all uses, they must be withdrawn in increasing amounts from other industries in order to produce given quantities of the good.

3. Both capital and technology increase the productivity of the production process. More output can be produced with the same amount of resources. A farmer with a tractor is far more productive than one with a digging stick. This is the story of American agriculture. The enormous productivity increases in the U.S. farm sector have been made possible by the mechanization of agriculture.

4. The United States not only sacrifices output of consumer goods and services in the short run but also sacrifices a higher rate of future economic growth and living standards.

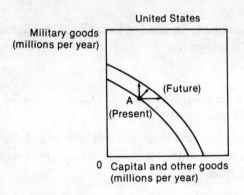

Western Europe, in contrast, is able to consume both more capital and other goods in the short run and because of greater capital investments will realize a faster rate of GNP growth in the future.

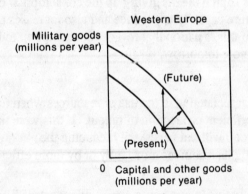

Analyzing the News

1. By avoiding or delaying the transition to more efficient forms of technology, the rate of growth in the United States could be slowed. The production possibilities curve would not shift out as much as it would otherwise, limiting the growth of product development and preventing consumers from consuming goods and services that otherwise would have been available.

2. Nations such as Germany and Japan, with highly educated labor forces and large investments in capital, stand to benefit from the use of robotic technology by putting lower cost, and thus more price-competitive goods on world markets.

PART II

SUPPLY AND DEMAND: MARKETS AND THE PRICE SYSTEM

PART EXERCISE

Inside Information: *Getting Information on Financial and Commodity Markets*

In Part II, you will learn about supply and demand and the price system. You will also learn about the loanable funds market and the determination of interest rates. Use *The Wall Street Journal* over a two week period and record changes in interest rates. Be sure to identify the specific interest rates that you use. What possible changes in the supply of and demand for loanable funds could cause these observed changes? Explain.

3 MARKET TRANSACTIONS: BASIC SUPPLY AND DEMAND ANALYSIS

CHAPTER CONCEPTS

After studying your text, attending class, and completing this chapter, you should be able to:

1. Discuss the purposes and functions of markets.
2. Explain how a demand curve shows the law of demand and distinguish between a change in demand and a change in quantity demanded.
3. Show how a supply curve illustrates the law of supply and distinguish between a change in supply and a change in quantity supplied.
4. Describe the conditions required for market equilibrium and locate the equilibrium point on a supply and demand diagram.
5. Explain the consequences of shortages and surpluses in markets and how prices adjust in a free and unregulated competitive market to eliminate shortages or surpluses.
6. Show how changes in supply and demand affect market equilibrium.

THE CHAPTER IN BRIEF

Fill in the blanks to summarize chapter content.

Understanding the concept of a market and the role it plays in the allocation of resources and the distribution of output is critical to an understanding of how economies function. (1)_____ (Markets, Trade publications) communicate information to buyers and sellers alike. The forces of supply and demand, which are basic to every market, interact to produce a (2)_____ (market quantity, market price) that acts as a vehicle for communicating the wants of buyers to sellers. (3)_____(Cost-benefit analysis, Supply and demand analysis) is a method of isolating the forces of supply and demand so that the factors determining market prices can be understood. This allows us to better understand the communication and rationing functions of the price system.

Quantity demanded constitutes amounts of goods and services that buyers are willing and able to buy at a given price during a given period. A (4)_____(demand schedule, demand curve) is a table of data showing the relationship between the prices of a good and the associated quantities demanded, holding all other influencing factors unchanged. A (5)_____(demand curve, demand schedule) is a plot of the price-quantity demanded coordinates. The demand schedule and its demand curve show that price and quantity demanded are negatively related. This relationship is known as the law of (6)_____(increasing returns, demand). When there is a change in price, quantity demanded changes. This is called a (7)_____(change in demand, change in quantity demanded). A change in demand determinants other than the price of the good will shift the demand curve. A shift in the demand curve means that, at a given price, quantity demanded will either increase or decrease. This is called a (8)_____(change in demand, change in quantity demanded). Changes in demand are caused by changes in (a) income, (b) wealth, (c) the prices of related goods, (d) price expectations, (e) tastes, and (f) the number of buyers in the market.

Quantity supplied represents the quantities that sellers are willing and able to produce and make available to the market at a given price during a given period. A (9)_____(supply schedule, supply curve) is a table of data showing the relationship between the prices of a good and the associated quantities supplied by sellers, all other influences on supply remaining the same.

A (10)_____(supply curve, supply schedule) is a plot of the price-quantity supplied coordinates. The relationship between price and quantity supplied is a positive one and is called the law of (11)_____ (monetary incentives, supply). A (12)_____(change in quantity supplied,change in supply) is caused by a price change. This is shown by a movement along a given supply curve. A (13)_____(change in quantity supplied, change in supply) is the result of influences other than price, such as (a) the price of inputs, (b) prices of other goods, (c) technology, (d) price expectations, and (e) the number of sellers in a market. These nonprice influences shift the supply curve.

The forces of supply and demand interact to produce a market (14)_____ (outcome, equilibrium), or state of balance, where the quantities demanded by buyers are just equal to the quantities supplied by sellers. In a state of equilibrium, buyers and sellers have no incentive to alter levels of consumption or production. It is the market (15)_____(price, quantity) that equates the quantities supplied and demanded.

A price above a market equilibrium price results in a (16)_____(shortage, surplus) because the quantity supplied at this price exceeds the quantity demanded. A price below the equilibrium price causes a (17)_____(shortage, surplus) because the quantity demanded exceeds the quantity supplied. In a competitive market, a seller tries to get rid of surpluses by (18)_____ (increasing inventories, cutting prices). Falling prices will reduce surpluses. When the price falls enough to equal the market equilibrium price, the (19)_____ (shortage, surplus) is eliminated completely.

Shortages require some form of rationing. Sellers ration the limited supply of goods among competing buyers by (20)_____(increasing, decreasing) prices. But price increases reduce the quantities demanded and increase the quantities supplied, which in turn reduce the shortage. Shortages are completely eliminated when the price has risen (21)_____(above, equal to) the market equilibrium price. Market prices remain unchanged in a competitive market unless the underlying forces of supply or demand change. A change in demand, a change in supply, or a change in both supply and demand (22)_____ (can, cannot) alter the market equilibrium price and quantity.

KEY TERMS REVIEW

Write the key term from the list below next to its definition.

Key Terms

Market
Change in quantity
  demanded
Supply and demand
  analysis
Quantity demanded
Demand schedule
Law of demand
Complements
Demand curve
Surplus
Change in relative
  price
Change in demand

Market equilibrium
Quantity supplied
Demand
Supply
Law of supply
Supply schedule
Supply curve
Change in quantity
  supplied
Substitutes
Change in supply
Shortage
Equilibrium

Definitions

1. _____: an increase or decrease in the price of a good relative to an average of the prices of all goods.

2. _____: a graph that shows how quantity demanded varies with the price of a good.

3. _____: a table that shows how the quantity supplied of a good is related to the price.

4. _____: the quantity of a good sellers are willing and able to make available in the market over a given period at a certain price, other things being equal.

5. _____: a relationship between the price of an item and the quantity supplied by sellers.

6. _____: other things being equal, the higher the price of a good, the greater the quantity of that good sellers are willing and able to make available over a given period.

7. _____: an arrangement through which buyers and sellers meet or communicate in order to trade goods or services.

8. _____: explains how prices are established in markets through competition among many buyers and sellers, and how those prices affect the quantities traded.

9. _____: attained when the price of a good adjusts so that the quantity buyers are willing and able to buy at that price is just equal to the quantity sellers are willing and able to supply.

10. _____: exists if the quantity demanded exceeds the quantity supplied of a good over a period of time.

11. _____: prevails when economic forces balance so that economic variables neither increase nor decrease.

12. _____: exists if the quantity supplied exceeds the quantity demanded of a good over a period of time.

13. _____ : a change in the relationship between a good's price and the quantity supplied in response to a change in a supply determinant other than the good's price.

14. _____ : a change in the amount of a good buyers are willing and able to buy in response to a change in the price of the good.

15. _____ : a change in the relationship between the price of a good and the quantity demanded caused by a change in a demand determinant other than the price of the good.

16. _____ : goods whose use together enhances the satisfaction a consumer obtains from each.

17. _____ : goods that serve a purpose similar to that of a given good.

18. _____ : a graph that shows how the quantity supplied varies with the price of a good.

19. _____ : in general, other things being equal, the lower the price of a good, the greater the quantity of that good buyers are willing and able to purchase over a given period.

20. _____ : a change in the amount of a good sellers are willing to sell in response to a change in the price of the good.

21. _____ : a relationship between an item's price and the quantity demanded.

22. _____ : a table that shows how the quantity demanded of a good would vary with price, given all other demand determinants.

23. _____ : the amount of an item that buyers are willing and able to purchase over a period at a certain price, given all other influences on their decision to buy.

CONCEPT REVIEW

Concept 2:   *Demand, law of demand, changes in demand and quantity demanded*

1. The following is a demand schedule for corn:

Price per Bushel	Quantity Demanded (000s bushels per week)	
	(a)	(b)
$4.00	850	_____
3.75	900	_____
3.50	950	_____
3.25	1,000	_____
3.00	1,050	_____
2.75	1,100	_____
2.50	1,150	_____

a. Put the demand curve on the diagram below.

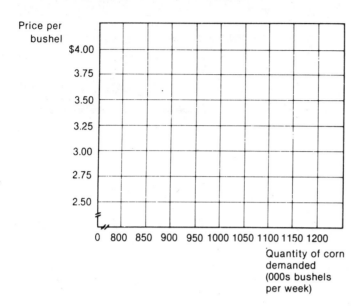

Price per bushel

$4.00
3.75
3.50
3.25
3.00
2.75
2.50

0   800 850 900 950 1000 1050 1100 1150 1200

Quantity of corn
demanded
(000s bushels
per week)

b. What kind of relationship exists between the price per bushel of corn and the quantity of corn demanded?
c. Assume that the prices of other vegetables are falling relative to the price of corn. Will this cause the demand curve to shift? Why?
d. Assume that the quantity of corn demanded decreases by 50,000 bushels at every price level. Show the impact of this by completing column b above.
e. Show the impact from part d on the demand curve that you plotted in part a.

2. List six nonprice determinants of demand:
   a. _____
   b. _____
   c. _____
   d. _____
   e. _____
   f. _____

3. Indicate for each of the following if a demand curve for automobiles will shift to the right (R), left (L), or remain unchanged (U):
   a. _____ Auto prices fall
   b. _____ Price of gasoline triples
   c. _____ Incomes decrease
   d. _____ Stock market gains increase wealth
   e. _____ Public transit fares fall to zero
   f. _____ Auto price increase expected

67

Concept 3: *Supply, law of supply, changes in supply and quantity supplied*

4. The following is a supply schedule for corn:

Price per Bushel	Quantity Supplied (000s of bushels per week)	
	(a)	(b)
$4.00	1600	_____
3.75	1400	_____
3.50	1200	_____
3.25	1000	_____
3.00	800	_____
2.75	600	_____
2.50	400	_____

a. Plot the supply curve on the diagram below.

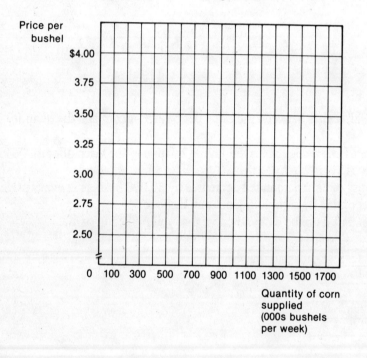

b. Is there a positive or negative relationship between the price of corn and the quantity of corn supplied? Explain.

c. Suppose a serious drought reduces corn output at each price by 100,000 bushels. Show the impact in column b above by completing the table.

d. Plot the new supply curve from column b on the diagram from part a.

5. List five nonprice determinants of supply:

a. _____

b. _____

c. _____

d. _____

e. _____

6. Which of the following will cause the supply curve for hamburgers to shift to the right (R), left (L), or remain unchanged (U)?

a. _____ Increase in the price of hamburger meat

b. _____ Increase in the price of hamburgers

c. _____ Increase in the price of chicken nuggets

d. _____ Introduction of new cost-saving technology in the hamburger industry

Concepts 4 and 5: *Market equilibrium price and quantity; shortages and surpluses*

7. The table below contains the price, quantity supplied, and quantity demanded data from column a of questions 1 and 4.

Price per Bushel	Quantity Demanded		Quantity Supplied	
	(000s of bushels per year)			
	(a)	(b)	(c)	(d)
$4.00	850	_____	1600	_____
3.75	900	_____	1400	_____
3.50	950	_____	1200	_____
3.25	1000	_____	1000	_____
3.00	1050	_____	800	_____
2.75	1100	_____	600	_____
2.50	1150	_____	400	_____

a. From the table above, determine the market equilibrium price and quantity in bushels.

b. On the diagram below, plot both the demand and supply curves. Identify the equilibrium price and quantity.

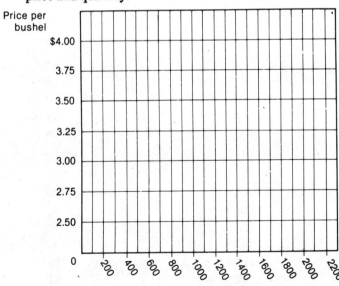

Quantity of corn demanded and supplied
(000s of bushels per week)

c. At a price of $3.75, a _____ exists in the amount of _____ because quantity demanded is _____ than quantity supplied.

d. At a price of $2.75, a _____ exists in the amount of _____ because quantity demanded is _____ than quantity supplied.

e. What is meant by the statement that competitive markets are self-equilibrating?

Concept 6: *Changes in supply and demand and market equilibrium*

8. Referring to the supply and demand schedules in question 7 above:
   a. Suppose that an increase in income causes the demand for corn to increase by 250,000 bushels at each price. Show the change in question 7, column b. Plot the new demand curve on the diagram in question 7.
   b. The market equilibrium price has _____ from $_____ to $_____. Market equilibrium output has _____ from _____ bushels to _____ bushels.
   c. Suppose that because of excellent weather, corn production increases at every price by 500,000 bushels. Show the change by completing column d from question 7. Plot the new supply curve on the diagram in question 7.
   d. Comparing the original equilibrium—demand curve a and supply curve c—to the new equilibrium with supply curve d, market equilibrium price has _____ from $_____ to $_____. Market quantity has _____ from _____ bushels to _____ bushels.
   e. Comparing the original equilibrium—demand curve a and supply curve c—to a new equilibrium with demand curve b and supply curve d, market equilibrium price has _____ from $_____ to $_____ and market quantity has _____ from _____ to _____ bushels.

9. Indicate below if the market price and quantity of concert tickets increases (+), decreases (-), or is indeterminate (0):

		Price	Quantity
a.	Stock market losses reduce wealth	_____	_____
b.	Income increases	_____	_____
c.	Season ticket prices are expected to rise	_____	_____
d.	Musicians' union wins large pay increase	_____	_____
e.	Price of movie tickets falls	_____	_____
f.	Population increases	_____	_____

Advanced Application: Changes in supply and demand and market equilibrium

10. Let the following equations represent demand and supply curves for some good:

Demand curve:	$Qd = a - bP$
Supply curve:	$Qs = c + dP$
where	a, b, c, and d are positive
	constants
	Qd = quantity demanded
	Qs = quantity supplied
	P = price

   a. Solve the above equations for the market equilibrium price.
   b. Solve for the equilibrium quantity.
   c. Interpret the equations for price and quantity. What causes price or quantity to rise or fall?

MASTERY TEST

Select the best answer.

1. In a free and unregulated competitive economy:
   a. wants are communicated to producers by the purchase orders of wholesalers.
   b. wants of buyers are communicated to sellers through the determination of prices in markets.
   c. sellers use market survey instruments to determine what and how much to produce.
   d. markets play an insignificant role.

2. The quantities of goods that buyers are willing and able to purchase at a specific price over a period of time, other influences held unchanged, is a definition for:
   a. quantity demanded.
   b. supply.
   c. total sales.
   d. demand.

3. The demand _____ is a table of price and quantity demanded data in which the *ceteris paribus* assumption is employed. The _____ is a plot of that data.
   a. table/scatter diagram
   b. schedule/marginal cost curve
   c. curve/schedule
   d. schedule/demand curve

4. The law of demand states that, other things being the same:
   a. price and income are positively related.
   b. income and sales are positively related.
   c. price and quantity demanded are positively related.
   d. price and quantity demanded are inversely related.

5. Which of the following will not cause a change in demand?
   a. Change in income
   b. Change in the price of the good in question
   c. Change in the prices of related goods, such as complements or substitutes
   d. Expectation of higher prices

6. If two goods are substitutes and the price of one good increases, the demand for the other good will:
    a. not change.
    b. increase.
    c. not be related.
    d. decrease.

7. If two goods are complementary goods and the price of one good increases, the demand for the other will:
    a. not change.
    b. increase.
    c. not be related.
    d. decrease.

8. If a good is a normal good, an increase in income will:
    a. increase supply.
    b. decrease demand.
    c. increase demand.
    d. decrease supply.

9. The quantities of a good that sellers are willing and able to produce and make available to the market at a specific price over a given period, other things being constant, is a definition of:
    a. demand.
    b. equilibrium.
    c. demand curve.
    d. quantity supplied.

10. The law of supply states that, other influences being unchanged:
    a. price and quantity demanded are inversely related.
    b. price and quantity supplied are inversely related.
    c. income and quantity supplied are unrelated.
    d. price and quantity supplied are positively related.

11. A change in quantity supplied can be caused by a change in
    a. price.
    b. income.
    c. technology.
    d. price of inputs.

12. A shift in a supply curve is known as a:
    a. supply shift.
    b. change in quantity supplied.
    c. rotation.
    d. change in supply.

13. Which of the following will not cause a leftward shift in the supply curve?
    a. Decrease in input prices
    b. Increase in the prices of other goods that could be produced with the same resources and technology
    c. Expectation of lower product prices
    d. Decrease in the number of sellers

14. Market equilibrium occurs when:
    a. the forces of supply and demand oppose each other.
    b. the forces of price and quantity oppose each other.
    c. a market price just equates quantity demanded and quantity supplied.
    d. a market quantity just equates quantity supplied and quantity demanded.

15. A price above the market equilibrium price results in:
    a. a shortage.
    b. inflation.
    c. excess demand.
    d. a surplus.

16. A price below the market equilibrium price results in:
    a. a shortage.
    b. inflation.
    c. insufficient demand.
    d. a surplus.

17. An increase in the demand for a good will _____ price and _____ quantity.
    a. decrease/decrease
    b. increase/decrease
    c. increase/increase
    d. decrease/increase

18. A decrease in supply of a good will _____ price and _____ quantity.
    a. decrease/decrease
    b. increase/decrease
    c. increase/increase
    d. decrease/increase

19. An increase in both demand and supply will _____ price and _____ quantity.
    a. decrease/ decrease
    b. have an indeterminate effect on/increase
    c. increase/increase
    d. increase/have an indeterminate effect on

20. If the price of movie tickets increases significantly, then the price of VCRs will probably _____ and the market quantity of VCRs will _____.
    a. increase/decrease
    b. increase/increase
    c. decrease/decrease
    d. decrease/increase

21. Assume that consumer incomes increase as a result of increases in wage rates. Using supply and demand analysis, which of the following best explains the impact on market price? Assume that the good in question is an inferior good.
    a. Market price increases because the demand for the good increases relative to supply.
    b. Market price increases because supply increases and demand decreases.
    c. Market price is indeterminate because the supply decreases as demand increases.
    d. Market price is indeterminate because supply and demand both decrease.

22. What will likely happen to market price and market quantity of a good if technological improvements occur simlutaneously with decreases in the price of a substitute good?
    a. Market price will rise and market quantity will fall.
    b. Market price will fall and market quantity will rise.
    c. Both market price and quantity will rise.
    d. Both market price and quantity will fall.
    e. Market price will fall, but market quantity is indeterminate.

23. Suppose farms produce both wheat and barley. What will happen to the market price and quantity of wheat if the price of barley increases?
    a. Market price falls and market quantity rises.
    b. Both market price and quantity increase.
    c. Both market price and quantity decrease.
    d. Market price increases and market quantity decreases.

24. Which answer best explains the following statement? "An increase in income increases quantity supplied."
    a. Producers behave according to the law of supply which says that income and supply are positively related.
    b. As income increases, demand increases if the good is a normal good, causing market price and quantity supplied to rise.
    c. If the good is an inferior good and income increases, spending on the good will increase, inducing firms to increase quantity supplied.
    d. This statement is incorrect because changes in income change demand, not quantity supplied.

25. Which of the following best explains the cause and effect process associated with an increase in demand?
    a. An increase in demand increases price and causes a surplus at the existing level of output. Producers respond by apportioning that surplus among consumers.
    b. An increase in demand causes price to increase, producing shortages and the need to increase supply.
    c. An increase in demand increases price and causes a shortage at the existing level of output. Producers respond to the shortage by discounting prices so quantity supplied will increase.
    d. An increase in demand initially will cause a shortage as quantity demanded exceeds quantity supplied at the existing price. Firms respond by increasing price, producing an incentive to increase quantity supplied.

THINK IT THROUGH

1. A market economy is a type of economy that relies on the market to .... (Complete the statement as thoroughly as you can.)

2. Use supply and demand analysis to assess the impact of the drought that occurred in the farm belt in the Spring and Summer of 1988.
    a. Discuss the impact of the drought on the market for corn.
    b. Discuss the probable impact on feedlots that use corn as feed.

3. If a market is currently in equilibrium and an increase in demand occurs, what happens to the market price? *Explain.*

4. If the price of golf course greens fees increases nationally, using supply and demand analysis, discuss the impact on the market for golf balls.

5. Suppose that you operate a dry cleaning firm in a small city and you and the other dry cleaners are earning handsome profits. Because of the profit potential, a national dry cleaning firm enters the area and opens several new dry cleaners. Assess the impact on the market for dry cleaning in this city.

ANALYZING THE NEWS

Using the skills derived from studying this chapter, analyze the economic facts that make up the following article and answer the questions below, using graphical analysis where possible.

1. Explain the causes of the decline in salmon prices?

2. What, if anything, could the fisherman do to reverse this trend?

Salmon fishermen stay in port in price protest

From Chicago Tribune wires

ANCHORAGE—Thousands of salmon fishermen stayed in port Thursday to protest low prices they blame on the Japanese, and the governor delayed the opening of fishing in one area to prevent violence.

Representatives for processors and fishermen were to meet in the Bristol Bay village of Naknek Thursday to discuss the strike, involving about 3,000 fishermen. Alaska's salmon catch was worth more than $500 million last year.

Fishermen in the Bristol Bay area started the strike Tuesday, at the beginning of the brief Bristol Bay harvest, to protest prices that tumbled from more than $1 a pound last year to about 47 cents this year. Processors paid more than $2 a pound in 1988.

Bristol Bay is in Alaska's southwest, just north of where the Aleutian Island chain begins. Nearly all its harvest is shipped to Japan.

The strike spread Wednesday to Kodiak and Cook Inlet, and Gov. Walter J. Hickel postponed the opening of red-salmon fishing in the Egegik district of Bristol Bay for 24 hours to prevent violence between striking and non-striking fishermen.

"I think the Japanese are just trying to find out how cheap we will fish," said Drew Sparlin, a fisherman from Kenai. "I assume somewhere along the line if Bristol Bay went fishing for 50 cents and we went fishing for 75 cents or a dollar, next year we would have to fish for 50 cents and they would have to fish for 25."

But Alec Brindle, president of Seattle-based Ward Cove Packing, said prices are low because "there's just a pile of fish around."

"This is just the operation of the law of supply and demand," he said. "Anybody who's been reading the statistics would know that there's a worldwide surplus of salmon. Alaska's no longer the sole source."

Ownership of the 10 major seafood-processing plants in the Bristol Bay region is dominated by Maurbeni, according to a 1990 state legislative study. Other Japanese companies with controlling ownership shares in Bristol Bay-area processors are Nichiro G.K. Ltd. and Yuasa-Funashoku, according to the study.

Local government offices and businesses shut down Tuesday for 24 hours in solidarity with the fishermen, according to borough manager Ed Pefferman.

"The community is dependent on fishing, so the borough is very sympathetic to the strike," he said.

Low salmon prices hurt the borough, which collects its revenues from a raw fish tax, he said.

Salmon fishermen throughout the state have been disappointed with this season's prices, depressed by high inventories worldwide of frozen and farmed salmon, officials said.

"We want to focus national attention on what's happening out in Bristol Bay," said salmon fisherman Fred Pike, mayor of the Bristol Bay Borough and an organizer of the strike.

Source: "Salmon Fishermen Stay in Port in Price Protest," *The Chicago Tribune*.

CHAPTER ANSWERS

The Chapter In Brief

1. Markets 2. Market price 3. Supply and demand analysis 4. Demand schedule 5. Demand curve 6. Demand 7. Change in quantity demanded 8. Change in demand 9. Supply schedule 10. Supply curve 11. Supply 12. Change in quantity supplied 13. Change in supply 14. Equilibrium 15. Price 16. Surplus 17. Shortage 18. Cutting prices 19. Surplus 20. Increasing 21. Equal to 22. Can

Key Terms Review

1. Change in relative price 2. Demand curve 3. Supply schedule 4. Quantity supplied 5. Supply 6. Law of Supply 7. Market 8. Supply and demand analysis 9. Market equilibrium 10. Shortage 11. Equilibrium 12. Surplus 13. Change in supply 14. Change in quantity demanded 15. Change in demand 16. Complements 17. Substitutes 18. Supply curve 19. Law of demand 20. Change in quantity supplied 21. Demand 22. Demand schedule 23. Quantity demanded

Concept Review

1. a.

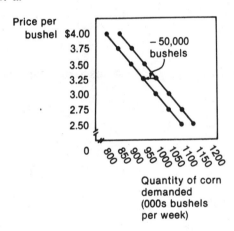

b. Negative or inverse
c. If other vegetables are considered substitutes for corn, the demand for corn falls and the demand curve shifts leftward as the prices of other vegetables are falling.
d.   (b)
       800
       850
       900
       950
       1000
       1050
       1100
e. The demand curve shifts leftward as shown in the diagram above in part a.

2. a. Income b. Wealth c. Prices of substitutes and complements d. Price expectations e. Tastes
f. Number of buyers

3. a. U b. L c. L d. R e. L f. R

4. a.

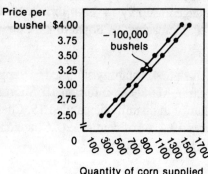

Price per bushel

Quantity of corn supplied
(000s bushels per week)

b.   Positive, higher prices increase the willingness and ability of suppliers to increase production.

c.   (b)
            1500

            1300

            1100

             900

             700

             500

             300

d.   The supply curve shifts leftward as shown in the diagram above in part a.

5. a. Prices of other goods b. Prices of inputs c. Technology d. Price expectations e. Number of
sellers

6. a. L b. U c. L d. R

7. a. $3.25, 1,000,000
   b.

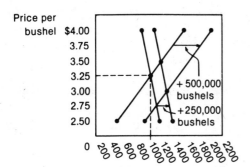

Price per bushel

Quantity of corn demanded
and supplied (000s of bushels)

c. Surplus, 500,000 bushels, less
d. Shortage, 500,000 bushels, greater
e. Competitive markets are self-equilibrating because market forces will eliminate shortages and surpluses. Shortages are eliminated as market prices rise and surpluses are eliminated as suppliers lower prices to sell excess inventory.

8. a.   (b)
             1100
             1150
             1200
             1250
             1300
             1350
             1400
   b. Increased, $3.25, $3.50, increased, 1,000,000, 1,200,000
   c.   (d)
             2100
             1900
             1700
             1500
             1300
             1100
             900
   d. Decreased, $3.25, $2.75, increased, 1,000,000, 1,100,000
   e. Decreased, $3.25, $3, increased, 1,000,000, 1,300,000

9.

	Price	Quantity
a.	—	—
b.	+	+
c.	+	+
d.	+	—
e.	—	—
f.	+	+

10. Market equilibrium requires that Qd = Qs. Setting the supply and demand curves equal to each other:

$$a - bP = c + dP$$

and solving for P, the market equilibrium price, gives:

a. $P = (a - c)/(d + b)$

Substituting this expression for P into either the demand or supply equation and solving for Q, the market equilibrium quantity, yields:

b. $Q = (ad + bc)/(d + b)$

c. Q is positive and P must be positive. P is positive if the intercept of the demand curve a exceeds the intercept of the supply curve c. This always is expected to be the case. Changes in the nonprice determinants of supply and demand influence the supply and demand equations by changing the value of the intercept terms, a or c. For instance, an increase in income would increase a assuming the good is a normal good. If it is an inferior good, the increase in income will reduce a. As can be seen from the equations above, an increase in a will increase P and Q. A decrease in a will decrease P and Q. An increase in c caused by a nonprice determinant of supply causes P to decrease and Q to increase.

Mastery Test

1. b 2. a 3. d 4. d 5. b 6. b 7. d 8. c 9. d 10. d 11. a 12. d 13. a 14. c 15. d 16. a 17. c 18. b 19. b 20. b 21. d 22. e 23. d 24. b 25. d

Think it Through

1. A market economy is a type of economy that relies on the market to allocate resources and distribute output. The impersonal interaction of the forces of supply and demand communicate the wishes of consumers to sellers via the market price. Changes in demand alter the price, and it is the change in price that causes a supplier to respond by altering production. As producers alter levels of production, they alter their levels of employment of resources. Thus markets determine what is to be produced and in what quantities. Resources flow to markets experiencing increases in quantity and away from markets experiencing decreases in production. Output is distributed based upon a buyer's ability to pay. Other things being constant, rising market prices reduce the ability to pay, whereas decreases in market prices increase the ability to pay.

2. a. As is shown in the diagram below, the drought reduces the supply of corn increasing the price per bushel of corn and reducing the market quantity of corn.

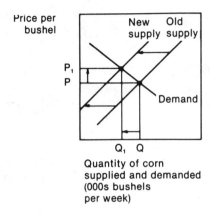

b. If corn is an input to feedlot operations and the price of corn is increasing, the supply of feedlot services will decrease, causing the price of those services to increase and the quantity of feedlot services to fall.

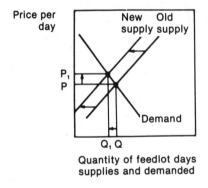

3. If demand increases, then at the current market price there is a shortage because quantity demanded exceeds quantity supplied. In order to ration the limited number of goods or services among many buyers, the price of the good or service is increased. Increases in price reduce quantity demanded but increase quantity supplied. This in turn reduces the shortage. As long as a shortage exists, the rationing function of prices implies that prices will continue to rise. Prices will no longer increase when the shortage is eliminated. The shortage no longer exists at the new market equilibrium.

4. Greens fees and golf balls are complementary goods. If the price of greens fees increases, the demand for golf balls will decrease. As can be seen in the figure below, a decrease in the demand for golf balls reduces the market price and quantity.

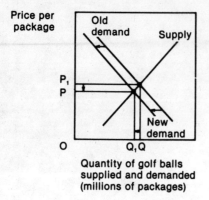

Quantity of golf balls
supplied and demanded
(millions of packages)

5. If several new dry cleaners open for business, the local market supply of dry cleaning services will increase. This causes a decrease in the price of dry cleaning services, but an increase in total market quantity.

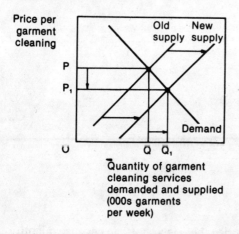

Quantity of garment
cleaning services
demanded and supplied
(000s garments
per week)

Analyzing The News

1. An increase in the number of salmon placed on the market by Japanese fishermen increased the market supply of fish. As the supply of fish increased, Alaska fishermen found that the equilibrium price was no longer $2 per pound. The increase in supply put downward pressure on prices as fishermen were faced with surpluses at $2 per pound. Surpluses will persist until a lower market equilibrium price is established where fishermen can sell all the fish they desire and consumers can purchase all the fish they want at the prevailing price. Apparently at $.47 per pound, surpluses of salmon still exist, indicating that the price could fall even more.

2. Given the realities of market forces, there is very little Alaskan fishermen can do to increase prices. Of course, some fishermen might go out of business at such low prices, shifting the market supply curve leftward and increasing prices. Alaskan fishermen could advertise and promote the consumption of salmon, such as is done in the dairy and beef industries. This might shift the demand curve for salmon rightward and increase salmon prices.

4   USING SUPPLY AND DEMAND ANALYSIS

CHAPTER CONCEPTS

After studying your text, attending class, and completing this chapter, you should be able to:

1. Demonstrate how market equilibrium prices deal with the problem of scarcity by rationing goods and services and explain why prices would be zero for nonscarce goods.
2. Explain how supply and demand conditions affect the price and sales potential for new products.
3. Show how wages and interest rates are determined in competitive markets.
4. Use supply and demand analysis to show how government control of prices in competitive markets can result in shortages or surpluses.

THE CHAPTER IN BRIEF

Fill in the blanks to summarize chapter content.

Supply and demand analysis is a useful tool for analyzing personal, business, and social problems and issues. It shows the importance of prices in the allocation of resources. Prices help us deal with the problem of scarcity in both the allocation of resources and the distribution of output. Do prices have a role when scarcity does not exist? Goods in abundant supply such as air are called (1)_____ (essential commodities, nonscarce goods) because there is no positive price for which quantity demanded exceeds quantity supplied. If a positive price is not possible, markets do not develop. Markets develop only when positive prices are possible.

But even at positive prices, a market may not develop if the minimum price required by sellers exceeds the maximum price that buyers are willing and able to pay for the first unit of output. A market for new products can only develop when demand and supply have reached a point where the (2)_____(maximum, minimum) price buyers are willing and able to pay for the first unit of output exceeds the (3)_____(maximum, minimum) price sellers are willing to take for that unit.

In addition to the markets for goods and services, supply and demand analysis can be used to assess changes in competitive labor and credit markets. The price per unit of labor is called the (4)_____(labor cost, wage). When the supply of labor equals the demand, there is a market wage and quantity of labor employed. Everyone who wants to work at that wage is employed. If the demand for the product produced by that labor increases, the demand for labor by employers will likewise increase. This causes the wage to (5)_____(rise, fall) and the quantity of labor employed to (6)_____(decrease, increase). In a recession, as the demand for goods and services falls, the demand for labor declines, causing both wages and employment to also (7)_____(rise, fall).

Changes in the demand and supply of loanable funds determine interest rate movements. In an economic expansion, individuals, businesses, and government as a group borrow more. Interest rates (8)_____(rise, fall) as the demand for loanable funds increases. If the supply of loanable funds increases, say as a result of an increase in savings by both businesses and individuals, interest rates will (9)_____(rise, fall) and (10)_____(more, less) credit will be extended by lenders.

Prices are not always allowed to perform the rationing function. Society will often sanction government price controls as an attempt to aid certain interest groups, such as farmers, unskilled workers, and low-income renters and borrowers. (11)_____ (Price ceilings, Price floors) are government-mandated prices that are set below market equilibrium prices. A price below the market price causes (12)_____(surpluses, shortages). Rent controls, while helping those fortunate enough to pay controlled rents, cause (13)_____(surpluses, shortages) of low-income housing and reduce the incentive of landlords to maintain properties. Usury laws that prevent interest rates from rising to their market levels, while benefiting those people able to obtain the regulated credit, will cause a (14)_____ (surplus, shortage) of loanable funds. The least credit worthy (and also the lowest income) members of society will have difficulty finding credit. Price ceilings will cause (15)_____ (surpluses, shortages) only when the regulated price is (16)_____(below, above) the market price. If market interest rates were to fall, for example, below the usury ceiling, there would be no (17)_____(shortage, surplus) of loanable funds.

When shortages develop there must be a way to allocate the limited goods and services among the buyers. A market system relies on prices to do this. But with price ceilings, prices are not allowed to perform that function. Waiting in line, eligibility criteria, and ration stamps are three methods of nonprice rationing. All three are less efficient than prices in responding to shortages. There will still be those people willing and able to pay prices above the controlled price. In response to this potential market, illegal or (18)_____ (new markets, black markets) develop.

(19)_____(Price ceilings, Price floors) are controlled prices that are set above the market price. Prices above market equilibrium prices cause (20)_____(surpluses, shortages). Whereas prices fall to eliminate the surplus, other means have to be used to deal with surpluses, such as with agricultural price-support programs. Farmers either have to be rewarded to reduce plantings or the surpluses have to be purchased, stored, and distributed by government. Resources that could have been used elsewhere in the economy are being used to eliminate or deal with surpluses that would have been efficiently eliminated by a functioning price system. Although farmers as a special interest group benefit, consumers lose in that they pay (21)_____(lower, higher) prices, and the allocation of resources in the economy is (22)_____(less, more) efficient.

Minimum wage laws set minimum wages at a level above the market wage in most labor markets. The intent of such legislation is to increase the income of the poorest members of society, those individuals who also happen to have the lowest skill levels. But as was the case with agricultural price supports, (23)_____(surpluses, shortages) develop. The unemployment rate among the unskilled is (24)_____(lower, higher). The minimum wage benefits those lucky enough to find employment at that wage, but causes (25)_____(more, less) unemployment in that segment of society that can least afford to be unemployed.

Price controls distort the economy. They benefit some at the expense of others and prohibit a competitive economy from efficiently rationing resources. If the motives underlying price controls are socially desirable, society would gain if methods other than price controls could be employed to make certain interest groups better off without impairing the functioning of a competitive economy.

KEY TERMS REVIEW

Write the key term from the list below next to its definition.

Key Terms

Nonscarce good   Price ceiling
Wages   Nonprice rationing
Credit   Black market
Interest   Price floor

Definitions

1. _____ : a good for which the quantity demanded does not exceed the quantity supplied at a zero price.

2. _____ : establishes a maximum price that can legally be charged for a good or service.

3. _____ : the price paid for labor services.

4. _____ : the price for the use of funds, expressed as a percentage per dollar of funds borrowed.

5. _____ : a minimum price established by law.

6. _____ : a market in which sellers sell goods to buyers for more than the legal prices.

7. _____ : the use of loanable funds supplied by lenders to borrowers, who agree to pay back the funds borrowed, according to an agreed-upon schedule.

8. _____ : a device that distributes available goods and services on a basis other than willingness to pay.

CONCEPT REVIEW

Concept 3:   *The determination of wages and interest rates in competitive markets*

1. You are a manager of a business and you are trying to decide if you should borrow funds for plant expansion today at the current interest rate of 12%. The morning newspaper reports that the Federal Reserve System has announced that within the next month it will begin to expand the funds that banks have on hand to extend credit.

    a.   Show the impact on the supply of loanable funds curve in the diagram below.

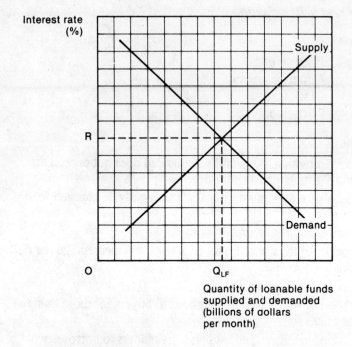

Interest rate (%)

Quantity of loanable funds
supplied and demanded
(billions of dollars
per month)

  b. How will your analysis of future interest rates influence your decision to borrow today?

2. You are a college sophomore trying to decide if you should major in mechanical engineering. Employability and income prospects are important considerations in your choice. As shown in the diagram below, the market for engineers is currently producing high entry market wages.

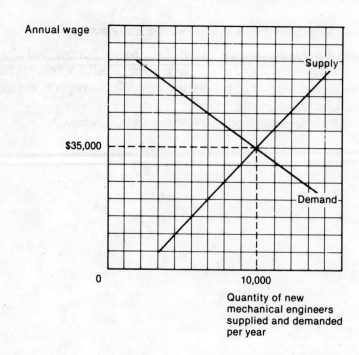

Annual wage

Quantity of new
mechanical engineers
supplied and demanded
per year

88

a. If you and thousands of other college students are induced by the high entry wages to become majors in engineering, in time the supply of engineers will _____. Show the future supply curve on the diagram above.

b. Entry wages in the future would _____, and the total employment of engineers would _____.

c. How might these expected future wages and employment levels influence your decision today to major in engineering?

Concept 4: *Government price controls—shortages and surpluses*

3. The diagram below represents the market for good X.

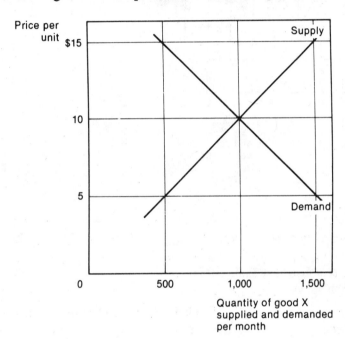

a. The market price is $_____, and the market quantity equals _____ units of X.

b. If a price ceiling is established at $5, a _____ would exist in the amount of _____ units. Show on the diagram above the impact of this price ceiling.

c. If a price floor is set at $15, a _____ would exist in the amount of _____ units. Show this on the graph above.

89

4. Given the market for unskilled labor in the diagram below:

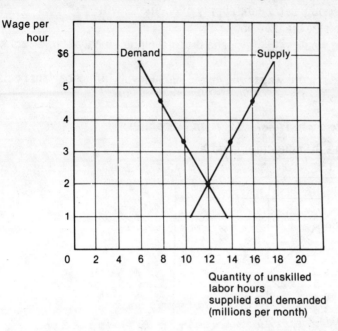

a. The market wage and level of employment equals $_____ and _____ hours, respectively.

b. A minimum wage is now established at $3.35 per hour.
   (1) Show on the graph above.
   (2) Wages _____ from $_____ to $_____ and employment _____ from _____ hours to _____ hours.

c. What would happen if the minimum wage increased from $3.35 to $4.70 per hour?
   (1) Show on the above graph.
   (2) Wages _____ from $_____ to $_____ and employment _____ from _____ hours to _____ hours.

5. List three forms of nonprice rationing:
   a. _____
   b. _____
   c. _____

Advanced Application: Determination of interest rates

6. As a portfolio manager you must react to anticipated changes in interest rates with respect to your company's holding of financial assets such as stocks, cash, and bonds. Based on the current interest rate of 10%, your research shows that for each one percentage point change in the interest rate, the quantity of loanable funds supplied changes by $2 billion and the quantity of loanable funds demanded changes by $3 billion. If you anticipate that the demand for loanable funds will increase by $5 billion, what would you predict regarding the future rate of interest?

MASTERY TEST

Select the best answer.

1. Markets for new products would not develop if:
   a. the price required by producers to produce the first unit of output exceeded the price that buyers are willing and able to pay for that first unit.
   b. profits exceeded that which could be earned on financial assets.
   c. the price required by producers to produce the first unit of output was less than the price buyers are willing and able to pay for the first unit.
   d. None of the above

2. Goods for which there is no positive price in which the quantity demanded exceeds the quantity supplied, are known as:
   a. scarce goods.
   b. normal goods.
   c. inferior goods.
   d. nonscarce goods.

3. An important function of prices in competitive markets is:
   a. the rationing function.
   b. to ensure that producers make profits.
   c. to eliminate any unemployment.
   d. to communicate to buyers the wishes of sellers.

4. In a competitive labor market, wages are determined:
   a. by buyers.
   b. by unions.
   c. by sellers.
   d. by the forces of supply and demand.

5. An increase in the demand for labor by businesses _____ wages and _____ employment.
   a. increases/decreases
   b. decreases/decreases
   c. increases/increases
   d. decreases/increases

6. If because of a recession the demand for loanable funds decreases, what would happen to market interest rates and the quantity of credit extended?
   a. Interest rates would increase and the quantity of credit would decrease.
   b. Interest rates would decrease and the quantity of credit would not change.
   c. Interest rates would not change but the quantity of credit would fall.
   d. Both interest rates and the quantity of credit would decline.

7. Usury laws that prevent interest rates from rising to market levels are called:
   a. monetary regulations.
   b. price ceilings.
   c. price floors.
   d. rationing methods.

8. Rents controls:
   a. are price ceilings.
   b. cause shortages of low-income housing.
   c. result in the deterioration of low-income housing through the lack of maintenance.
   d. All of the above.

9. The minimum wage law is an example of:
   a. an employment enhancement strategy.
   b. a price ceiling.
   c. a price floor.
   d. a well-designed policy intended to reduce teenage unemployment.

10. Price ceilings cause:
   a. no change in market quantities.
   b. shortages.
   c. quantity supplied to increase.
   d. surpluses.

11. Price floors cause:
   a. no change in market quantities.
   b. shortages.
   c. quantity demanded to increase.
   d. surpluses.

12. Agricultural price supports:
   a. benefit farmers.
   b. harm consumers.
   c. require the use of scarce resources to deal with surpluses.
   d. All of the above

13. If in some labor markets the market wage for unskilled labor exceeds the minimum wage:
   a. unemployment would result.
   b. wages would rise.
   c. the minimum wage law would not have an adverse impact on unemployment.
   d. wages would fall.

14. Which of the following cannot be considered true regarding price controls?
   a. Some people within special interest groups gain.
   b. Some people within the targeted special interest groups may actually lose.
   c. Resources are more efficiently used in the economy.
   d. Resources are less efficiently used in the economy.

15. Which of the following is not a nonprice form of rationing?
   a. Grouped staging
   b. Waiting in line
   c. Ration stamps
   d. Eligibility criteria

16. Price ceilings create an environment conducive to the development of:
    a. new products.
    b. black markets.
    c. higher employment.
    d. a saving ethic.

17. Suppose a firm introduces a radically-advanced stereo speaker system to the market, but finds that the system is not selling. What might be a likely cause for the apparent lack of consumer interest?
    a. The market demand and supply curves intersect at too high of a price.
    b. The market demand and supply curves intersect at a low price, but product quality is poor.
    c. The market demand curve's intercept on the horizontal axis is at a lower level of output than the market supply curve's intercept.
    d. The market demand curve's intercept on the vertical axis is at a lower price that the market supply curve's intercept.

18. Which of the following statements best explains the existence of black markets?
    a. There will always be a depraved segment of the population engaged in illegal activities.
    b. Black markets only exist in centralized socialist nations where people are not free to exercise their will.
    c. Black markets arise where prices are kept below market equilibrium prices, suggesting that some consumers would be willing and able to pay higher prices for these goods rather than to go without.
    d. Government price floors cause shortages and provide incentives for black market entrepreneurs to violate government price controls.

19. What might happen to market interest rates if households increase saving while federal government borrowing is increasing?
    a. The interest rate increases because the demand for loanable funds increases.
    b. The supply of loanable funds increases and the demand for loanable funds decreases, causing the market rate of interest to rise.
    c. Both the supply of and demand for loanable funds decrease, causing the market rate of interest to fall.
    d. The supply of and demand for loanable funds increase, resulting in an indeterminate change in the market rate of interest.

20. Suppose you work in an area where the market wage rate for unskilled labor is $5.00. New federal legislation is passed, increasing the minimum wage to $4.25. What happens to the level of unemployment?
    a. Unemployment increases because price floors always produce surpluses.
    b. Unemployment increases because there are some labor force participants that are willing and able to work at the minimum wage, but cannot find employment.
    c. Unemployment decreases because a minimum wage above the market wage causes labor shortages.
    d. Unemployment does not change because a below-market minimum wage has no impact on business employment decisions.

21. The air we breathe is essential for life, yet it does not command a price in the market. Why?
    a. The supply curve for air intercepts the horizontal axis at a level of output greater than the level of output at which the demand for air intercepts the horizontal axis.
    b. The demand curve for air intercepts the vertical axis at a price greater than the price at which the supply of air intercepts the vertical axis.
    c. The demand curve for air intercepts the horizontal axis at a level of output greater than the level of output at which the supply of air intercepts the horizontal axis.
    d. The supply curve of air intercepts the vertical axis at a price greater than the price at which the demand for air intercepts the vertical axis.

THINK IT THROUGH

1. Discuss the importance of the price system in a market-based economy.

2. Discuss how interest rates are determined in a competitive market for loanable funds. Identify the gainers and losers from usury laws. Under what conditions would the usury laws be ineffective? If it is socially desirable to make credit available at below-market interest rates, what are other ways to benefit the targeted interest group without resulting in as much economic inefficiency as usury laws.

3. The minimum wage increased to $4.25 in 1991. Identify the likely gainers and losers. If it is socially desirable to increase the incomes of the unskilled beyond the levels that would prevail in a competitive labor market, what are other ways of doing this so that unskilled workers can be better off without causing as much inefficiency as would be the case with price controls?

4. In the early 1970s, President Nixon installed a series of wage and price controls. Prices were temporarily frozen on all goods and services. The supply of and demand for gasoline put upward pressure on gasoline prices, but these prices were temporarily controlled. In effect, the price freeze acted as a price ceiling. What do you think occurred in the gasoline market? Explain.

ANALYZING THE NEWS

Using the skills derived from studying this chapter, analyze the economic facts that make up the following article and answer the questions below, using graphical analysis where possible.

1. Was the market for satellite phones in equilibrium during the Pursian Gulf War?

2. Are waiting lists the most efficient way to ration output?

'Desert Storm' Demand Buffets Satellite-Phone Firm

Orders for Portables Sweep In From Reporters, Saudis and Pentagon

By Mark Robichaux
And Gilbert Fuchsberg
Staff Reporters of The Wall Street Journal

In the old days, foreign correspondents didn't roam far without their trench coats. But in the Persian Gulf, a new essential has emerged: the portable satellite telephone.

Jordan's King Hussein once gave the devices to visiting heads of state, and sheiks saw them as exotic toys. But today, Cable News Network depends on one to beam audio reports out of Baghdad. Other networks, wire services and big newspapers all lug them around the area—as do allied military commanders, diplomats and relief groups. And they want more—lots more.

For **Mobile Telesystems** Inc. of Gaithersburg, Md., a leading maker of the high-tech phones, the boom is both a windfall and a headache.

Since the war erupted, demand for the company's most popular model—a $52,000 single-suitcase version—has skyrocketed. The backlog of orders now exceeds 100 units; months ago, the company had hoped it might sell 20 phones in January. Having met projections for the entire first quarter in just one month, officials now expect 1991 sales to easily exceed 1990 sales of $15 million and "significantly" surpass the $19 million they had projected. They describe the closely held concern as "very" profitable.

But sudden success has a flip side. Mobile Telesystems must struggle to cut a three-month backlog, a major task for a firm that hand-makes its products. It can't get some parts fast enough. And juggling customers is growing tougher, as priority orders for the Pentagon delay deliveries for other clients.

Around-the-Clock Pressure

Customers press their case around the clock. One day last week, Shafiq A. Chaudhuri, the company's vice president for marketing and sales, was awakened at home at 4:45 a.m. by a Saudi Arabian official wanting to buy a dozen phones. "People are very anxious," Mr. Chaudhuri says. A company salesman even took over his newborn son's nursery and installed a fax machine and phone line, so he could field a surge of late-night calls from Middle East customers.

Desperate to speed their orders, three customers, wanting five phones apiece,

each wired $250,000 last week to company accounts, rather than wait for letters of credit and invoices to clear. Another client offered a 20% premium to move up on the waiting list.

To meet demand, a dozen U.S. assembly workers, augmenting a production facility in Taiwan, now arrive at 5 a.m., to start 12-hour shifts. They work Saturdays, too.

Unlike cellular telephones, which rely on local receivers to relay calls, satellite phones work virtually anywhere. A user aligns a small satellite dish with a satellite positioned to handle such transmissions and dials a special code. The satellite

Mobile's Satellite Phone

bounces the call to a ground station, which feeds it into the regular phone network. Calls take 45 seconds to connect and cost from $7 to $10 a minute.

System Isn't Perfect

The system isn't perfect. Mobile Telesystems' one-suitcase model weighs 65 pounds and can blink out if atmospheric conditions aren't right. Still, its yardwide dish pops open like an umbrella. It can connect to a fax or computer, and it plugs into wall outlets. With a $400 accessory, it can operate off a car battery.

Users cite the phone's simplicity. "Peter Arnett isn't exactly known around here as a 'techno-nerd,'" Leon Harris, assistant director of satellites and circuits at CNN, says of the network's man in Baghdad. "Our guys showed him how to use it

Continued on next page

95

Continued from previous page

in five minutes on his way out of the country."

National Broadcasting Co. staffers in the Gulf use the phones to help coordinate video feeds with Stuart Pearman, a network manager in New York. "In certain situations, they're indispensable," Mr. Pearman says.

Though five companies world-wide sell portable satellite phones, only Mobile Telesystems sells one as compact as its single-suitcase model. The company claims an 80% share of the portable satellite phone market, though some familiar with the industry contend the figure is closer to 50%. Few dispute, however, that Mobile Telesystems leads a growing field. According to Inmarsat, the London-based consortium that runs the satellites and bills users, a total of 2,150 land-based satellite phones are now in use, up 71% from a year earlier.

Communications Satellite Corp., a telecommunications concern, started Mobile Telesystems a decade ago but set it off as a private entity three years ago, retaining a 23% stake. The company first sold satellite phones for marine use, and in 1987 packaged the technology into its first portable, a two-suitcase model.

After the single-suitcase model emerged last year, it found quick success. Federal officials bought dozens for presidential trips, air-crash investigation teams and far-flung embassies—where phones aren't always up to snuff. "The ambassador would rather play golf than wait four hours to get a call through," says Mr. Chaudhuri, the marketing vice president.

The company began suffering from its own success last summer, after Iraq invaded Kuwait and allied troops moved in. Orders began piling up. And capacity, which stood at 15 units a month last summer, quickly proved inadequate. The company has since managed to double production, but it can't easily squeeze suppliers to speed delivery of special, hard-to-make parts.

One supply snag: synthetic crystals that take two months to grow and can't be rushed. Meanwhile, a Swiss maker of watertight cable fittings for the phones balked at boosting output, for fear the surge in orders wouldn't last.

"We can go over the cliff, but they don't want to go with us," explains Kenneth A. Homon, Mobile Telesystems president.

The company is now adding to its supplier base when it can, and for unique parts it's paying higher prices—and signing long-term commitments for larger orders.

Customers, of course, don't want to hear about production problems. But with Pentagon orders getting priority, the company can't accommodate everybody. Some who order five may get only three; others are taking two-suitcase models to tide them over; a few are going to agents who lease the devices. Even mighty **Coca-Cola** Co. has had to wait three months for a phone it ordered as a backup for its offices in hurricane-prone Puerto Rico.

Nissho Iwai, a California-based Japanese trading company, is especially desperate to speed delivery of 10 phones it wants from Mobile Telesystems; the phones will eventually be used in the Gulf. Yoji Hirakata, the company's electronics manager, asks a reporter: "Is there any way you can you push them to get the units over here sooner?"

CHAPTER ANSWERS

The Chapter in Brief

1. Nonscarce goods 2. Maximum 3. Minimum 4. Wage 5. Rise 6. Increase 7. Fall 8. Rise 9. Fall 10. More 11. Price ceilings 12. Shortages 13. Shortages 14. Shortage 15. Shortages 16. Below 17. Shortage 18. Black markets 19. Price floors 20. Surpluses 21. Higher 22. Less 23. Surpluses 24. Higher 25. More

Key Terms Review

1. Nonscarce good 2. Price ceiling 3. Wages 4. Interest 5. Price floor 6. Black market 7. Credit 8. Nonprice rationing

Concept Review

1. a.

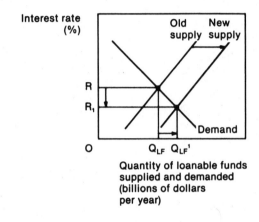

b. If you expect interest rates to fall, then other things being equal, you could lower borrowing costs by delaying borrowing until interest rates have fallen.

2. a. Increase

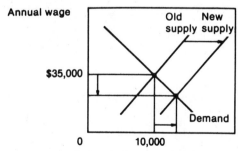

97

b. Decease, increase

c. You might be deterred from becoming an engineering major in anticipation of lower market wages that might prevail at the time you graduate and enter the labor force. This, of course, assumes that nothing else is expected to influence wages in the future and that you are placing a very high priority on entry level wages relative to other benefits received from an occupation or course of study.

3. a. $10, 1000

   b. Shortage, 1000

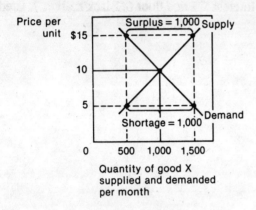

   c. Surplus, 1000

4. a. $2, 12 million

   b.   (1)

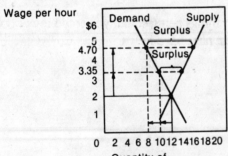

       (2) Increase, $2, $3.35, decreases, 12 million, 10 million

  c.   (1) Answer on the above diagram

       (2) Increase, $3.35, $4.70, decreases, 10 million, 8 million

5. a.   Waiting in line
   b.   Ration stamps
   c.   Eligibility criteria

6. This question can be solved graphically or algebraically with just the information given. Assume that the demand and supply curves for loanable funds are linear. This means that the slopes of both curves are constant. Assume also that no other influences are shifting the supply or demand curves other than the increase in demand of $5 billion. We are told that the current interest rate is 10%. This is the rate at which the supply and demand curves intersect. Increasing or decreasing the interest rate by one percentage point increases or decreases the quantity of loanable funds supplied by $2 billion and decreases or increases the quantity of loanable funds demanded by $3 billion. As can be seen in the figure below, this produces supply and demand curves that intersect at a market interest rate of 10%. Shifting the demand curve rightward by $5 billion increases the market interest rate to 11%.

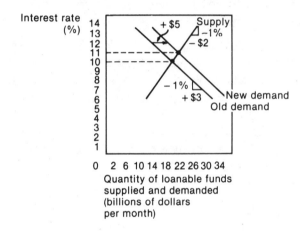

Another way to solve the problem would be to use the equilibrium price equation derived in question 10 from Chapter 5. Except in this case let's call the price the interest rate.

       Let $R = (a - c)/(d + b)$, where R = the interest rate

       A change in $R = 1/(d + b)$ x the change in $(a - c)$

Recall that we are assuming constant slopes. Therefore d and b remain unchanged. The a term is the constant term that reflects noninterest rate influences on the demand for loanable funds—that shifts the demand curve. Since we are making the *ceteris paribus* assumption, the c term is held constant.

       A change in $R = 1/(2 + 3)$ x $5 billion

       $= 1\%$

Interest rates are expected to rise from 10% to 11%

Mastery Test

1. a 2. d 3. a 4. d 5. c 6. d 7. b 8. d 9. c 10. b 11. d 12. d 13. c 14. c 15. a 16. b 17. d 18. c 19. d 20. d 21. a

Think it Through

1. Your answer needs to emphasize the rationing function of prices. Price changes will in time eliminate shortages or surpluses. The price system allocates resources efficiently. Prices represent the vehicle by which the wishes of buyers are communicated to sellers. In short, prices coordinate the purchase plans of buyers with the production plans of sellers.

2. In a competitive market for loanable funds, the forces of supply and demand determine the market rate of interest and the market quantity of credit. Usury laws benefit those lucky enough to obtain loans at the controlled rate (those people with higher incomes and credit ratings), but impose costs on those who must go without credit (those people with lower incomes and poorer credit ratings). One alternative to regulated interest rates might be subsidies to low-income borrowers or those with poor credit ratings to be used to defer the cost of borrowing at the market rate of interest. Lenders could be encouraged to make loans to these people if lenders were protected from loan defaults by some form of government guarantee. This alternative would still require the use of scarce resources that would not have been required in a market involving no intervention. But at least the price system can perform its rationing function.

3. An increase in the minimum wage will increase the incomes of those able to find employment at that wage. But the level of unemployment will increase among those least able to afford the loss of a job—the poor and unskilled. Incomes and employability can be increased a number of ways without having to resort to price controls. Job training programs that increase the productivity of the unskilled will increase their prospects for employment and better wages. Income transfers (such as Aid to Families with Dependent Children) can be used to supplement the incomes of the poor and unskilled. Again, these alternatives require the use of scarce resources but at least do not prevent the price system from functioning.

4. Severe gasoline shortages developed at the frozen price. Because prices could not perform their rationing function, people waited endlessly in line at service stations all across the nation. The problem continued to be serious until the price controls were removed.

Analyzing the News

1. During the Persian Gulf War, the market for satellite phones was clearly not in equilibrium. As the threat of information interruptions mounted, the demand for these phones skyrocketed. However, due to the lags that occur between production and distribution, the quantity of phones supplied did not increase fast enough to meet the increase in demand. As a result, severe shortages developed. Evidence of a shortage can be found in the firm's need to resort to a waiting list. If no shortage existed, the price premiums offered by buyers to move up on the list would not have occurred.

2. By using a waiting list to distribute the satellite phones, the firm was able to buy time to correct production difficulties but did not ration the good in an efficient manner. The price system will automatically ration the limited supply as price rises. Rising prices ration consumers out of the market who are unwilling or unable to pay the higher price. Those who are willing and able to purchase the product at the higher equilibrium price pay a price equal to their marginal benefit. Higher prices also induce firms to increase production. Therefore, rising prices increase quan-

tity supplied and reduce quantity demanded until the shortage is eliminated. A waiting list creates an artificial price ceiling that prevents the market from reaching the socially-optimal market-clearing price.

5   THE PRICE SYSTEM: FREE MARKETS AND THE ECONOMY

CHAPTER CONCEPTS

After studying your text, attending class, and completing this chapter, you should be able to:

1. Examine the framework of a pure market economy and show how the circular flow of income and expenditure in a capitalistic economy keeps it functioning.
2. Explain the price system as a means to allocate resources in terms of what is produced, how it is produced, and how it is distributed.
3. Identify the defects of a pure market system.
4. Briefly outline the functioning of the modern mixed and open economy.

THE CHAPTER IN BRIEF

Fill in the blanks to summarize chapter content.

(1)_____ (Capitalism, Socialism) is an economic system characterized by private owner-ship, freedom of choice and enterprise, and a limited economic role for government. A capitalistic economy relies on the (2)_____ (benevolence of sellers, price system) to answer the "what, how, and to whom" questions basic to all economies. (3)_____ (Profit, Money) is the guiding force in capitalistic systems. It is what induces sellers to acquire resources to produce goods that are profitable to produce and to withdraw resources from other uses that are less profit-able or involve no profit. (4)_____ (Economic dominance, Economic rivalry) is also an essential characteristic in which there are large numbers of both buyers and sellers in markets and in which economic power is dispersed among many sellers and buyers such that no one seller or buyer dominates market outcomes.

For a market system to operate efficiently, it must not only produce output efficiently, but buyers and sellers must also be allowed to engage in mutually gainful trades or transactions. Transactions in a (5)_____(money, barter) economy do not involve the exchange of money for goods, but the exchange of goods for goods. It is an inefficient form of exchange because of the high transac-tion costs involved in finding "producers-consumers" with which to trade. Barter requires a (6)_____ (single coincidence of wants, double coincidence of wants). Money greatly facilitates the exchange process because it allows individuals to specialize in the production of a single good, to convert any surplus into money by selling it in the market, and to spend the money on goods and services produced by other sellers. With money, a double coincidence of wants (7)_____(is, is not) required.

A (8)_____(supply and demand diagram, circular flow diagram) is a useful way of identifying the major sectors in a pure market economy and the relationships among those sectors. Businesses purchase resources from households in order to produce the output of goods and services consumed by households. Households derive their income from the sale of resources to the business sector. It is in this market for resources that supply and demand conditions determine the market prices that businesses must pay for resources and therefore the market wages, rents, and interest plus profits received by households. A household's income is the result of the quantities of resources sold in the resource market and the market prices at which those resources sell.

Households use their income, in part, to purchase the output of business. Household expenditures become the firm's sale revenue. The revenue from sales is used by businesses to purchase the resources necessary to produce output. In the markets for goods and services, supply and demand determine prices, which in turn influence the quantities of goods and services demanded and supplied.

In a pure market economy, the price system answers the three basic questions: What is produced? How are goods produced? To whom are goods distributed? Goods are produced if they are profitable to produce. Resources are used first to produce the most (9)_____(profitable, desirable) goods and services. Profitability depends, in part, upon the prices prevailing in both product and resource markets. Because of economic rivalry, successful producers are those that are able to earn enough income over time to continue in business. Sellers who introduce new technology can realize lower costs and, as a result, higher profits. But increased production resulting from higher profits increases market supply and reduces prices. This requires other sellers to adopt the new technology just to maintain profits. The (10)_____(newest, least costly) methods of production are adopted and quickly disseminated among other sellers. The market distributes goods based upon a buyer's willingness and ability to pay. Ability to pay is determined by household income and the prices of goods and services purchased.

The market system has several common defects. Private firms will not produce some goods that benefit society because prices cannot be used to exclude those unwilling to pay. These goods are known as (11)_____(private goods, public goods). Markets may overproduce or underproduce if market prices do not reflect all benefits and costs associated with the production or consumption of output. (12)_____(Negative, Positive) externalities occur when costs accrue to parties other than sellers and buyers. Sellers in this case make decisions based upon marginal costs that do not reflect these external or "third-party" costs. Their costs are lower than if all costs were considered and that induces them to produce (13)_____(less, more) than they would otherwise. In contrast, the production or consumption of goods may confer benefits on third parties, implying that market demand curves do not reflect all benefits associated with goods, but just those benefits received by the buyer of the good. (14)_____(Negative, Positive) externalities result in too (15)_____(much, little) output in that persons other than direct consumers benefit from the good. Sellers respond only to the effective demands registered by buyers, not third parties.

Externalities occur because property rights do not exist or because the property rights are not enforced. Property rights are not enforced when the transaction costs involved in enforcing these rights are very (16)_____(high, low). Some of the environment, such as air and navigable waterways, involve common ownership and are often polluted because no one individual has a property right or the capacity to enforce the right.

Other problems of a market system involve the absence of competition in markets and the ability of sellers to control market outcomes to the disbenefit of society. A market system can produce a skewed distribution of income in which a small percentage of families receive a much larger percentage of income and own an even larger percentage of the nation's wealth. A market system does not guarantee the absence of unemployment or poverty. Because of market shortcomings, modern economies rely on (17)_____(significant, no) government intervention in the economy to improve upon the allocation of resources or to correct other market problems. These modern market economies are known as (18)_____(mixed economies, pure market economies) because decisions regarding resource use are made by both the private and public sectors of the economy.

Modern market economies also engage in international trade. Exports of goods and services result in inflows of business revenue and income, whereas imports require payments to foreigners. Foreign income-producing assets purchased and owned by citizens of the United States and foreign-owned assets in the United States produce similar income flows and payments. Economies linked to the rest of the world through international trade are known as (19)_____ (open economies, common market economies).

KEY TERMS REVIEW

Write the key term from the list below next to its definition.

Key Terms

Capitalism	Free market
Mixed economy	Public goods
Price system	Externalities
Open economy	Property rights
Barter	Transaction costs
Money	

Definitions

1. _____: costs incurred in enforcing property rights to traded goods, locating trading partners, and actually carrying out the transaction.

2. _____: goods that are consumed equally by everyone whether they pay or not.

3. _____: what sellers usually accept as payment for goods and services.

4. _____: a mechanism by which resource use in an economy is guided by market prices.

5. _____: privileges to use or own goods, services, and economic resources.

6. _____: characterized by private ownership of economic resources and freedom of enterprise in which owners of factories and other capital hire workers to produce goods and services.

7. _____: the process of exchanging goods (or services) for goods (or services).

8. _____: one which is linked to the rest of the world through international trade.

9. _____: costs or benefits of market transactions that are not reflected in the prices buyers and sellers use to make their decisions.

10. _____: an economy in which governments as well as business firms provide goods and services.

11. _____: exist when there are no restrictions that prevent buyers and sellers from entering or exiting a market.

CONCEPT REVIEW

Concept 1:   *Framework of a pure market economy; circular flow of income and expenditure*

1. List six characteristics of a pure market economy:

    a. _____

    b. _____

    c. _____

    d. _____

    e. _____

    f. _____

2. In the diagram below, match the flow or box with one of the following:

    a. _____ 1. Market for goods and services (product markets)

    b. _____ 2. Resource markets (input markets)

    c. _____ 3. Rents, interest, wages, and profits

    d. _____ 4. Economic resources

    e. _____ 5. Goods and services

    f. _____ 6. Expenditures on goods and services

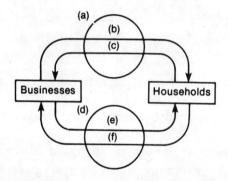

Concept 3:   *Defects of a pure market economy*

3. List four common defects of a market economy:

    a. _____

    b. _____

    c. _____

    d. _____

4. The diagram below represents the market for electricity. Electric power companies are burning bituminous coal and emitting sulfur into the atmosphere, creating acid rain that destroys forests and kills lakes.

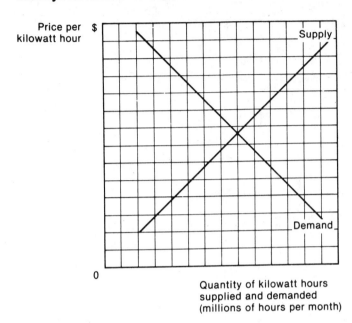

Price per $ kilowatt hour

Supply

Demand

0

Quantity of kilowatt hours supplied and demanded (millions of hours per month)

a. This is an example of a good involving _____ externalities.
b. On the diagram, show what would happen if these electric power companies were required to install scrubbers to remove sulfur from their emissions?
c. Market price of electricity _____ and market quantity _____.
d. Why is government required to correct the market failure?

5. Suppose the following diagram represents the market for AIDS therapy. Private pharmaceutical companies and health suppliers are in a race to discover and market a successful treatment. The demand for AIDS therapy reflects only the private demand of those infected with the virus and willing and able to pay for the treatment. Society as a whole, however, benefits from successful AIDS therapy because individuals who would have otherwise been infected are not infected because of the treatment that persons with AIDS are receiving.

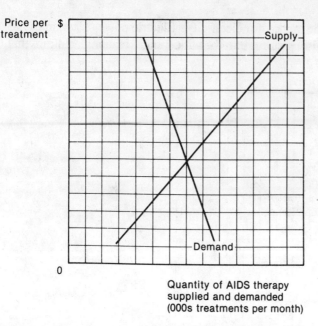

Price per $
treatment

Supply

Demand

0

Quantity of AIDS therapy
supplied and demanded
(000s treatments per month)

a. This is an example of a good involving _____ externalities.
b. According to the diagram above, there are too _____ resources allocated to AIDS therapy.
c. If government subsidizes AIDS research and the development of successful treatments, show on the diagram the likely impact on the market for AIDS therapy.
d. Market price of AIDS treatment _____ and market quantity _____.
e. Why must government be involved?

Advanced Application: Externalities

6. The Sleaze E Chemical Company is presently dumping untreated effluent into a river. Downstream residents and other users of the river suffer from pollution. You are a policy maker in charge of determining the socially desirable level of pollution for the river and the appropriate effluent tax or charge per gallon of untreated effluent to impose on Sleaze E. You want to impose a tax high enough to induce Sleaze E to treat its discharge up to the point at which the proper level of pollution is reached.

Sleaze E Treated Discharge (000s gallons)	Units of Pollution Reduction	Marginal Benefits	Marginal Costs
0	0	$0	$0
10	1	10	2
20	2	8	4
30	3	6	6
40	4	4	8
50	5	2	10

108

a. Using the marginal benefits and marginal costs columns, determine the units of pollution reduction that maximize the net gain to society. Assume that the marginal benefit and cost data include external costs and benefits. How many gallons of discharge will Sleaze E have to treat in order to reach that level of pollution reduction?

b. The diagram below represents the relationship between Sleaze E's marginal cost of treating discharge and the quantity of discharge treated. What tax per unit of untreated effluent would be sufficient to induce Sleaze E to treat its effluent up to the level desired by society?

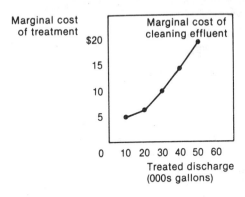

MASTERY TEST

Select the best answer.

1. Which of the following is not true of a pure market system?
   a. Private ownership
   b. Freedom of enterprise and choice
   c. Significant government income redistribution programs
   d. Presence of economic rivalry

2. A pure market economy relies on which of the following to answer the three basic questions: (1) What is produced? (2) How are goods produced? (3) To whom are goods distributed?
   a. Barter
   b. Money
   c. Property rights
   d. Price system

3. The catalyst or driving force in a market system that induces sellers to acquire resources to produce products is:
   a. money.
   b. profit.
   c. price.
   d. benevolence.

4. Economic rivalry means:
   a. that there are large numbers of consumers, but not sellers in markets.
   b. that the survival of the fittest criterion of business behavior is operative in the economy.
   c. there are large numbers of buyers and sellers in markets such that no one buyer or seller dominates market outcomes.
   d. that competitive firms produce profitable goods.

5. The advantage of a money economy as compared to a barter economy is :
   a. the avoidance of a double coincidence of wants.
   b. that money allows economic specialization and the division of labor.
   c. that money greatly facilitates the process of exchange.
   d. All of the above

6. In a circular flow diagram of the economy, households represent the _____ side of the input market, whereas business represents the _____ of the product market.
   a. demand/demand
   b. supply/supply
   c. demand/supply
   d. supply/demand

7. In a circular flow diagram of the economy, households provide _____ and receive _____, which when _____ become the _____ of businesses.
   a. goods/money/saved/capital
   b. money/bonds/employed/capital
   c. economic resources/money income/expended/sales revenue
   d. money income/employment/used/property

8. Economic rivalry in a pure market economy ensures that:
   a. only the healthiest firms use the most advanced technology.
   b. new cost-saving technology is rapidly disseminated among sellers in the economy.
   c. firms will adopt the least-cost combination of resources.
   d. b and c
   e. a and c

9. Goods are distributed in a pure market economy:
   a. by government.
   b. by both the private and public sectors.
   c. on the basis of the buyer's willingness and ability to pay for goods and services.
   d. to those with the highest wages.

10. Private businesses will not allocate resources to the production of goods when prices cannot be used to exclude those unwilling to pay. These goods are known as:
    a. inferior goods.
    b. public goods.
    c. loss goods.
    d. external goods.

11. Goods that when consumed or produced impose costs on third parties involve:
    a. public external effects.
    b. positive externalities.
    c. marginal costs.
    d. negative externalities.

12. Goods that when consumed or produced confer benefits on third parties involve:
    a. public external effects.
    b. positive externalities.
    c. marginal benefits.
    d. negative externalities.

13. Goods involving positive externalities result in :
    a. an efficient allocation of resources.
    b. productive efficiency, but not allocative efficiency.
    c. an overallocation of resources to the production of the good.
    d. an underallocation of resources to the production of the good.

14. Externalities exist because:
    a. businesses are often operated by uncaring individuals.
    b. businesses do not investigate production problems as thoroughly as they should.
    c. property rights are completely assigned and enforced.
    d. property rights either do not exist, are not enforced, or are too costly to enforce.

15. High transaction costs associated with the assignment and enforcement of property rights increase the likelihood that:
    a. externalities will not exist.
    b. government will not intervene in the economy.
    c. externalities will exist.
    d. allocative efficiency will be achieved.

16. Actual market economies give rise to all but one of the following:
    a. a skewed distribution of income
    b. poverty among plenty
    c. full employment
    d. less than competitive markets

17. In a market economy subject to market failures, society's well-being can be improved:
    a. by no government intervention.
    b. by government intervention that corrects resource misallocation and modifies other market outcomes consistent with the desires of society.
    c. by the price system.
    d. if decisions regarding public goods production are left to the private sector.

18. Modern market economies that rely on both the private and public sectors of the economy to answer the three basic questions are known as:
    a. modern market economies.
    b. pure market systems.
    c. pure capitalistic economies.
    d. mixed economies.

19. Which of the following is true regarding the three basic economic questions?
    a. A pure market economy answers the what, how, and to whom questions with a combination of private and public planning.
    b. The "to whom" question in any economic system must be answered by the public sector, whereas the other two questions are answered by self-interested government bureaucrats.
    c. In a mixed market economy, both private and government decision makers ultimately answer the three basic questions.
    d. In a pure market economy, the price system (or system of markets) coordinates the decisions of private producers, consumers, and suppliers of inputs, but government planning is required to answer the "to whom" question.

20. Suppose the demise of the Yugoslav federation results in the emergence of a new nation having the following characteristics: a) a system of markets coordinates the choices of self-interested individuals, b) the government intervenes in markets to improve the allocation of resources and achieve an equitable distribution of income, and c) the nation engages in international trade. Which of the following characterizes this nation?
    a. This nation is a pure market economy.
    b. This nation is an open pure market economy.
    c. This nation is a socialist system because government intervenes to influence the allocation of resources and the distribution of output.
    d. This nation is an open mixed market economy.

21. "Markets fail when resources are overallocated to the production of certain goods." Which of the following best explains this statement?
    a. As markets mature, firms grow large and unresponsive to consumers, often producing more output than is desired.
    b. Producers do not face the full costs of production if negative externalities exist. Firms produce more than they would if they were forced to realize all costs of production.
    c. When prices rise above market equilibrium prices, markets fail because surpluses grow, resulting in an overallocation of resources.
    d. It is impossible for markets to overallocate resources because prices will fall, eliminating surplus production.

22. Which of the following is an example of market failure?
    a. Monopolistic pricing
    b. The production of a good with external benefits
    c. A skewed distribution of income
    d. Periodic episodes of rising unemployment
    e. All of the above

23. What are key features associated with public goods?
    a. Public goods are desired by citizens and must be priced low enough for median-income households to purchase.
    b. Public goods are rival in consumption, but cannot be priced.
    c. Public goods are nonrival in consumption and once provided, entail a zero marginal cost of provision.
    d. Public goods can be provided by either the private or public sector, but because of tradition, most public goods are produced and provided by government.

THINK IT THROUGH

1. During inflationary periods of the 1970s, a number of barter services were established as a means of combatting inflation. These barter arrangements made use of computers to register the goods and services that the users were willing to supply and the goods that would be acceptable in exchange. Would such a barter system be as efficient as one with money? Explain.

2. A basic function of government in a pure market economy is to facilitate the functioning of the economy, but not to modify market outcomes. Discuss.

3. For a pure market economy, explain why producers employ the least costly techniques of production. If the price of labor rises relative to the price of capital and other inputs, how would this affect a competitive seller's combination of resources employed in production?

4. Education in the United States is provided by both the private and public sectors. Why?

CHAPTER ANSWERS

The Chapter in Brief

1. Capitalism 2. Price system 3. Profit 4. Economic rivalry 5. Barter 6. Double coincidence of wants 7. Is not 8. Circular flow diagram 9. Profitable 10. Least costly 11. Public goods 12. Negative 13. More 14. Positive 15. Little 16. High 17. Significant 18. Mixed economies 19. Open economies

Key Terms Review

1. Transaction costs 2. Public goods 3. Money 4. Price system 5. Property rights 6. Capitalism 7. Barter 8. Open economy 9. Externalities 10. Mixed economy 11. Free market

Concept Review

1. a. Private ownership
    b. Freedom of choice and enterprise
    c. Limited economic role for government
    d. Reliance on the price system to allocate resources
    e. Profit motive
    f. Economic rivalry

2. a. 2 b. 3 c. 4 d. 1 e. 5 f. 6

3. a. Externalities
    b. Lack of competition in markets
    c. Skewed distribution of income
    d. Doesn't eliminate poverty or unemployment

4. a. Negative
    b. If power companies are required to bear the cost of cleaning their emissions, the market supply curve would shift leftward.

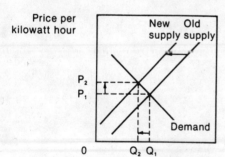

Quantity of kilowatt hours
supplied and demanded
(millions of hours per month)

c. Increases, decreases

d. Individual property rights do not exist to the atmosphere and to most lakes and a good portion of timber lands. Where property rights do exist in the ownership of forests and lakes, it is far too costly for any one property owner to identify the source of pollution and to seek remedy in court. Therefore government must intervene and enforce the collective property rights of society to commonly owned resources. Government can also reduce the transaction costs of enforcing property rights for individual property owners. In both cases, government improves resource allocation.

5. a. Positive

   b. Few

   c. Government subsidies increase the net gain to those conducting AIDS research and developing therapies. In time there will be a rightward shift in the supply curve.

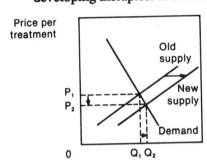

Price per treatment

Old supply

New supply

P_1
P_2

Demand

0    $Q_1 Q_2$

Quantity of AIDS therapy supplied and demanded (000s treatments per month)

   d. Decreases, increases

   e. A market system relies on pricing to allocate resources. Market prices do not reflect the external benefits accruing to third parties. Markets will underproduce goods involving positive externalities. Governments can produce net gains for society by engaging in activities that reallocate more resources to the production of goods with positive externalities.

6. a. Marginal benefits and costs become equal at three units of pollution reduction. This is the level of pollution that maximizes society's net gain. Sleaze E will have to treat 30,000 gallons of discharge for this level of pollution reduction to be realized.

   b. $10. A tax of $10 per unit of untreated discharge will result in a net gain to Sleaze E for each unit of treated discharge up to 30,000 gallons. This is because the marginal cost of treating a gallon of effluent is less than the additional benefit associated with not having to pay the pollution tax on that gallon. This holds true up to the level of 30,000 gallons at which the marginal cost of treatment is $10. Treatment beyond this level would not take place because Sleaze E would be better off by paying the tax than treating the discharge.

Mastery Test

1.c 2. d 3. b 4. c 5. d 6. b 7. c 8. d 9. c 10. b 11. d 12. b 13. d 14. d 15. c 16. c 17. b 18. d 19. c 20. d 21. b 22. e 23. c

Think It Through

1. Barter systems, whether or not they use computers, must develop "prices" or exchange ratios for the goods involved. This requires scarce resources. A double coincidence of wants is required, which reduces the efficiency of exchange. A middleman must be paid to provide a service that is naturally provided as part of the functioning of a market economy using money.

2. In a pure market system, there are no failures. There are no externalities, markets provide employment for everyone willing and able to work at prevailing wages, all markets involve economic rivalry, and incomes are based strictly on the resources that households supply to the market and the prices at which they sell. In short, the market operates efficiently without government interference. Government, nevertheless, performs a vital economic role by assigning property rights and enforcing those rights via a system of laws, courts, and police protection. Government also provides money and the basic infrastructure of roads, water supply, sewerage, etc., necessary for the efficient functioning of a market system.

3. Economic rivalry implies that sellers must operate at least cost. If they did not, in time they would incur insufficient profits to remain in business. Firms that stay in business in a pure market system are those that are able to use the least costly combination of inputs and technology in order to at least generate a minimally sufficient level of profit. If the price of labor rises relative to the cost of other inputs, a least cost producer will substitute the relatively less costly resources for labor. By making capital more productive relative to labor, technology reduces the cost of capital relative to labor in the production of output. This is what happened in American agriculture. Technology made farm labor more expensive relative to capital, inducing farmers to mechanize.

4. Education is a good involving positive externalities. A market system produces too little education from society's point of view. Government can increase the net gain to society by providing more education than that provided by a market system alone. But this does not necessarily mean the we have to have the current public-private system in order to achieve this outcome. Education could be entirely publicly provided or it could be provided entirely by a private sector encouraged to produce more with subsidies. Alternatively, students could be given education vouchers that supplement their own funds for education. These funds could be spent entirely in the private sector or even in the current public-private system.

PART III

PRODUCT MARKETS: MICROECONOMIC ANALYSIS

PART EXERCISE

Inside Information: *The Economic Bulletin Board*

In this part of the text, you will learn about cost and productivity relationships. Using the *Economic Bulletin Board,* find a measure of labor productivity. Does it correspond more closely to average product of labor or marginal product of labor? Has your measure of labor productivity increased, decreased, or has it remained unchanged? Given these observed changes in labor productivity, what are the implications for production costs? Explain.

6 ELASTICITY OF SUPPLY AND DEMAND

CHAPTER CONCEPTS

After studying your text, attending class, completing this chapter, you should be able to:
1. Explain the uses of the concept of price elasticity of demand and show how it can be calculated for points on a given demand curve.
2. Use information on price elasticity of demand to forecast changes in total expenditures on a product and total revenue from its sale when the item's price changes.
3. Explain how to use other elasticity measures, including the income elasticity of demand, the cross-elasticity of demand, and the price elasticity of supply.
4. Show how the price elasticities of demand and supply are relevant for explaining the impact of taxes on market prices of goods and services.

THE CHAPTER IN BRIEF

Fill in the blanks to summarize chapter content.

The laws of supply and demand indicate the direction in which quantity supplied or demanded changes in response to a price change but they do not reveal the sensitivity of sellers or buyers to given price changes. The concept of elasticity is employed to gauge the sensitivity of buyers and sellers to price changes. Specifically, the (1)_____(income, price) elasticity of demand is a number measuring the sensitivity of buyers to a 1% change in price. If the percentage change in quantity demanded is (2)_____(greater, smaller) than the percentage change in price, demand is said to be elastic, and the price elasticity of demand coefficient is (3)_____(greater, smaller) than 1 (ignoring the minus sign). If the percentage change in quantity demanded is (4)_____ (greater, smaller) than the percentage change in price, demand is said to be inelastic, and the price elasticity of demand coefficient is (5)_____ (more, less) than 1 (ignoring the minus sign) but greater than 0. A coefficient equal to (6)_____(1, 0) means that demand is unit elastic. Unit elasticity means that a given percentage change in price will result in (7)_____(a greater, the same) percentage change in quantity demanded.

The price elasticity of demand is determined by taking the percentage change in (8)_____ (price, quantity demanded) divided by the percentage change in (9)_____ (price, quantity demanded). The elasticity coefficient or number is influenced by (a) the availability of substitutes, (b) time, and (c) the percentage of income spent on a good. Demand becomes (10)_____(more, less) elastic with increases in the availability of substitute goods, time, and increases in the proportion of income spent on the good. Decreases in the availability of substitutes, time, or the percentage of income expended on a good cause demand to become (11)_____(more, less) elastic.

The price elasticity of demand is not the slope of the demand curve. For a linear demand curve with a constant slope, the price elasticity of demand changes from being (12)_____ (inelastic, elastic) in the upper portion of the demand curve to being (13)_____(inelastic, elastic) in the lower segment of the curve. Exceptions to this would be the cases of perfectly elastic and perfectly inelastic demand curves. A vertical demand curve is perfectly inelastic and has a price elasticity coefficient of (14)_____(1, 0). A horizontal demand curve is perfectly elastic and has a price elasticity coefficient of (15)_____(0, infinity).

A useful application of the price elasticity of demand is an analysis of the behavior of total revenue or expenditures given percentage price changes. If demand is elastic over the range of a price decrease, total revenues and expenditures will (16)_____(fall, rise). This is because the increase in quantity demanded more than offsets the decline in price. If demand is inelastic over the range of a price increase, total revenue and expenditures also (17)_____(fall, rise). In this case, the price increase more than dominates the decline in quantity demanded. Therefore price and total revenue or expenditures are positively related when demand is inelastic and are negatively related when demand is elastic. When the price elasticity of demand is unit elastic, a change in price (18)_____ (increases, has no impact on) revenue or expenditures.

Other elasticity concepts include the income elasticity of demand, the cross-elasticity of demand, and the price elasticity of supply. The income elasticity of demand measures the sensitivity of consumer purchases to changes in income. If the income elasticity coefficient is (19)_____ (greater, smaller) than 0, the good in question is a normal good. If the coefficient is (20)_____(greater, smaller) than 0, the good is an inferior good. The cross-elasticity of demand is a way to identify goods as being substitutes, complements, or unrelated. If the cross-elasticity is (21)_____ (negative, positive), the two goods in question are substitutes. The percentage quantity demanded of one good increases when the price of the other good increases by a given percentage. Two goods are complements when the cross-elasticity coefficient is (22)_____(negative, positive). In this case, the percentage quantity demanded of one good decreases when the price of the other good increases by a given percentage. Two goods are unrelated when the cross-elasticity is (23)_____(1, 0).

The price elasticity of supply measures the sensitivity of sellers to percentage price changes. If the percentage change in quantity supplied is greater than the percentage change in price, supply is (24)_____ (elastic, inelastic), with an elasticity coefficient greater than 1. If the percentage change in quantity supplied is less than the percentage change in price, supply is (25)_____ (elastic, inelastic), with an elasticity coefficient greater than 0 but less than 1. A coefficient of 0 represents unit supply elasticity, where quantity supplied does not change given a change in price. Supply is (26)_____(more, less) elastic when (a) the additional costs of producing a unit of output rise slowly with increases in output and (b) sufficient time is allowed for the firm or industry to respond to price changes. As with demand, supply can also be perfectly inelastic or perfectly elastic. A vertical supply curve, one that is perfectly (27)_____ (elastic, inelastic), has a supply elasticity coefficient of 0. A horizontal supply curve is perfectly (28)_____(elastic, inelastic) with a coefficient of infinity.

Price elasticities of supply and demand can be used in determining the portion of a tax levied on producers that is shifted to buyers. A tax per unit of output levied on sellers will shift the supply curve (29)_____ (downward, upward) by the amount of that tax per unit. Prices rise, but if they rise less than the tax, some of the tax is borne by sellers and the remainder is borne by consumers. A firm would be successful in passing or shifting all of the tax to consumers when the demand curve is perfectly (30)_____ (inelastic, elastic) or when the supply curve is perfectly (31)_____(inelastic, elastic). In the opposite case, where the demand curve is (32)_____ (horizontal, vertical) and the supply curve is (33)_____(horizontal, vertical), the entire tax would be borne by sellers. With conventionally sloped demand and supply curves, both sellers and buyers bear a portion of the tax.

KEY TERMS REVIEW

Write the key term from the list below next to its definition.

Key Terms

Price elasticity of demand
Elastic demand
Inelastic demand
Total revenue
Unit elastic demand
Total expenditure
Income elasticity of demand

Normal goods
Inelastic supply
Inferior goods
Price elasticity of supply
Elastic supply
Unit elastic supply
Tax shifting
Cross-elasticity of supply

Definitions

1. _____: goods that have positive income elasticity of demand.

2. _____: prevails if the price elasticity of demand for a good is a number that exceeds 1, ignoring the minus sign.

3. _____: occurs when a tax levied on sellers of a good causes the market price of the good to increase.

4. _____: a number representing the percentage change in quantity demanded of a good resulting from each 1% change in the price of a good.

5. _____: a number used to measure the sensitivity of consumer purchases of one good to each 1% change in the prices of related goods.

6. _____: prevails when the price elasticity of supply is equal to or greater than 0 but less than 1.

7. _____: the dollars sellers of a product take in; the amount sold over a period multiplied by the price (PQ).

8. _____: prevails if the price elasticity of demand for a good exactly equals 1 when the minus sign is ignored.

9. _____: goods that have negative income elasticity of demand.

10. _____: a number used to measure the sensitivity of changes in quantity supplied to each 1% change in the price of a good, other things being equal.

11. _____: prevails if the price elasticity of demand for a good is equal to or greater than 0, but less then 1, ignoring the minus sign.

12. _____: prevails when the price elasticity of supply is greater than 1.

13. _____: over any given period, the number of units of a product purchased multiplied by the price of the product (PQ); equals the total revenue of sellers.

14. _____: a number that measures the sensitivity of consumer purchases to each 1% change in income.

15. _____: prevails when elasticity of supply just equals 1.

CONCEPT REVIEW

Concepts 1 and 2: *Price elasticity of demand; measurement, uses, determinants*

1. Referring to the diagram below:
   a. Calculate the price elasticity of demand over the demand curve segment a-b. _____
      Demand is _____.
   b. Calculate the price elasticity of demand over segment e-f.
      _____ Demand is _____.
   c. Calculate the price elasticity of demand over segment c-d.
      _____ Demand is _____.
   d. Total revenue (P X Q) at point

   a = _____
   b = _____
   c = _____
   d = _____
   e = _____
   f = _____

   e. A decline in price from $6 to $5 _____ total revenue by $_____.
   f. A decline in price from $2 to $1 _____ total revenue by $_____.
   g. A decline in price from $4 to $3 _____ total revenue by $_____.

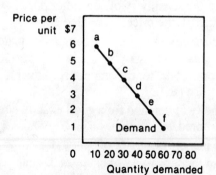

2. Will the following make the elasticity of demand more elastic or less elastic?
   a. _____ Decrease in the percentage of income spent on a good
   b. _____ Import tariffs reduce the availability of substitute goods
   c. _____ More time to respond to price changes
   d. _____ Increase in the availability of substitutes

3. Given your knowledge of the determinants of the price elasticity of demand, which of the following goods are likely to have elastic demands and which are likely to be inelastic?

a. _____ Diamonds

b. _____ Hamburgers

c. _____ Toothpaste

d. _____ Automobiles

e. _____ Gasoline

f. _____ Cigarettes

g. _____ Movies

Concept 3: *Other concepts of elasticity; measurement, uses, determinants*

4. Suppose you observe that as incomes increase by 10%, the quantity of some good purchased:

a. Increases by 20%. Determine the income elasticity of demand. The good in question is a/an_____ good.

b. Decreases by 5%. Determine the income elasticity of demand. The good is a _____ good.

5. Determine the cross-elasticity of demand if a 5% decrease in the price of good X:

a. Increases the quantity of good Y purchased by 15% _____. Good Y is a _____ to good X.

b. Decreases the quantity of good Y purchased by 5% _____. Good Y is _____ to good X.

c. Does not change the quantity of good Y purchased _____. Good Y is _____ to good X.

6. Referring to the diagram below:

a. Calculate the elasticity of supply over the supply curve segment a-b. _____ Supply is _____.

b. Calculate the elasticity of supply over segment e-f. _____ Supply is _____.

c. List two determinants of the elasticity of supply:

(1) _____

(2) _____

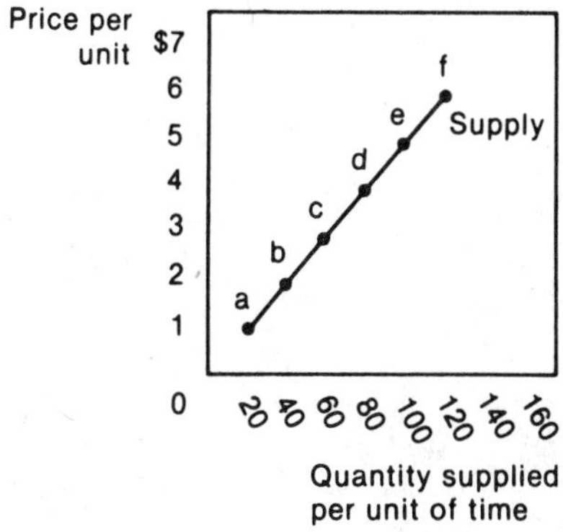

123

Concept 4: *Price elasticity of demand and supply; impact of taxes on prices*

7. Referring to the diagram below:

    a. Show the impact on the supply curve for cigarettes of a tax of $1 per pack.

    b. Market price _____ from $_____ to $_____.

    c. Consumers pay _____ cents of the tax and sellers pay the other _____cents.

    d. Assume that cigarette smoking is such an addiction that the demand for cigarettes is perfectly inelastic.

        (1) Show a perfectly inelastic demand curve on the diagram.

        (2) How much of the tax is paid by consumers? _____ cents By sellers? _____ cents

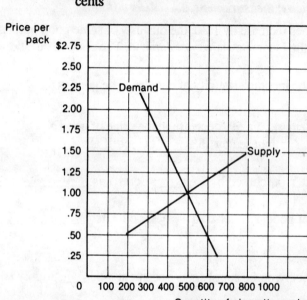

Price per pack

Quantity of cigarette packs supplied and demanded (millions of packs per year)

8. For which of the following diagrams is a per unit tax completely borne by:
   a. Consumers?_____
   b. Sellers?_____

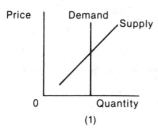

(1)

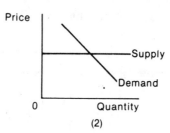

(2)

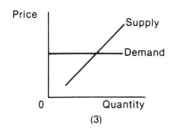

(3)

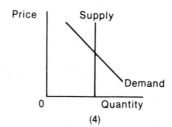

(4)

Advanced Application: Tax shifting

9. The market demand and supply equations from Chapter 3, question 10, are as follows:

$$Qd = a - bP$$

$$Qs = c + dP$$

where a, b, c, and d are positive constants

Qd = quantity demanded

Qs = quantity supplied

P = price

Suppose that in the absence of per unit taxes on output, Qs is a positive function of P. If a tax, T, is levied on sellers, Qs becomes a function of the after-tax price rather than the before-tax price, P.
   a. Modify the supply equation to incorporate a per unit tax, T.
   b. Derive an expression for the market equilibrium price.
   c. How can that expression be used to determine the portion of a tax, T, that is shifted to buyers?

MASTERY TEST

Select the best answer.

1. The price elasticity of demand is measured by:
   a. dividing the percentage change in quantity demanded into the percentage change in income.
   b. dividing the percentage change in quantity demanded into the percentage change in supply.
   c. dividing the percentage change in price into the percentage change in quantity demanded.
   d. dividing price into quantity demanded.

2. If the price elasticity of demand is greater than 1, it is said to be:
   a. unit elastic.
   b. elastic.
   c. inelastic.
   d. a normal good.

3. If the price elasticity of demand is greater than 0, but less than 1, it is said to be:
   a. unit elastic.
   b. elastic.
   c. inelastic.
   d. a normal good.

4. A _____ elastic demand curve is one where the price elasticity coefficient is infinity.
   a. unit
   b. less
   c. completely
   d. perfectly

5. A demand curve for insulin is likely to be:
   a. very inelastic.
   b. perfectly elastic.
   c. somewhat elastic.
   d. moderately inelastic.

6. Moving from the upper range of a linear demand curve southeast to the lower portions is associated with a price elasticity of demand that becomes increasingly:
   a. elastic.
   b. inelastic.
   c. large.
   d. difficult to estimate.

7. Which of the following is a determinant of the price elasticity of demand?
   a. Time
   b. The percentage of income spent on the good
   c. The availability of substitutes
   d. All of the above

126

8. Other things being equal, an increase in the availability of substitutes:
   a. has no impact on the price elasticity of demand.
   b. decreases the price elasticity of demand.
   c. increases the price elasticity of demand.
   d. None of the above

9. If demand is elastic and the price falls, total revenue will:
   a. not change.
   b. increase.
   c. decrease.
   d. increase if the supply elasticity is not 0.

10. If demand is inelastic and the price falls, total revenue will:
    a. not change.
    b. increase.
    c. decrease.
    d. increase if the supply elasticity is not 0.

11. A good having a positive income elasticity of demand is called a:
    a. positive good.
    b. public good.
    c. inferior good.
    d. normal good.

12. A good having a negative income elasticity of demand is called a:
    a. positive good.
    b. public good.
    c. inferior good.
    d. normal good.

13. Two goods that are substitutes in consumption have a _____ cross-elasticity of demand.
    a. positive
    b. elastic
    c. inelastic
    d. negative

14. Two goods that are complements in consumption have a _____ cross-elasticity of demand.
    a. positive
    b. elastic
    c. inelastic
    d. negative

15. Which of the following is not a determinant of the price elasticity of supply?
    a. Availability of substitutes
    b. Time
    c. The marginal cost associated with producing additional units of output
    d. Percentage of income spent on a good
    e. A and d

16. A perfectly elastic supply curve is:
    a. positively sloped.
    b. vertical.
    c. negatively sloped.
    d. horizontal.

17. If the supply of some good is unit elastic and the price of the good increases by 10%:
    a. quantity supplied increases by more than 10%.
    b. quantity demanded decreases by at least 10%.
    c. quantity supplied increases by 10%.
    d. quantity supplied does not change.

18. If a per unit tax is levied on sellers and the demand for the good is perfectly elastic, sellers:
    a. will pass all of the tax to consumers in the form of higher prices.
    b. will not be able to shift the tax.
    c. will share the burden of the tax equally with buyers.
    d. None of the above

19. If a per unit tax is levied on sellers and the demand for the good is perfectly inelastic, sellers:
    a. will pass all of the tax to consumers in the form of higher prices.
    b. will not be able to shift the tax.
    c. will share the burden of the tax equally with buyers.
    d. will pay most of the tax.

20. If a per unit tax is levied on sellers and the supply and demand curves are conventionally sloped, sellers:
    a. will pass all of the tax to consumers in the form of higher prices.
    b. will not be able to shift the tax.
    c. will share the burden of the tax equally with buyers.
    d. will share the burden of the tax with buyers.

21. Assume that the demand for unskilled labor is elastic. As an administrator for the federal government, you have been asked what change in the federal minimum wage is necessary in order to increase total wages received by unskilled labor as a group? Which of the following is the correct response?
    a. The minimum wage must be increased in order to increases total wages.
    b. The minimum wage must be increased so that the gain in wages from the higher wage rate more than offsets the loss in total wages from higher unemployment.
    c. The minimum wage must be increased so that the higher wage rate and level of employment result in higher total wages.
    d. The minimum wage must be decreased so that the loss in total wages from the lower wage rate is more than offset by the gain in total wages from more employment.

22. Assume that the cross-elasticity of demand for coffee with respect to tea is .5. Further assume that for every 1% change in the demand for coffee, the price of coffee changes by 1/2%. The current market price for coffee is $3.00 per pound. What happens to the price of coffee if the price of tea increases by 20%?
    a. The price of coffee does not change.
    b. The price of coffee decreases to $2.40.
    c. The price of coffee increases to $3.30.
    d. The price of coffee increases to $3.15.
    e. The price of coffee decreases to $2.70.

23. As a physician and owner of a medical practice, you wish to increase revenue. You decide to lower your fees because you believe that increased business will more than offset a fee reduction, resulting in more revenues. Is your decision correct?
    a. Yes, because the demand for physician services is unit elastic.
    b. No, because the demand for physician services is elastic.
    c. No, because the demand for physician services is inelastic.
    d. Yes, because the demand for physician services is inelastic.

24. Suppose the labor supply elasticity with respect to the after-tax wage is .2. What is the impact of an income tax increase that lowers the after-tax wage from $5.00 to $4.00?
    a. Labor hours supplied will decrease by 4%.
    b. Labor hours supplied always fall when income taxes are increased.
    c. Labor hours supplied will increase by 20%.
    d. Labor hours supplied will decreases by 10%.

25. Which of the following is true regarding tax incidence?
    a. The statutory incidence of a tax is equivalent to the actual incidence of a tax.
    b. A business always passes an excise tax to consumers in the form of a higher product price.
    c. Depending on the elasticity of demand and supply, a business may or may not raise price in response to an excise tax.
    d. A business is unable to shift the burden of an excise tax to consumers when the supply curve is upsloping and the demand curve is perfectly inelastic.

THINK IT THROUGH

1. You have been asked by a physician to determine if his fees should be increased. He wants to generate additional revenues. Based upon what you know about the determinants of the price elasticity of demand, determine first if the demand for physicians services is elastic or inelastic and then determine what fee change will increase the physician's revenues.

2. The demand for unskilled labor is generally regarded as elastic. Why? An increase in the minimum wage will increase wages for those employed, but will reduce the total wages paid to unskilled labor as a whole. Why?

3. How could knowledge of the price, cross-price, and income elasticities of demand for various goods be useful in helping a discount store manager predict the probable consequences of price changes?

4. Sumptuary taxes are taxes intended to discourage the consumption of goods considered harmful to individuals. A tax per quart of whiskey is such a tax. Based upon what you know about determinants of the price elasticity of demand, is a per unit tax on whiskey likely to curb consumption?

ANALYZING THE NEWS

Using the skills derived from studying this chapter, analyze the economic facts that make up the following article and answer the questions below, using graphical analysis where possible.

1. What assumptions do you think this firm is making concerning the price elasticity of demand for this service? Why?

2. Suppose as a result of the reduction in air fares, quantity demanded for first-class flights rises by a smaller percentage than the percentage decrease in price. Explain what will happen to total revenue.

3. List 3 reasons why first-class airline flights might be characterized as a service with an inelastic demand.

BUSINESS TRAVEL

Midway discounts first-class fares

First-class seats on Midway Airlines will be easier to get and less expensive starting Aug. 5. In a bid to attract more corporate fliers, Midway Airlines Inc. said Monday, it will install more first-class seats and sell them for full-coach or discounted fares. For example, Midway's first-class, round-trip fare between Chicago and New York is now $898. Starting Aug. 5, a full-coach, round-trip fare of $838 will buy a first-class seat. Chicago-New York fliers who buy their round-trip tickets at least seven days in advance can sit in first class for $438. The deal does not include Midway's cheapest coach fares ($198 round trip on the Chicago-New York route), which require a Saturday night stay. First-class fliers will receive extras such as valet parking at Chicago's Midway Airport and, in flight, roomier seats.

The strategy will be familiar to those who flew Eastern Airlines in its final months. Midway, which serves 42 U.S. airports from its Midway Airport hub, now is in bankruptcy reorganization itself. David Kunstler — Midway's head of marketing who came from Eastern — is betting the first-class gambit can turn Midway around. Midway's average leisure flier pays $68 one-way, but the typical business flier pays $175 one-way. If Midway can get one more business flier on each flight, that will mean $10 million a year in additional revenue, he says.

CHAPTER ANSWERS

The Chapter in Brief

1. Price 2. Greater 3. Greater 4. Smaller 5. Less 6. 1 7. The same 8. Quantity demanded 9. Price 10. More 11. Less 12. Elastic 13. Inelastic 14. 0 15. Infinity 16. Rise 17. Rise 18. Has no impact on 19. Greater 20. Smaller 21. Positive 22. Negative 23. 0 24. Elastic 25. Inelastic 26. More 27. Inelastic 28. Elastic 29. Upward 30. Inelastic 31. Elastic 32. Horizontal 33. Vertical

Key Terms Review

1. Normal goods 2. Elastic demand 3. Tax shifting 4. Price elasticity of demand 5. Cross-elasticity of demand 6. Inelastic supply 7. Total revenue 8. Unit elastic demand 9. Inferior goods 10. Price elasticity of supply 11. Inelastic demand 12. Elastic supply 13. Total expenditure 14. Income elasticity of demand 15. Unit elastic supply

Concept Review

1. a. 3.67, elastic
   b. 0.27, inelastic
   c. 1, unit elastic
   d. (a) $60, (b) $100, (c) $120, (d) $120, (e) $100, (f) $60
   e. Increase, $40
   f. Decrease, $40
   g. Changes, $0

2. a. Less
   b. Less
   c. More
   d. More

3. a. Elastic
   b. Elastic
   c. Inelastic
   d. Elastic
   e. Inelastic
   f. Inelastic
   g. Elastic

4. a. +2, normal
   b. -1/2, inferior

5. a. -3, complement
   b. +1, substitute
   c. 0, unrelated

6. a. 1, unit elastic

   b. 1, unit elastic

   c. (1)Additional cost of producing a unit of output as more output is produced (2)Time

7. a.

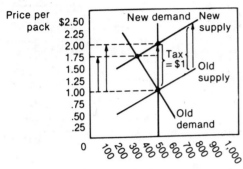

Quantity of cigarette packs
supplied and demanded
(millions of packs
per year)

   b. Increase, $1, $1.75

   c. 75, 25

   d. (1) Shown on diagram above

       (2) 100, 0

8. a. Figures (1) and (2)

   b. Figures (3) and (4)

9. a. Let $Qs = c + d (P - T)$

   b. Equilibrium requires setting $Qd = Qs$. Therefore:

       $$a - bP = a + d (P - T)$$

       Solving for P gives:

       $$P = (a - c + dT)/(b + d)$$

   c. Let the change in $P = [d/(b + d)]$ x change in T

       If $d/(b + d)$ is greater than 0 but less than 1, both sellers and buyers share the tax burden. If $d/(b + d)$ equals 0, the tax is borne by sellers. If $d/(b + d)$ equals 1, the tax is borne by buyers. When $d/(b + d)$ is 0, $d = 0$ or b equals infinity. $d = 0$ when supply is perfectly inelastic. $b =$ infinity when demand is perfectly elastic. $d/(b + d)$ is 1 when $b = 0$ or when $d =$ infinity. $b = 0$ when demand is perfectly inelastic and $d =$ infinity when supply is perfectly elastic. Conventionally sloped supply and demand curves yield a value for $d/(b + d)$ greater than 0 but less than 1.

Self-Test for Mastery

1. c 2. b 3. c 4. d 5. a 6. b 7. d 8. c 9. b 10. c 11. d 12. c 13. a 14. d 15. e 16. d 17. c
18. b 19. a 20. d 21. d 22. d 23. c 24. a 25. c

Think it Through

1. People perceive physician services as having few close substitutes. Because care usually cannot be delayed, the demand for physician services is regarded as inelastic. If the physician wants to increase revenues from his practice, he should increase his fees.

2. Unskilled labor is considered to have an elastic demand, in part because many types of labor can be substituted for unskilled labor, but unskilled workers are not substitutes for those requiring special skills, education, or training. Also, there is typically a ready pool of unskilled labor that can be employed with minimal training cost to the firm.

   If the demand for unskilled labor is elastic and the minimum wage increases, total wages (minimum wage x quantity of labor hours employed) paid to unskilled labor as a group will decrease, even though those employed at the minimum wage are better off. This occurs because the unemployment caused by the minimum wage more than offsets the impact of the higher wage on the total wages paid to labor.

3. Knowledge of price elasticities of demand for various goods would allow the manager to predict percentage changes in quantities demanded for given percentage price changes. Cross-price elasticities would allow predictions regarding the quantities demanded of complementary and substitute goods. Income elasticities of demand would allow predictions for those goods that are normal or inferior. This would be useful, for instance, in areas experiencing a significant influx of higher income households. All of this assumes that the national or regional data used to estimate these coefficients are applicable to a local economy. In other words, the relationships that hold for the economy as a whole are assumed to pertain to the local economy as well.

4. For whiskey consumers, there are probably few close substitutes for whiskey. The demand for whiskey is probably inelastic. A sumptuary tax would primarily increase the price of whiskey, having only a modest negative impact on the quantity of whiskey demanded.

Analyzing the News

1. The airline is assuming that the price elasticity of demand is greater than one (elastic). They apparently believe that the percentage increase in quantity demanded will exceed the percentage decrease in price. By cutting fares, they expect revenues will increase.

2. If the percentage increase in quantity demanded is smaller than the percentage decrease in prices, total revenues will fall. Price cuts will reduce total revenue more than increases in quantity demand will raise revenues.

3. a. Business flyers often fly on short notice. The less time one has to react to price changes, the smaller the change in quantity demand, resulting in a less elastic demand.
   b. For business travellers, there are few substitutes for airline travel. Demand is less elastic the fewer the number of substitutes.
   c. Since business flyers typically fly at the expense of the firm, the share of firm income allocated to airline travel is small relative to the share of income spent by a household on airline travel. If the price of a good is insignificant relative to the firm's budget, demand will tend to be less elastic.

7   CONSUMER CHOICE AND THE THEORY OF DEMAND

CHAPTER CONCEPTS

After studying your text, attending class, and completing this chapter, you should be able to:

1. Distinguish between the concepts of total and marginal utility and show how the way marginal utility varies with purchases can reflect a person's preferences.
2. Describe the conditions for consumer equilibrium as expressed by the equimarginal principle for purchases.
3. Show how total and marginal benefits relate to total and marginal utility.
4. Demonstrate that buying a good up to the point where its marginal benefit equals its price maximizes net benefit of giving up money to purchase it.
5. Analyze the impact of changes in prices and incomes on consumer choices.
6. Use marginal analysis data to draw a single buyer's demand curve for a good. Show how marginal benefit and therefore demand shift as income changes.
7. Derive a market demand curve from the demand curves of individual buyers.

THE CHAPTER IN BRIEF

Fill in the blanks to summarize chapter content.

An understanding of the demand side of the market requires an understanding of consumer choice. Marginal analysis is used to explain the choices made by consumers. Consumers seek to maximize their net gain from consumption. The consumption of goods increases a consumer's total satisfaction or (1)_____ (marginal, total) utility. But the additional satisfaction realized from the consumption of each additional unit of a good decreases. The law of diminishing (2)_____ (returns, marginal utility) states that marginal utility falls as more of a good is consumed over a period. Consumers will try to allocate their income such that they consume goods up to the point where the marginal utility per dollar expended on a good (3)_____(equals, is greater than) the marginal utility per dollar spent on each and every other good. This is known as the equimarginal principle. Consuming according to the equimarginal principle will maximize a consumer's utility.

To a consumer, total and marginal utility is valued by the (4)_____ (minimum, maximum) sum of money that the consumer is willing and able to give up to have the total quantity or additional unit, respectively. Because of (5)_____ (declining, increasing) marginal utility, the maximum sum that consumers are willing and able to give up to obtain an additional unit of a good (6)_____ (increases, declines) as more of the good is consumed. This is known as the law of declining marginal benefit. As long as buyers consume goods for which marginal benefits (7)_____(are less than, exceed) the price of the good, their net benefits increase. Net benefit is maximized when consumption is carried to the point where marginal benefit (8)_____ (is still greater than, equals) the price. On units of goods consumed up to the point where marginal benefits equal price, the consumer realizes a surplus. Consumer surplus is the total benefit received in excess of the (9)_____(dollar expenditure, marginal benefit) necessary to obtain the goods.

Consumers will not necessarily prefer to purchase an additional unit of a good having a high marginal benefit over one yielding less additional satisfaction if the price of the former good is high. Nor will a consumer purchase any units of a good when the price (10)_____ (exceeds, is greater than) the marginal benefit received. This is because the value of the goods and services that the consumer will have to give up are worth more than the marginal benefits received from consuming the good. Consumers will prefer those goods for which marginal benefits exceed the price by the greatest margin.

Income affects a consumer's ability to pay. Total and marginal benefits are the maximum sum of dollars that buyers are willing and able to give up to obtain some total or additional quantity of a good. An increase in income therefore increases the consumer's ability to give up dollars for benefits. For (11)_____(inferior goods, normal goods), an increase in income causes the marginal benefit curve to shift upward. At any quantity, the maximum additional dollars that a buyer is willing and able to give up for an additional unit of output increases. For (12)_____ (inferior goods, normal goods), an increase in income shifts the marginal benefit curve downward. The maximum additional dollars that a buyer is willing and able to give up for an additional unit of output decreases.

(13)_____(Market, Individual) demand curves can be derived from the individual's marginal benefit curve. A price-quantity demanded coordinate on a demand curve represents a point of consumption at which a utility-maximizing consumer has equated price and marginal benefit. If the price falls, the buyer's marginal benefit temporarily exceeds price. The consumer can increase net benefits by increasing consumption to the point where price and marginal benefit are once again equal. Thus lower prices are associated with higher quantities demanded. This assumes that income, tastes, and other influences are held unchanged.

Price changes have two effects: the income effect and the substitution effect. A decrease in price, for instance, increases the purchasing power of a given income and increases the consumer's ability to consume more of all normal goods, including the one for which prices have decreased. This is known as the (14)_____(substitution, income) effect. A decrease in price relative to the prices of other goods will induce the buyer to substitute the relatively less costly good for more expensive goods. With the income effect neutralized, the (15)_____(substitution, income) effect means that price and quantity demanded are always inversely related. For normal goods, the income effect (16)_____(complements, offsets to some extent) the substitution effect in that both effects work to increase quantities consumed as the price decreases. For inferior goods, the income effect (17)_____ (complements, to some extent offsets) the substitution effect of a price change. For a special variety of goods called Giffen goods, the income effect (18)_____(more than offsets, does not offset) the substitution effect, causing prices to be positively related to quantity demanded!

The market demand curve is a horizontal summation or aggregation of the demand curves of individual buyers in the market. The market demand is downsloping and shifts when individual demand curves shift.

KEY TERMS REVIEW

Write the key term from the list below next to its definition.

Key Terms

Preferences
Utility
Total utility
Marginal utility
Law of diminishing
  marginal utility
Consumer equilibrium
Equimarginal principle

Net benefit
Marginal benefit
Paradox of value
Income effect
Substitution effect
Total benefit
Market demand curve
Consumer surplus

Definitions

1. _____: a change in consumption of a good only as a result of the variation in the purchasing power of money income caused by a price change.

2. _____: a change in consumption of a good only as a result of a change in its price relative to the prices of other goods.

3. _____: shows the relationship between the price of a product and the total quantity demanded by all consumers willing and able to purchase the product at each price, other things being equal.

4. _____: states that the marginal utility of any item tends to decline as more is consumed over any given period.

5. _____: the maximum sum of money a consumer is willing and able to give up to obtain another unit of a good.

6. _____: the difference between the total benefit of a given quantity purchased by a consumer and the expenditure necessary to purchase that quantity.

7. _____: people are willing to give up zero or very small amounts of money to obtain certain items that provide them great total benefit.

8. _____: the total satisfaction enjoyed from consuming any given quantity of a good.

9. _____: the maximum sum of money a consumer would give up to obtain a certain quantity of a good.

10. _____: the total benefit of the quantity of a good purchased less the dollar sacrifice necessary to purchase that quantity.

11. _____: the extra satisfaction received over a given period by consuming one extra unit of a good.

12. _____: the satisfaction consumers receive from items they acquire, activities they engage in, or services they use.

13. _____: states that to maximize utility, a consumer must equalize the marginal utility per dollar spent on each good.

14. _____: individual likes and dislikes.

15. _____: attained when a consumer purchases goods over a period until the marginal utility per dollar is the same for all goods consumed.

CONCEPT REVIEW

Concept 1:   *Total and marginal utility*

1. The table below contains quantity and total utility data for consumption of good X.

Units of Good X	Total Utility	Marginal Utility
1	50	_____
2	90	_____
3	120	_____
4	140	_____
5	150	_____
6	150	_____
7	140	_____

    a.   Complete the marginal utility column above.

    b.   Plot the total and marginal utility data on the diagrams below.

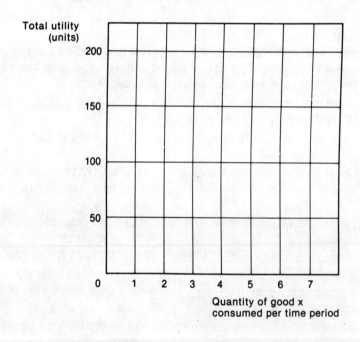

138

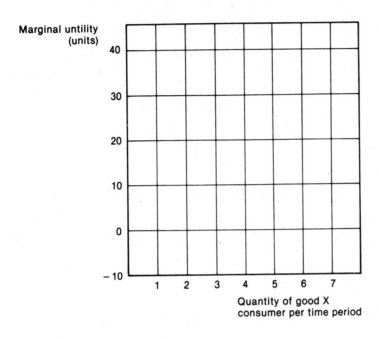

Marginal untility (units)

Quantity of good X consumer per time period

c. Marginal utility is the _____ of the total utility curve. When total utility reaches a maximum, marginal utility equals _____.

Concept 2: *Equimarginal principle*

2. Assume that an individual has an income of $150 per week to be spent on either ballpark tickets or sweaters. The price of each ballpark admission is $5 and the price of a sweater is $25. The individual is assumed to spend all income each week. Given the total utility data below:

a. Complete the marginal utility (MU) columns.

b. Complete the marginal utility per dollar (MU/P) columns.

c. Determine the individual's utility-maximizing combination of ballpark tickets and sweaters. _____ tickets and _____ sweaters

d. Determine the total utility (TU) associated with the combination of goods consumed from part c. _____ units of utility

Ballpark Tickets					Sweaters			
Units	TU	MU	MU/P		Units	TU	MU	MU/P
1	60	——	——		1	400	——	——
2	115	——	——		2	750	——	——
3	165	——	——		3	1050	——	——
4	210	——	——		4	1300	——	——
5	250	——	——		5	1500	——	——
6	285	——	——		6	1650	——	——
7	315	——	——					

Concepts 3, 4, 5, and 6: *Total and marginal benefits; the impact of price and income*

3. The following represent total and marginal benefit data for a consumer:

Units of Good X	Total Benefits ($)	Marginal Benefits ($)
1	$150	——
2	280	——
3	390	——
4	480	——
5	550	——
6	600	——
7	630	——

a. Complete the marginal benefits column.

b. Plot the marginal benefits curve below.

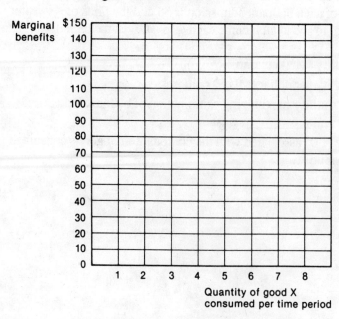

140

c. If price equals $90 per unit, how many units of good X would be consumed?_____units. At this level of consumption, total benefits equal $_____, consumer surplus equals $_____.

d. If price equals $50 per unit, how many units of good X would be consumed?_____units. At this level of consumption, total benefits equal $_____, consumer surplus equals $_____.

e. If price equals $200, how many units of the good would be consumed?_____ units Why?

f. Plot the price-quantity demanded coordinates from parts c and d above in the diagram below. This curve is called a/an _____.

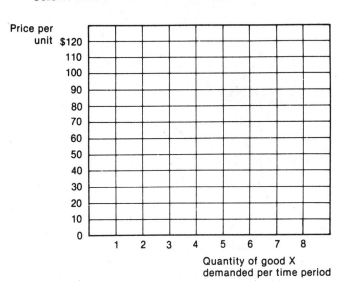

4. The following diagram represents the price and marginal benefits curve associated with a consumer's purchases of a good.

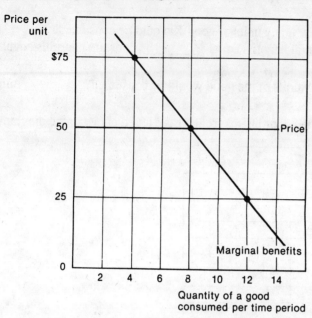

a. In the diagram, show the impact of an increase in income if the good is a normal good. Quantity consumed _____.

b. In the diagram, show the impact of an increase in income if the good is an inferior good. Quantity consumed _____.

5. a. For normal goods:

    (1) A decrease in price, via the income effect, will _____ quantity demanded.

    (2) A decrease in price, via the substitution effect, will _____ quantity demanded.

    (3) The net effect of a price decrease is an _____ in quantity demanded.

  b. For inferior goods:

    (1) A decrease in price, via the income effect, will _____ quantity demanded.

    (2) A decrease in price, via the substitution effect, will _____ quantity demanded.

    (3) The net effect of a price decrease is an _____ in quantity demanded.

  c. For Giffen goods,

    (1) A decrease in price, via the income effect, will _____ quantity demanded.

    (2) A decrease in price, via the substitution effect, will _____ quantity demanded.

    (3) The net effect of a price decrease is an _____ in quantity demanded.

Concept 7: *Market demand curve*

6. Derive the market demand curve in diagram d below from the individual demand curves shown in figures a, b, and c.

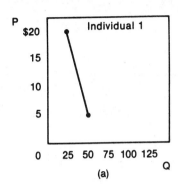

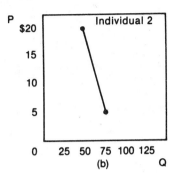

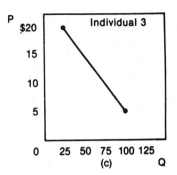

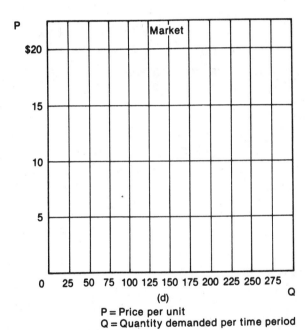

P = Price per unit
Q = Quantity demanded per time period

MASTERY TEST

Select the best answer.

1. The total satisfaction received by a consumer from a given quantity of consumption per time period is known as:
   a. marginal utility.
   b. marginal benefit.
   c. total benefit.
   d. total utility.

2. The additional satisfaction received by a consumer from the consumption of an additional unit of a good is known as:
   a. marginal utility.
   b. marginal benefit.
   c. total benefit.
   d. total utility.

3. Which of the following defines the law of diminishing marginal utility?
   a. Total utility rises at an increasing rate as additional units of a good are consumed.
   b. Marginal utility rises at an increasing rate as additional units of a good are consumed.
   c. Marginal utility falls as more of a good is consumed over a period.
   d. Total utility falls as more of a good is consumed over a period.

4. If the marginal utility per dollar (MU/P) of good A exceeded the MU/P of good B, a consumer could increase utility by:
   a. not altering the combination of goods A and B consumed.
   b. consuming more of good B and less of good A.
   c. consuming less of both goods A and B.
   d. consuming more of good A and less of good B.

5. Utility is maximized in the consumption of goods when:
   a. the marginal utility per dollar is the same for each good.
   b. goods are consumed to the point of satiation.
   c. the marginal utility of each good is the same.
   d. the satisfaction from each good is equal.

6. The maximum sum of money that consumers are willing and able to pay for the additional satisfaction associated with the consumption of an extra unit of output is called:
   a. income.
   b. total benefit.
   c. marginal benefit.
   d. marginal utility.

7. The marginal benefit curve is downsloping because:
   a. of the law of diminishing returns.
   b. it is the slope of the total utility curve.
   c. most goods are normal goods.
   d. of the law of diminishing marginal utility.

8. A consumer can maximize net benefits by consuming a good to the point where marginal benefit:
   a. equals the price.
   b. equals marginal utility.
   c. equals total benefit.
   d. is equal for all goods.

9. If goods A and B are associated with marginal benefits of $5 and $10, respectively, for the first unit consumed, a consumer would _____ if the price of good A equaled $6 and the price of good B equaled $12.50.
   a. purchase both goods A and B
   b. not purchase either good
   c. prefer A to B
   d. prefer B to A

10. Which of the following terms represents total benefits received in excess of the dollar expenditure necessary to obtain goods?
   a. Consumer excess
   b. Net gain
   c. Consumer surplus
   d. B or c

11. If the excess of marginal benefits over the product price for good A exceeds that of good B, a consumer:
   a. is indifferent regarding the purchase of goods A and B.
   b. would prefer A to B.
   c. would not prefer either good.
   d. would prefer B to A.

12. An increase in income shifts the marginal benefit curve _____, resulting in an increase in consumption if the good in question is a _____ good.
   a. upward, inferior
   b. downward, normal
   c. upward, normal
   d. upward, Giffen

13. The income effect reinforces the substitution effect for:
    a. normal goods.
    b. inferior goods.
    c. giffen goods.
    d. public goods.

14. The income effect to some extent offsets the substitution effect for:
    a. normal goods.
    b. inferior goods.
    c. public goods.
    d. all goods and services.

15. The income effect more than offsets the substitution effect for:
    a. normal goods.
    b. inferior goods.
    c. public goods.
    d. giffen goods.

16. A market demand curve:
    a. is a horizontal summation of individual demand curves.
    b. is downsloping.
    c. is the culmination of utility-maximizing choices by consumers.
    d. All of the above.

17. The utility associated with the consumption of the next apple is 4 units of utility whereas the consumption of the next banana produces a gain in utility of 10 units. The price per banana is $.50 and the price per apple is $.25. A consumer will maximize utility:
    a. if equal quantities of bananas and apples are consumed.
    b. if less is spent on apples and more on bananas until the marginal utilities per dollar for each good are equal.
    c. only if bananas are consumed.
    d. if more is spent on apples and less on bananas until the total utilities per dollar for each good are equal.

18. When the extra benefit associated with the consumption of the next unit of a good exceeds that good's price, a consumer will:
    a. be maximizing consumer surplus.
    b. reduce the quantity purchased in order to increase net benefits.
    c. want to increase consumption of the good in order to increase consumer surplus.
    d. either increase or decrease consumption of the good depending on the elasticities of demand and supply.

19. Which of the following represents the chain of events associated with an increase in income? Assume the good in question is a normal good.
    a. An increase in income causes an upward shift in a consumer's marginal benefit curve, causing marginal benefit to rise above the product price. This, in turn, causes the individual's demand curve to shift rightward. The market demand curve will shift rightward if a significant number of consumers are affected.
    b. An increase in income causes prices to rise, causing the marginal benefit and market demand curves to shift rightward.
    c. An increase in income causes the price line to shift downward, causing marginal benefit to exceed price. As consumers increase consumption, both individual and market demand curves shift rightward.
    d. An increase in income shifts the market demand curve rightward, increasing market price. Rising market prices allow producers to pay higher wages to workers. As wages and consumption rise, individual demand curves shift rightward.

20. If the income effect of a price change outweighs the substitution effect for an inferior good and the demand curve for the good is less steeply sloped than the supply curve, an increase in demand for the good will:
    a. cause both price and quantity demanded to increase.
    b. cause both price and quantity demanded to decrease.
    c. cause price to rise and quantity demanded to fall.
    d. cause price to fall and quantity demanded to rise.

21. Which of the following can result in a positively-sloped demand curve?
    a. Substitution effect outweighs the income effect for a normal good.
    b. Substitution effect outweighs the income effect for a substitute good.
    c. Income effect outweighs the substitution effect for an inferior good.
    d. Income effect outweighs the substitution effect for complementary goods.

THINK IT THROUGH

1. You go to a restaurant, look at the menu, and find that the price of a cheese omelette is $3.50 and the price of a short stack of pancakes is $2. Your marginal benefits associated with the next order of an omelette or pancakes are $5 and $2.75, respectively. Which do you prefer? Why?

2. Explain the logic underlying the equimarginal principle.

3. You complain because your spouse always purchases the more expensive good when confronted with a choice. Assume that price and product quality are not always positively related. Is your spouse a utility maximizer? Discuss.

4. Why are people often willing and able to spend large sums on goods with limited usefulness like gold money clips when these same people are willing to spend little if any money for essential goods like air or water?

CHAPTER ANSWERS

The Chapter in Brief

1. Total 2. Marginal utility 3. Equals 4. Maximum 5. Declining 6. Declines 7. Exceed 8. Equals
9. Dollar expenditure 10. Exceeds 11. Normal goods 12. Inferior good 13. Individual 14. Income
15. Substitution 16. Complements 17. To some extent offsets 18. More than offsets

Key Terms Review

1. Income effect 2. Substitution effect 3. Market demand curve 4. Law of diminishing marginal
utility 5. Marginal benefit 6. Consumer surplus 7. Paradox of value 8. Total utility 9. Total benefit
10. Net benefit 11. Marginal utility 12. Utility 13. Equimarginal principle 14. Preference
15. Consumer equilibrium

Concept Review

1. a.

Units	MU
1	50
2	40
3	30
4	20
5	10
6	0
7	-10

b.

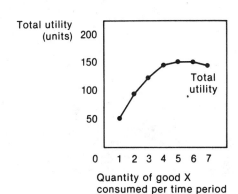

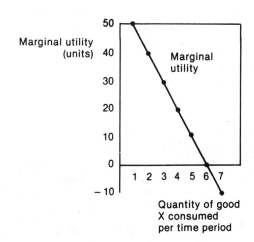

c. Slope, zero

2. a. and b.

	Tickets			Sweaters		
Units	MU	MU/P		Units	MU	MU/P
1	60	12		1	400	16
2	55	11		2	350	14
3	50	10		3	300	12
4	45	9		4	250	10
5	40	8		5	200	8
6	35	7		6	150	6
7	30	6				

c. 5, 5

d. 1750

3. a.

Units	MB($)
1	150
2	130
3	110
4	90
5	70
6	50
7	30

b.

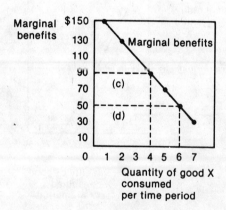

150

c.   4, $480, $120

d.   6, $600, $300

e.   None. Price exceeds marginal benefits for the first unit consumed.

f.   Individual demand curve

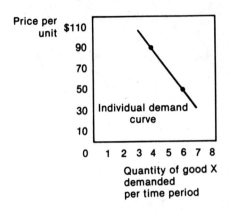

4. a.   Increases

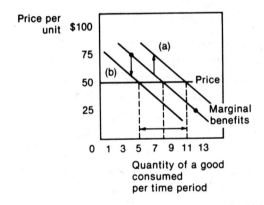

b.   Decreases

5. a.   (1) Increase (2) Increase (3) Increase

   b.   (1) Decrease (2) Increase (3) Increase

   c.   (1) Decrease (2) Increase (3) Decrease

6.

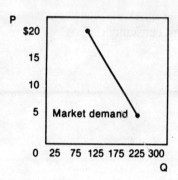

Mastery Test

1. d 2. a 3. c 4. d 5. a 6. c 7. d 8. a 9. b 10. d 11. b 12. c 13. a 14. b 15. d 16. d 17. b 18. c 19. a 20. b 21.c

Think it Through

1. For both goods, marginal benefits exceed price. But for an omelette, the difference between the marginal benefit and price is greater than it is for pancakes. The net gain to you is greater if you purchase an omelette rather than pancakes. You prefer, therefore, an omelette to pancakes.

2. A consumer maximizes utility when the marginal utility per dollar for each good consumed is the same. If the MU/P for some good exceeded that for other goods, dollars could be reallocated away from other goods and spent on the good with the higher MU/P. A consumer could increase utility by reallocating a given income. The reverse holds true for goods having a smaller MU/P.

3. Your spouse probably gets satisfaction from purchasing more expensive goods. It might be the perception of higher quality or an attempt to keep up with the Joneses or the need to not feel "cheap" that gives your spouse "tastes" for higher priced goods. Remember that a consumer's preferences depend on both prices and marginal benefits associated with goods. For higher priced goods, your spouse is simply expressing a willingness and ability to pay a higher maximum sum—a higher marginal benefit curve. But for the higher priced good to be chosen, the excess of marginal benefits over the price must be larger than for lower priced goods, or it would be irrational to purchase the more expensive good.

4. Plentiful goods such as air or water command either no market price or a very minimal price. The additional benefit of a gallon of water is very small. The price you are willing to pay is likewise very small even though the total benefit associated with water consumption is quite large. Because of their scarcity, the additional benefit of a gold clip is high. Some people are willing to pay high prices for gold money clips even though the total benefits received from the clips are very small relative to the consumption of water.

APPENDIX TO CHAPTER 7:
INDIFFERENCE CURVE ANALYSIS

THE APPENDIX IN BRIEF

Fill in the blanks to summarize appendix content.

(1)_____(Marginal analysis, Indifference curve analysis) is a technique for analyzing the choices that consumers make between alternatives. The indifference curve and budget constraint are the essential elements of the analysis. Applied to goods, an indifference curve shows the various combinations of two goods that can be consumed while maintaining (2)_____ (the same level, different levels) of utility. The curve is negatively sloped because in order to keep utility unchanged, the consumer must give up some consumption of a good in order to increase the consumption of another good. The slope of the indifference curve becomes less negative as more of the good on the horizontal axis is consumed. The slope is called the (3)_____ (marginal utility, marginal rate of substitution). It indicates the quantity of one good that a consumer is willing to give up to have a unit of another good, while maintaining the level of utility. The marginal rate of substitution of x for y (MRSxy) (4)_____ (decreases, increases) as more of good X is consumed. This is known as the diminishing marginal rate of substitution. The consumer is willing to give up large quantities of Y in order to have the first few units of good X. As more and more units of X are consumed, the consumer is willing to sacrifice smaller and smaller quantities of good Y. Marginal utility and marginal benefits fall as additional units of X are consumed. But reducing the consumption of Y increases the marginal utility and benefit of Y. At the margin, units of X become increasingly less valuable in terms of the sacrifice of good Y. Indifference curves (5)_____(closer to, further from) the origin are associated with higher levels of utility.

(6)_____(The budget constraint, Income) determines the consumer's ability to maximize satisfaction from the consumption of goods X and Y. The budget constraint is determined by the income per period available to the consumer and the relative prices of the two goods consumed. The slope of the budget line is negative and is the ratio of the price of good X to the price of good Y. Changes in (7)_____(income, prices) shift the budget line, whereas changes in (8)_____(income, prices) alter the slope.

Consumer equilibrium occurs when the market value of good Y that you are willing to give up just equals what the market requires you to pay for a unit of good X. This occurs where the budget line (9)_____(intersects, is just tangent to) the highest indifference curve. Here the marginal rate of substitution equals the ratio of the price of good X to the price of good Y. The consumer spends all income and allocates it in a way that maximizes utility. It can be shown that the MRSxy also equals the ratio of the marginal utility of good X to the marginal utility of good Y. MUx/MUy also equals the price ratio. The point of tangency between the indifference curve and budget constraint is equivalent to the equimarginal principle when the slope of the indifference curve is interpreted as the ratio of these marginal utilities.

An increase in income shifts the budget constraint curve (10)_____ (outward, inward) parallel to the old budget line such that a new point of tangency is reached on a higher indifference curve. For instance, if goods are normal, an income increase will cause the consumption of both goods to (11)_____(fall, rise). A decrease in the price of X will cause the budget line to become less steep. The consumption of X increases, and the consumer attains a higher level of utility. A demand curve for good X can be derived by changing the price of good X, all other things being equal, and determining the consumer's utility-maximizing quantity demanded. Plotting these price-quantity demanded coordinates yields the consumer's individual demand curve.

KEY TERMS REVIEW

Write the key term from the list below next to its definition.

Key Terms

Indifference curve analysis	Consumer equilibrium
Market basket	Budget constraint
Indifference curve	Indifference map
Marginal rate of substitution	Diminishing marginal rate of substitution

Definitions

1. _____: the marginal rate of substitution of good X for Y will tend to decline as more X is substituted for Y along any consumer's indifference curve.

2. _____: represents the combination of goods purchased that maximizes utility subject to the budget constraint.

3. _____: a technique for explaining how choices between two alternative are made.

4. _____: as defined by a consumer's income and its purchasing power; indicates that income must equal expenditure.

5. _____: a graph of various market baskets that provide a consumer with equal utility.

6. _____: the quantity of one good a consumer would give up to obtain one more unit of another good while being made neither better off nor worse off by the trade.

7. _____: a combination of goods and services.

8. _____: a way of drawing indifference curves to describe a consumer's preferences.

CONCEPT REVIEW

1. In the diagram below, draw a budget constraint where the consumer has income of $100 per week and the prices of goods X and Y are both $5.

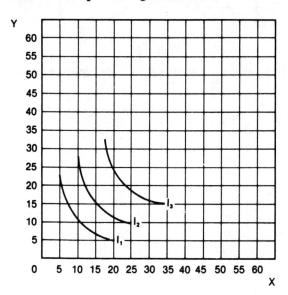

a. The consumer's utility-maximizing combination of goods X and Y are _____ units of good X and _____ units of good Y.

b. Show on the diagram above the effect of an increase in income to $150 per week. The consumption of good X _____ to _____ units and the consumption of good Y _____ to _____ units. The goods must be _____ goods.

c. Holding income at $150 per week, show the impact of a price reduction of good X to $2.50. The consumption of good X _____ to _____ units; the consumption of good Y _____ to _____ units.

2. Referring to the diagram below, let income equal $120 and assume that the prices of X and Y equal $10.

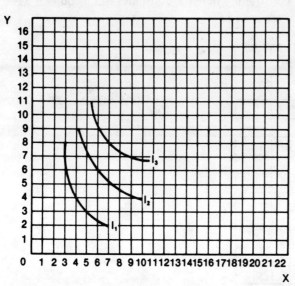

a. Determine the utility-maximizing combination of goods X and Y. _____
    units of X, _____ units of Y.

b. Let the price of X fall to $6. The utility-maximizing quantity of X consumed is
    _____ units. Of Y consumed the utility-maximizing quantity is
    _____ units.

c. Let the price of X rise from $10 to $20. The utility-maximizing combination of X and Y is
    _____ units of X and _____ units of Y.

d. Construct this consumer's individual demand curve in the diagram below for good X from the information in parts b and c above.

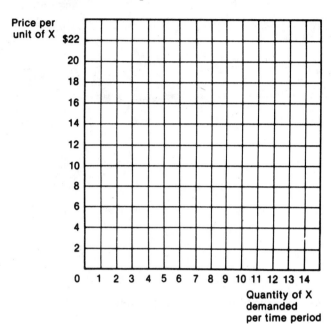

Price per unit of X

Quantity of X demanded per time period

MASTERY TEST

Select the best answer.

1. Which of the following are true regarding an indifference curve?
   a. The slope is negative.
   b. The MRS_{xy} increases as more of good X is consumed.
   c. The MRS_{xy} decreases as more of good X is consumed.
   d. Indifference curves farther from the origin imply a higher level of utility.
   e. A, c, and d.

2. The budget constraint:
   a. has a positive slope.
   b. must be curvilinear if the prices of the two goods are held unchanged.
   c. has a slope equal to $-(P_x/P_y)$.
   d. None of the above.

3. Increases in income shift the budget constraint:

    a. inward.

    b. outward.

    c. to a different slope.

    d. such that it no longer limits consumer purchases.

4. A change in price of either good X or Y will:

    a. shift the indifference curve.

    b. shift the budget constraint.

    c. rotate the indifference curve.

    d. rotate the budget constraint about one of its two intercepts.

5. Consumer equilibrium occurs when:

    a. the budget constraint and the indifference curve intersect.

    b. two indifference curves intersect.

    c. the highest indifference curve on the indifference curve map is attained.

    d. the budget constraint is just tangent to the highest indifference curve.

6. In an indifference curve system, an increase in the price of good X will _____ the budget constraint toward the origin and _____ the quantity of good X consumed.

    a. rotate, decrease

    b. rotate, increase

    c. shift, decrease

    d. shift, increase

7. In an indifference curve system, an increase in income will _____ the budget constraint away from the origin, and the quantity of good X consumed will _____ if good X is a normal good.

    a. rotate, decrease

    b. rotate, increase

    c. shift, decrease

    d. shift, increase

8. Which one of the following is true regarding consumer equilibrium?

    a. $MRSxy = MUx = MUy$

    b. $MRSxy = (MUx/MUy) = (Px/Py)$

    c. $(Px/Py) + MRSxy = (MUx/MUy)$

    d. None of the above

THINK IT THROUGH

1. Every point on a consumer's individual demand curve represents a utility-maximizing decision. Discuss.

2. Explain how market demand curves can be derived from individual demand curves.

APPENDIX ANSWERS

The Appendix in Brief

1.Indifference curve analysis 2. The same level 3. Marginal rate of substitution 4. Decreases
5. Further from 6. Budget constraint 7. Income 8. Prices 9. Is just tangent to 10. Outward 11. Rise

Key Terms Review

1.Diminishing marginal rate of substitution 2. Consumer equilibrium 3. Indifference curve analysis
4.Budget constraint 5. Indifference curve 6. Marginal rate of substitution 7. Market basket
8. Indifference map

Concept Review

1.

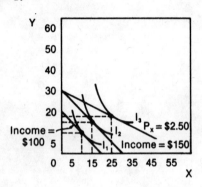

a. 10,10

b. Increases, 15, increases, 15, normal

c. Increases, 25, increases, 17 1/2

2.

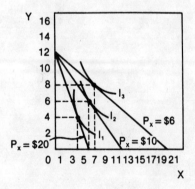

160

a. 6,6

b. 7,8

c. 4,4

d.

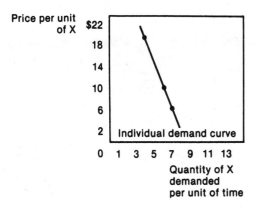

Price per unit of X

$22
18
14
10
6
2

Individual demand curve

0 1 3 5 7 9 11 13

Quantity of X
demanded
per unit of time

Mastery Test

1. c 2. c 3. b 4. d 5. d 6. a 7. d 8. b

Think it Through

1. A coordinate on the consumer's individual demand curve represents a utility-maximizing response to a given price of the good relative to other product prices, other things being equal. This is true of other coordinates on the demand curve. Each point on the demand curve represents a state of consumer equilibrium.

2. Market demand curves represent the utility-maximizing responses of all consumers to relative prices. It can be derived by horizontally summing the individual demand curves of all consumers in the market.

8 THE BUSINESS FIRM: A PROLOGUE TO THE THEORY OF MARKET SUPPLY

CHAPTER CONCEPTS

After studying your text, attending class, and completing this chapter, you should be able to:

1. Outline the advantages of alternative forms of business organization: the sole proprietorship, the partnership, and the corporation.
2. Explain the functions of firms and how various aspects of production and distribution are integrated within a single firm.
3. Describe a simplified view of the firm that is useful in constructing a model that explains market supply.
4. Show how the concept of opportunity cost must be applied to accurately measure the profit of a firm.

THE CHAPTER IN BRIEF

Fill in the blanks to summarize chapter content.

Business firms, each of which is under one management, are engaged in earning profits for the owners by producing items for sale in markets. They operate one or more plants producing one or more products and in some cases are vertically integrated. Vertical integration means that all stages of operation, including the acquisition of raw materials, the processing of resources to produce output, and the distribution and marketing of goods are handled by (1)_____ (several firms, a single firm). A (2)_____ (conglomerate, corporation) is a firm that produces many kinds of goods and services. Firms selling (3)_____(different, similar) products are in the same industry.

A firm can be structured as a sole proprietorship, a partnership, or a corporation. A (4)_____ (partnership, corporation) is a legal person. It has some distinct advantages over other business enterprises. Corporations can issue both stocks and bonds and the owners of the corporation (the stockholders) have (5)_____(limited, unlimited) liability. Both of these characteristics greatly (6)_____ (reduce, increase) the amount of funds that can be attracted for expansion and growth. Stockholders can easily sell their rights in the firm. Individuals can reduce the risk associated with owning firms by diversifying their holdings. This increases the total amount of funds available for stock ownership. Another factor that induces individuals to provide more funds to the corporation is (7)_____(limited, unlimited) liability. This too reduces the risk of ownership in that a stockholder's liability relates to the amount of stock held. Other business enterprises are at (8)_____ (an advantage, a disadvantage) compared to corporations in that they have unlimited liability and cannot issue stocks and bonds.

In corporations, ownership and management (9)_____(are, are not) separated. If management pursues goals that are inconsistent with the owners' goals, profits decrease because managers use corporate resources to attain managerial goals that would have otherwise been used to further the goals of the owners. Also, owners must use resources to monitor management to ensure that the owners' goals are met. Another disadvantage of corporations is that they are not only subject to a corporate income tax, but the (10)_____ (retained earnings, dividends) paid to stockholders are subject to individual income taxes as well. Thus the income of the corporation is taxed twice. This (11)_____(is, is not) the case for other business enterprises.

The functions of business firms include the production of goods and services, the assignment of tasks to either employees or to outside firms for various stages of production, and a determination of the appropriate division of labor within the firm. Managers assist in these functions by helping to decide what and how much to produce and whether certain operations should be handled internally or contracted out. Operations are likely to be (12)_____ (contracted out, kept within the firm) if a reliable flow of materials and services is considered important and there is a possibility that outside suppliers might prove unreliable. A firm might want to control a strategic input and thus put other firms in the industry at a disadvantage. Or a firm might put a premium on internal communication or the ability to easily adapt to new technology. All of these things would probably induce a firm to vertically integrate—to handle all production stages within the firm. Managers also have to assign labor-specific tasks or responsibilities so that the firm can operate at least cost. Managers reward efficient employees with a compensation system designed to maintain and enhance labor productivity.

In studying the behavior of firms, it is necessary to abstract from the complexities of the modern economy and make some assumptions regarding the structure or goals of firms so that the basic features of firm behavior can be understood. It is assumed that there (13)_____(is, is no) separation between ownership and management. Firms are assumed to be (14)_____ (multiproduct, single product), having owner-operators who make decisions regarding resource use and production that maximize (15)_____(revenues, profits).

Profit is defined as total revenue less total costs in which total costs include (16)_____(in addition to, only) the accounting costs, (17)_____(but not the, the) cost of owner-supplied resources. (18)_____ (Total, Accounting) costs are the explicit outlays by the firm for resources bought in resource markets. Owner-supplied inputs are not purchased by the firm but entail opportunity costs. These (19)_____ (explicit, implicit) costs must be imputed or estimated. They are estimated by determining the opportunity cost of the owner-supplied inputs. Revenues in excess of accounting and implicit costs are called (20)_____(economic, normal) profit. (21)_____(Economic, Normal) profit is treated as a cost (the implicit costs associated with owner-supplied resources). It is a return to the owner-operator just equal to the opportunity cost of self-owned resources.

KEY TERMS REVIEW

Write the key term from the list below next to its definition.

Key Terms

Business firm
Plant
Vertical integration
Conglomerate
Industry
Sole proprietorship
Partnership
Corporation
Dividend
Retained earnings
Limited liability

Manager
Personnel management
Multiproduct firm
Single-product firm
Profit
Economic cost
Implicit cost
Accounting cost
Normal profit
Economic profit

Definitions

1. _____: that portion of a firm's costs that is not included in accounting costs. A measure of the implicit cost of owner-supplied resources in a firm over a given period.

2. _____: the difference between total revenue and the cost of all inputs used by a firm over a given period.

3. _____: the portion of a corporation's profit paid to its stockholders.

4. _____: the portion of corporate profits not paid out as dividends.

5. _____: the monetary value of all inputs used in a particular activity or enterprise over a given period.

6. _____: the cost of nonpurchased inputs to which a cash value must be imputed because the inputs are not purchased in a market transaction.

7. _____: a group of firms selling a similar product in a market.

8. _____: a business that is legally established under state laws that grant it an identity separate from its owners.

9. _____: an organization under one management set up for the purpose of earning profits for its owners by making one or more items available for sale in markets.

10. _____: a business owned by one person.

11. _____: a physical structure in which a firm's owners or employees conduct business.

12. _____: a business owned by two or more persons, each of whom receives a portion of any profits.

13. _____: a firm that owns plants used in various stages of its production.

14. _____: measures the explicit costs of operating a business, those which result from purchases of input services.

15. _____: a firm operating plants that produce many different kinds of goods and services.

16. _____: a person who coordinates decisions within the firm.

17. _____: a firm that produces only one type of item for sale in markets.

165

18. _____: a firm that produces several different items for sale in markets.

19. _____: a legal provision that protects the owners of a corporation (its stockholders) by putting a ceiling equal to the purchase price of their stock on their liability for debts of the corporation.

20. _____: the difference between the revenues a firm takes in over any given period and the costs incurred in operating the firm over the same period.

21. _____: the process by which managers monitor worker performance and provide rewards for workers who perform efficiently.

CONCEPT REVIEW

Concept 1: *Alternative forms of business organization*

1. Which of the following characteristics are associated with corporations (C), sole proprietorships (PR), and/or partnerships (PT)?

   a. _____ Limited liability

   b. _____ Unlimited liability

   c. _____ Separation of ownership and management

   d. _____ Presence of owner-operators

   e. _____ Ability to issue stock and bonds

   f. _____ Can pay dividends

   g. _____ Income is subject to personal income taxes only

   h. _____ Income is subject to taxation twice

   i. _____ Is a legal person

Concepts 2, 3: *Functions of business; business management*

2. List three functions of business firms:

   a. _____

   b. _____

   c. _____

3. List three ways in which managers assist business firms in the fulfillment of their functions:

   a. _____

   b. _____

   c. _____

4. You manage a U.S.-based corporation, the XYZ Aluminum Company, and you are trying to decide whether to mine your own raw input, bauxite, internally or to purchase it from outside firms. Assume that bauxite is found only in Africa and must be processed into aluminum ingots before shipment to fabrication plants in the United States. For each of the scenarios below, are you *more* or *less* inclined to contract out? Explain.

a. _____ War develops, closing sea lanes.

b. _____ Civil wars are no longer occurring in African nations, raising the possibility of long-term peace and political stability.

c. _____There are no substitutes for bauxite in the production of aluminum.

d. _____ XYZ is battling with four other companies for a larger share of the aluminum market.

e. _____XYZ finds that closer managerial communication among the various stages of production enhances the firm's efficiency.

f. _____ XYZ patents a process that reduces the cost of mining bauxite.

g. _____Because the world supply of bauxite and aluminum ingots is produced by firms specializing in the production of these inputs, they produce a large volume, realizing efficiencies associated with large-scale production and specialization.

Concept 4: *Cost and profit measures*

5. Given the data in the table below for Fred's Bar and Grill, determine Fred's:

a. Accounting cost_____

b. Explicit cost _____

c. Implicit cost _____

d. Normal profit _____

e. Total cost_____

f. Economic profit_____

Fred's Bar and Grill
(annual data)

Wages	$25,000
Depreciation	15,000
Interest paid	7,000
Other expenditures for inputs	17,000
Imputed cost of owner-supplied labor	20,000
Imputed cost of owner-supplied plant	6,000
Imputed interest associated with owner-supplied resources	2,000
Total revenue	108,000

6. Discuss the implications if Fred's Bar and Grill earned $85,000 of revenue instead of $108,000.

MASTERY TEST

Select the best answer.

1. A business firm that engages in several stages of production from the acquisition of resources to the distribution of output is known as a:
   a. conglomerate.
   b. single-product firm.
   c. multiproduct firm.
   d. vertically integrated firm.

2. A business firm that sells output in many different industries is known as a:
   a. conglomerate.
   b. single-product firm.
   c. multiproduct firm.
   d. vertically integrated firm.
   e. a and c.

3. Which of the following best describes an industry?
   a. A collection of markets
   b. A group of firms
   c. A group of firms selling similar products
   d. A collection of markets for unrelated goods

4. Unlimited liability is a characteristic of:
   a. corporations.
   b. sole proprietorships.
   c. partnerships.
   d. b and c.

5. The ability to issue stock and bonds is a characteristic of:
   a. corporations.
   b. sole proprietorships.
   c. partnerships.
   d. b and c.

6. The separation of ownership and management is a characteristic of:
   a. corporations.
   b. sole proprietorships.
   c. partnerships.
   d. b and c.

7. Which of the following is a legal person?
   a. Corporation
   b. Sole proprietorship
   c. Partnership
   d. None of the above

8. The main advantage of a corporation over other forms of business enterprise is that:
   a. other forms of business enterprise have their incomes taxed twice.
   b. other forms of business enterprise have limited liability.
   c. corporations have unlimited liability.
   d. corporations can raise larger sums of money for expansion and growth.

9. That portion of corporate income which is not paid as dividends or used to meet the corporation's tax liability is called:
   a. depreciation.
   b. retained earnings.
   c. normal profit.
   d. implicit cost.

10. A business firm is less likely to contract out for production or services if:
    a. communication within the firm between various production stages is relatively unimportant.
    b. controlling a strategic input is unimportant to the firm.
    c. adapting to changing technology is considered unimportant.
    d. there is a possibility that outside suppliers might prove unreliable.

11. A business firm is more likely to contract out when:
    a. communication within the firm between various stages of production is important.
    b. controlling a strategic input is considered important.
    c. adapting to changing technology is important.
    d. outside suppliers are reliable.
    e. All of the above

12. Abstracting from the complexities of the modern economy to better understand the essential features of business firm behavior, several simplifying assumptions are made. Which of the following is not one of these?
    a. Ownership and management are not separated.
    b. The firm is a single-product firm.
    c. The goal of the firm is to maximize profits.
    d. The firm is vertically integrated.

13. The total actual payments made by a firm to acquire inputs are known as:
    a. accounting costs.
    b. normal profit.
    c. implicit costs.
    d. marginal costs.

14. Accounting costs are also called:
    a. explicit costs.
    b. total costs.
    c. total normal costs.
    d. imputed costs.

15. The cost of nonpurchased owner-supplied resources is known as:
    a. implicit costs.
    b. explicit costs.
    c. accounting costs.
    d. total costs.

16. Implicit costs are measured by the:
    a. accounting costs less the imputed costs.
    b. imputed costs plus the explicit costs.
    c. total revenues less total costs.
    d. opportunity cost of owner-supplied resources.

17. Total costs are the sum of:
    a. accounting costs and explicit costs.
    b. accounting costs and the opportunity costs of owner-supplied resources.
    c. imputed costs and the opportunity costs of owner-supplied resources.
    d. accounting costs and implicit costs.
    e. b and d.

18. A return to the owner just equal to the opportunity costs of the owner's self-owned resources provided to the firm is called:
    a. total revenue.
    b. imputed revenue.
    c. normal profit.
    d. economic profit.

19. Economic profit is defined as:
    a. a return to the owner just equal to the opportunity costs of the owner's self-owned resources provided to the firm.
    b. total revenue less accounting costs.
    c. total revenue less the sum of accounting costs and implicit costs.
    d. normal profit plus imputed revenues.

Answer questions 20 to 23 based upon the information provided below.

You are considering opening a restaurant. You estimate that the annual cost of labor will be $50,000, interest on borrowed funds will be $18,000, and other supplies will equal $65,000. Owner-supplied resources include a building that is currently renting for $12,000 per month and $25,000 in cash currently earning a 10% rate of interest. Annual revenues are projected to be $250,000.

20. What is the explicit cost (or accounting cost) associated with operating the restaurant described above?
    a. $146,500
    b. $133,000
    c. $170,000
    d. $115,000

21. What is the implicit cost (or normal profit) associated with operating the restaurant described above?
    a. $40,000
    b. $37,000
    c. $146,500
    d. $170,000

22. Based on the estimates described above, will the restaurant be opened?
    a. Yes, because projected normal profits equal the opportunity cost of the owner-supplied resources.
    b. Yes, because accounting profit is $117,000.
    c. No, because accounting profits exceed normal profits.
    d. No, because total costs exceed total revenue.

23. What amount of revenue would be required for the owner to just earn normal profits and have an incentive to open the restaurant?
    a. $279,500
    b. $250,000
    c. $133,000
    d. $147,500

THINK IT THROUGH

1. Of the three forms of business enterprise, why are sole proprietorships and partnerships so numerous and corporations so large?

2. The microcomputer industry is populated by many more firms operating at a single stage of production than by vertically integrated firms. Explain why.

3. Why is it necessary to consider implicit costs in decisions?

4. You are considering owning and operating a day care center. You determine that the annual cost to hire labor is $35,000. You plan to use one of your rental houses for the location of the center. You estimate that $25,000 of capital equipment is required. Because you have only $5,000 in cash, you expect to borrow $20,000. The interest cost on the loan would be $2,000 per year. Other miscellaneous inputs are expected to cost $15,000 annually. You would consider it a success if you just break even the first year—if your revenues just cover your costs. You estimate that you can do this if revenues for the first year are $52,000. Discuss.

CHAPTER ANSWERS

The Chapter in Brief

1. A single firm 2. Conglomerate 3. Similar 4. Corporation 5. Limited 6. Increase 7. Limited 8. A disadvantage 9. Are 10. Dividends 11. Is not 12. Kept within the firm 13. Is 14. Single product 15. Profits 16. In addition to 17. The 18. Accounting 19. Implicit 20. Economic 21. Normal

Key Terms Review

1. Normal profit 2. Economic profit 3. Dividend 4. Retained earnings 5. Economic cost 6. Implicit cost 7. Industry 8. Corporation 9. Business firm 10. Sole proprietorship 11. Plant 12. Partnership 13. Vertical integration 14. Accounting cost 15. Conglomerate 16. Manager 17. Single-product firm 18. Multiproduct firm 19. Limited liability 20. Profit 21. Personnel management

Concept Review

1. a. C b. PR, PT c. C d. PR, PT e. C f. C g. PR, PT h. C i. C

2. a. Production of goods and services
   b. Assignment of tasks to employees of the firm or to outside firms
   c. Determination of the appropriate division of labor and specialization of resources

3. a. Helps decide what and how much to produce
   b. Helps decide whether or not to contract out for production or services
   c. Assigns labor-specialized tasks, monitors their efforts, and rewards them accordingly

4. a. Less. If you rely on African suppliers to ship ingots to the United States, there is likely to be an interruption in supply. Whereas if you develop the resource yourself, you might be able to stockpile ingots or build fabrication plants in Africa in anticipation of impending events.
   b. More. The likelihood of interruptions in the availability of ingots is lessened.
   c. Less. If you must have ingots to produce aluminum and if survival is considered important, it might be wise to develop the capability to mine and process bauxite.
   d. Less. One way to lessen competition is to gain control over an input strategic to all competitors.
   e. Less. If least-cost production is important and it is found that for XYZ internal communication is critical to achieving that goal, it might make sense to vertically integrate.
   f. Less. If XYZ can mine and process bauxite at less cost than outside suppliers because of this new technology, it can reduce costs by vertically integrating. It could even compete as a seller in the bauxite market.
   g. More. Outside suppliers specializing in the production of aluminum ingots can deliver the ingots to you less expensively and more reliably than if you were vertically integrated.

5. a. $64,000
   b. $64,000
   c. $28,000
   d. $28,000
   e. $92,000
   f. $16,000

6. Fred would incur an economic loss of $7,000. Total revenues are less than total costs by $7,000. The opportunity cost of Fred's self-owned resources used in the firm are $28,000, but only $21,000 of this is earned in the current employment of these resources. Fred would in time probably consider employing his self-owned resources elsewhere.

Mastery Test

1. d 2. e 3. c 4. d 5. a 6. a 7. a 8. d 9. b 10. d 11. d 12. d 13. a 14. a 15. a 16. d 17. e 18. c 19. c 20. c 21. c 22. d 23. a

Think it Through

1. Sole proprietorships and partnerships involve limited resources and maximum freedom and are easy to establish. There are simply many more firms that have modest resource requirements than there are firms that require very large sums of money. The largest firms are corporations because of their ability to attract funds for expansion and growth.

2. The microcomputer industry has chip makers, producers of microprocessors, assemblers of cards or boards, component manufacturers such as producers of disk drives and modems, final assemblers, sales distributors, etc. In this case, technology is changing very fast and involves many small upstart companies. Because of the number of firms, the supply of inputs is reliable and available at competitive market prices. To stay abreast of the technology and to purchase inputs at minimum prices, many companies rely on a large network of outside suppliers.

3. It is necessary to consider implicit costs in a decision because if you did not, you would not be considering the total costs of some action or alternative. You would likely make a decision that would not result in the best use of your resources. You would be sacrificing more productive uses of your resources.

4. In this case, you are not considering total costs, but rather accounting costs. If you indeed realize revenues of $52,000, you are covering accounting costs but not providing any revenues toward your implicit costs of owner-supplied resources. You have sacrificed the opportunity to have used your own resources in their next-best employment. To break even, your revenues must be high enough to cover both accounting and implicit costs.

9   PRODUCTION AND COST

CHAPTER CONCEPTS

After studying your text, attending class, and completing this chapter, you should be able to:

1. Show how the law of diminishing marginal returns implies a certain pattern of variation in output in the short run when the use of some inputs can't be varied.
2. Distinguish between variable cost and fixed cost and describe the variation in total cost and other cost concepts as a single-product firm varies production.
3. Explain the relationship between cost and productivity of inputs and input prices.
4. Derive a long-run average cost curve from short-run average cost curves.

THE CHAPTER IN BRIEF

Fill in the blanks to summarize chapter content.

To understand the supply side of product markets, it is necessary to first examine productivity and costs associated with producing output. Inputs are used in the production process to produce output. Some inputs are in fixed quantities over a period, whereas other inputs can be varied. (1)_____ (Fixed, Variable) inputs can be varied over the short run. Some resources are fixed in the short run. These resources are known as (2)_____ (fixed, variable) inputs. In the (3)_____(long run, short run), all inputs are variable.

In the short run, if a variable input such as labor is increased to produce output, while other resources such as plant and equipment are held constant, then in time the extra output resulting from each additional unit of the variable input will decline. This is known as the law of diminishing marginal (4)_____(utility, returns). The total product curve will in time increase at a (5)_____ (decreasing, increasing) rate as additional units of the variable input are employed. The slope of the total product curve (change in total output/change in a unit of variable input) is known as the (6)_____ (total, marginal) product of a variable input. Marginal product begins to (7)_____(decline, increase) at the point at which diminishing marginal returns set in. Average product, or output per unit of the variable input, (8)_____(falls, rises) as long as marginal product is greater than average product and (9)_____(declines, increases) when marginal product is less than average product. Diminishing marginal returns occur when a variable input is continually added to a fixed quantity of other inputs. This is because continued employment of the variable input will eventually strain and surpass a plant's capacity to productively utilize the variable input.

Short-run costs can be derived from the short-run productivity relationships. (10)_____ (Fixed, Variable) costs are the costs of the variable inputs. These costs (11)_____ (do not vary, vary) with the level of output. They are determined by the quantity of variable inputs, valued at their market prices, required to produce output. In order to minimize variable costs for a given level of output, the firm must employ variable inputs up to the point where the marginal product per dollar spent on each input is the same. This principle is known as the (12)_____ (profit, equimarginal) principle for minimizing variable costs of production. (13)_____(Fixed, Variable) costs are the costs associated with fixed inputs. They (14)_____(do, do not) vary with levels of output. Total costs are the sum of variable costs and fixed costs. Other short-run cost concepts include (15)_____(average, total) cost, which is the sum of average fixed cost and average variable cost. (16)_____(Total, Average) fixed cost is total fixed costs divided by total output. (17)_____(Marginal, Average variable) cost is total variable costs divided by total output. Finally, (18)_____(marginal, average variable) cost is the cost associated with production of one additional unit of output.

The behavior of short-run costs and the shape of the short-run cost curves are related to the behavior of the short-run productivity relationships. Although total product initially increases at an increasing rate, total variable costs and total costs increase at a/an (19)_____(decreasing, increasing) rate. But when diminishing marginal returns set in, total product increases at a/an (20)_____(decreasing, increasing) rate and both the total and variable cost curves increase at a/an (21)_____(decreasing, increasing) rate. When the average productivity of the variable input is increasing, a unit of output can be produced with increasingly smaller quantities of the variable input. The average variable cost and average cost therefore (22)_____ (decrease, increase). When average product declines, the average variable and average cost (23)_____ (decrease, increase). When the marginal product of a variable input is rising, an additional unit of output can be produced with smaller quantities of the variable input. The marginal cost of producing that additional unit of output (24)_____ (decreases, increases). When marginal product declines, marginal cost (25)_____(decreases, increases). Thus short-run costs depend upon the quantity and productivity of the resources employed and the market prices at which they sell.

In the long run, (26)_____(only variable inputs, all inputs) are variable. Costs are not only influenced by the rate at which plants are utilized, but also by the size and number of plants operated. If the manager's objective is to find the combination of inputs that minimizes costs, the (27)_____ (largest, least cost) plant size must be utilized and it must be operated at minimum average cost. Long-run minimum average costs are attained at the minimum point on the average cost curve of the most efficient size plant. Declining long-run average costs are known as (28)_____ (diseconomies, economies) of scale, whereas increasing long-run average costs are called (29)_____(diseconomies, economies) of scale. Constant returns to scale mean that a number of plant sizes have the same minimum average cost.

KEY TERMS REVIEW

Write the key term from the list below next to its definition.

Key Terms

Production

Inputs

Production function

Short run

Variable input

Fixed input

Law of diminishing
  marginal returns

Total product curve

Point of diminishing
  returns

Total product of a
  variable input

Long run

Marginal product

Marginal cost

Fixed costs

Variable costs

Total cost

Average cost

Average variable cost

Average fixed cost

Long-run cost

Average product

Economies of scale
  (increasing returns to
  scale)

Diseconomies of scale
  (decreasing returns to
  scale)

Constant returns to
  scale

Definitions

1. _____: costs that do not vary as a firm varies its output; also called overhead costs.

2. _____: costs that change with output; the costs of variable inputs.

3. _____: the total output produced over a given period divided by the number of units of that input used.

4. _____: corresponds to the level of usage of a variable input at which its marginal product begins to decline.

5. _____: the sum of the value of all inputs used to produce goods over any given period; the sum of fixed costs and variable costs.

6. _____: the process of using the services of labor and capital together with other inputs, such as land, materials, and fuels, to make goods and services available.

7. _____: states that the extra production obtained from increases in a variable input will eventually decline as more of the variable input is used together with the fixed inputs.

8. _____: the increase in output from one more unit of an input when the quantity of all the inputs is unchanged.

9. _____: a period of production long enough that producers have adequate time to vary all the inputs used to produce a good.

10. _____: fixed costs divided by the number of units of output produced over a given period.

11. _____: the extra cost of producing one more unit of output.

12. _____: the labor, capital, land, natural resources, and entrepreneurship that are combined to produce products and services.

13. _____: total cost divided by the number of units of output produced over a given period; also called unit cost.

14. _____: describes how output varies in the short run as more of any one input is used with fixed amounts of other inputs under current technology.

15. _____: variable cost divided by the number of units of output produced over a given period.

16. _____: describes the relationship between any combination of input services and the maximum attainable output from that combination.

17. _____: the amount of output produced over any given period when that input is used along with other fixed inputs.

18. _____: a period of production during which some inputs cannot be varied.

19. _____: an input whose quantity can be changed.

20. _____: an input whose quantity cannot be changed over the short run.

21. _____: the minimum cost of producing any given output when all inputs are variable.

22. _____: reductions in unit costs resulting from increased size of operations; also called economies of mass production.

23. _____: increases in average costs of operation resulting from problems in managing large-scale enterprises.

24. _____: prevail when economies of scale no longer exist and when average costs do not increase as a result of diseconomies of scale in the long run.

CONCEPT REVIEW

Concept 1: *Productive relationships in the short run*

1. The following represents daily production data for a small manufacturer of cup holders.

Units of Labor	Total Product	Marginal Product	Average Product
		(number of cup holders)	
0	0		
1	50	____	____
2	130	____	____
3	230	____	____
4	320	____	____
5	400	____	____
6	465	____	____
7	525	____	____
8	575	____	____

a. Complete the marginal and average product columns in the table above.

b. Plot the total product (TP), marginal product (MP), and average product (AP) curves in the diagram below.

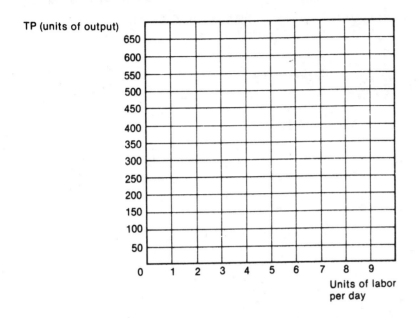

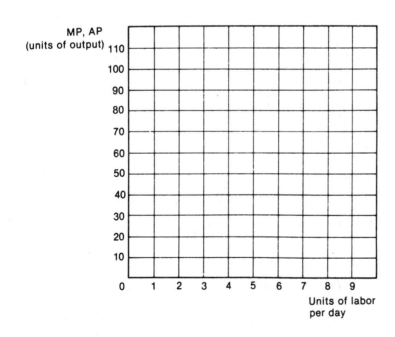

c. When MP exceeds AP, AP is _____. When MP is less than AP, AP is

_____.

d.   When TP is rising at an increasing rate, MP is _____. When TP is rising at a decreasing rate, MP is _____.

Concepts 2 and 3: *Costs in the short run; productivity relationships and costs*

2. Using the production data above and assuming that total fixed costs (FC) equal $50 and the price per unit of labor is $20:
   a.   Complete the table below.
   b.   Plot FC, VC, and TC in the diagram below.

Units of Output	Labor (units)	FC $	VC $	TC $
0	0	___	___	___
50	1	___	___	___
130	2	___	___	___
230	3	___	___	___
320	4	___	___	___
400	5	___	___	___
465	6	___	___	___
525	7	___	___	___
575	8	___	___	___

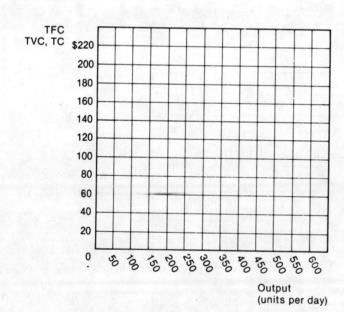

TFC
TVC, TC

Output
(units per day)

   c.   When TP is rising at an increasing rate, VC and TC are rising at a _____ rate. When TP is rising at a decreasing rate, VC and TC are rising at an _____ rate.

180

3. Given the cost and output data in question 2,
   a. Complete the table below (round to two decimal places).
   b. Plot the average fixed cost (AFC), average variable cost (AVC), average cost (AC), and marginal cost (MC) in the diagram below.

Units of Output	AFC $	AVC $	AC $	MC $
0				
50	—	—	—	—
130	—	—	—	—
230	—	—	—	—
320	—	—	—	—
400	—	—	—	—
465	—	—	—	—
525	—	—	—	—
575	—	—	—	—

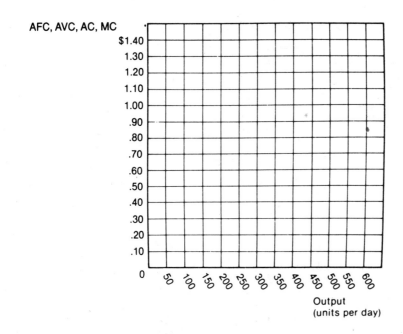

c. When MP is rising, MC is _____ and both VC and TC are rising at a/an
   _____ rate. When MP is falling, MC is _____ and both VC and TC
   are rising at a/an _____ rate.
d. When AP is rising, AVC is _____. When AP is falling, AVC is
   _____.
e. When MC is below AVC, AVC is _____. When MC is above AVC, AVC is
   _____. When MC is below AC, AC is _____. When MC is above AC,
   AC is _____.

181

4. If total fixed costs are $80 and marginal costs are given below:
   a. Complete the table below (round to two decimal places).
   b. Plot FC, VC, TC, AVC, AC, and MC on the diagrams below.

Units of Output	MC $	VC $	FC $	TC $	AFC $	AVC $	AC $
0		—	—	—			
1	75	—	—	—	—	—	—
2	65	—	—	—	—	—	—
3	55	—	—	—	—	—	—
4	65	—	—	—	—	—	—
5	75	—	—	—	—	—	—
6	85	—	—	—	—	—	—
7	95	—	—	—	—	—	—

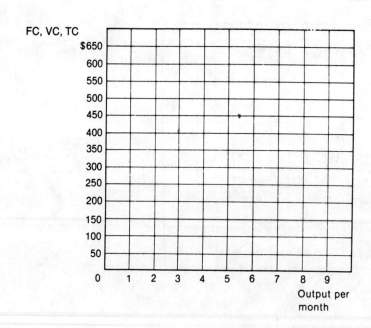

FC, VC, TC

$650
600
550
500
450
400
350
300
250
200
150
100
50

0   1   2   3   4   5   6   7   8   9

Output per month

182

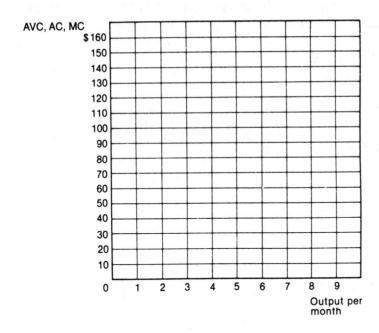

Concept 4: *Costs in the long run*

5. a. The figure below represents a set of short-run AC curves for various plant sizes. Determine the long-run AC curve by tracing over those segments of the short-run ACs that make up the long-run AC.

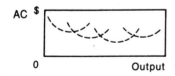

b. Determine for the levels of output designated on the long-run AC below whether there are economies of scale, diseconomies of scale, or constant returns to scale.

      (1) _____

      (2) _____

      (3) _____

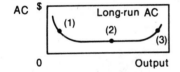

c. For the three long-run AC curves below, determine whether there are likely to be few or many producers or both and whether they are likely to be large or small or both.

(1) _____

(2) _____

(3) _____

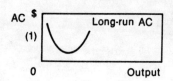

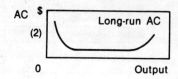

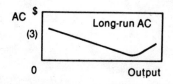

6. a. Economies of scale exist because:

1. _____

2. _____

3. _____

4. _____

b. Diseconomies of scale exist because:

1. _____

2. _____

Advanced Application: Short-run costs

7. If FC equals $100 and VC increases by $30 for every one unit increase in output:

a. Find equations for FC, VC, TC, AFC, AVC, AC, and MC.

b. Plot FC, VC, TC, AVC, AC, and MC on the diagrams below for levels of output from one to five units.

c. Does the MC curve ever intersect the AC curve?

184

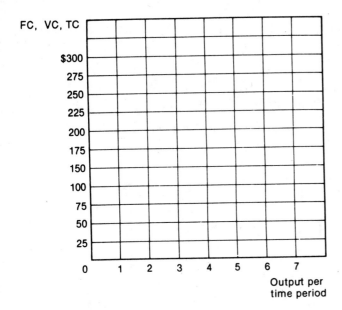

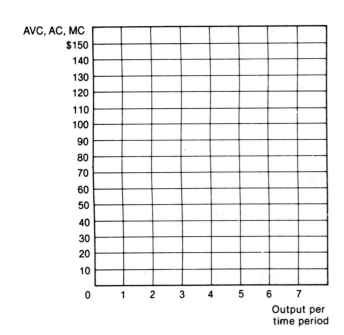

185

MASTERY TEST

Select the best answer.

1. A period of time during which some inputs are variable and some are fixed is known as the:
   a. market period.
   b. short run.
   c. interim period.
   d. long run.

2. A period of time during which all inputs can be varied is known as the:
   a. market period.
   b. short run.
   c. interim period.
   d. long run.

3. A _____ input is one that varies with output in the short run.
   a. marginal
   b. economic
   c. fixed
   d. variable

4. A _____ input is one that does not vary with output in the short run.
   a. marginal
   b. economic
   c. fixed
   d. variable

5. The law of diminishing marginal returns states that:
   a. Total product begins to fall as a result of continued employment of a variable input.
   b. Marginal product increases when the employment of variable inputs increases and falls when the employment of variable inputs falls.
   c. The extra production obtained from increases in a variable input will eventually decline as more of the variable input is used with the fixed inputs.
   d. The total production obtained from increases in a variable input will eventually decline as more of the variable input is used with the fixed inputs.

6. Marginal product is defined as:
   a. total product divided by total output.
   b. total product divided by the change in total output.
   c. the change in total product divided by total product.
   d. the change in total product divided by the change in variable input.

7. Average product
   a. increases when marginal product is greater than average product.
   b. is defined as total product divided by the quantity of variable input employed.
   c. reaches a peak when marginal product and average product are equal.
   d. All of the above.

8. _____ costs do not vary with the level of output.
   a. Accounting
   b. Explicit
   c. Variable
   d. Fixed

9. Total costs equal the sum of:
   a. variable costs and fixed costs.
   b. marginal costs and imputed costs.
   c. average variable costs and marginal costs.
   d. economic costs less implicit costs.

10. Average variable costs can best be defined as:
    a. variable costs times the average level of production.
    b. total product divided by variable costs.
    c. average costs less average fixed costs.
    d. None of the above.

11. Marginal cost is the:
    a. change in production costs divided by output.
    b. change in variable cost divided by a change in total product.
    c. change in total cost divided by a change in total product.
    d. B and c.

12. The marginal cost curve:
    a. intersects the average variable cost and average cost curves from below at their minimum points.
    b. falls when the point of diminishing marginal returns is reached.
    c. first rises and then declines.
    d. increases when the average cost curve lies above the average variable cost curve.

13. When the marginal product is rising, _____ is _____.
    a. average cost, rising
    b. average variable cost, rising
    c. marginal cost, rising
    d. marginal cost, falling

14. When marginal product is falling, marginal costs are _____ and both the total cost and variable cost curves are _____ at a/an _____ rate.
    a. falling, falling, decreasing
    b. falling, rising, increasing
    c. rising, falling, decreasing
    d. rising, rising, increasing

15. The point of diminishing returns occurs when:
    a. the average product curve has reached a peak.
    b. the marginal cost curve has reached a trough.
    c. the total product curve has reached a peak.
    d. the marginal product curve has reached a trough.

16. Economies of scale mean that:
    a. short-run average cost decreases.
    b. long-run average cost decreases.
    c. long-run total costs decrease.
    d. long-run marginal costs exceed long-run average costs.

17. The rising portion of the long-run average cost curve is called:
    a. diseconomies of scale.
    b. economies of scale.
    c. mass production economies.
    d. constant returns to scale.

18. An industry with firms having long-run average cost curves that initially decline sharply, flatten out over a range of output, and then begin to increase suggest that the industry is probably composed of firms:
    a. that are both large and small, producing at the minimum long-run average cost.
    b. that are large and few in number.
    c. that are numerous and very small.
    d. that must be large to realize economies of scale.

19. Which of the following is not considered a cause of economies of scale?
    a. Specialization and division of labor
    b. Inability to shift to new production methods as the firm becomes larger
    c. Ability to purchase inputs in large quantity at quantity discounts
    d. As output is increased, a proportionate increase in inputs is not required.

20. Which of the following has been suggested as a cause of diseconomies of scale?
    a. Inability to purchase inputs at a discount
    b. Ability to shift to new production methods as the firm becomes bigger
    c. Impaired managerial communication
    d. Government regulation

21. If the market wage rate is $10 and the change in output per hour of labor employed is 5 units, what is the marginal cost of producing the next unit of output?
    a. $50
    b. $15
    c. $2
    d. $.50

22. Assume that output per labor hour is increasing faster than the market wage rate. Also assume that firms set product prices èqual to the average cost of production. Product prices are:
    a. remaining constant.
    b. falling.
    c. rising.
    d. rising in the short-run only.

23. If the total variable cost curve is rising at an increasing rate, it follows that:
    a. marginal product is falling.
    b. average product is falling.
    c. the firm is experiencing diminishing returns.
    d. marginal cost is rising.
    e. All of the above.

24. Which of the following is a measure of average variable cost?
    a. (Total cost - fixed cost)/output
    b. Average cost - average variable cost
    c. (Cumulative sum of marginal cost)/output
    d. (Price of the variable input)/average product of the variable input
    e. All of the above

25. Suppose industry X has a few very large firms that produce for the national market. Which of the following might characterize the shape of each firm's long-run average cost curve?
    a. Economies of scale are realized over a wide range of output before constant costs or diseconomies of scale occur.
    b. Long-run average costs fall sharply as scale is increased, quickly becoming constant over a wide range of output and scale.
    c. Long-run average costs increase as small firms grow, but when firms become large average costs decline continuously until minimum possible average cost is attained.
    d. The long-run average cost curve is an envelope curve made up of many short-run average cost curves.

THINK IT THROUGH

1. A producer never produces at a level of output where marginal product is negative. Why?

2. Explain how changes in wages influence the average variable cost and marginal cost associated with the use of labor in producing output.

3. Why are fixed costs irrelevant to decisions in the short run involving marginal costs?

4. In many American industries a handful of very large capital-intensive firms dominate sales. Why?

5. Clearly explain why variable costs rise at an increasing rate when the point of diminishing returns is reached.

Analyzing the News

Using the skills derived from studying this chapter, analyze the economic facts that make up the following article and answer the questions below, using graphical analysis where possible.

1. What would be the outcome of a labor agreement that significantly increased wages and benefits, but did not increase labor productivity? Why should the firm be concerned with labor productivity?

Bethlehem Steel Seeks to Renegotiate Labor Agreement It Signed Last Year

By Dana Milbank
Staff Reporter of The Wall Street Journal

BETHLEHEM, Pa. — Bethlehem Steel Corp., threatening to shutter its troubled rod and wire division, said it wants to renegotiate a costly labor agreement it signed last year.

In exchange for labor concessions, Bethlehem, the nation's No. 2 steel concern, said it would invest more than $100 million to modernize facilities at the division's three sites, in Johnstown, Pa.; Lackawanna, N.Y., and Sparrows Point, Md. The division, which has estimated annual revenue of about $450 million, has been unprofitable every year since it opened in 1983.

The United Steelworkers union had no immediate response to the company's call for a new labor agreement. But the union and its 2,700 employees in Bethlehem's bar, rod and wire division may have no choice but to negotiate. If labor balks at Bethlehem's call, "there would be the risk of shutting it down entirely," a company spokesman said.

Whether the union will make concessions, a spokesman for USW Local 2635 in Johnstown said, "depends on how many carrots are out there."

The 50-month agreement, signed in May 1989, boosted wages and benefits an estimated 20%, following five years of reduced labor costs. Company officials, competitors and industry analysts agree that Bethlehem now suffers from a competitive disadvantage from both labor costs and outdated equipment.

Bethlehem declined to name specific concessions it would seek from the union. But analysts said it is likely to seek cuts in both wages and the work force, and better labor productivity. Labor, in return, will probably seek job security and, for terminated employees, improved compensation.

In seeking the renegotiation, Bethlehem is acknowledging that it cannot support the costs of the current contract, which saddled the company with some of the highest labor costs in the industry. But the company spokesman indicated that the company had anticipated possible problems when it included a renegotiation clause in the contract.

Charles Bradford, an analyst with UBS Securities, said Bethlehem's per-hour employee costs total $28, including high pension costs. The industry average is $26, he said, and the Bethlehem division's minimill competitors are paying in "the middle teens."

The outdated equipment in the mills has kept the division's productivity at five man-hours to produce each ton of steel, against an industry average of about three man-hours, the analyst added.

The capital improvements will include a continuous caster, which eliminates several laborious and costly steps in steelmaking, as well as the modernization of an existing bar mill. Analyst John Tumazos, of Donaldson Lufkin & Jenrette, said Bethlehem's offer to invest $100 million is something it had to do anyway to match the modernization plans of competitors.

CHAPTER ANSWERS

The Chapter in Brief

1. Variable 2. Fixed 3. Long run 4. Returns 5. Decreasing 6. Marginal 7. Decline 8. Rises
9. Declines 10. Variable 11. Vary 12. Equimarginal 13. Fixed 14. Do not 15. Average 16. Average
17. Average variable 18. Marginal 19. Decreasing 20. Decreasing 21. Increasing 22. Decrease
23. Increase 24. Decreases 25. Increases 26. All inputs 27. Least cost 28. Economics
29. Diseconomies

Key Terms Review

1. Fixed cost 2. Variable costs 3. Average product 4. Point of diminishing returns 5. Total cost
6. Production 7. Law of diminishing marginal returns 8. Marginal product 9. Long run 10. Average
fixed cost 11. Marginal cost 12. Inputs 13. Average cost 14. Production function 15. Average
variable cost 16. Total product curve 17. Total product of a variable input 18. Short run
19. Variable input 20. Fixed input 21. Long run cost 22. Economies of scale 23. Diseconomies of
scale 24. Constant returns to scale

Concept Review

1. a.

MP	AP
50	50
80	65
100	76.67
90	80
80	80
65	77.50
60	75
50	71.88

b.

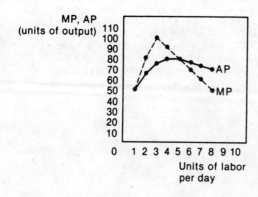

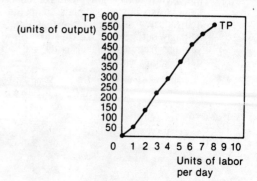

c. Rising, falling
d. Increasing, falling

2. a.

FC	VC	TC
50	0	50
50	20	70
50	40	90
50	60	110
50	80	130
50	100	150
50	120	170
50	140	190
50	160	210

b.

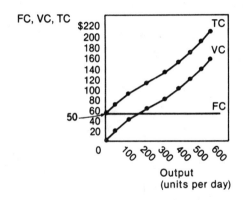

c. Decreasing, increasing

3. a.

AFC	AVC	AC	MC
1.00	.40	1.40	.40
.38	.31	.69	.25
.22	.26	.48	.20
.16	.25	.41	.22
.13	.25	.38	.25
.11	.26	.37	.31
.10	.27	.36	.33
.09	.28	.37	.40

b.

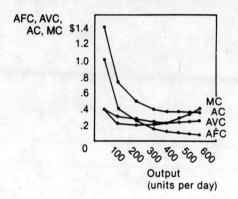

AFC, AVC, AC, MC

Output
(units per day)

c. Falling, decreasing, rising, increasing
d. Falling, rising
e. Falling, rising, falling, rising

4. a.

VC	FC	TC	AFC	AVC	AC
0	80	80			
75	80	155	80	75	155
140	80	220	40	70	110
195	80	275	26.67	65	91.67
260	80	340	20	65	85
335	80	415	16	67	83
420	80	500	13.33	70	83.33
515	80	595	11.43	73.57	85

b.

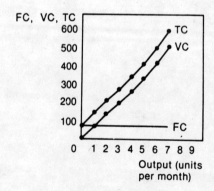

FC, VC, TC

Output (units per month)

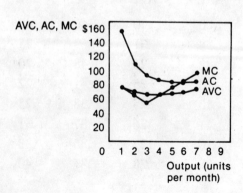

AVC, AC, MC

Output (units per month)

5. a.

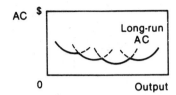

AC $

Long-run
AC

0   Output

b.   (1) Economies of scale

       (2) Constant returns to scale

       (3) Diseconomies of scale

c.   (1) Many small firms

       (2) Both large and small firms

       (3) A few large firms

6. a.   (1) Can increase output without proportionately increasing inputs

       (2) Quantity discounts

       (3) Specialization and division of labor

       (4) Ability of use new methods of production

b.   (1) Strained managerial communication

       (2) Shirking of labor and difficulty of monitoring performance

7. a. FC = $100

VC = $30 TP

TC = $100 + $30 TP

AFC = $100/TP

AVC = $30

AC = $100/TP + $30

MC = $30

b.

TP	FC	VC	TC	AC	AFC	AVC	MC
0	100	0	100				
1	100	30	130	130	100	30	30
2	100	60	160	80	50	30	30
3	100	90	190	63.33	33.33	30	30
4	100	120	220	55	25	30	30
5	100	150	250	50	20	30	30

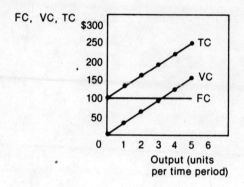

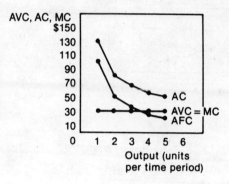

c.   For MC and AC to intersect, MC = AC. Let:

MC = $30 = $100/TP + $30 = AC

As TP approaches infinity, $100/TP approaches zero. AC approaches MC as TP approaches infinity, but never touches it.

Mastery Test

1. b 2. d 3. d 4. c 5. c 6. d 7. d 8. d 9. a 10. c 11. d 12. a 13. d 14. d 15. b 16. b 17. a 18. a 19. b 20. c 21. c 22. b 23. e 24. e 25. a

Think it Through

1. A negative marginal product means that using more variable inputs reduces output! No manager would increase total costs in order to reduce output.

2. Average variable costs equal variable costs divided by output. Variable costs equal the quantity of variable inputs purchased times the respective input prices per unit. With regard to labor:

     AVC = (Units of Labor x wage)/TP

     or

     AVC = Wage/(TP/units of labor) = Wage/AP

An increase in wages increases AVC and a decrease in wages decreases AVC. Notice that an increase in wages will not increase AVC if average labor productivity increases more than wages.

Similarly, marginal cost can be expressed as:

     MC = (Change in the units of labor x wage)/change in TP

     or

     MC = Wage/(change in TP/change in the units of labor) = Wage/MP

MC rises when wages increase and falls when wages decrease unless the marginal product of labor changes sufficiently to offset the impact of wages.

3. If a decision involves whether or not to increase output by a unit, fixed costs are unimportant in that they are "sunk" costs. If a goal of the firm is to maximize profits in the short run, the relevant comparison is between the marginal costs of producing that unit and the revenues received from the sale of that unit. Fixed costs influence average costs but not marginal costs.

4. These industries comprise a few very large firms that have long-run average cost curves that decline over a very large range of output. They must be large in order to realize economies of scale. This is because the least-cost combination of inputs requires a capital-intensive operation with large fixed costs in plant and equipment. It takes a large level of production to spread the overhead costs. Large-scale production runs take advantage of cost-saving technology. Purchasing inputs in mass quantity allows the firm to realize quantity discounts. And the larger the firm, the greater the extent to which the division of labor and the specialization of resources can be achieved.

5. When the point of diminishing returns is reached, production requires increasing quantities of a variable input in order to produce a given quantity of output. Therefore, the cost of the variable input must rise at an increasing rate for given increases in output.

Analyzing the News

1. If wages and benefits increase with no accompanying increase in labor productivity (average or marginal product), average and marginal costs of production increase. If prices have to at least cover average costs, the firm will be at a competitive price disadvantage with its rivals. One way the firm can avoid such an occurrence is to increase the productivity of labor by making investments in both human and physical capital.

APPENDIX TO CHAPTER 9
ISOQUANT ANALYSIS: CHOOSING
THE METHOD OF PRODUCTION

THE APPENDIX IN BRIEF

Fill in the blanks to summarize appendix content.

Indifference curve analysis can be used to analyze the choice of production methods. The analysis assumes that firms have a goal to minimize the costs of producing a given output.

An (1)_____(isoquant, isocost line) represents various combinations of two inputs that can be used to produce a given level of output. It is (2)_____(positively, negatively) sloped because the use of additional labor requires a/an (3)_____(reduction, increase) of capital in order to keep output unchanged. The slope is called the marginal rate of technical substitution (MRTS) of labor for capital. Because of the law of diminishing marginal (4)_____ (returns, utility), the slope of the isoquant becomes (5)_____ (less, more) negative as more labor is employed. This is because the MRTS of labor for capital equals the ratio of minus the change in capital to the change in labor. This ratio in turn equals the ratio of the marginal product of labor to the marginal product of capital. Therefore as more labor is used and less capital is employed along an isoquant, the marginal product of labor (6)_____ (decreases, increases), and the marginal product of capital (7) _____ (decreases, increases), causing the isoquant slope to become (8)_____ (less, more) steep. An isoquant map shows isoquants at various distances from the origin. Isoquants lying farther from the origin represent (9)_____ (higher, lower) levels of output.

Total costs can be thought of as the quantity of inputs employed in producing a given output multiplied by their respective market resource prices. An (10)_____ (isoquant, isocost line) can be derived by solving the total cost equation for capital in terms of labor. The slope of the isocost line is (11)_____ (positive, negative) and equals the ratio of the price of labor to the price of capital. Changes in the price of capital and the price of labor will (12)_____ (shift, alter the slope of) the isocost line—higher costs shift the line outward from the origin and vice versa.

Costs are minimized when an isoquant for a given level of output is just tangent to the isocost line (14)_____ (farthest, closest) to the origin. This occurs where the MRTS of labor for capital equals the ratio of the price of labor to the price of capital. The cost-minimizing combination of capital and labor used in producing a given output is influenced by the prices of labor and capital and technology that influences marginal products and the MRTS.

KEY TERMS REVIEW

Write the key term from the list below next to its definition.

Key Terms

Isoquant
Isocost line
Isoquant map

Marginal rate of technical
   substitution (MRTS) of labor for
   capital

Definitions

1. _____: a measure of the amount of capital each unit of labor can replace without increasing or decreasing production.

2. _____: gives all combinations of labor and capital that are of equal total cost.

3. _____: a curve showing all combinations of variable inputs that can be used to produce a given quantity of output.

4. _____: shows the combinations of labor and capital that can be used to produce several possible output levels.

CONCEPT REVIEW

1. Given the isoquant map in the diagram below:

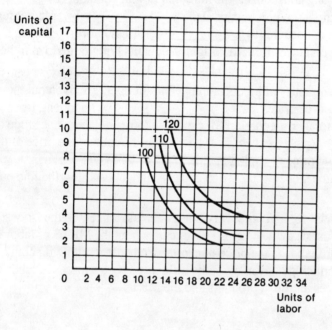

  a. Derive the isocost line, assuming that the price per unit to labor is $10, the price per unit of capital is $20, and total cost equals $300. Plot the line on the diagram.

b. Find the cost-minimizing combination of labor and capital:

   (1) _____ units of labor

   (2) _____ units of capital

   (3) _____ level of output at this combination of inputs

c. Show the effect on the diagram of an increase in the price of labor to $15. The cost-mini-mizing combination of labor and capital changes to _____ units of labor and _____ units of capital.

d. Show the effect on the diagram of an increase in the price of capital to $30, assuming the price of labor is $10. The cost-minimizing combination of inputs changes to _____ units of labor and _____ units of capital.

MASTERY TEST

Select the best answer.

1. An isoquant is:

   a. the level of production possible from a given stock of resources.

   b. a curve giving various combinations of two inputs that are equal in total cost.

   c. a curve showing all combinations of variable inputs that can be used to produce a given quantity of output.

   d. the producer's demand curve for labor and capital.

2. A_____gives all combinations of labor and capital that can be used to produce several possible output levels.

   a. isoquant

   b. isocost

   c. isoquant map

   d. isocost map

3. The slope of an isoquant is negative and equal to:

   a. the ratio of the change in capital to the change in labor.

   b. the ratio of the marginal product of labor to the marginal product of capital.

   c. the marginal rate of technical substitution of labor for capital.

   d. b and C.

   e. All of the above.

4. Which of the following concepts best explains the curvature of an isoquant?
   a. equimarginal principle
   b. law of decreasing costs
   c. law of diminishing marginal returns
   d. law of diminishing marginal utility

5. The slope of an isocost line is:
   a. the ratio of the marginal products of labor and capital.
   b. the product price divided by the price of labor and capital.
   c. the change in capital divided by the change in labor.
   d. negative and equal to the price per unit of labor divided by the price per unit of capital.

6. A/An _____ in the price of labor makes the isocost line _____ steep.
   a. increase, more
   b. decrease, more
   c. increase, less
   d. change, increasingly

7. A/An _____ in the price of capital makes the isocost line _____ steep.
   a. increase, more
   b. decrease, more
   c. decrease, less
   d. change, neither more nor less

8. The cost-minimizing combination of labor and capital can be found where
   a. the mrts of labor for capital = the change in capital/change in labor.
   b. the mrts of labor for capital = the ratio of input marginal products.
   c. the mrts of labor for capital = the ratio of the price of capital to the price of labor.
   d. the MRTS of labor for capital = the ratio of the price of labor to the price of capital.

THINK IT THROUGH

1. Explain why the slope of the isoquant becomes increasingly less steep as or labor is used relative to capital.

2. What condition must be satisfied in order to find the cost-minimizing combination of labor and capital? Explain.

202

APPENDIX ANSWERS

The Appendix in Brief

1. Isoquant 2. Negatively 3. Reduction 4. Returns 5. Less 6. Decreases 7. Increases 8. Less
9. Higher 10. Isocost line 11. Negative 12. Alter the slope of 13. Shift 14. Closest

Key Terms Review

1. Marginal rate of technical substitution of labor for capital 2. Iscost line 3. Isoquant 4. Isoquant map

Concept Review

a.

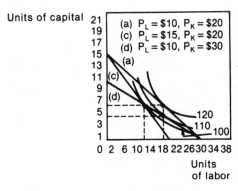

b.   (1) 18 (2) 6 (3) 120

c.   12, 6

d.   18, 4

Mastery Test

1. c 2. c 3. e 4. c 5. d 6. a 7. b 8. d

Think it Through

1. Output is constant along a given isoquant. An increase in labor times the marginal product of labor must equal the decrease in capital times the marginal product of capital in order to keep the production level unchanged. But as more labor is added and capital is reduced, the marginal product of labor decreases and the marginal product of capital increases. This is due to the law of diminishing marginal returns. Since the slope of the isoquant is the ratio of the marginal product of labor to the marginal product of capital, the slope becomes less negative as more labor is used.

2. To find the least-cost combination of labor and capital, the MRTS of labor for capital must equal the ratio of the price of labor to the price of capital. The rate at which it is technically feasible to substitute labor for capital is just equal to the rate at which labor can be exchanged for capital as determined by market prices and the total cost of production. The cost-minimizing condition can be alternatively expressed as follows:

(MP of labor/price of labor) = (MP of capital/price of capital)

Costs are minimized in producing a given output when the last dollar's worth of labor and capital yields the same marginal product.

10 THE PROFIT-MAXIMIZING COMPETITIVE FIRM AND MARKET SUPPLY

CHAPTER CONCEPTS

After studying your text, attending class, and completing this chapter, you should be able to:

1. Define perfect competition and explain why the demand curve for the product of a competitive firm is perfectly elastic at the market equilibrium price.
2. Use marginal analysis to explain how the firm chooses its output so as to maximize profits.
3. Use graphs to show the actual profits a firm earns and to show how a product's market price affects the firm's profitability.
4. Explain under what conditions a firm will cease operations in the short run.
5. Show how a supply curve can be derived for a competitive firm that maximizes profit from selling a single product and how the market supply curve can be derived from the supply curves of individual firms in an industry.
6. Tell how changes in input prices affect the supply curve in the short run.

THE CHAPTER IN BRIEF

Fill in the blanks to summarize chapter content.

In order to construct a theory of supply, it is necessary to make simplifying assumptions. The goal of the firm is (1)_____ (profit maximization, market share). The firm produces a single product and operates in a perfectly competitive market. The assumptions underlying perfect competition are: (a) (2)_____(few, many) sellers, (b) (3)_____ (homogeneous, heterogeneous) goods, (c) (4)_____ (large, very small) market shares, (d) firms are (5)_____ (unconcerned, concerned) about the decisions of competing firms, (e) information is (6)_____ (costly, freely available), and there is (f) freedom of (7)_____(entry and exit, enterprise). The firm is a price taker, producing the quantity of output that maximizes profit or minimizes losses in the short run.

The market demand curve for an industry is downward sloping, but the demand curve faced by a competitive firm is horizontal or perfectly (8)_____ (inelastic, elastic). The firm can sell any quantity it desires at the market price without influencing market supply and hence the equilibrium price. A firm maximizes profit in the short run by producing at that level of production where total revenue exceeds total cost by the (9)_____ (greatest, smallest) amount. At zero output, total costs (10)_____ (exceed, are less than) total revenues because of fixed costs and zero sales revenue. At high levels of output, total costs (11)_____'_____ (are also less than, will also exceed) total revenue because of the law of diminishing marginal returns. In between are levels of production where total revenues exceed total costs, but there is only one level of output where economic profit is at a maximum. If market prices are low enough, there may be no levels of output where total revenues exceed total costs.

Marginal analysis can also be used to determine the profit-maximizing level of production in the short run. A producer will increase or decrease output if there is a net gain from doing so. If the additional benefits from altering production (12)_____(exceed, equal) the additional costs, then it would be rational to change the level of output to the point where the net gain from doing so is at a maximum. If the marginal revenue associated with the sale of an additional unit of output (13)_____(exceeds, is less than) the marginal cost of producing that unit, more is added to revenue than to costs and profit must (14)_____(decrease, increase)—marginal profit is positive. If marginal cost (15)_____(is less than, exceeds) marginal revenue, profit can be increased by reducing output. Cutting output by one unit reduces total costs more than total revenues and as a result (16)_____ (decreases, increases) profit. Where marginal revenue and marginal cost are equal, marginal profit is (17)_____ (zero, negative), meaning that a one-unit increase or decrease in output will have no effect on profit. At this level of output, either profits are maximized or losses are minimized. For a perfectly competitive firm, price and marginal revenue are equal because the slope of the total revenue curve, marginal revenue, is constant and equal to the market price. Therefore the rule for maximizing profit in the short run for a competitive firm is either (18)_____ ($MR = MC$ or $P = MC$, $MR = AC$ or $P = MR$).

A competitive firm will operate in the short run and produce output as long as the market price exceeds the minimum average (19)_____(variable, total) cost. If price exceeds average variable cost, a portion of the firm's (20)_____ (marginal, fixed) costs will be covered by revenue. Even though the firm is not earning sufficient normal profits to retain the services of the entrepreneur for very long, it can minimize losses by producing at a positive level of output and deferring some of the firm's overhead or fixed costs. If the market price is (21)_____(above, below) average variable cost, the loss-minimizing strategy would be to shut down in the short run and not produce any output. This is because the firm's loss would be limited to the payment of fixed costs. If the firm produced output, its losses would (22)_____ (exceed, be less than) its fixed costs.

At prices above the minimum average variable cost, the firm is induced to produce output. As prices rise it is profitable to increase production. For the firm, the supply curve is that segment of the firm's (23)_____ (average variable, marginal) cost curve that lies above the (24)_____ (average variable, marginal) cost curve. The market supply curve is an aggregation or summation of the supply curves of all the individual firms in that industry.

Factors that influence and shift the market supply curve are: (a) the number of firms, (b) the average productive capacity of firms, (c) the prices of (25)_____(fixed, variable) inputs, and (d) technology. An increase or decrease in the number of firms will shift the market supply curve to the right or left, respectively. A change in productive capacity will shift the marginal cost curve to either the right or the left. A decrease in variable input prices or an improvement in technology will shift the marginal cost curve (26)_____ (downward, upward) and vice versa. Because the market supply curve is an aggregation of individual firms' supply curves, shifts in their marginal cost curves shift the market supply curve and affect market equilibrium prices. While a change in the price of a variable input affects marginal cost and the market supply curve, a change in the price of a fixed input has no effect on marginal costs, market supply, or price, but does influence the producer's (27)_____(market share, profits).

KEY TERMS REVIEW

Write the key term from the list below next to its definition.

Key Terms

Perfectly competitive market   Marginal profit
Competitive firm   Shutdown point
Average revenue   Short-run supply curve
Marginal revenue   Market supply curve

Definitions

1. _____: one that sells its product in a perfectly competitive market in which it is a price taker.

2. _____: total revenue per unit of a good sold.

3. _____: the change in profit from selling an additional unit of a good, representing the difference between the marginal revenue from that unit and its marginal cost.

4. _____: the portion of a competitive firm's marginal cost curve above the minimum point of its average variable cost curve.

5. _____: gives the sum of the quantities supplied by all firms producing a product at each possible price over a given period.

6. _____: exists when (1) there are many sellers in the market; (2) the products sold in the market are homogeneous; (3) each firm has a very small market share of total sales; (4) no seller regards competing firms as a threat to its market share; (5) information is freely available on prices; (6) there is freedom of entry and exit by sellers.

7. _____: the extra revenue obtained from selling an additional unit of a good.

8. _____: the point a firm reaches when price has fallen to a level below that which just allows the firm to cover its minimum possible average variable cost.

CONCEPT REVIEW

Concept 1: *Perfectly competitive market*

1. List six conditions necessary for the existence of a perfectly competitive market.

   a. _____

   b. _____

   c. _____

   d. _____

   e. _____

   f. _____

Concept 1:   *Perfectly elastic demand curve; economic profit and output*

2. If you operate a business in a perfectly competitive market and the current market equilibrium price is $12 per unit:

  a.   Show on the diagram below the demand curve you face.

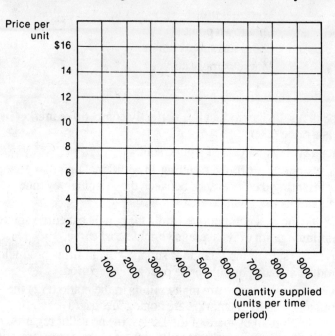

  b.   On the diagram above, show the effect of an increase in price from $12 to $15.

  c.   On the diagram above, show the effect of a decrease in price from $12 to $10.

3. a.   Find total revenue from the quantity and P1 columns in the table below and enter the results in the TR1 column. Plot the total revenue curve, TR1, in the diagram below the table.

Quantity	P1	P2	P3	TR1	TR2	TR3
0	$12	$___	$___	$___	$_____	$_____
10	12	___	___	___	_____	_____
20	12	___	___	___	_____	_____
30	12	___	___	___	_____	_____
40	12	___	___	___	_____	_____
50	12	___	___	___	_____	_____
60	12	___	___	___	_____	_____

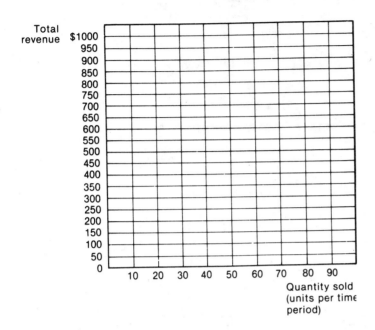

Total
revenue $1000
950
900
850
800
750
700
650
600
550
500
450
400
350
300
250
200
150
100
50
0

10 20 30 40 50 60 70 80 90

Quantity sold
(units per time
period)

b. Assume price increases from $12 to $15. Enter the price in column P2 in the table above and find TR2. Plot the new total revenue curve, TR2, on the figure above.

c. Assume price decreases from $12 to $10. Enter the price in column P3 in the table above and find TR3. Plot TR3 on the diagram above.

4. Consider the following quantity and total cost data:

Quantity	Total Cost
0	$ 50
10	120
20	220
30	330
40	450
50	600
60	780

a. Plot the total cost curve, TC, on the figure above in question 3.

b. Referring to TC and TR1, at zero output, economic profit (or loss) equals
    $_____.

c. As output increases, what happens to profit (or loss)?

Quantity	Profit (Loss)
10	$_____
20	_____
30	_____
40	_____
50	_____
60	_____

d. At what level of output are profits at a maximum? _____ units

e. Referring to TC and TR3, what relationship exists between output and profit or loss? The profit-maximizing or loss-minimizing level of output is _____ units.

Concepts 2 and 3: *Marginal analysis and profit maximization*

5. a. Complete the table.

Q	$P1$	$TR1$	$MR1$	$P2$	$TR2$	$MR2$	$P3$	$TR3$	$MR3$
0	$12	$___		$15	$___		$10	$___	
10	12	___	$ ___	15	___	$ ___	10	___	$ ___
20	12	___	___	15	___	___	10	___	___
30	12	___	___	15	___	___	10	___	___
40	12	___	___	15	___	___	10	___	___
50	12	___	___	15	___	___	10	___	___
60	12	___	___	15	___	___	10	___	___

b. In the diagram below, plot the MR curves: MR1, MR2, and MR3.

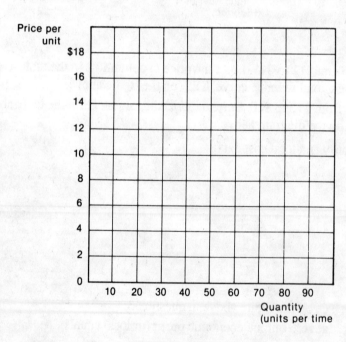

Price per unit

Quantity
(units per time

210

6. a. Complete the table.

Q	TC	VC	MC	AVC	AC
0	$ 50	$_____			
10	120	_____	$_____	$_____	$_____
20	220	_____	_____	_____	_____
30	330	_____	_____	_____	_____
40	450	_____	_____	_____	_____
50	600	_____	_____	_____	_____
60	780	_____	_____	_____	_____

b. Plot the MC, AVC, and ATC curves in the diagram below.

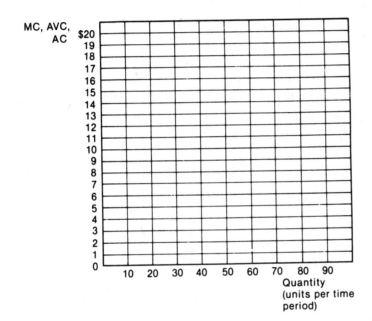

c. On the figure above, show the MR1 curve from question 5 (b) (P1 = MR1 = $12). Profit is maximized where _____ equals _____ at _____ units of output.

Concepts 4 and 5: *Shutdown point; a competitive firm's short-run supply curve*

7. a. On the figure above, show the marginal revenue curve, MR2, from question 5 (P2 = MR2 = $15). The profit-maximizing output is _____ units, and profit equals $_____.

   b. On the figure above, show the marginal revenue curve, MR3, from question 5 (P3 = MR3 = $10). The profit-maximizing (or loss-minimizing) output is _____ units, and profit (or loss) equals $_____. Will the firm shut down at this price? Why or why not?

   c. If the market price falls to $7, will the firm shut down? Why or why not?

211

8. a. Complete the profit-maximizing quantity column in the table below using the results derived in questions 6 and 7.

Price	Profit-Maximizing or Loss-Minimizing Quantity (units)
$15	_____
12	_____
10	_____
7	_____

b. In the figure below, plot the price and quantity supplied data from the completed table above.

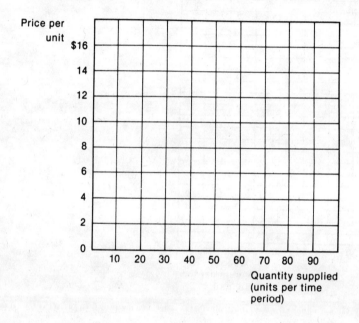

c. The curve that you have plotted above is called the firm's _____ and is that segment of the _____ curve lying above the _____ curve.

Concepts 5 and 6: *Market supply; determinants of market supply*

9. Assume there are 100 firms comprising an industry with cost curves identical to that plotted in question 6.

a. Complete the table below.

Price	Profit Maximizing (Loss-Minimizing) Quantity from Question 8	Quantity Supplied in the Market
$15	_____	_____
12	_____	_____
10	_____	_____
7	_____	_____

b. Plot the market supply curve from the data above.

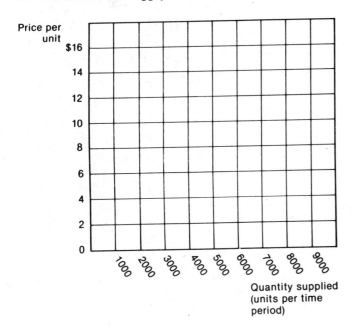

10. List four factors that shift the market supply curve and indicate for each one, whether the effect of an increase or improvement in the factor shifts the supply curve up or down or right or left, whichever is appropriate.

   a. _____

   b. _____

   c. _____

   d. _____

Advanced Application: Profit maximization

11. A perfectly competitive firm's MR and MC curves can be expressed as follows:

$$MR = P$$
$$MC = a + bQ$$

where P and Q are price and quantity a is a constant term reflecting the forces that influence marginal cost other than quantity, and b is the slope of the MC curve reflecting the extent to which diminishing marginal returns are encountered.

a. Find an expression for the profit-maximizing quantity.

b. If price increases, the profit-maximizing quantity _____ and vice versa.

c. If marginal costs increase due to influences other than quantity—if a increases—the profit-maximizing output _____ and vice versa.

d. If new technology reduces the effect of diminishing returns such that the slope, b, of the MC curve decreases, the profit-maximizing output _____.

MASTERY TEST

Select the best answer.

1. Which of the following is a characteristic of perfectly competitive markets?
   a. Many sellers
   b. Very small market shares of firms
   c. Information on prices is freely available
   d. Freedom of entry and exit
   e. All of the above

2. The demand curve faced by a perfectly competitive firm is:
   a. perfectly inelastic.
   b. horizontal.
   c. downward sloping.
   d. perfectly elastic.
   e. b and d

3. An increase in market price shifts the firm's demand curve _____ and rotates its total revenue curve _____.
   a. downward, counterclockwise
   b. upward, clockwise
   c. upward, counterclockwise
   d. downward, upward parallel to the old total revenue curve

4. At a zero level of output, the loss incurred is equal to
   a. variable costs.
   b. fixed costs.
   c. marginal costs.
   d. price.

5. If market price is high enough, profits increase as output increases up to a maximum level of profits and then begins to decline as output continues to increase. Which of the following concepts accounts for this relationship?
   a. The law of supply
   b. The law of marginal profit
   c. The law of diminishing marginal returns
   d. Marginal analysis
   e. None of the above

6. For the case of perfect competition, which of the following is true?
   a. Price always equals average revenue.
   b. Profit maximization occurs at the level of output where MR = MC.
   c. Profit maximization occurs at the level of output where P = MC.
   d. A and c.
   e. All of the above.

7. When price exceeds marginal cost, a profit-maximizing producer will:
   a. increase production.
   b. decrease production.
   c. lower price and increase production.
   d. leave the level of output unchanged.

8. When price is less than marginal cost, a profit-maximizing producer will:
   a. increase production.
   b. decrease production.
   c. raise the price and decrease output.
   d. leave the level of output unchanged.

9. If at the level of output where MR = MC the market price is less than a competitive firm's ATC but is greater than its AVC the firm would:
   a. continue to operate indefinitely.
   b. shut down.
   c. continue to operate in the short run.
   d. increase output to increase sales and profit.

10. If at the level of output where MR = MC the market price is less than the competitive firm's AVC:
    a. the total fixed-cost loss exceeds the operating loss and the firm will shut down.
    b. the variable-cost loss is less than the fixed-cost loss and the firm will continue to operate in the short run.
    c. the firm can minimize losses by producing where MR = MC.
    d. the firm can minimize losses by raising prices.
    e. the firm will raise prices and increase production.

11. A firm's short-run supply curve is:
    a. the segment of the variable cost curve below the total cost curve.
    b. the marginal cost curve.
    c. the market supply curve.
    d. the section of the marginal cost curve below the average total cost curve.
    e. the segment of the marginal cost curve above the minimum point of the average variable cost curve.

12. Which of the following does not influence the firm's short-run supply curve?
    a. The number of firms
    b. The productivity of the firm
    c. The prices of variable inputs
    d. Improvements in technology

13. The market supply curve is a horizontal summation of:
    a. industry output.
    b. the marginal cost curves of all the firms selling in the market.
    c. the total cost curves of all the firms selling in the market.
    d. prices times quantity demanded for all the firms selling in the market.
    e. the short-run supply curves of all the firms selling in the market.

14. An increase in the number of firms in an industry:
    a. shifts the market supply curve upward at each level of output.
    b. shifts the market supply curve downward at each level of output.
    c. shifts the marginal cost curve upward.
    d. shifts the market supply curve rightward at each price.
    e. shifts the market supply curve leftward at each price.

15. An increase in wages will:
    a. shift the market supply curve upward at each price.
    b. shift marginal cost curves downward at each level of output and shift the market supply curve leftward.
    c. shift the total cost curve upward, shifting the market supply curve to the right.
    d. shift marginal cost curves upward at each level of output and shift the market supply curve leftward.

16. A decrease in the price of a variable input will shift the market supply curve _____ and cause the equilibrium price to _____.
    a. rightward, fall
    b. leftward, fall
    c. rightward, rise
    d. leftward, rise
    e. the supply curve will not shift, and the market price will not change.

17. An increase in insurance premiums (a fixed input) will shift the market supply curve
    _____ and cause the equilibrium price to _____.
    a. rightward, fall
    b. leftward, fall
    c. rightward, rise
    d. leftward, rise
    e. the supply curve will not shift, and the market price will not change.

18. The perfectly elastic demand curve faced by a perfectly competitive firm derives from which
    of the following characteristics of a competitive market?
    a. Many sellers and consumers
    b. Costless and available information
    c. Firms with small market shares
    d. Firms produce a homogeneous good
    e. None of the above

19. Assume that a competitive firm has the following cost and revenue characteristics at its current
    level of output: average revenue = $8.00, average variable cost = $6.00, and average fixed
    cost = $4.00. This firm is:
    a. incurring a loss of $2.00 per unit and should shut down.
    b. realizing only a normal profit.
    c. realizing an economic profit of $2.00 per unit.
    d. incurring a loss per unit of $2.00, but should continue to operate in the short run.

20. Which of the following best explains why a competitive firm's supply curve does not include
    that portion of the marginal cost curve that lies below the average variable cost curve?
    a. If price equals marginal cost below the average variable cost curve, the fixed cost loss is
       less than the operating loss and the firm will shut down.
    b. At points below the average variable cost curve, firms incur losses and will shut down.
    c. If price equals marginal cost below the average variable cost curve, operating losses ex-
       ceed the fixed cost losses associated with shutting down.
    d. At points below the average variable cost curve, revenues are just sufficient to cover fixed
       costs, causing the firm to shut down.

21. Which of the following explains the chain of events associated with improvements in
    technology?
    a. Technological improvements reduce marginal product and marginal cost, thus shifting the
       competitive market supply curve rightward.
    b. Technological improvements increase marginal product and marginal cost, thus shifting
       the competitive market supply curve leftward.
    c. Technological improvements decrease marginal product and increase marginal cost, thus
       shifting the competitive market supply curve rightward.
    d. Technological improvements increase marginal product and decrease marginal cost, thus
       shifting the competitive market supply curve rightward.

22. Which of the following explains the impact of wage increases on market prices?
    a. Wage increases increase marginal cost, causing the market supply curve to shift rightward and the market price to fall.
    b. Wage increases decrease marginal cost, causing the market supply curve to shift leftward and the market price to rise.
    c. Wage increases increase marginal cost, decreasing market supply and increasing market price.
    d. Wage increases increase accounting costs and are passed on to the consumer in the form of higher product prices.

THINK IT THROUGH

1. Why is the market for wheat considered to be a competitive market?

2. This is a free country. You can raise or lower the price of a good or service if you wish. Why then do we say that the competitive firm is a price "taker" rather than a price "maker"?

3. Discuss the rationale underlying the MR = MC rule for profit maximization. If it is a rule for the maximization of profits, then how can it also be a rule for the minimization of losses?

4. You are a manager in a firm within a competitive industry that is heavily reliant upon electricity as a source of power to propel the assembly line. An embargo of oil from the Middle East causes increases in the price of oil and its substitutes such as natural gas and coal. Coal-fired electric power plants will experience an upward shift in their marginal cost curves, resulting in an increase in the price of electricity. What are the implications for your industry and your firm?

ANALYZING THE NEWS

Using the skills derived from studying this chapter, analyze the economic facts that make up the following article and answer the questions below, using graphical analysis where possible.

1. Should the cost of electric power to large companies be regarded as a fixed or variable cost? Why?

2. What would be the impact of an increase in the price of electric power for a firm operating just above the minimum point on the average variable cost curve?

CP&L power rates trouble industries

Some companies take their jobs elsewhere

By C.E. YANDLE
Staff writer

Carolina Power & Light Co. historically has prided itself for being a cog that moves North Carolina's economic-development wheel, helping the state attract new industries and jobs.

In recent years, however, some companies have rejected the Raleigh utility's advances, choosing instead to open plants in other states. The companies — which use extremely high volumes of electricity — were turned off by CP&L's comparatively high electrical rates, the executives said.

And some of CP&L's biggest customers have complained that their competitors — which are served by other utilities — have an edge because of lower electrical rates.

"CP&L's higher electrical rates are one of the factors that are hurting economic development in Eastern North Carolina," said Jerry T. Roberts, executive director of the Carolina Utility Customers Association in Raleigh, an industry trade group.

One state official estimated that during the past two to three years, North Carolina lost to neighboring states a handful of companies that represented a potential economic investment of $1 billion and hundreds of jobs.

"We haven't lost a lot of companies, just ones that are very energy-sensitive," said Alvah H. Ward Jr., who heads industrial recruiting for the state Department of Economic and Community Development. "So you would think maybe that since the numbers are small, we shouldn't be concerned, but we're losing the real cream of the crop. It's the Fortune 500 companies."

CP&L executives, however, said they knew of no specific instances in which companies chose to open plants elsewhere because of CP&L's higher rates. "We have no evidence that would support that," said Norris L. Edge, CP&L's senior vice president of customer and operating services. "We have no evidence that industries are not locating in our area because of electrical rates."

Holding up a sheet of paper that listed the names of several companies that had opened new plants in CP&L's service area over the past 18 months, Mr. Edge added: "We do know of a lot of industries that are locating in our area."

Choosing Camden

One company that apparently was concerned by CP&L's rates was Allied-Signal Corp. in Morristown, N.J. Earlier this year, Allied-Signal announced plans to open a new copper foil plant near Camden, S.C., that would employ about 100 people. The company had considered putting the plant near Asheboro.

Instead, it chose South Carolina because of CP&L's higher rates, according to testimony at a House Utilities Committee meeting in April by D.A. McCaig, an executive at Allied-Signal's Moncure plant. Allied officials declined further comment.

Dale B. Carroll, economic-development supervisor for CP&L, was involved in North Carolina's negotiations to woo Allied-Signal. He acknowledged that Allied-Signal representatives had expressed concerns about electric rates, but said the company had been attracted to South Carolina for other reasons as well.

Those included about $900,000 in economic incentives offered by the state, and a close relationship between the president of Allied-Signal and South Carolina Gov. Carroll A. Campbell Jr., he said.

But the Allied-Signal decision highlights how South Carolina and its state-owned electric utility, Santee Cooper, have benefited from CP&L's higher rates.

Santee Cooper, with headquarters near Charleston in Monck's Corner, charges electric rates that are among the lowest in the Southeast, according to industry publications.

Those same surveys have ranked CP&L in recent years as one of the region's most expensive utilities. The surveys are based on what utilities charge per kilowatt hour. In North Carolina CP&L charged 5.63 cents per kilowatt hour for industrial users in 1990 compared with 3.3 cents for Santee Cooper.

CP&L has the highest rates of the utilities that serve customers in North Carolina. The state's other two utilities are Duke Power Co. in Charlotte and Virginia Power in Richmond, Va., which does business in North Carolina as North Carolina Power.

Millions at stake

The cost of electricity can mean millions of dollars to certain types of industries, such as paper mills and textile plants.

Such companies might use as much as 32 million kilowatt-hours of electricity a month, according to a survey by Carolina Utility Customers Association. By comparison, a typical residential customer uses about 1,000 kilowatt-hours a month.

National Spinning Co. Inc., for example, a Washington, N.C., maker of textile yarns, paid CP&L 8.7 cents for every pound of yarn it made at its four North Carolina plants, said Henry Moore Jr., the company's director of purchasing. The company's other plants are in Warsaw, Beulaville and Whiteville.

Mr. Moore, who spoke April 25 at a legislative hearing in Raleigh, said that if those four National Spinning plants had been in Duke Power's service area, his company would have spent only 6.5 cents for each pound of yarn. That would have saved the company $2 million.

At the same hearing, William M. Sue of E.I. du Pont de Nemours & Co. said the giant conglomerate had paid more per kilowatt hour at its seven North Carolina operations in 1990 than at any of its more than 100 other U.S. plants.

The company employs more than 6,000 people in North Carolina. Last year, DuPont purchased more than 920 million

Continued on next page

Source: "CP&L Power Rates Trouble Industries: Some Companies Take Their Jobs Elsewhere," *The News and Observer*, Raleigh, N.C., June 23, 1991, p. 10A.

Continued from previous page

kilowatt-hours of electricity in the state, paying about $45 million, Mr. Sue said. Five of DuPont's Tar Heel operations are served by CP&L.

Shearon Harris' price

The reason for CP&L's higher electrical rates can be summed up in two words, said Robert P. Gruber, executive director of the state's Public Staff, a consumer-advocacy group.

"Shearon Harris," said Mr. Gruber, referring to the Shearon Harris Nuclear Plant in southwestern Wake County. "It's really that simple ... I think CP&L's rates are a problem for industry recruitment."

Shearon Harris was completed in 1987 at a cost of $3.9 billion. Paying for the plant has added about 16 percent to the average monthly electricity bill of CP&L's customers, Mr. Gruber said.

Mr. Edge, the CP&L executive, acknowledged that the company had higher rates than other nearby utilities. But he noted that Shearon Harris was one of the country's newest nuclear plants, which goes hand-in-hand with higher rates. As other utilities build large, expensive plants to keep up with demand, the rates those utilities charge will increase to levels as high as, or higher than, CP&L's, he said.

"I believe that you'll find that existing industries and new industries are looking at the long-term," Mr. Edge said. "If you look at us long-term, you'll see our rates have been very competitive."

Nonetheless, some industries that had shown interest in opening plants in North Carolina have slipped across the border to South Carolina and Santee Cooper's lower rates.

"You tell your folks in North Carolina: 'Anybody you can't handle, we'll be glad to help them down here,' " quipped Charles C. Gunnin, Santee Cooper's manager of economic development.

Economic incentives

Mr. Ward of the Department of Economic and Community Development said North Carolina had lost at least four or five companies to South Carolina and Santee Cooper in 1990 because of lower electric rates.

The total economic investment by those companies could reach $1 billion, he said. He emphasized that Santee Cooper had succeeded in attracting companies that had considered opening new plants throughout North Carolina, and not just in CP&L's service area.

Santee Cooper is a non-profit utility, so it does not pay state or federal taxes and does not have stockholders who expect to receive quarterly dividend checks and an increase in the value of their shares.

The South Carolina utility works closely with a state-run economic-development group that offers to industries considering the Palmetto State a laundry list of financial incentives worth millions of dollars.

The incentives include low-interest loans, relocation assistance and outright grants.

North Carolina typically has offered few — if any — of the types of monetary incentives offered by South Carolina.

South Carolina's strategy has prompted representatives from CP&L, Duke Power and North Carolina Power to say that Santee Cooper has a competitive advantage in recruiting industries.

"It isn't a level playing field," said Joseph J. Maher, a Duke Power spokesman.

But Duke Power fares well against in-state rival CP&L. Even if a 9.2 percent rate increase that Duke has asked for is approved by the state Utilities Commission, Duke would continue to have rates lower than CP&L's.

The difference between Duke's and CP&L's rates has prompted complaints from some of CP&L's larger customers.

The issue of CP&L's rates at times has been the subject of corporate boardroom discussions, acknowledged Ernest C. Pearson, an assistant secretary with the state Department of Economic and Community Development.

"We talk to them all the time about it," said Mr. Pearson, referring to CP&L. "They're well aware of the problem ... but at the same time, CP&L is entitled to make a fair profit.

"But, companies have made decisions to locate their industries elsewhere in part because they can get better rates in other states. It's business, and we understand that."

CHAPTER ANSWERS

The Chapter in Brief

1. Profit maximization 2. Many 3. Homogeneous 4. Very small 5. Unconcerned 6. Freely available 7. Entry and exit 8. Elastic 9. Greatest 10. Exceed 11. Will also exceed 12. Exceed 13. Exceeds 14. Increase 15. Exceeds 16. Increases 17. Zero 18. MR = MC or P = MC 19. Variable 20. Fixed 21. Below 22. Exceed 23. Marginal 24. Average variable 25. Variable 26. Downward 27. Profits

Key Terms Review

1. Competitive firm 2. Average revenue 3. Marginal profit 4. Short-run supply curve 5. Market supply curve 6. Perfectly competitive market 7. Marginal revenue 8. Shutdown point

Concept Review

1. a. Many sellers b. Homogeneous goods c. Firms with very small market share d. Firms unconcerned about rivals e. Information on prices is freely available f. Freedom of entry and exit

2.

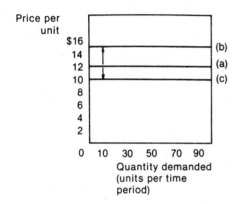

3.

P2	P3	TR1	TR2	TR3
$15	$10	$ 0	$ 0	$ 0
15	10	120	150	100
15	10	240	300	200
15	10	360	450	300
15	10	480	600	400
15	10	600	750	500
15	10	720	900	600

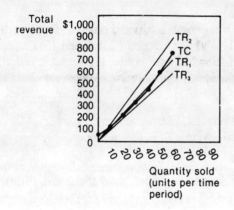

Total revenue

Quantity sold
(units per time
period)

4. a.   TC plotted on figure above.

   b.   -$50

   c.   Profit (Loss)   d. 40

        $ 0   e. There is a loss at every
           20   output, but the loss is
           30   minimized at an output of
           30   20 units.
            0
         (60)

5. a.

TR1	MR1	TR2	MR2	TR3	MR3
$ 0		$ 0		$ 0	
120	$12	150	$15	100	$10
240	12	300	15	200	10
360	12	450	15	300	10
480	12	600	15	400	10
600	12	750	15	500	10
720	12	900	15	600	10

   b.

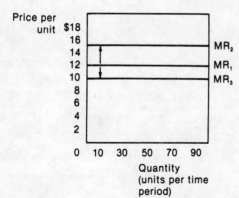

Price per unit

Quantity
(units per time
period)

222

6. a.

VC	MC	AVC	AC
$ 0	$	$	$
70	7	7	12
170	10	8.50	11
280	11	9.33	11
400	12	10	11.25
550	15	11	12
730	18	12.10	13

b.

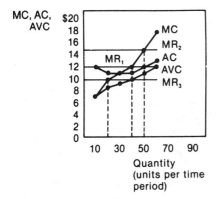

c. MR, MC, 40

7. a. 50, 150

b. 20, -20 ; No, because the operating loss is less than the fixed-cost loss.

c. At $7, the firm is indifferent because the operating loss is equal to the fixed-cost loss. Any price below this, however, will force the firm to shut down because the operating loss will exceed the fixed-cost loss.

8. a. Profit-Maximizing (Loss-Minimizing)

Quantity (units)

50

40

20

10

b.

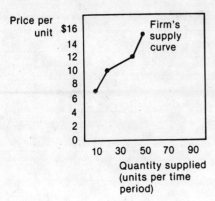

c. Short-run supply curve, MC, minimum point of the average variable cost curve

9. **a.**

Quantity Supplied (Firm)	Quantity Supplied (Market)
50	5,000
40	4,000
20	2,000
10	1,000

b.

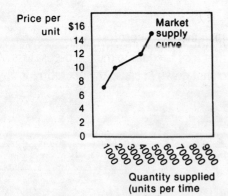

10. a. Number of firms, right b. Technology, down c. Prices of variable inputs, up d. Average productive capacity, right

11. a. Set marginal revenue equal to marginal cost and solve for the profit-maximizing quantity.

$$MR = MC$$

$$P \ \ = \ \ a + bQ$$

$$Q \ \ = \ \ (P - a)/b$$

b. Increases c. Falls d. Increases

Mastery Test
1. e 2. e 3. c 4. b 5. c 6. e 7. a 8. b 9. c 10. a 11. e 12. a 13. e 14. d 15. d 16. a 17. e 18. c 19. d 20. a 21. d 22. c

Think it Through

1. There are a number of characteristics similar to those required for perfectly competitive markets. There are many producers, so no one farmer can change production enough to affect market prices. Wheat farmers are price takers and have very small market shares. Wheat is not strictly homogeneous in terms of quality, but the wheat produced by one farmer is a very close substitute if not a perfect substitute for the wheat produced by other farmers. Wheat farmers can sell all they produce at the market price and are therefore unconcerned with decisions of rival farmers. Information regarding wheat prices is freely available in that prices are published daily in most newspapers and announced on many television stations. There are certainly freedom of entry and exit, but the financial investment required to enter the wheat-farming industry as a competitive producer would probably be sizable and thus to some extent would impede entry.

2. Because there are many firms with very small market shares producing goods that are perfect substitutes for each other, any one firm choosing to raise price above the market price would experience a loss of most if not all sales. Consumers would simply go elsewhere and buy the identical product at the lower market price.

3. If marginal revenue exceeds marginal cost, an increase in output by a unit will increase revenues more than costs and will either increase profits or reduce losses, depending on whether or not the market price exceeds average total cost. If marginal revenue is less than marginal cost, a one-unit decrease in output will increase profits or reduce losses. If marginal revenue equals marginal cost, a one-unit change in output will change revenues and costs by the same amount, leaving the profit or loss unchanged. At this point profits are at a maximum or losses are at a minimum again, depending on whether or not the price exceeds average total cost. It should be noted that the losses being referred to are operating losses.

4. Because electricity is an important variable input to the manufacture of your good, an increase in the price of electricity will cause an upward shift in your marginal cost curve, causing marginal cost to exceed marginal revenue at your current rate of production. As a manager of a profit-seeking firm, you have to make decisions regarding production levels that increase profit. In this case, a reduction in output will reduce costs more than revenues and result in a higher profit than if you continued to produce at your current level of output. For the industry, rising marginal costs will shift the market supply curve upward at each level of output, resulting in an eventual increase in the market price of the good.

Analyzing the News

Using the skills derived from studying this chapter, analyze the economic facts that make up the following article and answer the questions below, using graphical analysis where possible.

1. A firm's cost of electric power is a variable cost of production. Increasing use of machinery, computers, lights, and so forth requires additional electricity. The firm's total power bill will vary with the level of production.

2. If a perfectly competitive firm sells its goods or services at prices that just barely exceed the minimum point on the average variable cost curve, an increase in electric power rates could push the average variable cost curve above the market price and force the firm to shut down.

11 LONG-RUN SUPPLY IN COMPETITIVE MARKETS

CHAPTER CONCEPTS

After studying your text, attending class, and completing this chapter, you should be able to:
1. Discribe the conditions that exist when long-run competitive equilibrium is achieved in a market.
2. Show how profits and losses act as signals that cause shifts in market supply over the long run.
3. Derive long-run supply curves for products sold in perfectly competitive markets and show how long-run supply differs from short-run supply.
4. Analyze the long-run impact of technological advance, taxes, and subsidies on prices and quantities traded in perfectly competitive markets.
5. Show how allocative efficiency is achieved in competitive markets.

THE CHAPTER IN BRIEF

Fill in the blanks to summarize chapter content.

Firms in a competitive industry are in long-run equilibrium when there is neither entry to nor exit from the industry and when firms within the industry are neither expanding nor contracting. In long-run competitive equilibrium, economic profits are (1)_____(zero, positive), but the opportunity costs of the owner's self-owned resources (2)_____(are not, are) being covered. The existence of short-run economic profits in a competitive industry induces firms to (3)_____(enter, exit) the industry. Entry of new firms (4)_____ (decreases, increases) market supply and (5)_____ (increases, reduces) market prices and economic profits in the long run. Prices (6)_____(fall, rise) until entry stops. This occurs at a market price equal to minimum (7)_____(average variable, average total) cost in the long run. Here economic profits equal zero although normal profits are being earned. Consumers are paying a price equal to the minimum possible average cost of production.

Assuming competitive long-run equilibrium initially, the impact of an increase in market demand for a good (8)_____ (decreases, increases) the market price, causing existing firms to experience economic (9)_____ (profits, losses) and the incentive to (10)_____(decrease, increase) production. Firms (11)_____(decrease, increase) output because marginal revenue has risen relative to marginal cost. But short-run profits induce firms to (12)_____ (exit, enter) the market, causing the market supply curve to shift (13)_____ (leftward, rightward). As market supply (14)_____ (rises, falls) relative to market demand, the equilibrium price (15)_____(rises, falls) until the economic profits are eliminated—where price equals both short- and long-run marginal cost and minimum average cost. If the expansion of the industry does not affect input prices, the price will return to its former level. The long-run market supply curve is (16)_____ (horizontal, upward sloping) for the above case of constant costs. If industry expansion is significant enough to cause the market prices of inputs to rise, the marginal and average cost curves will shift upward. Thus prices will not have to fall as much in the long run to restore market equilibrium. For the case of increasing costs, the long-run market supply curve is (17)_____(horizontal, upward sloping).

227

An improvement in technology increases the productivity of inputs and reduces both marginal and average costs. As average costs (18)_____(fall, rise) relative to the market price, firms realize economic (19)_____(losses, profits). Also, as marginal costs fall relative to marginal revenue, firms have an incentive to (20)_____(contract, expand) production. The economic profits result in new firms entering the industry and cause an increase in market supply. As supply rises relative to demand, prices fall, but in this case prices will fall (21)_____(below, to) their initial level because the long-run minimum average cost has (22)_____(declined, increased) due to the technological improvement and prices must equal this minimum to establish the new equilibrium.

For the case of constant costs, an increase in a tax per unit of output will shift the long-run average cost curve upward by the amount of the tax. If firms were in long-run equilibrium prior to the tax, the tax would impose losses on the firms, causing some of them to (23)_____(enter, exit) the industry. Market supply would (24)_____(rise, fall) and price would (25)_____(rise, fall) eventually to equal the higher average costs. Prices would therefore increase by the upward shift in the average cost curve or by the increase in the tax since average costs and taxes increase by the same amount. For the case of increasing costs, market prices would increase by (26)_____ (less, greater) than the tax per unit because the industry decline would reduce input prices and keep average costs from increasing as much as in the constant-costs case.

A competitive market in long-run equilibrium achieves allocative efficiency when the marginal benefit associated with the use of resources (27)_____(equals, is greater than) the marginal cost of those resources. The value consumers place on an additional unit of a good consumed is just equal to the producer's opportunity cost of the resources employed to produce that unit. Net gains to both consumers and producers are maximized. A point on the market demand curve represents marginal benefit—the (28)_____ (minimum, maximum) price that the consumer is willing and able to pay for an additional unit of a good rather than go without. The market supply curve, being a summation of individual firm marginal cost curves, represents the marginal cost of producing an additional unit of output. Market equilibrium occurs where the demand and supply curves intersect or, in terms of benefits and costs, where the marginal benefit and marginal cost curves intersect. A perfectly competitive market results in a level of output where marginal benefit and marginal cost are (29)_____(unequal, equal) and net gains to producers and consumers are at a maximum. Consumers are maximizing utility and producers are maximizing profit, although in the long run only normal profits are earned and consumers pay a price equal to the lowest possible average cost of production.

KEY TERMS REVIEW

Write the key term from the list below next to its definition.

Key Terms

Long-run competitive equilibrium

Constant-costs industry

Long-run industry supply curve

Increasing-costs industry

Definitions

1. _____ : one for which the prices of at least some of the inputs used increase as a direct result of the expansion of the industry.

2. _____ : a relationship between price and quantity supplied for points where the industry is in long-run competitive equilibrium.

3. _____ : exists in an industry when there is no tendency for firms to enter or leave the industry or to expand or contract the scale of their operations.

4. _____ : one for which input prices are unaffected by the quantity of a good produced or the number of firms in the industry.

CONCEPT REVIEW

Concepts 1 and 2: *Long-run equilibrium for a firm and market; role of profits and losses*

1. a. On the diagram below, draw the competitive firm's demand curve and label the curve d1.

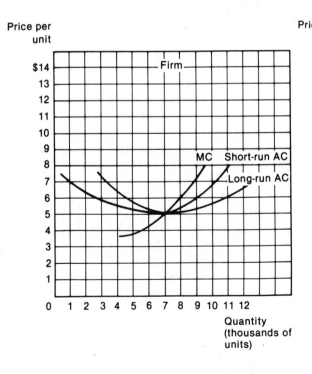

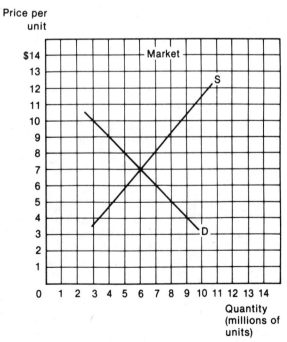

b. Given the figure above, determine whether the firm is realizing economic profits or losses.

    (1) The firm's short-run economic profits (losses) = $_____

    (2) The firm's level of output = _____ units

    (3) Market price = $_____

    (4) Market quantity = _____ units

c.   (1) In time, _____ (entry, exit) will occur because of the presence of economic _____ (profits, losses).

    (2) Show graphically in the figure above the long-run adjustment of both the market and the firm assuming the firm operates in a constant-costs industry.

    (3) As a result of _____ (entry, exit), economic _____ (profits, losses) will _____ (rise, fall). _____(Entry, Exiting) will continue until market price _____ (rises, falls) sufficiently to eliminate economic _____ (profits, losses).

d. In the long run, price equals both short- and long-run _____ and _____. Consumers pay a price equal to the minimum _____. Producers earn _____ economic profits but continue to earn _____ profits. Referring to the figure above, in long-run equilibrium the firm's economic profit (or loss) equals $_____ and its level of production is _____ units. Market price and quantity are $_____ and _____ units, respectively.

2. a. On the diagram below, draw the firm's demand curve and label it d2.

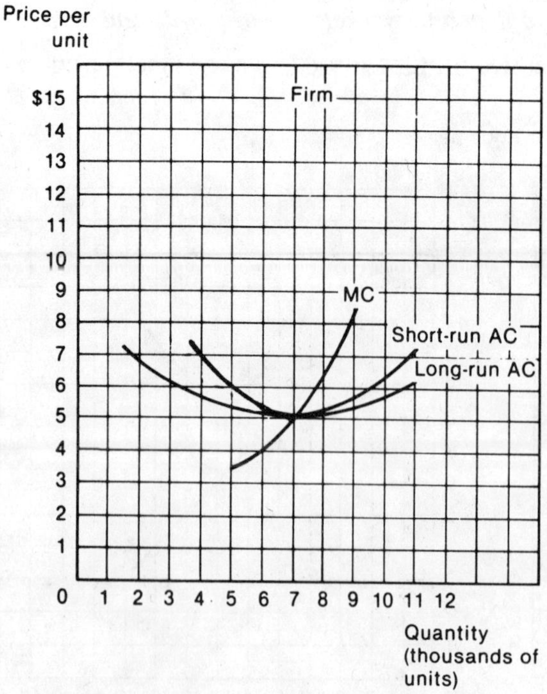

Price per unit (Firm)

$15
14
13
12
11
10
9 —MC
8
7 Short-run AC
6 Long-run AC
5
4
3
2
1
0   1 2 3 4 5 6 7 8 9 10 11 12
Quantity (thousands of units)

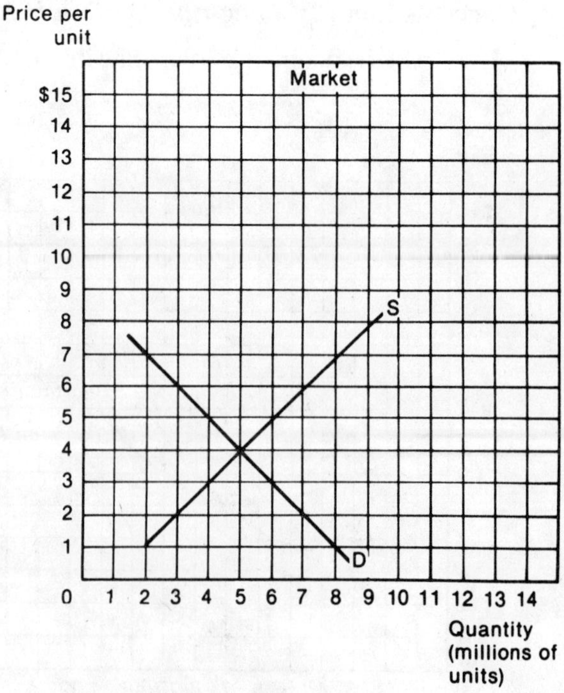

Price per unit (Market)

$15
14
13
12
11
10
9
8 S
7
6
5
4
3
2
1 D
0   1 2 3 4 5 6 7 8 9 10 11 12 13 14
Quantity (millions of units)

b. Given the figure above, determine whether the firm realizes economic profits or losses.

    (1) The firm's economic profit (or loss) = $_____

    (2) The firm's level of output = _____ units

    (3) Market price = $_____

    (4) Market quantity = _____ units

c.   (1) In time, _____ (entry, exiting) will occur because of the presence of economic _____ (profits, losses).

    (2) Show graphically in the figure above the long-run adjustment of both the market and the firm assuming the firm operates in a constant-costs industry.

    (3) As a result of _____ (entry, exiting), economic _____ (profits, losses) will _____ (rise, fall). _____ (Entry, Exiting) will continue until market price _____ (rises, falls) sufficiently to eliminate economic _____ (profits, losses).

d. In long-run equilibrium, price equals both short-and long-run _____ and _____. Consumers pay a price equal to the minimum _____. Producers earn _____ economic profits but continue to earn _____ profits. Referring to the figure above, in long-run equilibrium the firm realizes economic _____ (profits, losses) of $_____ and produces _____ units of output. Market price and quantity equal $_____ and_____ units, respectively.

Concept 3: *Long-run market supply curves*

3. a. Given the figure below representing a competitive firm and market in long-run equilibrium, show the short-run impact of an increase in market demand of 20 million units at every price.

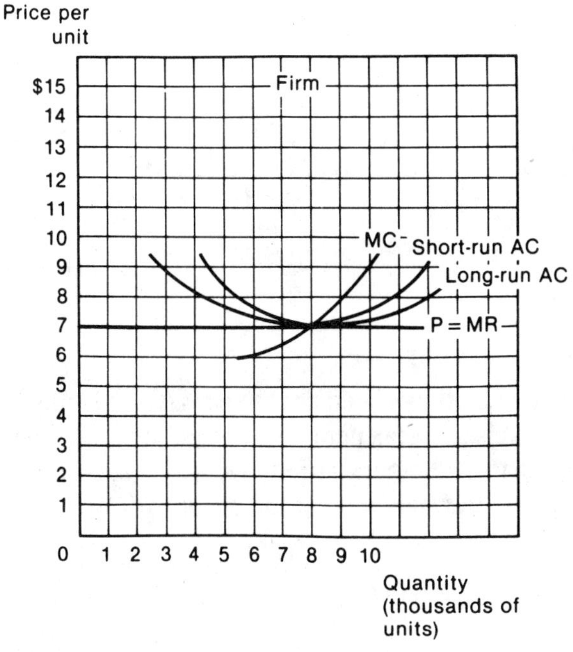

Price per unit — Firm
Quantity (thousands of units)

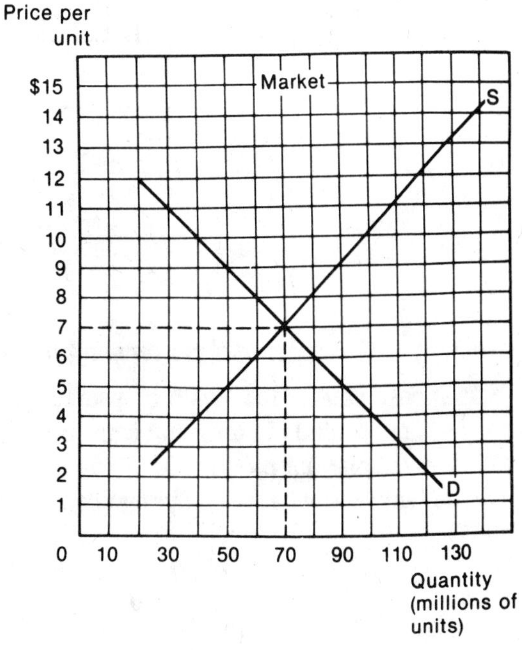

Price per unit — Market
Quantity (millions of units)

Market price _____ to $_____, and market quantity _____ to _____ units.

b. Assuming the case of constant costs, on the figure above show the adjustments that move the firm and the market to long-run equilibrium.

c. Show the long-run supply curve in the figure above. The long-run supply curve has a _____ slope.

4. For the case of an increasing-costs industry, show graphically on the figure below:

a. The short-run effect of an increase in market demand of 40 million units at every price.

b. The impact of industry expansion on the firm's costs (assume that the marginal and average cost curves shift upward by $1 at each level of output).

c. The adjustment of the firm and market to long-run equilibrium.

d. The long-run market supply curve. The long-run market supply curve has a _____ slope.

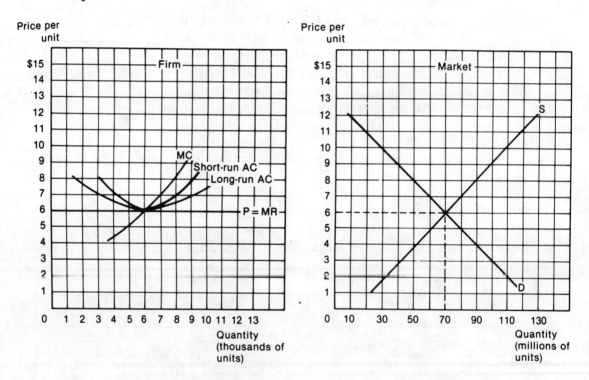

Concept 4: *Impact of taxes on market price and quantity*

5. Suppose you are the owner of a small vineyard operating in a competitive market in California and are currently in long-run equilibrium. An excise tax (tax per unit of output) of $1 per bottle is levied on your production of wine. Assuming that all other California wineries are subject to the same tax, what would you expect to happen to the market price and quantity of wine?

232

a. Using the figure below, show the short-run impact of the tax.

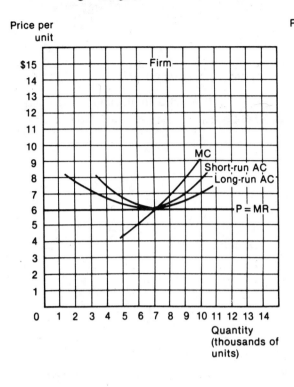

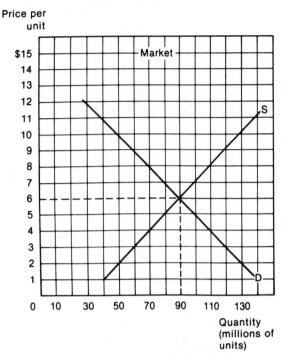

b. In the short run, you and other producers of wine will experience _____ (losses, profits). In the long run, assuming the case of a constant-costs industry, firms _____ (enter, exit), causing market price to _____ by $_____ to $_____ and market quantity to _____ to _____ units. Prices _____ (rise, fall) by what percentage of the $1 excise tax? _____%

MASTERY TEST

Select the best answer.

1. Long-run competitive equilibrium occurs when:
   a. firms are neither entering nor exiting the industry.
   b. firms within the industry are neither expanding nor contracting.
   c. economic profits are zero.
   d. the opportunity costs of the owner's self-owned resources are just being covered.
   e. All of the above.

2. In long-run competitive equilibrium, price equals not only _____, but also _____.
   a. average variable costs, marginal cost
   b. marginal cost, minimum possible average cost
   c. marginal cost, total benefit
   d. the lowest price available to the consumer, total revenues to the firm.

3. Which of the following is correct regarding profits in long-run competitive equilibrium?

   a. Normal profits are zero.

   b. Normal profits are zero, but economic profits are being covered.

   c. Accounting profits are zero.

   d. Economic profits are zero, but normal profits are being covered.

4. The existence of economic profits induces _____ from/into an industry, which in turn _____ market supply and _____ market price.

   a. exiting, increases, increases

   b. exiting, decreases, increases

   c. entry, increases, increases

   d. entry, increases, decreases

5. The existence of losses induces _____ from/into an industry, which in turn _____ market supply and _____ market price.

   a. exiting, increases, increases

   b. exiting, decreases, increases

   c. entry, increases, increases

   d. entry, increases, decreases

6. For the case of a constant-costs industry, an increase in demand will:

   a. result in a higher price in the short run and a lower price in the long run as compared to the current market price.

   b. increase the firm's profits in the long run.

   c. result in a higher price in the short run and the same price in the long run as compared to the current market price.

   d. cause short-run profits but long-run losses.

   e. c and d.

7. The long-run market supply curve for a constant-costs industry is:

   a. vertical.

   b. upward sloping.

   c. downward sloping.

   d. horizontal.

8. For the case of an increasing-costs industry, an increase in demand will:
   a. result in a higher price in the short run, but in the long run price will fall to a level above the original market price.
   b. result in short-run profits but long-run losses.
   c. increase profits in the long run.
   d. cause an expansion of the industry that will increase input prices and shift the firm's average cost curve downward.

9. The long-run market supply curve for an increasing-costs industry is:
   a. vertical.
   b. upward sloping.
   c. downward sloping.
   d. horizontal.

10. An improvement in technology in an industry:
    a. shifts the marginal cost curve upward and causes production and profit to rise.
    b. shifts the average cost curve upward due to increased labor productivity.
    c. results in short-run economic profits and a decline in price below the initial market price in the long run.
    d. produces an upward sloping market supply curve.

11. For the case of a constant-costs industry, a per-unit tax levied on a good:
    a. shifts the competitive firm's average cost curve down by less than the amount of the tax and increases the market price.
    b. increases supply and causes the price to fall.
    c. shifts the competitive firm's average and marginal cost curves upward by the amount of the tax per unit and in the long run results in an increase in the market price that is equal to the unit tax.
    d. None of the above.

12. For the case of an increasing-costs industry, a per-unit tax:
    a. results in an increase in the long-run market price equal to the tax per unit.
    b. results in an increase in the short-run market price equal to the tax per unit.
    c. results in an increase in the long-run market price less than the tax per unit.
    d. results in an increase in the long-run market price greater than the tax per unit.

13. Net gain is maximized where:
    a. price equals marginal revenue.
    b. marginal cost equals marginal benefit.
    c. the average variable cost is low.
    d. economic profits are high.

14. A market demand curve can be thought of as a marginal benefit curve because:

    a. the price reflects the opportunity costs of scarce resources.

    b. quantities consumed yield benefits.

    c. the price represents a measure of the additional benefit received from consuming one unit of a good—the price on a demand curve represents the maximum price that the consumer is willing and able to pay rather than go without.

    d. price times marginal benefit equals total net gain.

15. Allocative efficiency occurs where:

    a. marginal benefits equal marginal costs.

    b. net benefits are maximized from the allocation of resources.

    c. the maximum price that consumers are willing and able to pay for an additional unit of a good just equals the price required by firms to produce that unit.

    d. All of the above.

16. Competitive markets can maximize the net gain to both buyers and producers because:

    a. marginal benefits exceed the supply of the good.

    b. the market demand curve reflects marginal benefits and the market supply curve reflects marginal costs, and in equilibrium, supply equals demand; hence marginal benefits equal marginal costs.

    c. they are efficient and do not waste resources.

    d. optimal exchange takes place to the point where total benefits equal total costs.
        Challenge Questions

17. Assume that a perfectly competitive industry is an increasing cost industry. If the industry is initially in long-run equilibrium and demand increases, what happens to short and long-run market equilibrium price, output, and average cost?

    a. Price, output, and average cost rise in the short run, but they fall to their original levels in the long-run.

    b. Price and output rise in the short run, but average cost, price, and output are lower than initial levels in the long run.

    c. Price, output, and average cost rise in the short-run. In long-run equilibrium, they are higher than initial levels.

    d. Price, average cost, and output fall in the short run, but rise to higher than initial levels in the long run.

18. Assume that a perfectly competitive industry is a constant cost industry. If the industry is initially in long-run equilibrium and demand decreases, what happens to short- and long-run market equilibrium price, output, and average cost?

a. Price and output fall and average cost rises in the short run, but they return to their original levels in the long run.

b. Price and output fall in the short run, but average cost, price, and output are higher than initial levels in the long run.

c. Price, output, and average cost fall in the short run. In long-run equilibrium, they are lower than initial levels.

d. Price, average cost, and output rise in the short run, but fall to lower than initial levels in the long run.

19. In a constant-cost perfectly competitive industry, improvements in technology will:

a. raise the average and marginal cost of production, causing the long-run market price to rise above its initial level.

b. increase the productivity of labor and decrease both short- and long-run average costs, resulting in a decrease in market price in the long run.

c. shift average cost curves upward, but increased productivity makes it possible for firms to realize economies of scale and lower market price.

d. shift the market demand curve more than the market supply curve, causing the market price to fall.

20. Assume that the market for tomatoes is perfectly competitive and the industry experiences constant costs. Suppose the elasticity of demand for tomatoes is -2 and the elasticity of supply is .5. If an excise tax of $.10 per tomato is levied on tomato producers, what percentage of the tax is shifted to consumers?

a. .5%

b. 50%

c. 0%

d. 100%

e. Cannot tell from the information given.

21. Which of the following statements best describes the relationship between competitive markets and allocative efficiency?

a. Markets allocate resources efficiently as long as producers act in their own self interest.

b. Competition forces producers to quickly adopt the latest technology.

c. At market equilibrium, consumers are maximizing net benefits and producers are maximizing profits. The benefit a consumer associates with the consumption of the next unit of a good is just equal to the opportunity costs of producing that good.

d. Markets produce full employment and the most efficient use of scarce resources. In long-run equilibrium, the economy is on its consumption possibilities curve.

THINK IT THROUGH

1. Oil prices are determined by the world supply of and demand for oil. In the early 1970s, the member nations of OPEC reduced production of the world's available supply of oil. Although the oil industry is not perfectly competitive, the forces of supply and demand determine prices. Using your knowledge of the short- and long-run adjustments in markets, what would you predict to happen to oil prices in the short run and the long run as a result of OPEC's restriction of output?

2. Discuss the impact of technological improvement on the competitive firm, the competitive market, and the long-run market supply curve.

3. How do perfectly competitive markets maximize the net gains to producers and consumers?

ANALYZING THE NEWS

Using the skills derived from studying this chapter, analyze the economic facts that make up the following article and answer the questions below, using graphical analysis where possible.

1. What impact do you think the second tier computer manufacturers, superstores, mail order businesses and Japanese producers have had on the computer market? Describe in detail the short- and long-term effects.

These Prices Are Insane!

Computer industry's pain means consumers gain

What a difference a season makes. When Bob Vanderheiden, a newspaper systems manager from San Francisco, priced an Apple Macintosh IIfx computer for the office this winter, it was $7,369. By the time he closed the deal on the equipment a few weeks ago, the tab had dropped to $5,300. Vanderheiden also picked up two additional Macintoshes, three monitors, software, keyboards and a printer for a total savings of $12,000 over the midwinter estimate. "It was awfully nice to get some essential equipment at an incredible price," he says.

As the Crazy Eddie ads used to say, the prices are ... well, you know. Strained by the recession and increased competition, manufacturers are slashing prices with the kind of frenzy usually exhibited by electronics discounters and used-car salesmen. According to Susan Yamada, an analyst for Merrin Information Services in Palo Alto, Calif., street prices for some models have dropped by as much as 15 percent. Apple kicked it off late last year with new, lower-priced Macintosh models—and cut prices on its high-end products in March. Compaq Computer Corp., whose stock sank 27 percent one day last week on disappointing profit projections, slashed its suggested retail prices by as much as 34 percent in April. Toshiba quickly followed with its own round of cuts on selected models, as did IBM—and Big Blue is expected to announce new cuts this week of up to 24 percent on some models. Even scrappy Dell Computer Corp., already a low-price manufacturer, reduced systems by as much as $900. "Manufacturers need to move product," says JoeAnn Stahel of the market research firm StoreBoard/Computer Intelligence. "The result is that it's the greatest time in the world to purchase a computer."

Economic fears and the erosion of brand loyalty are keeping the pressure on prices. As the recession drags on, many buyers are taking a wait-and-see attitude toward updating their aging computer equipment. "Companies that don't have a cheap product to offer lose the customer who's hunting for a bargain," says Richard Shaffer, editor of industry publication ComputerLetter. While the demand for machines made by second-tier "clone" manufacturers is increasing, allegiance to companies with cachet like IBM and Compaq is on the decline. Many retailers are feeling the heat, too, thanks to increased competition from new "superstores" and a growing mail-order computing business. "It's a much more price-sensitive market than ever before," says Bruce Lupatkin, a technology analyst with Hambrecht & Quist in San Francisco. "Computers have become commodities—almost like TV sets."

Japanese turf: That may be good news for consumers, but could be bad news for the U.S. computer industry. American manufacturers are being forced to compete with their Asian rivals on price, rather than quality. And that's a problem, because it's often cheaper to manufacture computers overseas than in the United States. "As soon as you're in the consumer-products area, you're on Japanese turf," says Sheridan Tatsuno, publisher of NeoJapan Newsletter. "It's very much like what happened with the VCR. At first, it was a high-end professional machine. Then, the Japanese turned it into a consumer product."

Just how much more squeezing can the industry take? Rick Martin, an analyst for Prudential Securities in New York, believes these cuts might just be the beginning. "If the market doesn't turn around by Labor Day, then the next round of price cuts will be deeper," he says. Those prices won't just be insane. They'll be painful.

ANNETTA MILLER

Compaq LTE 386s/20 Model 30 $5,499 NOW $4,399

Toshiba T2000SX/20 Notebook $4,499 NOW $3,399

Apple Macintosh (entry model) $1,500 NOW $999

Source: "These Prices Are Insane: Computer Industry's Pain Means Consumers Gain," *Newsweek*, May 27, 1991, p. 43.

CHAPTER ANSWERS

The Chapter in Brief

1. Zero 2. Are 3. Enter 4. Increases 5. Reduces 6. Fall 7. Average total 8. Increases 9. Profits 10. Increase 11. Increase 12. Enter 13. Rightward 14. Rises 15. Falls 16. Horizontal 17. Upward sloping 18. Fall 19. Profits 20. Expand 21. Below 22. Declined 23. Exit 24. Fall 25. Rise 26. Less 27. Equals 28. Maximum 29. Equal

Key Terms Review

1. Increasing-costs industry 2. Long-run industry supply curve 3. Long-run competitive equilibrium 4. Constant-costs industry

Concept Review

1. a.

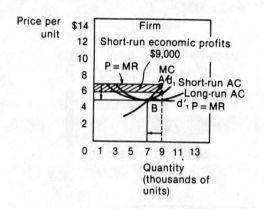 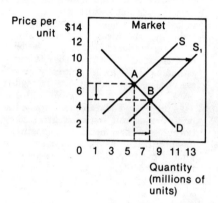

b. (1) Profits, $9,000 (2) 9,000 units (3) $7 (4) 6 million

c. (1) Entry, profit

(2) On figure above

(3) Entry, profits, fall; Entry, falls, profit

d. Marginal cost, minimum possible average cost; possible average cost of production; zero, normal; $0, 7,000 units; $5, 8 million

2. a.

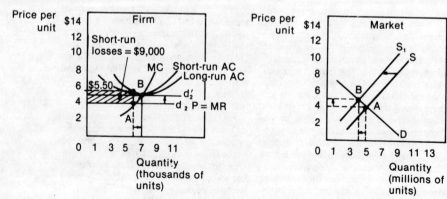

b. (1) Loss, $9,000 (2) 6,000 units (3) $4 (4) 5 million

c. (1) Exiting, losses
   (2) On figure above
   (3) Exiting, losses, fall; Exiting, rises, losses

d. Marginal cost, minimum possible average cost; possible average cost of production; zero, normal; $0, 7,000 units; $5, 4 million

3. a.

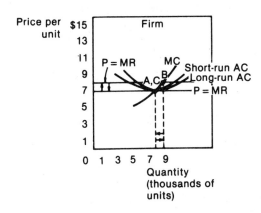
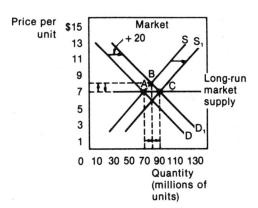

Increases, $8, increases, 80 million

b. On figure above

c. On figure above, zero or horizontal

4. a.

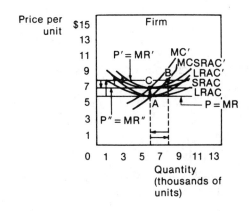
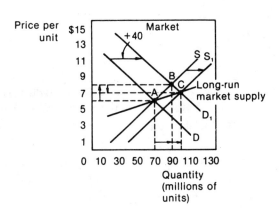

b. On figure above

c. On figure above

d. On figure above, positive

5. a.

b. Losses; exit, increase, $1, $7, decrease, 80 million; rise, 100%

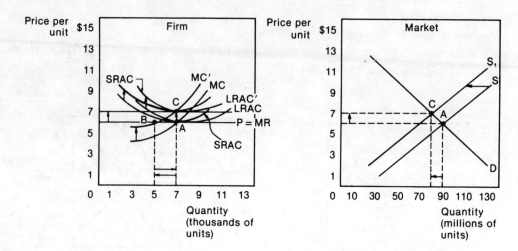

Mastery Test

1. e 2. b 3. d 4. d 5. b 6. c 7. d 8. a 9. b 10. c 11. c 12. c 13. b 14. c 15. d 16. b 17. c 18. a 19. b
20. d 21. c
Think it Through

1. In the short run, the restriction of oil production reduces market supply relative to market demand and increases the price per barrel of oil. This results in greater short-run profits associated with the production of oil and in the long run results in firms entering the industry such as
wildcats and other independent oil producers. It will also cause existing oil producers other
than the members of OPEC to expand exploration and production efforts. The latter represents
a movement up the supply curve in response to higher prices, and the former represents a
rightward shift in the supply curve. As the supply curve shifts rightward, the market price in
the long run will fall.

2. Technological improvement increases the productivity of variable inputs, causing the marginal
and average cost curves to shift downward. The minimum possible average cost of production
likewise falls. As marginal costs fall relative to marginal revenue, the firm has an incentive to
increase production in order to maximize short-run profits. But short-run profits induce entry
into the industry, shifting the market supply curve rightward and reducing the market price. In
the long run, (assuming a constant-costs industry) the market price is likely to fall below the
original market price because price will fall to equal the minimum average cost, which has
fallen below its original level due to the technological improvement.

3. Consumers maximize utility by consuming goods to the point where price equals marginal benefit. Producers maximize profits by producing to the point where price equals marginal cost.
The market equilibrium occurs where demand equals supply. But since a point on the market
demand curve represents the consumer's marginal benefit of consuming an additional unit of a
good and a point on the market supply curve represents the price necessary to just cover the
firm's marginal cost, marginal benefits and marginal costs are equal where the market supply

and demand curves intersect. When the market is in equilibrium, net gains to consumers and producers are maximized from the allocation of resources.

Analyzing the News

1. As discussed in this article, the United States computer market has undergone rapid and irreversible changes. Apparently, higher than "normal" profits lured potential entrants into this market. As sellers entered the market, two effects seem to dominate. First, an increase in the short-run market supply of computers in the United States drove prices downward as existing manufacturers found it difficult to sell computers at previously higher prices. Second, as "clone" manufacturers introduced lower priced computers of comparable quality, the demand for name-brand models fell. This also caused prices to fall. Consumers view these clones as close substitutes for name-brand models—a sign of increasing competition.

   In the long-run, any economic profits that were earned previously may be reduced as more sellers with sufficient capital enter this market with newer models and lower prices. This market may never become perfectly competitive in the theoretical sense, but it exhibits characteristics associated with more competitive markets. There are now *many sellers,* the good is more *homogeneous*, and *market shares have fallen.*

12   MONOPOLY

CHAPTER CONCEPTS

After studying your text, attending class, and completing this chapter, you should be able to:

1. Define pure monopoly, discuss how it can be maintained in a market, and show how the demand curve for a product sold by a monopoly firm implies that the firm can control the market price.
2. Show how the marginal revenue from a monopolist's output is less than the price the monopolist charges for its product.
3. Show how a profit-maximizing monopoly seller chooses how much of its product to make available to buyers, and demonstrate how the decision of how much to sell is inseparable from that of how much to charge.
4. Compare market outcomes under pure monopoly with those that would prevail under perfect competition and discuss the social cost and possible social benefit of monopoly.
5. Discuss government regulation of natural monopoly.
6. Discuss how monopolies react to taxes on their output or price ceilings and why they sometimes engage in price discrimination.

THE CHAPTER IN BRIEF

Fill in the blanks to summarize chapter content.

A pure monopoly exists when there is a single seller of a product or service for which there are (1)_____ (close, no close) substitutes. The monopolist controls the market price by restricting output and preventing entry into the industry. Barriers to entry include government franchises and licenses, patents and copyrights, (2)_____ (control of an important resource, government influence), and economies of scale made possible by large size. Some monopolies that exist because of economies of scale are regulated by government so that the economies associated with large-scale production can be passed on to consumers in the form of lower prices than would be possible if the industry were made up of many small firms operating inefficiently small plants. These monopolies are called (3)_____ (natural, pure) monopolies.

The monopolist faces (4)_____ (a horizontal, the market) demand curve because it is the only seller in the market. Because the market demand curve is downward sloping, prices must be lowered in order to increase sales. Therefore marginal revenue (5)_____(increases, falls) as output sold increases and is also (6)_____(less, greater) than the product price. A monopoly firm will maximize profits by finding the level of output where marginal revenue (7)_____ (is greater than, equals) marginal cost. Once the profit-maximizing level of output is found, the monopolist will set a price on the market demand curve at a level that will ensure that quantity of output will be sold. Because price (8)_____(equals, exceeds) marginal revenue and because at the profit-maximizing output marginal revenue equals marginal cost, price must also (9)_____ (equal, exceed) marginal cost. The monopolist will never operate where marginal revenue is negative. This means that the monopoly seller will operate on the (10)_____ (inelastic, elastic) portion of the market demand curve where marginal revenue is positive and increases in output resulting from decreases in price will increase total revenue. No unique monopoly supply curve can be found because it is possible to have more than one price associated with the same level of monopoly output.

As compared to perfect competition, the monopolist charges a (11)_____ (higher, lower) price by (12)_____ (expanding output above, restricting output below) the level that would prevail in a competitive market. The monopolist's price (13)_____(equals, exceeds) marginal cost, whereas the competitive market results in a price (14)_____(equal to, greater than) marginal cost. Because of the presence of barriers to entry, the monopolist (15)_____ (cannot, can) earn economic profits in the long run. With perfect competition, economic profits are competed away in the long run due to entry into the competitive industry. Further, the monopolist's price (16)_____ (equals, exceeds) the minimum possible average cost of production. Consumers pay more for the good than they would have to pay in a competitive market. Monopolization of markets in effect redistributes income from consumers to the owners of monopoly firms. Since price exceeds marginal cost, the marginal benefit to a consumer from the consumption of an additional unit of the monopolist's good will (17)_____ (be less than, exceed) the opportunity costs of the resources used to produce that good. Society's net gain (18)_____ (is, is not) maximized. That loss of potential net benefit is the (19)_____ (external, social) cost of monopoly and is measured by the triangular area between the demand and marginal cost curves from the monopolist's level of output to the level of output that would prevail in a perfectly competitive market.

Other comparisons between monopoly and perfect competition include analyses of the impact of taxes and price ceilings on a monopolist vs. a competitive firm and the effect of a price-discriminating monopolist on market quantity and price. An increase in a tax per unit of output increases the market price by an amount (20)_____(greater than, equal to) the increase in the tax for the case of perfect competition, but will result in an increase in price by (21)_____(less, greater) than the increase in the tax for a monopolist. A price ceiling (22)_____(increases, reduces) output in a perfectly competitive market, but (23)_____(increases, reduces) it in a monopoly. Price discrimination by a monopolist can result in a level of output (24)_____ (greater than, equal to) that produced by a competitive market, but price will equal marginal cost (25)_____ (for all units, only for the last unit) of output sold. All other buyers have to pay a price in excess of marginal cost. Price discrimination is feasible if the firm can control the price, the good produced (26)_____(is, is not) resalable, and customers can be differentiated according to their willingness and ability to pay.

KEY TERMS REVIEW

Write the key term from the list below next to its definition.

Key Terms

Pure monopoly	Natural monopoly
Monopoly power	Social cost of monopoly
Barrier to entry	Price discrimination

Definitions

1. _____ : the ability of a firm to influence the price of its product by making more or less of it available to buyers.

2. _____ : a constraint that prevents additional sellers from entering a monopoly firm's market.

3. _____ : a measure of the loss in potential net benefits from the reduced availability of a good stemming from monopoly control of price and supply.

4. _____ : a firm that emerges as a single seller in the market because of cost or technological advantages contributing to lower average costs of production.

5. _____ : occurs when there is a single seller of a product that has no close substitutes.

6. _____ : the practice of selling a certain product of given quality and cost per unit at different prices to different buyers.

CONCEPT REVIEW

Concept 1: *Pure monopoly*

1. List four characteristics of a pure monopoly.

a. _____

b. _____

c. _____

d. _____

Concept 2: *A monopoly firm's demand, marginal revenue and total revenue*

2. The following price and quantity demanded data are for a monopolistic market.

Price per Unit	Quantity Demanded (000s units)	Total Revenue	Marginal Revenue
$10	1	$_____	
9	2	_____	$_____
8	3	_____	_____
7	4	_____	_____
6	5	_____	_____
5	6	_____	_____
4	7	_____	_____

a. Complete the marginal revenue and total revenue columns in the above table.

b. Plot the firm's total revenue curve in a in the figure below, and plot the demand and marginal revenue curves in b.

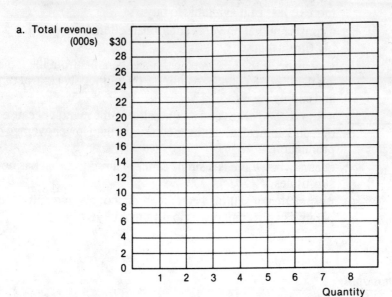

a. Total revenue (000s)

Quantity (000s units)

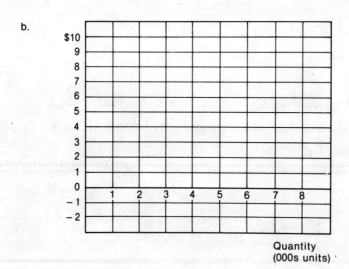

b.

Quantity (000s units)

c. Total revenue _____ when marginal revenue is positive and _____ when marginal revenue is negative. The elastic segment of the demand curve is that section over the range of output where marginal revenue is _____ and total revenue is

_____.

Concept 3: *Profit maximization of a monopolist*

3. Consider the monopoly seller's cost and demand data in the table below.

Quantity Supplied (000s)	TC (000s)	AC	MC	Quantity Demanded (000s)	Price	TR (000s)	MR	Profit (Loss) (000s)
1	$12	$12.00		1	$10	$_____		$_____
2	14	7.00	$2	2	9	_____	$_____	_____
3	17	5.67	3	3	8	_____	_____	_____
4	21	5.25	4	4	7	_____	_____	_____
5	26	5.20	5	5	6	_____	_____	_____
6	32	5.33	6	6	5	_____	_____	_____
7	39	5.57	7	7	4	_____	_____	_____

a. Complete the table.

b. Determine the monopolist's profit-maximizing price and quantity. Price = $_____, quantity = _____ units, and total profit = $_____.

c. Plot the total revenue and total cost curves in a in the figure below and identify the profit-maximizing level of output and the level of profits. Plot the marginal cost, average cost, demand, and marginal revenue curves in b and identify the level of profits and the profit-maximizing level of output and price.

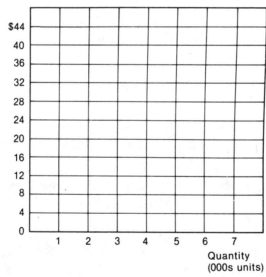

a. Total revenue, total costs (000s)

Quantity (000s units)

b.

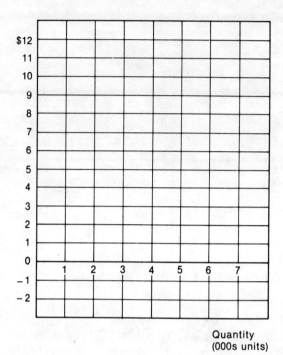

Quantity
(000s units)

d. A monopolist maximizes profits by producing at a level of output where _____ equals _____.

e. The monopolist shown in b in the figure above is operating on the _____ segment of the market demand curve.

Concept 4: *Comparison of monopoly and perfect competition*

4. Referring to b in the figure above:

a. Price _____ (exceeds, equals, is less than) marginal cost and is _____ than would be the case for perfect competition. For perfect competition, price _____ marginal cost.

b. Price _____ (exceeds, equals, is less than) marginal revenue, whereas with perfect competition, price _____ marginal revenue.

c. Price _____ (exceeds, equals, is less than) average cost, whereas with perfect competition, price _____ the minimum average cost of production.

d. Output for a monopolist occurs where _____ equals _____. A monopoly firm produces _____ output than a perfectly competitive industry.

e. In the long run, monopolists may earn _____ profits, but a perfectly competitive firm earns only _____ profits.

250

Concept 6: *Monopoly and excise taxation*

5. Suppose a tax of $1 per unit of output is levied on the monopolist shown in the figure below.

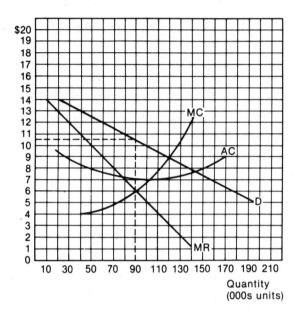

   a. Show the effect of a $1 per unit tax on the marginal and average cost curves above.

   b. The profit-maximizing price _____ and the level of output _____.
   Price _____ (increases, decreases) _____ than the $1 tax. With perfect
   competition in long-run equilibrium, the price _____ (increases, decreases) by an
   amount _____ the $1 tax.

Advanced Application: Monopoly profit maximization

6. Below are expressions for a monopolist's demand, marginal revenue, and marginal cost curves.

Demand	$P = a - bQ$
Marginal revenue	$MR = a - 2bQ$
Marginal cost	$MC = c + dQ$

   a. Find and interpret an equation for the profit-maximizing level of output.

   b. Find and interpret an equation for the monopolist's price.

   c. If $a = \$20$, $b = .1$, $c = \$5$ and $d = .25$, find the profit-maximizing price and quantity.

MASTERY TEST

Select the best answer.

1. Which of the following is not a characteristic of a pure monopoly?
   a. Single seller
   b. No close substitutes
   c. Barriers to entry
   d. Control over price
   e. Operates on the inelastic portion of the demand curve

2. Which of the following are not barriers to entry?
   a. Government franchises and licenses
   b. Copyrights and patents
   c. Control of an important resource
   d. Advantages of government lobbying efforts
   e. Economies of scale

3. Monopolies that are allowed to exist because of scale economy advantages but are regulated by the government are called:
   a. normal monopolies.
   b. natural monopolies.
   c. pure monopolies.
   d. regulated monopolies.
   e. None of the above.

4. A monopolist's marginal revenue is:
   a. equal to the product price.
   b. greater than the market price.
   c. less than the price on the market demand curve.
   d. measured by the change in output divided by the change in total revenue.
   e. c and d.

5. Marginal revenue is more steeply sloped than the demand curve because:
   a. price must be lowered in order to increase sales and the lower price pertains not just to the additional units sold but to the monopolist's total output.
   b. the monopolist restricts output.
   c. the monopolist raises price and reduces marginal revenue.
   d. the monopolist restricts output and to do that it must raise price, which applies to all units sold.

6. The monopolist maximizes profit when:
   a. marginal revenue equals average cost.
   b. price equals marginal revenue.
   c. marginal revenue equals marginal cost.
   d. price equals marginal cost.
   e. total revenue equals total cost.

7. At the monopoly seller's profit-maximizing output:
   a. price exceeds marginal revenue.
   b. price exceeds marginal cost.
   c. price exceeds average cost.
   d. economic profits are being earned.
   e. All of the above.

8. A monopolist operates on the _____ portion of the market demand curve because that is where marginal revenue is _____ and total revenue is _____.
   a. elastic, positive, increasing
   b. elastic, negative, increasing
   c. inelastic, negative, decreasing
   d. inelastic, positive, decreasing

9. A monopolist's supply curve:
   a. is the segment of its marginal cost curve above its average variable cost curve.
   b. is the market supply curve because the monopolist is the sole producer of output in the industry.
   c. is represented by the price - marginal revenue coordinates from a zero level of output to the level where price equals marginal cost.
   d. None of the above.

10. Compared to the case of perfect competition, a monopolist that does not experience significant economies of scale:
    a. charges a higher price.
    b. produces a lower level of output.
    c. earns long-run economic profits.
    d. operates at a level of output where average cost is not minimized.
    e. All of the above.

11. The social cost of monopoly is the:
    a. sacrificed net benefit to society that results from the monopolist restricting output below the competitive output.
    b. cost incurred by the justice department to control monopoly behavior.
    c. income that consumers lose as a result of paying higher monopoly prices.
    d. explicit outlays by the monopolist to acquire scarce resources.

12. The social cost of monopoly is measured by:
    a. the accounting costs of the monopolist's production.
    b. the area underlying the marginal revenue curve.
    c. the triangular area between the demand and marginal cost curves from the monopolist's level of output to the level of output that would prevail in a perfectly competitive market.
    d. the area above the average cost curve and below the demand curve.

13. A per-unit tax on output _____ the monopolist's price by _____ the tax.
    a. decreases, an amount equal to
    b. increases, an amount less than
    c. increases, an amount greater than
    d. increases, an amount equal to

14. A price ceiling _____ output in a competitive market but _____ it for a monopoly.
    a. decreases, increases
    b. decreases, decreases
    c. increases, decreases
    d. increases, increases

15. Price discrimination by a monopolist can result in a level of output _____ that produced by a competitive market, but price will equal marginal cost _____.
    a. greater than, only occasionally
    b. equal to, for all levels of output
    c. less than, for all levels of output
    d. equal to, only for the last unit of output sold

16. Which of the following best defines price discrimination?
    a. Charging different prices on the basis of race
    b. Charging different prices for goods with different costs of production
    c. Selling a certain product of given quality and cost per unit at different prices to different buyers
    d. Charging different prices based upon cost-of-service differentials

17. Which of the following is not a condition necessary to enable a monopolist to engage in price discrimination?

   a.   Must operate on the inelastic portion of the demand curve

   b.   Must be able to set the price of the product

   c.   The product must not be resalable

   d.   Must be able to differentiate customers according to willingness and ability to pay

18. If the market demand faced by a monopolist can be expressed as $P = a - bQ$ and total revenue equals PQ, which of the following gives the slope of the marginal revenue curve?

   a.   -b

   b.   Price

   c.   Marginal Revenue

   d.   -2b

19. Why does a monopolist operate on the elastic portion of a market demand curve?

   a.   Monopolists maximize profits by raising price, total revenue, and profits along the elastic segment of the demand curve.

   b.   At levels of output along the inelastic segment of the demand curve, marginal revenue is negative. Monopolists will not operate in this range because an increase in output reduces both revenues and costs.

   c.   Along the elastic segment of the demand curve, marginal revenue is negative. An increase in output will reduce total revenue less than cost, causing profits to rise.

   d.   In recessions, monopolists must operate on the elastic segment of their market demand curve, but in economic expansions they can operate further down the market demand curve in the inelastic region.

20. If a monopolist is the sole producer of a particular good, then the monopolist's marginal cost curve must be the market supply curve. True or False?

   a.   True, the intersections of marginal revenue and marginal cost determine output levels and price and those intersections occur along a given marginal cost curve.

   b.   True, that portion of the marginal cost curve above the average variable cost curve is the monopolist's supply curve.

   c.   False, it is possible to have more than one price associated with a level of output where marginal revenue and marginal cost equal.

   d.   False, the market supply curve is unrelated to the monopolist's cost curve.

21. Assume a monopolist takes over a competitive industry having constant costs. Also assume that the monopolist faces a linear market demand curve. If the monopolist restricts output by 1000 units in order to increase price by $10 per unit, what is the social loss?

    a. $5,000

    b. $10,000

    c. $5,000,000

    d. Insufficient information to answer question.

22. If a price ceiling is imposed in a monopolistic market:

    a. surpluses occur as they would in a perfectly competitive market.

    b. shortages occur as they would in a perfectly competitive market

    c. shortages occur in a perfectly competitive market, but output increases in a monopolistic market.

    d. shortages occur in a perfectly competitive market and the monopolist is induced to further restrict output.

THINK IT THROUGH

1. A monopolist produces a good for which no close substitutes exist. The monopolist therefore faces an inelastic demand. True or false? Explain.

2. Discuss the social cost of monopoly. How does society benefit from efforts by government to reduce, eliminate, or regulate monopolies?

3. Compare a perfectly competitive industry with one in which a monopolist is engaged in price discrimination.

4. Society is generally better off with perfect competition than with pure monopoly. But why does government promote regulated monopolies or natural monopolies in some industries rather than insist upon perfect competition?

ANALYZING THE NEWS

Using the skills derived from studying this chapter, analyze the economic facts that make up the following article and answer the questions below, using graphical analysis where possible.

1. What barrier to entry does NutraSweet currently enjoy?

2. How could the market for sugar substitutes be affected by the end of this entry barrier? Who stands to gain from this change? Why?

3. Why might the NutraSweet Co. not be as concerned about the loss of a barrier to entry as one might expect?

End of patent to alter market for NutraSweet

By Nancy Ryan

As NutraSweet Co. celebrates a decade of unprecedented growth and brand-name recognition on its 10th anniversary Monday, the aspartame producer faces a not-so-sweet competitive environment in the next 10 years.

Its exclusive patent on the sugar substitute, which helped revolutionize the diet-soda industry, expires in December 1992—a milestone most experts agree will dramatically change the carbonated beverage industry and the Deerfield-based manufacturer.

But "the winner in all of this is going to be the consumer," said Jesse Meyers, publisher of Beverage Digest newsletter. "We're going to have the technology of Monsanto (NutraSweet's parent company) and its competitors giving the consumers better products at lower retail prices."

A number of businesses are expected to attempt to sell aspartame as a generic commodity or under their own brand names, and several major manufacturers have come up with other sweeteners that may end up replacing aspartame for some products.

"Over the next two to five years, as the FDA approves more products, there will be better and improved sweeteners," said Tom Pirko, head of BevMark, a Los Angeles-based consultant to the beverage industry.

Johnson & Johnson's McNeil Specialty Products is awaiting Food and Drug Administration approval of its sucralose, which can be used in baked goods and other foods currently off limits to NutraSweet, and the government agency already has approved acesulfame-k, made by the German manufacturer Hoechst Celanese, for limited use.

FDA approvals for Pfizer Inc.'s alitame and NutraSweet's Sweetener 2000, which is 10,000 times sweeter than sugar, also are pending.

"They will chip away at NutraSweet as companies try out new blends. But NutraSweet is going to hang around for a long time," Pirko said. "It's part of the landscape."

No other food ingredient has gained the kind of brand identity that NutraSweet has. Its trademark red swirl has helped make the name known to almost 98 percent of Americans, according to NutraSweet's president and chief operating officer, Lauren S. Williams.

"That's up there with Pepsi-Cola and Coca-Cola, and that's for a product that has only been on the market for 10 years," Williams said.

The so-called "branded ingredient strategy," launched by former NutraSweet chairman and chief executive officer Robert Shapiro, has been a brilliant success—but not without what some have called strong-arm tactics with customers.

Though NutraSweet, which is part of Monsanto's G.D. Searle division, also produces the tabletop sweetener Equal and is included in foods and other beverages, Coke and Pepsi make up some two-thirds of the company's sales.

And it's that business relationship that has enabled the company to peddle its brand. As the sole manufacturer of aspartame, Monsanto was able to force the two giants and others to include the NutraSweet logo on their labels.

Now NutraSweet has almost complete control over the $730 million annual demand in the U.S. for artificial sweeteners, or 97 percent of the market in value.

Other factors helped pave the way for NutraSweet. Among those are aspartame's taste advantage over the previous leading sweetener, saccharine; growing concern over health and weight control; and shifting tastes in beverages—with carbonated ones outpacing fruit juices, coffee, milk, beer and even tap water. Carbonated beverages account for 27 percent of American beverage consumption, more than any other category, including water.

But the strength of NutraSweet's exclusive patent, most agree, played the largest role in its success, and the carbonated beverage industry, primarily Coke and Pepsi, are looking forward to gaining more leverage after a decade of having uncomfortable conditions imposed on them by the patentholder.

"Coke and Pepsi are accustomed to dictating to suppliers, but the tables were turned and NutraSweet could really dictate the rules of the game," said Gary Hemphill, editor of Beverage Industry magazine.

The most immediate change after 1992 will be a drop in prices, though NutraSweet and others have said that the company has already started lowering its prices. In 1982, NutraSweet cost $90 per pound, compared with $3 per pound for saccrine, according to Meyers.

It later dropped to approximately $60, then to its current $50. After the patent expires in 1992 it is expected to fall to about $20. One pound of NutraSweet can sweeten approximately 105 cases of soda.

Whether potential competitors can sell aspartame for less remains unanswered, though some analysts doubt they could beat NutraSweet's price.

"NutraSweet will fight to keep market share. If it means cutting the price, then it will mean cutting the price," said William R. Young, analyst at Donaldson, Lufkin and Jenrette.

Competitors most likely will bypass the high cost of advertising and brand development and simply produce a generic product they could offer to beverage companies at a price lower than NutraSweet, Pirko said.

Continued on next page

Source: "End of Patent to Alter Market for NutraSweet," The Chicago Tribune, July 15, 1991, Section 4, pp. 1 and 5.

Continued from previous page

The only likely competitor in the brand-name category is Holland Sweetener, a joint venture of Dutch State Mines of the Netherlands and Tosoh Corp., a Japanese industrial company, according to Manuel K. Pyles, an analyst with A.G. Edwards in St. Louis.

Holland Sweetener, which has taken NutraSweet to court a number of times to challenge its patent in the U.S., has said it intends to launch a competing brand here.

The biggest question that remains is whether Coke and Pepsi will stay with NutraSweet and, if so, for how long.

"Will Coke or Pepsi drop it knowing full well that their competitor will not drop it?" Meyers said. "Who will blink first? If one drops it, will the other than embark on an ad campaign showing consumers they still use NutraSweet while the other is fooling around with an unproven product?"

The stakes are too high for either producer to experiment with their diet formulas, and with lower prices after the patent expiration, Coke and Pepsi likely will stay with NutraSweet for at least a few years after 1992, Pyles said. Neither company would comment on its plans.

Smaller beverage producers, such as 7-Up, Royal Crown or Dr. Pepper, might take the first plunge in experimenting with new artificial sweeteners since "they wouldn't have much to lose, but they'd have a lot to gain," Hemphill said.

Such decisions will become even more critical over the next 25 years, during which time observers expect diet soda to outsell regular sugared sodas.

Diet carbonated beverages now account for 29.4 percent of all industry sales and have been the fastest growing category in the last decade, growing by 8.9 percent in the last year. Sugared soda has grown by only 2 to 5 percent in each of the last five years, according to Gary Gerdemann, spokesman for Pepsi.

None of these factors has gone unnoticed by NutraSweet, and the manufacturer has taken a number of steps to prepare for the transition, Williams said.

The company, which reported almost $1 billion in sales and $183 million in net earnings last year, completed a reorganization in April. Some 170 employees were laid off and departments were restructured to help NutraSweet focus more on its customers.

Additionally, NutraSweet, which spends $41 million annually on research, will continue to develop new products and to market its fat substitute Simplesse as a food ingredient.

Just as other U.S. food companies are looking to new overseas markets, NutraSweet is investigating ways to expand in countries where diet sodas are still new. The high cost of importing sugar in some countries has sparked interest in aspartame, Williams said.

Though NutraSweet has 75 percent of the artificial sweetener market worldwide, it makes up less than 1 percent of all sweeteners, Williams said.

"There's a tremendous opportunity for us to replace sugar," Williams said. "In many markets, NutraSweet costs less than sugar.... It's more cost-effective for them."

CHAPTER ANSWERS

The Chapter in Brief

1. No close 2. Control of an important resource 3. Natural 4. The market 5. Falls 6. Less 7. Equals 8. Exceeds 9. Exceed 10. Elastic 11. Higher 12. Restricting output below 13. Exceeds 14. Equal to 15. Can 16. Exceeds 17. Exceed 18. Is not 19. Social 20. Equal to 21. Less 22. Reduces 23. Increases 24. Equal to 25. Only for the last unit 26. Is not

Key Terms Review

1. Monopoly power 2. Barrier to entry 3. Social cost of monopoly 4. Natural monopoly 5. Pure monopoly 6. Price discrimination

Concept Review

1. a. Single seller b. No close substitutes c. Can control price d. Barriers to entry

2. a.

Total Revenue	Marginal Revenue
$10,000	
18,000	$8
24,000	6
28,000	4
30,000	2
30,000	0
28,000	-2

b.

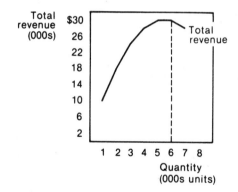

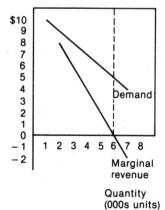

c. Increases, decreases; positive, rising

3. a.

TR	MR	Profit (loss)
$10,000		($2,000)
18,000	$8	4,000
24,000	6	7,000
28,000	4	7,000
30,000	2	4,000
30,000	0	(2,000)
28,000	-2	(11,000)

b. $7, 4,000 units, $7,000

c.

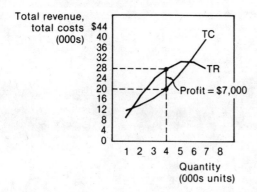

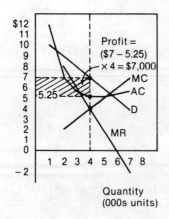

d. Marginal revenue, marginal cost

e. Elastic

4. a. Exceeds, greater; equals b. Exceeds, equals c. Exceeds, equals d. Marginal revenue, marginal cost; less e. Economic, normal

5. a.

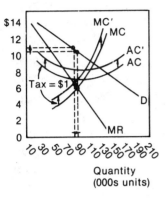

b. Increases, decreases; increases, less; increases, equal to

6. a. The profit-maximizing output equation can be found by first setting marginal revenue equal to marginal cost and then solving for output.

$$MR = MC$$

$$a - 2bQ = c + dQ$$

$$Q = (a - c)/(d + 2b)$$

An increase in a—an upward shift in the demand and marginal revenue curves—will increase the profit-maximizing output. An increase in c—an upshift in the marginal cost curve—will decrease the profit-maximizing quantity. As can be seen in the denominator of the quantity equation, changes in the slopes of the demand, marginal revenue, and marginal cost curves will also influence the profit-maximizing output.

b. Substituting the profit-maximizing quantity equation, Q, for Q in the demand curve yields the price required to maximize profit.

$$P = a - bQ$$

$$P = a - bQm \qquad \text{where } Qm=(a - c)/(d + 2b)$$

$$P = [bc + a(b + d)]/(d + 2b)$$

An increase in c or a will result in the monopolist raising price. Changes in the slopes of the curves will also likely affect the monopolist's price.

c. Qm = 33.33 units; Pm = $16.67

Mastery Test

1. d 2. d 3. b 4. c 5. a 6. c 7. e 8. a 9. d 10. e 11. a 12. c 13. b 14. a 15. d 16. c 17. a 18. d 19. b 20. c 21. a 22. c

Think it Through

1. False. The monopolist will never operate on the inelastic portion of the market demand curve because marginal revenue is negative and increases in production reduce total revenues while costs continue to increase.

2. The social cost of monopoly is the sacrificed net benefit that could have been realized if the market operated at the higher competitive level of output where price equals marginal cost. Social policies designed to replace monopoly with competition or to regulate monopolies such that output is not restricted and price equals marginal cost will allow society to realize the maximum net benefits from the allocation of resources. This assumes that the monopolies in question exist for reasons other than significant scale economies.

3. A price-discriminating monopolist produces at the same level of output as does a perfectly competitive industry—where price equals marginal cost, or in other words, where the market demand curve intersects the marginal cost curve. The monopolist, however, is able to redistribute the net gains to society of this level of output away from consumers to the monopolist's owners. Price equals marginal cost as it does for perfect competition, but only for the last unit of output sold.

4. Some monopolies exist largely because of scale economies. They must be large in order to realize an efficient use of plant and an efficient scale of operation. Even though economic profits are earned, a monopolist with significant scale economies might produce more output at a lower price than would be the case if the industry were made up of many small, inefficiently sized firms. States allow utilities such as electric power companies to exist as regional monopolies, but the states regulate prices so that the benefits of large-scale production can be passed on to consumers.

Analyzing the News

1. NutraSweet's barrier to entry is a patent on its product. Such patents prevent other firms from entering this market with identical products for 17 years.

2. When the patent expires, firms that were previously kept out of this lucrative and expanding sugar-substitute market will be able (theoretically) to compete with NutraSweet by introducing their own sugar-substitutes at potentially lower prices. If or when competition intensifies, the price elasticity of demand for NutraSweet should become more elastic, and all sugar-substitute prices will fall. Consumers stand to benefit from the expiration of the patent with the arrival of new products and lower prices. It could be argued that NutraSweet recognizes the fact that competitive pressures will mount when their patent expires, since they have already begun to lower prices. This price reduction in effect concedes the market to competition as the barrier to entry approaches extinction.

3. As is often the case, firms that have established monopoly power enjoy profit reserves high enough to invest in the establishment of brand name loyalty through advertising. As customers grow to identify certain popular products with certain companies, and if these companies are fortunate enough to face little or no competition, once artificial barriers to entry are reduced the firm that has achieved brand name identification and loyal customers may not lose considerable market share to new rivals. As the article mentions, NutraSweet currently enjoys a 97 percent market share, and 98 percent of Americans recognize its products name. Therefore, brand name identification can help maintain market share and can become yet another barrier to entry for potential competitors of NutraSweet.

13 MONOPOLISTIC COMPETITION AND OLIGOPOLY

CHAPTER CONCEPTS

After studying your text, attending class, and completing this chapter, you should be able to:

1. Define monopolistic competition in markets and show how outcomes in such markets differ from those expected under perfect competition and pure monopoly.
2. Define oligopoly and analyze market outcomes under oligopoly.
3. Explain the concept of a cartel and show how it differs from a pure monopoly.
4. Discuss price leadership, price rigidity, entry-limit pricing, and advertising in oligopolistic markets.

THE CHAPTER IN BRIEF

Fill in the blanks to summarize chapter content.

Perfect competition and pure monopoly represent extreme market structures. Virtually all markets fall somewhere in between. Monopolistic competition and oligopoly are two such imperfectly competitive markets. Monopolistic competition is characterized by (a) (1)_____ (few firms, a large number of firms) with small market shares, (b) the production of goods that (2)_____ (are not, are) perfect substitutes, (c) (3)_____ (concern, lack of concern) regarding rivals' reactions to price and production policy, (d) relative freedom of entry and exit, and (e) (4)_____ (no, significant) opportunity or incentive to collude to limit competition.

In the short run, the monopolistic competitor finds the profit-maximizing price and quantity by producing at a level of output where (5)_____(marginal revenue, price) equals marginal cost. The firm must set a price to achieve sales at this level of output because it faces a (6)_____ (market, downward-sloping) demand curve. The demand and marginal revenue curves are flatter or (7)_____(less, more) elastic than in the case of monopoly because the goods in question, while not perfect substitutes, are nevertheless substitutes in consumption. In contrast, the monopolist produces a good for which there are no close substitutes. A perfectly competitive firm faces a horizontal demand curve because the goods produced in the market by various firms are perfect substitutes.

Short-run profits or losses will have the same effect on the monopolistic competitor as they do on the perfect competitor. Economic profits result in (8)_____(exiting from, entry into) the industry, whereas losses result in (9)_____ (exiting from, entry into) the industry. (10)_____(Profits, Losses) that cause firms to enter an industry will shift an existing firm's demand and marginal revenue curves leftward until they are just tangent to the firm's (11)_____ (marginal, average) cost curve. (12)_____ (Profits, Losses) cause exiting of firms in the long run and cause a rightward shift in a firm's demand and marginal revenue curves until they are again just tangent to the (13)_____(marginal, average) cost curve. In the long run, the monopolistically competitive firm will earn (14)_____ (zero economic, zero normal) profits and will charge a price (15)_____(greater than, equal to) average cost, but the price charged will (16)_____ (equal, exceed) both marginal cost and the minimum average cost of production. The industry operates in long-run equilibrium with too (17)_____ (many, few) firms, each having (18)_____(insufficient, excess) capacity.

Whereas neither the perfectly competitive firm nor the monopolist has an incentive to advertise, the monopolistic competitor often uses substantial resources to advertise, establish brand names, and develop and improve products. In the short run, such efforts can shift the demand and marginal revenue curves (19)_____(rightward, leftward) and may even make them steeper or (20)_____(more, less) elastic. But the selling costs associated with product promotion and advertising increase average costs as well. In the long run, however, entry or exiting ensure that such efforts (21)_____ (produce, have no lasting effect on) economic profits. The consumer can benefit from the information content in advertisements and the variety of products that are produced as firms try to differentiate their products. But prices (22)_____(may be higher, are always lower) as a result of the product promotion and differentiation.

(23)_____(Monopolistic competition, Oligopoly) is a market structure with (24)_____ (a few, many) dominant firms having large market shares and producing either standardized or differentiated goods. Other characteristics include the necessity of considering rivals' reactions and the presence of barriers to entry. There is no single behavioral model of oligopoly. The oligopolistic market results in different outcomes depending upon how rivals react to a given oligopolist's decision to change price or promotion policy and other decisions. If each oligopolist assumes that rival oligopolists will not react to a price cut, then each firm believes it can increase market share by reducing price. This results in (25)_____ (price leadership, a price war), causing the price to fall to the (26)_____(average, marginal) cost of production. A (27)_____ (cartel, contestable) market is one in which oligopolists reduce price to average cost in order to eliminate the incentive for new firms to enter the market.

Price warring and contestable markets benefit consumers through lower prices, but deplete economic profits. Since oligopolists have large market shares and are few in number, there is an incentive to collude to restrict industry output and increase market price and profit. In effect, there is an incentive to coordinate their activities such that they can jointly produce an outcome identical to that of (28)_____(monopoly, monopolistic competition). A (29)_____(cartel, contestable market) is created by an agreement among oligopolists to restrict market output and share in the sales and profits resulting from the higher market price. There is an incentive to form cartels if barriers to entry (30)_____(exist, do not exist), market and firm production targets can be agreed upon, and the agreement can be enforced. But once a cartel is formed, members have an incentive to cheat and to produce beyond their quota in order to increase profits. Cheating will work for a firm only if the change in market supply resulting from its increase in production (31)_____ (influences, does not influence) the market price and if it can be carried out undetected.

Two other models of oligopoly are the price leadership and price rigidity models. In a (32)_____ (price leadership, cartel) oligopoly, the dominant oligopolist takes the lead and establishes the market price and the less dominant firms follow shortly with similar prices. This behavior avoids price warring and brings some stability to the industry. Even though the dominant firm's price may not maximize the profits of the other oligopolists, the fear of predatory pricing by the dominant firm may be great enough to keep the other firms in a price follower pattern.

If oligopolists react to a price cut by reducing prices but do not match price increases, a kink in the demand curve results where there is a noticeable change in the elasticity of demand. Demand is more elastic above the kink and less elastic or even inelastic below the kink. A change in price above or below the kink will likely reduce total revenues. Therefore the price tends to (33)_____(be flexible, remain rigid) at the kink. Changes in costs that shift the marginal cost curve over a given range (34)_____(may not have any, always have an) impact on the profit-maximizing level of output and price and are another reason why the price is rigid.

KEY TERMS REVIEW

Write the key term from the list below next to its definition.

Key Terms

Imperfect competition	Oligopoly
Monopolistic competition	Price war
Product group	Contestable market
Excess capacity	Cartel
Selling costs	Price leader

Definitions

1. _____: exists when more than one seller competes for sales with other sellers of competitive products, each of whom has some control over price.

2. _____: represents several closely related, but not identical, items that serve the same general purpose for consumers.

3. _____: all costs incurred by a firm to influence the sales of its product.

4. _____: a market structure in which a few sellers dominate the sales of the product and where entry of new sellers is difficult or impossible.

5. _____: a market in which entry of sellers is easy and exit is not very costly.

6. _____: a group of firms acting together to coordinate output decisions and control prices as if they were a single monopoly.

7. _____: exists when many sellers compete to sell a differentiated product in a market in which entry of new sellers is possible.

8. _____: the difference between the output corresponding to minimum possible average cost and that produced by the monopolistically competitive firm in the long run.

9. _____: a bout of continual price cutting by rival firms in a market; one of many possible consequences of oligopolistic rivalry.

10. _____: one dominant firm in an industry that sets its price to maximize its own profits, after which other firms follow its lead by setting exactly the same price.

CONCEPT REVIEW

Concept 1: *Monopolistic competition; comparison to perfect competition and pure monopoly*

1. List five characteristics of a monopolistically competitive market.

    a. _____

    b. _____

    c. _____

    d. _____

    e. _____

2. The diagram below represents a monopolistically competitive firm in short-run equilibrium.

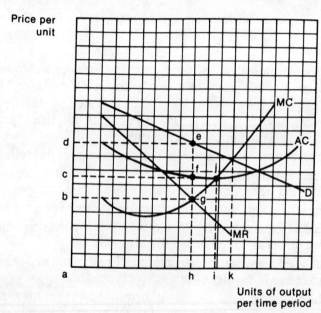

    a. Short-run profits are maximized where _____ equals _____. The profit-maximizing price = $_____, and quantity = _____ units.

    b. This firm has short-run economic _____ (profits, losses) equal to area _____ in the figure above.

    c. In the long run, _____ causes the firm's demand and marginal revenue curves to shift _____ until the demand curve is just tangent to the _____ curve.

    d. Show the long-run equilibrium on the figure above.

e. In long-run equilibrium:
  (1) Price _____ marginal cost
  (2) Price _____ average cost
  (3) Price _____ minimum average cost
  (4) Economic profits = $_____

3. The figure below represents a monopolistically competitive firm in short-run equilibrium.

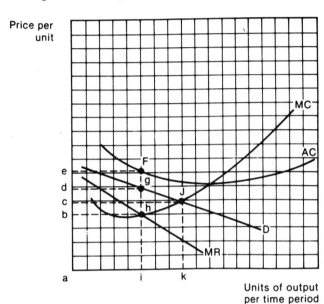

a. The profit-maximizing or loss-minimizing level of output and price are _____ units and $_____, respectively.

b. The firm has short-run economic _____ (profits, losses) equal to area _____ in the figure above.

c. In the long run, _____ causes the firm's demand and marginal revenue curves to shift _____ until the demand curve is just tangent to the _____ curve.

d. Show the long-run equilibrium on the figure above.

e. In long-run equilibrium:
  (1) Price _____ marginal cost
  (2) Price _____ average cost
  (3) Price _____ minimum average cost
  (4) Economic profit = $_____

4. As compared to perfect competition, monopolistic competition results in:
   a. (Same, higher, lower) price.
   b. (Same, higher, lower) output.
   c. (Same, higher, lower) average cost.
   d. (Same, more efficient, less efficient) capacity utilization.
   e. (Same, more, less) economic profit.
   f. (Same, more, less) net benefits to society.
   g. (Same, more, less) product promotion and development.

5. List four similarities and four dissimilarities between monopolistic competition in long-run equilibrium and pure monopoly.
   a. Similarities
      (1) _____
      (2) _____
      (3) _____
      (4) _____
   b. Dissimilarities
      (1) _____
      (2) _____
      (3) _____
      (4) _____

Concepts 2, 3, and 4: *Oligopoly; oligopoly behavior and market outcomes*

6. List three characteristics of oligopoly.
   a. _____
   b. _____
   c. _____

7. The figure below represents an oligopolist in short-run equilibrium in an industry in which each oligopolist believes that a price decrease will *not* be matched by rival oligopolists.

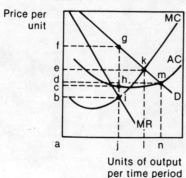

270

a. The oligopolist maximizes profit by equating _____ and _____. Economic profits equal area _____, price = $_____, and quantity = _____ units.

b. Suppose this oligopolist cuts price in order to increase market share. Show the effect graphically in the figure below.

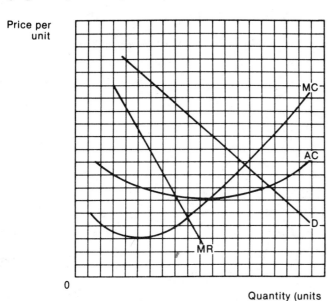

c. If other oligopolists react by also cutting prices, the oligopolist that initiated the price reduction must _____ (match, not match) the price decrease in order to maintain market share. If a price war develops, price could potentially fall to a level equal to _____. Show the effect of price warring in the figure above. What happens to economic profit?

d. Price wars create an incentive for rival oligopolists to _____. A formal agreement of output restriction and market sharing is known as a _____. The intent of such a restriction and market sharing is to approximate the market outcome of a _____.

8. Consider the following figure of an oligopolist.

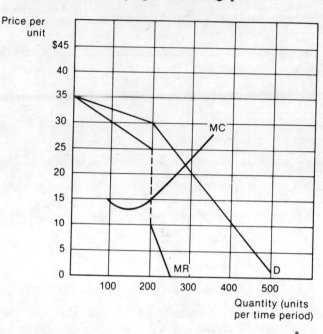

a. Explain the behavioral reactions of rival oligopolists that produce the "kink" in the demand curve.

b. Profits are maximized at a level of output where _____ equals _____.
   Price = $_____ and quantity = _____ units.

c. Show on the figure above the effect of an increase in marginal cost of $5 at each level of output and a decrease of $5. An increase in marginal cost of $5 at each level of output causes the profit-maximizing price and quantity to _____. A decrease in marginal cost of $5 at each level of output causes the profit-maximizing price and quantity to _____.

d. Prices are _____ (rigid, flexible) given certain shifts in the marginal cost curve in the discontinuous section of the marginal revenue curve.

MASTERY TEST

Select the best answer.

1. Which of the following is not a characteristic associated with monopolistic competition?
   a. There is a large number of firms with small market shares.
   b. Goods produced by firms within the industry are not perfect substitutes.
   c. Firms are unconcerned with the reaction of rival firms.
   d. There are barriers to entry.
   e. There is no opportunity or incentive to collude to limit competition.

2. The demand and marginal revenue curves faced by a monopolistic competitor are flatter or more elastic than the demand and marginal revenue curves faced by a monopolist because:

   a. the demand for the good is very responsive to changes in income.

   b. the goods produced in the industry, while not perfect substitutes, are nevertheless close substitutes.

   c. the goods in the industry are unique and are not substitutes.

   d. entry and exiting by firms makes consumers more responsive to price changes.

3. A monopolistically competitive firm maximizes profit at the level of output where:

   a. price equals marginal revenue.

   b. price equals marginal cost.

   c. marginal cost equals average revenue.

   d. marginal revenue equals marginal cost.

4. In the short run, economic profits cause _____ the monopolistically competitive industry and a _____ shift in the demand and marginal revenue curves.

   a. entry into, leftward

   b. entry into, rightward

   c. exiting from, leftward

   d. exiting from, rightward

5. In the short run, losses cause _____ the monopolistically competitive industry and a _____ shift in the demand and marginal revenue curves.

   a. entry into, leftward

   b. entry into, rightward

   c. exiting from, leftward

   d. exiting from, rightward

6. In a monopolistically competitive industry, short-run losses or economic profits will cause the demand curve to shift to the point where in long-run equilibrium, it:

   a. intersects the supply curve.

   b. intersects the average variable cost curve.

   c. is just tangent to the average cost curve.

   d. is just tangent to the marginal cost curve.

7. Monopolistic competition and perfect competition are similar in which of the following ways?

   a. In long-run equilibrium, economic profits are zero.

   b. Price exceeds marginal cost.

   c. Price equals minimum average cost.

   d. There is relative freedom of entry and exit.

   e. A and d.

8. Which of the following market structures is associated with significant advertising and product development?
    a. Perfect competition
    b. Pure monopoly
    c. Monopolistic competition
    d. Oligopoly
    e. C and d

9. Because the monopolistic competitor charges a price _____ marginal cost, net benefits to society _____.
    a. equal to, are maximized
    b. less than, are maximized
    c. equal to, are not maximized
    d. greater than, are not maximized

10. Which of the following is not a characteristic associated with oligopoly?
    a. Few firms
    b. Standardized or differentiated goods
    c. Lack of concern regarding a rival's behavior
    d. Large market shares
    e. Barriers to entry

11. If each oligopolist in a given industry believes that its rivals will not match price cuts:
    a. price wars can develop resulting in economic profits for all but the smallest oligopolists.
    b. there is no incentive to reduce prices and risk a price war.
    c. a price war can develop, resulting in prices falling to a level equal to average cost.
    d. a kink appears in the oligopolist's demand and marginal revenue curves.

12. If each oligopolist in a given industry matches price cuts but does not match price increases:
    a. price wars develop, resulting in zero economic profits.
    b. prices become rigid at the intersection of the marginal revenue and average cost curves.
    c. prices become flexible due to the price-cutting behavior.
    d. prices become rigid at the kink in the demand curve.

13. Prices are rigid at the kink of an oligopolist's demand curve because:

    a. of the distinct change in the elasticity of demand at the kink.

    b. changes in fixed costs have no impact on the profit-maximizing price.

    c. changes in marginal cost in the discontinuous section of the marginal revenue curve do not alter the profit-maximizing price and output.

    d. a and c.

    e. All of the above.

14. A contestable market is one in which

    a. there are significant transaction costs associated with exiting an industry.

    b. entry is difficult, but exiting is costless.

    c. entry is easy and exiting is not very costly.

    d. rival oligopolists engage in predatory pricing.

15. In order to prevent entry into a contestable market, oligopolists:

    a. set prices very high to earn monopoly profits.

    b. set prices equal to marginal costs to maximize profits.

    c. set prices to reduce normal profits to zero.

    d. set prices at a level equal to average cost.

16. Price warring creates an incentive by oligopolists to collude. A formal agreement to restrict output and share markets is called a:

    a. pure monopoly.

    b. restrictive oligopoly.

    c. cartel.

    d. quota.

17. Which of the following conditions are necessary for a cartel to exist?

    a. Barriers to entry

    b. Agreement on total market production levels

    c. Agreement on individual firms' share of total output

    d. Ability to police and enforce the agreement

    e. All of the above

18. An oligopolistic market in which the dominant oligopolist establishes the industry price, which subsequently is matched by the other oligopolists, is characterized by:

    a. illegal collusion.

    b. price leadership.

    c. predatory pricing.

    d. price discrimination.

19. Which of the following statements is true regarding monopolistic competition and allocative efficiency?

   a. Monopolistic competition achieves allocative efficiency because price equals average cost in long-run equilibrium.

   b. In the long run, price equals marginal cost but exceeds average cost, causing the monopolistic competitor to fall short of allocative efficiency.

   c. In the long run, allocative efficiency is not achieved in monopolistic competition because price is greater than marginal cost.

   d. Allocative efficiency is achieved in monopolistic competition because economic profits are eliminated in the long run.

20. Suppose you are a manager of laundry, a monopolistically competitive firm, and your firm is in long-run equilibrium. You decide to advertise in order to increase sales and to distinguish your services from that of your rivals. What adjustments occur as your firm moves to a new long-run equilibrium?

   a. Average cost curve shifts upward, demand and marginal revenue curves shift rightward and become less elastic, and price rises.

   b. Marginal cost curve shifts downward, demand and marginal revenue curves shift rightward and become more elastic, and price falls.

   c. Sales increase, causing supply to rise and price to fall.

   d. Marginal cost curve shifts rightward, causing output and price to rise.

21. Cartels may fail in the long run to restrict output and charge monopolistic prices because:

   a. the elasticity of demand and supply will decrease in the long run, causing price to fall and output to rise.

   b. price (and marginal revenue) exceeds marginal cost at the restricted level of output, creating an incentive for cartel members to cheat by secretly selling output at prices below the cartel price but above marginal cost.

   c. they are against the law and eventually will be successfully prosecuted.

   d. price and marginal revenue equal marginal cost at the restricted level of output, inducing cartel members to engage in clandestine price cutting.

22. Which of the following models of oligopoly may result in price falling to a level equal to average cost?

   a. Price leadership

   b. Kinked demand curve

   c. Cartel

   d. Contestable market

23. Assume an oligopoly exists in which rivals match price cuts, but do not match price increases. Which of the following models of oligopoly characterizes this interdependent behavior?

   a. Price war

   b. Kinked demand curve

   c. Price leadership

   d. Cartel

   e. Contestable market

THINK IT THROUGH

1. Discuss the advantages and disadvantages of monopolistic competition relative to perfect competition.

2. Which market structure best fits the video rental business in your community? Explain. What are your expectations for that industry as it attains long-run equilibrium?

3. Discuss the forces that tend to make cartels unworkable over the long run.

4. Why is it difficult to compare the market outcomes of oligopoly to those of other market structures?

ANALYZING THE NEWS

Using the skills derived from studying this chapter, analyze the economic facts that make up the following article and answer the questions below, using graphical analysis where possible.

1. How can General Motors or Ford announce or set prices that are expected to be followed? Do they not operate in a purely competitive market?

2. Suppose the price elasticity of demand for Ford automobiles is elastic. Considering the competitive role of foreign car manufacturers in United States markets, how might a price increase affect Ford's total revenue?

3. Explain the impact higher safety and emission standards can have on car producers. How are consumers affected?

Ford sets 4.7% price increase for '92 models

By Jim Mateja
Auto writer

Ford Motor Co. has put General Motors on the spot by informing its dealers that tentative 1992 model prices will be an average of 4.7 percent, or $700, higher.

Traditionally, as the industry's largest automaker, GM sets the pricing pattern each model year. Ford and Chrysler announce tentative prices that free dealers to take orders on the coming models, but it's not until GM announces its prices that Ford and Chrysler adjust their own up or down to remain competitive.

Ford is the first of the Big Three to announce tentative prices. The 4.7 percent boost is a test to see how GM will respond, by initiating even higher prices or by holding the line.

Some analysts questioned how big a price increase the market will bear.

"They can't sell cars at the prices they're asking now. How can they raise prices any more?" asked Thomas O'Grady, president of Integrated Automotive Resources in Wayne, Pa.

"What Ford is doing is role-playing, telling GM, 'OK, we bet $700, now what are you going to do?' " he said.

Robert Rewey, vice president of sales for Ford, said the tentative price increase "only partially recovers Ford's costs for 1992."

He said, "When the government dictates how you design cars to meet federal safety and emissions laws, you have to recover your investment through price increases."

Tentative prices typically are announced in the summer to encourage advance orders on the new models and allow dealers to sell early arrivals from the factory as soon as they reach showrooms. Tentative pricing also gives fleet customers, early buyers of the new models, an idea of what they can expect to pay.

The Ford price boost can let GM portray itself as the industry hero and come out with a smaller increase, making it appear to be holding the line on prices at a time when the economy is weak and sales are soft.

Alternately, GM can top the mark set by Ford and look like a greedy villain trying to make up for lost profits at the expense of the consumer.

GM gave an early clue as to what to expect.

Based on Olds' pricing of its early '92 model arrivals in the full-size 88 lineup, it appears that a significant, but somewhat camouflaged, price increase is in the works at GM.

In June, for example, Oldsmobile said its 1992 Royale and Royale LS, now arriving in showrooms, were to be priced $280 and $770 lower, respectively, than the 1991 models.

In order to save $280 or $770, however, the consumer would be spending $1,300 to $2,600 more for the '92s. The difference is in the options that have become standard. The resulting price increases amounted to 7.5 to 13.8 percent.

The base price of the Olds 88 Royale for '92 is $18,495, a $1,300 increase from $17,195 for the '91 model. The '92 Royale LS was priced at $21,395, a $2,600 jump from $18,795 for '91.

Olds arrived at its "savings" for '92 by saying the optional driver-side air bag that cost $850 for '91 is standard for '92; so don't count the $850 built into the '92 sticker price as an increase. Other previous options made standard for 1992 were a split bench seat ($133 option in 1991), power windows ($340 option in 1991), 15-inch wheels and whitewall tires ($104), dual visor mirrors ($20), hood and trunk lamps ($14), temperature gauge and oil sensors ($39), heavy-duty cooling system ($40) and pass-key theft deterrent system ($40).

In informing its dealers of tentative 1992 prices, Ford said the price of the slow-selling Probe built in cooperation with Mazda would not be increased. A new Probe will be introduced later in the year. But dealers also were told the F-Series truck, Ford's best-selling vehicle, would go up 8 percent.

Firm 1992 prices usually are set by the carmakers in September.

Source: "Ford Sets 4.7% Price Increase for '92 Models," *The Chicago Tribune*.

CHAPTER ANSWERS

The Chapter in Brief

1. A large number of firms 2. Are not 3. Lack of concern 4. No 5. Marginal revenue 6. Downward-sloping 7. More 8. Entry into 9. Exiting from 10. Profits 11. Average 12. Losses 13. Average 14. Zero economic 15. Equal to 16. Exceed 17. Many 18. Excess 19. Rightward 20. Less 21. Have no lasting effect on 22. May be higher 23. Oligopoly 24. A few 25. A price war 26. Average 27. Contestable 28. Monopoly 29. Cartel 30. Exist 31. Does not influence 32. Price leadership 33. Remain rigid 34. May not have any

Key Terms Review

1. Imperfect competition 2. Product group 3. Selling costs 4. Oligopoly 5. Contestable market 6. Cartel 7. Monopolistic competition 8. Excess capacity 9. Price war 10. Price leader

Concept Review

1. a. There is a large number of firms with small market shares.

   b. Goods are close but not perfect substitutes.

   c. There is lack of concern regarding the reaction of rivals.

   d. There is freedom of entry and exit.

   e. There is no opportunity or incentive to collude to limit competition.

2. a. Marginal revenue, marginal cost; $ad, ah units

   b. Profits, cdef

   c. Entry, leftward, average cost

   d.

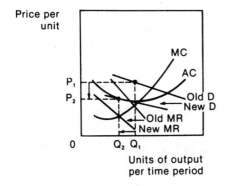

   e. (1) Exceeds (2) Equals (3) Exceeds (4) $0

3. a. ai units, $ad

   b. Losses, defg

   c. Exiting, rightward, average cost

   d.

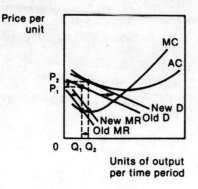

   e. (1) Exceeds (2) Equals (3) Exceeds (4) $0

4. a. Higher b. Lower c. Higher d. Less efficient e. Same f. Less g. More

5. a. (1) Price exceeds minimum average cost.

      (2) Price exceeds marginal cost.

      (3) Price exceeds the competitive price.

      (4) Output is less than the competitive output.

   b. (1) Price equals average cost for monopolistic competition, but exceeds average cost for a monopolist.

      (2) Economic profit is zero for the monopolistic competitor but positive for the monopolist.

      (3) Monopolistic competition is associated with ease of entry, whereas monopoly has barriers to entry.

      (4) Monopolistic competitors have incentives to advertise and engage in product development, whereas monopolists have little if any incentive to promote or improve their product.

6. a. Few firms with large market shares

   b. Standardized or differentiated goods

   c. Barriers to entry

7. a. Marginal revenue, marginal cost; cfgh, $af, aj units

b.

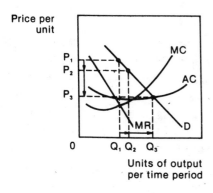

Price per unit — P₁, P₂, P₃, MC, AC, MR, D, Q₁, Q₂, Q₃
Units of output per time period

c. Match, average cost; economic profits fall to zero

d. Collude; cartel; monopolist

8. a. The kink in the demand curve results from rival oligopolists matching price cuts but not matching price increases. The logic is that the firm must match price cuts or lose market share. With price increases, a firm could increase market share by not matching the price increase and capturing a portion of the market share previously held by the oligopolist that raised its price. As a result, below the kink demand is much less elastic or inelastic because a price reduction does not increase sales very much since other oligopolists are also reducing prices. In contrast, an increase in price results in large sales losses because other firms have maintained their prices at the lower level. Here demand is much more elastic.

b. Marginal revenue, marginal cost, $30, 200 units

c.

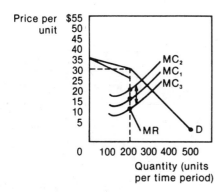

Price per unit — $55, 50, 45, 40, 35, 30, 25, 20, 15, 10, 5; MC₂, MC₁, MC₃, MR, D
0, 100, 200, 300, 400, 500
Quantity (units per time period)

Not change, not change

d. Rigid

Mastery Test

1. d 2. b 3. d 4. a 5. d 6. c 7. e 8. e 9. d 10. c 11. c 12. d 13. d 14. c 15. d 16. c 17. e 18. b 19. c 20. a 21. b 22. d 23. b

Think it Through

1. Monopolistic competition results in product differentiation. Perfect competition is associated with a homogeneous good. Consumers benefit by having a greater variety of goods. Consumers, however, pay a higher price for less efficiently produced goods. Allocative efficiency is not achieved because the price charged by the monopolistic competitor exceeds marginal cost. While product advertising may increase the information available to consumers, resulting in more efficient choices, the selling costs represent resources that would otherwise be available for the production of goods in a perfectly competitive economy.

2. In a local market, the video rental industry is a monopolistically competitive market. There are numerous firms each with a small market share. Short-run economic profits attract new entrants to the industry. The product is differentiated by advertising, the length of the rental period, store hours, method of payment, and convenience in pickup and return. Even price discrimination is practiced in that popular new releases have a less elastic demand than older releases and often carry a higher rental fee. Because of the number of firms and the certainty of entry in response to economic profits, it would be very difficult to collude to limit competition. In the long run, the video rental business will have too many firms, each with excess capacity and earning only normal profits.

3. The monopoly price resulting from a cartel's restriction of output will likely not be the price that maximizes profit for the individual cartel members. Each firm will probably have somewhat different average and marginal costs of production. Beyond the firm's share of cartel profits resulting from the sale of a specified level of output at the cartel price, the firm could increase profits even more by reducing prices to other buyers. This will work only if the increase in production does not affect market price and the cartel either does not detect the clandestine price cutting or cannot enforce the cartel agreement. If several of the members are doing this, market price will fall and the cartel will effectively be broken.

4. The market outcomes of oligopoly depend, among other considerations, upon the reactions of rival oligopolists, the scope of the market—local, regional, national, or international—and the ease of entry and exit. An oligopolist may operate where price equals average cost or, because of scale economies, may even charge a price less than that of a perfectly competitive firm. On the other hand, an oligopolist may charge a price in excess of marginal and average cost and earn economic profits in the long run. There is no given model of oligopolistic behavior that fits all oligopolistic industries. Differences in firm behavior produce differences in outcomes. In order to assess oligopoly relative to other market structures, each oligopolistic market must be considered unique and studied individually.

Analyzing the News

1. The domestic automobile market is not purely competitive. The market is an oligopolistic market structure where Ford, General Motors, and Chrysler are the dominant domestic automobile manufacturers. These firms rely on product differentiation and advertising to distinguish their products from their rivals'. The key to their ability to set or announce prices is that they enjoy market power (although this power has been and will continue to be eroded by foreign competition). Additionally, each firm realizes its mutual interdependence. This interdependence forces

each company to consider the choices its rival will make in response to any "announced" price changes. Obviously, Ford is assuming General Motors and Chrysler will follow with price hikes as well. What is unusual about the current situation is that Ford, not GM (the historical price leader), was the first to announce higher prices. As the dominant firm among the "big three" automakers, GM could theoretically punish Ford by refusing to raise prices.

2. If the price elasticity of demand for Ford automobiles is elastic—which is not unrealistic given the availability of substitutes in the United States automobile market—then a price hike could cause total revenues to fall. Just because a firm sets a price does not mean it will be immune to the laws of supply and demand. If the price increase comes at a time when there is a large inventory of unsold autos, then the price increase will increase inventories.

3. Emission and safety standards increase input costs and cause the production of automobiles to fall and prices to rise. Consumers benefit from these standards because there is less pollution and more lives saved, but these gains are to some extent offset by higher car prices.

APPENDIX TO CHAPTER 13
OLIGOPOLY STRATEGIES AND
THE THEORY OF GAMES

THE APPENDIX IN BRIEF

Fill in the blanks to summarize appendix content.

Oligopolists (1)_____ (are, are not) mutually interdependent. Strategies of one oligopolist (2)_____ (do not influence, influence) the strategies of other oligopolists. The theory of games analyzes the impact of decisions assuming various reactions on the part of rivals. The payoff matrix shows the expected gains or losses from each possible strategy (3)_____ (assuming firms are unconcerned with the reactions of rivals, given the reactions of rivals). Among many possible strategies, one possibility is to choose the strategy that (4)_____ (minimizes, maximizes) the worst possible outcome of all possible strategies. This is known as the maximin strategy. If the decisions involve whether to cut price or leave it unchanged, and if each oligopolist hopes that a price cut will not induce rivals to also cut prieces, a maximin strategy on the part of each firm that causes rivals to cut prices will result in a price war. Each firm (5)_____ (increases, loses) profit. This creates an obvious incentive to reduce uncertainty by (6) _____ (colluding and agreeing to maintain, increasing) price.

KEY TERMS REVIEW

Write the key term from the list below next to its definition.

Key Terms

Theory of games

Payoff matrix

Maximin strategy

Definitions

1. _____: the strategy that maximizes the minimum (or worst) outcomes of all possible strategies.

2. _____: shows the gain or loss from each possible strategy for each possible reaction by the rival player of the game.

3. _____: analyzes the behavior of individuals or organizations with conflicting interests.

CONCEPT REVIEW

Suppose there are two newspapers in a community—The Times and *The Daily*. *The Times* is trying to decide whether it should cut price. It expects to increase profits by 10% if *The Daily* does not react by cutting prices. If *The Daily* does match the price cut, it expects profits to fall by 4%. If *The Times* maintains price and *The Daily* cuts price, profits are expected to fall by 8%.

    a. Set up the payoff matrix.

    b. Assuming each firm employs the maximin strategy, what will *The Times* do? How will *The Daily* react? What are the long-run consequences for the local newspaper market?

MASTERY TEST

Select the best answer.

    1. The theory of games is useful:

       a. in understanding the operations of a monopolist.

       b. when the decisions of one firm are unrelated to the decisions of other firms.

       c. in understanding the behavior of monopolistic competitors.

       d. in understanding the behavior of oligopolists when their decisions are mutually interdependent.

    2. The payoff matrix:

       a. shows the potential profits or losses associated with a given price.

       b. shows the gains or losses associated with various strategies given various reactions by rival firms.

       c. ranks profitable strategies in descending order.

       d. shows the relationship between oligopolistic profits and product price.

    3. When each rival employs the maximin strategy to protect the level of profits:

       a. monopolistic profits arise.

       b. price wars develop, resulting in a decrease in profits and an incentive to collude.

       c. one oligopolist succeeds at the expense of the others and becomes the industry leader.

       d. profits are maximized only when average-cost pricing accompanies the strategy.

APPENDIX ANSWERS

The Appendix in Brief

1. Are 2. Influence 3. Given the reaction of rivals 4. Maximizes 5. Loses 6. Colluding and agreeing to maintain

Key Terms Review

1. Maximin strategy 2. Payoff matrix 3. Theory of games

Concept Review

a.

		Times	
		Reduce price	No change
Daily	Reduce price	-4%	-8%
	No change	+10%	———

b.   If both firms pursue the maximin strategy, they will cut prices, thus reducing profits and likely starting a price war. In the long run, the firms might decide that collusion is necessary to reduce the uncertainty and to protect profits.

Mastery Test

1. d 2. b 3. b

PART IV

GOVERNMENT AS A REGULATOR IN MARKETS
AND AS A PROVIDER OF SERVICES:
MICROECONOMIC ANALYSIS

PART EXERCISE

Inside Information: *Economic Report of the President*

In Part IV, you will learn about some of the economic roles of government. Choose an issue of interest, such as environmental policy, regulation of business, or government spending, and do a brief report using current and recent issues of the *Economic Report of the President*.

14 ANTITRUST POLICY AND REGULATION OF MARKETS

CHAPTER CONCEPTS

After studying your text, attending class, and completing this chapter, you should be able to:

1. Describe how governments use the law and the courts to prevent establishment of monopoly positions through unfair business practices.
2. Discuss antitrust laws and how they affect business behavior and mergers.
3. Describe the impact of government policies that limit the freedom of sellers to choose their own prices and to enter markets.

THE CHAPTER IN BRIEF

Fill in the blanks to summarize chapter content.

The goal of antitrust policy is to prevent abuses of market power in less competitive markets and to prevent the monopolization of markets that are presently competitive. The first antitrust law was the (1)_____ (Clayton, Sherman) Act of 1890. The intent of the law was to prohibit activities that restrain trade. The (2)_____ (Clayton, Sherman) Act of 1914 identified specific business practices that restrict competition, such as price discrimination, tying contracts, interlocking directorates, and anticompetitive mergers via the acquisition of corporate (3)_____ (assets, stock). The Federal Trade Commission, established in 1914, regulates methods of competition and today it (4)_____ (targets deceptive and false advertising, is mainly interested in violations of U.S. pricing statutes). The Robinson-Patman Act of 1936 was intended to protect small retailers from unfair competition from chain and discount stores. The Celler-Kefauver Act of 1950 closed a major loophole in the Clayton Act by making illegal the acquisition of (5)_____ (stock, assets) that lessens competition.

The antitrust laws have been interpreted in different ways by the courts over the years. In 1911, (6)_____(U.S. Steel, Standard Oil) was broken up because it engaged in practices considered to constitute an intent to monopolize. In 1920, (7)_____ (U.S. Steel, Standard Oil) had a high market share but was not dissolved because it was found that it did not use its size to limit competition. In the Standard Oil case, the (8)_____ ("rule of reason," relevant market rule) was established in which it had to be shown that the monopolist or firm with a very large market share was a "bad" monopolist—engaging in anticompetitive activities. This interpretation held until the Alcoa case of (9)_____ (1926, 1945). Alcoa had a 90% share of its market. It was found to have not engaged in anticompetitive activities, but it was found guilty of monopolization and broken up because its expansion of capacity was viewed as an attempt to monopolize the market. This essentially reversed the rule of reason—market share alone was enough to be convicted of monopolization. Another major interpretation relating to market share had to do with the concept of the "relevant" market. Although du Pont had a monopoly in the production of cellophane, if the definition of the relevant market was broadened to include all flexible wrappings, it had a much smaller market share. Du Pont was found (10)_____(guilty, innocent) of monopolization. Similar considerations were relevant when the Justice Department dropped its antitrust case against IBM in 1982.

Are high market concentration and profits evidence of monopoly power? In many cases the answer is yes, but not always. For instance, a firm may have a large market share because economies of scale require a large production run. The large firm may be large because it offers a superior product. High accounting profits do not necessarily mean high economic profits because implicit costs are not considered in accounting profit. If firms face competition from abroad, even firms with large domestic market shares must contend with numerous foreign firms. This tends to (11)_____ (lessen, increase) market power and the potential for market abuses. Concentration ratios can be misleading in that a firm with a small national concentration ratio may have a high ratio in some local or regional markets, allowing it to exercise market power.

An important portion of the market share concentration in business today is the result of mergers. Mergers can be horizontal, vertical, or conglomerate. (12)_____ (Horizontal, Vertical, Conglomerate) mergers occur between firms that operate at a given stage of production, such as refining in the oil industry, whereas (13)_____ (horizontal, vertical, conglomerate) mergers are between firms that operate at different stages of production, such as oil exploration and refining. (14)_____ (Horizontal, Vertical, Conglomerate) mergers are between firms in dissimilar industries.

Regulation by federal and state governments in some industries such as airlines, railroads, and trucking, has actually prevented entry of potential new firms and prohibited price competition. The commissions set up to regulate these industries had the intent to ensure the continuation of a vital service at stable prices and to prevent monopolization. But in controlling service routes, rate structures, etc., they (15)_____ (promoted, in effect prevented potential) competition. Several of these industries have been deregulated, resulting in generally lower prices to the public, but in the airline industry there is concern regarding the quality of service and the threat of oligopolization as the market stabilizes.

KEY TERMS REVIEW

Write the key term from the list below next to its definition.

Key Terms

Antitrust statutes   Rule of reason
Horizontal merger   Vertical merger
Conglomerate merger

Definitions

1. _____: holds that acts beyond normal business practice that unduly restrain competition for the purpose of excluding rivals can be used to infer intent to monopolize an industry.

2. _____: seeks to prevent "unfair" business practices that give rise to monopoly power.

3. _____: a merger of a firm with its suppliers.

4. _____: occurs when competing sellers in the same market merge into a single firm.

5. _____: a merger of firms selling goods in unrelated markets.

CONCEPT REVIEW

Concept 2:   *Antitrust laws*

1. Identify the antitrust legislation designed to prevent each of the following activities.

   Law/Date

   a. _____ anticompetitive price discrimination

   b. _____ anticompetitive mergers resulting from the acquisition of corporate assets

   c. _____ anticompetitive mergers resulting from the acquisition of corporate stock

   d. _____ monopolization that results in a restraint of trade

   e. _____ false and deceptive advertising

   f. _____ chain stores taking over markets from independent retailers

   g. _____ tying contracts

   h. _____ interlocking directorates

2. Which antitrust cases are associated with the following?

   Case/Date

   a. _____ establishment of the rule of reason

   b. _____ market share itself or how it is acquired, whether or not the firm engages in anticompetitive activities, is evidence of intent to monopolize

   c. _____ the "relevant" market must be identified in order to use market share as evidence of monopolization

   d. _____ mere size itself is not an offense

3. List five reasons why the presence of high market share and profits may not be evidence of monopoly power.

   a. _____

   b. _____

   c. _____

   d. _____

   e. _____

Concept 4:   *Deregulation of regulated industries*

4. List four effects of the Airline Deregulation Act of 1978.

   a. _____

   b. _____

   c. _____

   d. _____

MASTERY TEST

Select the best answer.

1. Which of the following acts made it illegal to "restrain trade"?
   a. Sherman Act of 1890
   b. Clayton Act of 1914
   c. Federal Trade Act of 1914
   d. Robinson-Patman Act of 1936
   e. Celler-Kefauver Act of 1950

2. Which of the following acts prohibited specific anticompetitive business practices such as price discrimination?
   a. Sherman Act of 1890
   b. Clayton Act of 1914
   c. Federal Trade Act of 1914
   d. Robinson-Patman Act of 1936
   e. Celler-Kefauver Act of 1950

3. Under which act is false and deceptive advertising prohibited?
   a. Sherman Act of 1890
   b. Clayton Act of 1914
   c. Federal Trade Act of 1914
   d. Robinson-Patman Act of 1936
   e. Celler-Kefauver Act of 1950

4. Which of the following acts is designed to protect small independent retailers from large chain store operations?
   a. Sherman Act of 1890
   b. Clayton Act of 1914
   c. Federal Trade Commission Act of 1914
   d. Robinson-Patman Act of 1936
   e. Celler-Kefauver Act of 1950

5. Which act prohibits anticompetitive mergers resulting from the acquisition of a firm's assets?
   a. Sherman Act of 1890
   b. Clayton Act of 1914
   c. Federal Trade Commission Act of 1914
   d. Robinson-Patman Act of 1936
   e. Celler-Kefauver Act of 1950

6. The "rule of reason":
   a. holds that monopolists must be reasonably competitive when dealing with smaller rivals.
   b. was established in the alcoa case of 1920.
   c. holds that acts beyond normal business practice that unduly restrain competition for the purpose of excluding rivals can be used to infer intent to monopolize an industry.
   d. holds that the entire market must be considered rather than just the relevant market.

7. The "rule of reason" was established in which of the following cases?
   a. Standard Oil case of 1911
   b. U.S. Steel case of 1920
   c. Alcoa case of 1945
   d. Du Pont case of 1956

8. The concept that mere size was not an offense was established in the:
   a. Standard Oil case of 1911.
   b. U.S. Steel case of 1920.
   c. Alcoa case of 1945.
   d. Du Pont case of 1956.

9. The concept of the "relevant" market was important in which of the following cases?
   a. Standard Oil case of 1911
   b. Du Pont case of 1956
   c. IBM case, which was terminated in 1982
   d. U.S. Steel case of 1920
   e. B and c

10. High market concentration and profit are not necessarily evidence of monopoly power because:
   a. of the presence of economies of scale.
   b. the firm may simply produce superior products.
   c. a firm with a high domestic concentration ratio might nevertheless face significant competition from imports.
   d. high accounting profits do not necessarily mean high economic profits.
   e. All of the above.

11. A merger of two firms operating in different markets producing dissimilar goods is called a:
   a. horizontal merger.
   b. vertical merger.
   c. multinational merger.
   d. conglomerate merger.

12. A merger of two firms operating in the same market is known as a:

    a. horizontal merger.

    b. vertical merger.

    c. multinational merger.

    d. conglomerate merger.

13. Some transportation industries, such as airlines, railroads, and trucking, were regulated:

    a. because violent unions required the government to intervene in order to establish stability.

    b. to ensure or guarantee service and to prevent the monopolization of the industry.

    c. because such industries are considered natural monopolies.

    d. to avoid the destructive effects of price wars.

14. Regulation in the transportation industries resulted in:

    a. price competition and freedom of entry and exit.

    b. lower prices.

    c. the absence of both price competition and the freedom of entry and exit.

    d. the establishment of the ftc as the major oversight body in charge of reviewing rate structures.

    e. b and d.

15. The Airline Deregulation Act of 1978 has resulted in all but one of the following.

    a. A reduction in fares

    b. A more complex price structure

    c. An increase in the quality of service

    d. Increased entry to and exit from the industry

16. U. S. Steel had a large market share, but was found innocent of monopolization in 1920 because:

    a. it violated the "rule of reason."

    b. the relevant market concept was used to define market share.

    c. it did not engage in anticompetitive business practices.

    d. it did not have 100 percent of the market share.

17. The duPont case of 1956 and the IBM case of 1982 are similar in that:

    a. the relevant market concept was important for determining market share.

    b. the "rule of reason" was overturned in both cases.

    c. both firms were virtual monopolists.

    d. they both involved anticompetitive mergers.

18. Which of the following is true regarding the relationship between profits and market share?

    a. Rising market share and profits always signal monopolization.

    b. Monopolization may occur even though a firm may have a small national market share.

    c. High profits may not be the result of monopolization, but may be due to economic cost excluding accounting cost and resulting in overstated economic profits.

    d. Large market shares can be obtained only by deliberate attempts to restrict competition.

19. Which of the following are considered objectives of trucking regulation?

    a. Ensuring the continuation of a vital service

    b. Avoiding price warring or monopolization that might threaten the availability of the service

    c. To stabilize the industry

    d. To prevent rich railroad barons from capturing market share

    e. a and b

THINK IT THROUGH

1. Discuss the how the interpretation of the antitrust laws has changed over time and identify the important court cases associated with the changes.

2. Large market share and high profits are evidence of the exercise of monopoly power. True or false? Explain.

3. Interstate trucking was deregulated in the 1970s, but many states continue to regulate intrastate trucking. Discuss the intent or objectives of regulatory commissions. Can you think of any reasons why some of the strongest objections to the deregulation of intrastate trucking often come from trucking firms with dominant market shares rather than small firms?

ANALYZING THE NEWS

Using the skills derived from studying this chapter, analyze the economic facts that make up the following article and answer the questions below, using graphical analysis where possible.

1. How could any firm benefit from the establishment of *minimum* prices?

Nintendo's Latest Novelty Is a Price-Fixing Settlement

By Paul M. Barrett

Staff Reporter of The Wall Street Journal

WASHINGTON—Nintendo Co., the colossus of the home video-game market, joined the growing list of Japanese electronic giants nailed by state antitrust regulators for allegedly fixing prices of popular consumer products.

This time, the Federal Trade Commission got in the act, joining prosecutors from New York and Maryland in charging that Nintendo's U.S. arm illegally colluded with some dealers, and bullied others, to set minimum prices for the company's home-video consoles.

In an unusual twist, however, the federal and state prosecutors announced yesterday that they had agreed to settle the charges in a fashion that could boost Nintendo's already robust sales.

Under a proposed agreement to settle the state charges, the company would provide up to $25 million in coupons to some nine million consumers nationwide—in effect, requiring home-video buffs to purchase more Nintendo products if they are to benefit from the settlement. Nintendo of America Inc. controls 80% of the estimated $5 billion domestic video-game market.

Nintendo would also pay the states $4.75 million in damages and legal costs under the settlement, which requires the approval of a federal judge in New York. The proposed settlement of the parallel but separate federal charges would require Nintendo to refrain from price fixing but wouldn't involve a monetary penalty. The federal settlement requires final FTC approval after a 60-day period for public comment.

Prosecutors insisted that the state monetary penalties, combined with the company's vow to obey the law in the future, would "send a message" to corporate price-fixers in the U.S. and Japan.

But Nintendo of America said it "did not violate antitrust laws" and agreed to settle only to avoid "lengthy court proceedings." Howard Lincoln, senior vice president of Nintendo of America, asserted: "We decided to enter into this comprehensive and nationwide settlement in order to maintain the good will our company enjoys with millions of consumers who play Nintendo games."

The company may not yet have disposed of all of its antitrust difficulties, though. Lawyers from the FTC and the office of New York Attorney General Robert Abrams are investigating separate allegations that Nintendo has attempted to monopolize the home video-game industry by using product designs and licensing policies to lock others out of its business and keep prices artificially high. Nintendo has denied those allegations.

Nintendo has been accused in a series of private lawsuits of designing its video console so that consumers can use only Nintendo game cartridges with the machines. In private litigation, the company has aggressively tried, often successfully, to block rivals from selling unauthorized imitations of Nintendo game cartridges.

At yesterday's joint federal-state announcement here, Mr. Abrams of New York said Nintendo was the fourth Japanese electronics giant caught in "conspiracies by manufacturers to strangle competition and hurt consumers by controlling retail prices." He estimated that such conspiracies in the electronics industry and other businesses cost American consumers "hundreds of millions of dollars a year."

Just last month, a U.S. unit of Mitsubishi Electric Corp. agreed to refund nearly $8 million to consumers to settle charges that it illegally fixed the retail prices of 242,000 television sets. In earlier cases, Minolta Corp. and Panasonic Co. were charged with similar antitrust violations. Minolta agreed in 1987 to pay $7 million to settle charges that it tried to manipulate camera prices; Panasonic, a unit of Matsushita Electric Industrial Co., agreed in 1989 to refund $16 million to purchasers of answering machines, stereo parts and other products.

In the Nintendo case, prosecutors said the company's sales representatives enforced prices set by the manufacturer. Retailers who resisted Nintendo's pressure were threatened with a slowdown of shipments, a reduction in the number of consoles delivered or a complete lockout, prosecutors said.

Nintendo required retailers to sell its Nintendo Entertainment System consoles at a uniform price of $99.95 from June 1988 through December 1990, according to prosecutors. Some discount retailers resisted Nintendo's price policy and helped government investigators; other dealers eagerly cooperated with Nintendo to increase their profit, prosecutors said. But no retailers were named in the charges because the state and federal governments hadn't gathered enough evidence to implicate dealers, prosecutors said.

State prosecutors agreed to the refund-by-coupon plan, fully understanding that the plan would boost Nintendo's sales. Mr. Abrams said the coupon arrangement was a response to the failure of many consumers to apply for cash rebates available to them in the Minolta and Panasonic cases.

"Very, very, very few consumers responded" to the earlier rebate offers, Mr. Abrams said. In fact, consumers sought and received less than one-tenth of the money made available by Minolta and Panasonic, according to an Abrams aide.

Under the Nintendo settlement, the company automatically would mail $5 coupons to consumers who bought the video consoles and filed warranty cards. Other purchasers will be mailed coupons if they call an 800 telephone number and provide a legitimate console serial number.

The company would redeem a minimum of $5 million and a maximum of $25 million in coupons. If consumers request less than $5 million in coupons, the value of the left-over coupons would be given to the states in cash, bringing the company's total minimum liability to $9.75 million. Thirty-four states and the District of Columbia, in addition to New York and Maryland, have signed the Nintendo settlement, and other states may join the agreement during the next 75 days.

The FTC's joining in the action against Nintendo reflects the commission's increased aggressiveness on antitrust matters in the past 18 months. Though far more circumspect than Mr. Abrams, a feisty liberal Democrat, the FTC's antitrust chief, Kevin Arquit, celebrated the first joint federal-state prosecution of so-called resale-price maintenance. "This combined . . . effort is without precedent in the antitrust area," Mr. Arquit said, "and we look forward to continuing this partnership in the future."

Under the federal portion of the settlement, Nintendo has agreed to refrain from setting prices or pressuring discounters. The company has also agreed to send a letter to all of its dealers, informing them of their right to sell the video-game consoles at whatever price they choose.

Said Mr. Arquit: "Where retailers are not permitted to discount, comparison shopping does no good."

CHAPTER ANSWERS

The Chapter in Brief

1. Sherman 2. Clayton 3. Stock 4. Targets deceptive and false advertising 5. Assets 6. Standard Oil 7. U.S. Steel 8. "Rule of reason" 9. 1945 10. Innocent 11. Lessen 12. Horizontal 13. Vertical 14. Conglomerate 15. In effect prevented potential

Key Terms Review

1. Rule of reason 2. Antitrust statutes 3. Vertical merger 4. Horizontal merger 5. Conglomerate merger

Concept Review

1. a. Clayton Act of 1914

   b. Celler-Kefauver Act of 1950

   c. Clayton Act of 1914

   d. Sherman Act of 1890

   e. Federal Trade Commission Act of 1914

   f. Robinson-Patman Act of 1936

   g. Clayton Act of 1914

   h. Clayton Act of 1914

2. a. Standard Oil (1911) b. Alcoa (1945) c. Alcoa (1945), du Pont (1956), IBM (suit terminated in 1982) d. U.S. Steel (1920)

3. a. Economies of scale require a large production run and may result in a lower price than if the industry was made up of several inefficiently sized firms.

   b. The firm might produce a superior product.

   c. Accounting profit is likely to be larger than economic profit.

   d. The presence of foreign competition will likely result in more competition among firms having high domestic concentration ratios than among firms having lower ratios but no foreign competition.

   e. A firm may have a low national concentration ratio but have a regional monopoly.

4. a. Lower fares b. More complex fares c. Increased entry and exit d. Reduced quality of service

Mastery Test

1. a 2. b 3. c 4. d 5. e 6. c 7. a 8. b 9. e 10. e 11. d 12. a 13. b 14. c 15. c 16. c 17. a 18. b 19. e

Think it Through

1. Standard Oil was found guilty in 1911 of monopolization and broken up. It engaged in business practices, in excess of those considered normal, that resulted in a restraint of trade. The "rule of reason" was established in which a firm could be found guilty of monopolization if it engaged in activities beyond normal business practices where the effect was to lessen competition. Although U.S. Steel was a firm with a large share of the market, in 1920 it was found innocent of monopolization because it *did not* engage in anticompetitive business practices.

From 1920 until the Alcoa case of 1945, the interpretation of the antitrust laws was that size is itself not an offense, but anticompetitive business practices together with size were sufficient to show the intent to exercise market power. In 1945, this interpretation changed in the Alcoa case in that Alcoa was not found to have engaged in anticompetitive business practices, but was convicted of monopolization because of Alcoa's large market share and the way in which Alcoa's production capacity was acquired. The concept of the relevant market became important in the Alcoa case of 1945, the du Pont case of 1956, and the IBM case terminated in 1982. To be convicted of monopolization, the firm has to have a very high share in the relevant product market, not just a large market share in general.

2. False. A large market share and high profits may many times indicate the exercise of monopoly power, but there are a number of reasons other than the exercise of market power why a firm could have a large market share and high profits. For instance, accounting costs do not include implicit costs and therefore accounting profits will likely always be higher than economic profits. A firm may have a low national market share but be a monopolist in regional or local markets. A firm with economies of scale may have a large market share in order to operate at an efficient level of production. Because of the scale economies, the firm may even charge a price lower than that charged by many small but inefficiently sized firms. A firm might have a large market share because of its reputation for quality and service.

3. Objectives of regulation regarding the trucking industry include (a) ensuring the continuation of a vital service, and (b) avoiding price warring or monopolization that might threaten the availability of the regulated good or service. Trucking regulation has been in the form of strict control over rates and service routes, thus prohibiting price competition and entry of new firms. Established firms, often having large market shares of the intrastate trucking business, are sheltered and protected by the very commissioners who are ostensibly acting in the public interest to promote lower rates and reliable and universal service. Thus the sheltered firm may have much to lose if the market is opened up to competitive pricing and entry.

Analyzing the News

1. While many firms would like to practice the policy of requiring distributors to charge prices that cannot fall below some specified level, firms that produce high-tech products often find it necessary and lucrative to create minimum prices for a variety of reasons. First, by preventing distributors from selling their goods below a specified price, firms have the potential to enjoy profits from artificially high prices. This generally is a result of significant market power on the part of the price setter. Second, minimum prices can prevent price competition among dealers who can use profit margins from the sale of high-tech items to finance the cost of ongoing service and training sessions provided to customers who purchase the product. Third, minimum prices prevent dealers from selling the product as a "loss leader"—a product that is sold at a very low and loss-generating price in order to attract customers to the store to buy other products as well. Fourth, minimum prices maintain the firms brand name image. This point has as much to do with psychology as it does with economics. How often do you see a popular brand name product at a high price and think, "If this product is expensive it must be high-quality." By associating high-quality with high prices, the firm that establishes minimum prices may succeed in maintaining or improving their image.

15 MARKET FAILURE AND THE ROLE OF GOVERNMENT IN ALLOCATING RESOURCES

CHAPTER CONCEPTS

After studying your text, attending class, and completing this chapter, you should be able to:

1. Define externality and show how externalities prevent free and competitive markets from allocating resources efficiently.
2. Describe the causes of externalities and show how government can help achieve efficiency by intervening in markets when externalities exist.
3. Explain the concept of a public good and show how provision of public goods by government can result in net gains to consumers.
4. Describe and evaluate social regulation by government to correct for market failure.

THE CHAPTER IN BRIEF

Fill in the blanks to summarize chapter content.

Markets often fail to allocate resources efficiently. Governments may be able to correct the misallocation, thus enhancing society's well-being. Externalities are a common cause of market failure. (1)_____ (Positive, Negative) externalities are costs associated with the use of resources that are not reflected in price and are imposed on third parties—those other than the buyers or sellers of the good. Marginal social costs (2)_____ (are less than, exceed) the producer's marginal cost by the marginal external cost. Because profit-maximizing producers equate marginal cost and marginal revenue rather than the (3)_____ (higher, lower) marginal social cost and marginal revenue, too (4)_____ (much, little) is produced and market price (or marginal benefit) is (5)_____ (above, below) the marginal social cost. Thus society would benefit if (6)_____ (more, less) of the good were produced.

(7)_____ (Positive, Negative) externalities are benefits associated with the use of resources that are not reflected in price and accrue to third parties. Marginal social benefits (8)_____ (are less than, exceed) marginal benefits by the marginal external benefit. Since the market equates marginal benefit and marginal cost rather than the (9)_____ (lower, higher) marginal social benefit and marginal cost, the market (10)_____ (underproduces, overproduces) output, which results in a price that is too (11)_____ (high, low). It allocates too (12)_____ (many, few) resources to the production of the good. Society would gain if (13)_____ (more, less) of the good were produced.

Both negative and positive externalities result because (14)_____ (prices, property rights) either do not exist, are poorly defined, or are not enforced. Common property resources such as navigable rivers are often polluted in the absence of government regulation because no one individual has a property right to the river and therefore cannot prevent others from imposing external costs such as pollution on users of the river. The producer of a positive externality does not have a property right to the (15)_____ (benefits conferred, costs imposed) on others. There is no way to be compensated for these external benefits by the market.

Government can potentially correct an externality by internalizing the externality—forcing the external costs of negative externalities on those that generate them and requiring those that benefit from positive externalities to compensate the producer of the benefits. A (16)_____ (corrective subsidy, corrective tax) can be used to internalize a negative externality. A tax equal to the marginal (17)_____ (social, external) cost of some action will cause the firm's marginal cost to equal the marginal social cost. A profit-maximizing firm will be induced to (18)_____ (cut, increase) output and (19)_____ (lower, raise) price. The adjusted market price now equals the marginal social cost, and the level of output is the level that maximizes the net gain to society from the use of resources. The tax revenue can be used to compensate those that have suffered as a result of the negative externality.

A corrective (20)_____ (subsidy, tax) can be used to internalize a positive externality. A (21)_____ (subsidy, tax) to consumers equal to the marginal external benefit would cause the marginal benefit or demand curve to shift to the higher marginal social benefit curve. Consumers would be induced to purchase (22)_____ (less, more) of the subsidized good, ultimately causing market price and quantity to (23)_____ (decrease, increase). Price would (24)_____ (rise, fall) to equal marginal social benefit, which would also equal marginal cost. Again society's net benefit is maximized. Alternatively, a subsidy could be given to the producer, causing the producer to (25)_____ (increase, decrease) output, but price would (26)_____(rise, fall) and be less than the marginal social benefit. Subsidies can be financed via specific taxes levied on the beneficiaries of the positive externality. If the beneficiaries cannot be easily identified or the extent of the benefit cannot be precisely measured, then general tax revenues can be used.

In a small-numbers case, it is possible to assign property rights such that bargaining results in the internalization of externalities and eliminates the need for corrective taxes or subsidies. This trade of property rights for cash payments resulting in maximum social welfare is known as the (27)_____ (Pareto Rule, Coase Theorem). For the case of environmental pollution, a negative externality, the allocation of resources, and extent of pollution that maximizes society's welfare (28)_____ (are achieved only when property rights are assigned to the victims of pollution; are achieved regardless of whether polluters or victims are assigned property rights).

Public goods are (29)_____ (rival, not rival) in consumption, are (30)_____ (subject, not subject) to the exclusion principle, and are associated with (31)_____ (zero, positive) marginal costs of production. If the public good is provided to one, it is provided to all and at zero marginal cost. A profit-maximizing firm equating price and marginal cost would not produce a good at zero price. Even if a positive price could be charged, there is no way to exclude nonpayers from enjoying the benefits of the good. The market will therefore (32)_____ (produce, not produce) public goods. Yet these goods bestow benefits on society. Many government-provided goods are not pure public goods, but have characteristics similar to both private (excludable and rival) and public (nonexcludable and nonrival) goods. Public education is excludable, but is provided by the government in the belief that it is associated with positive externalities.

Government can reallocate resources from private goods production to public goods production by taxing the private sector and using the tax revenues to purchase or produce public goods. In order to maximize net benefits from the use of resources, government should produce public goods up to the point at which marginal (33)_____ (social, external) benefits (the sum of individual marginal benefits) equal the marginal social cost of providing the public good. Beneficiaries can be forced to share the cost of the public good through taxation. Taxation is necessary because of the (34)_____ (democratic process, free-rider problem). If some people pay for the public good and it is provided, it is provided to all whether they pay or not. Since people can receive the benefits without having to contribute, many people have to be coerced to pay, and this is done via a mandatory tax.

Markets also fail in other areas, such as providing the socially desirable levels of product safety, occupational safety, and racial integration. Often these failures stem from lack of information or faulty information used by consumers and producers in making decisions. (35)_____ (Antitrust legislation, Social regulation) is the use of government power to intervene in markets to achieve social goals such as product and occupational safety, the absence of discrimination, and an equitable distribution of income.

KEY TERMS REVIEW

Write the key term from the list below next to its definition.

Key Terms

Negative externality   Corrective tax
Marginal external cost   Corrective subsidy
Positive externality   Private goods
Marginal external benefit   Pure public good
Internalization of an   Free rider
    externality   Social regulation

Definitions

1. _____: the extra benefit that accrues to third parties when a positive externality is present.

2. _____: a tax levied on polluters to simulate a charge equal to the marginal external cost of their actions.

3. _____: an amount paid to consumers or producers of a good equal to the marginal external benefit of the good.

4. _____: a good that provides benefits to all members of a community as soon as it is made available to any one person.

5. _____: the extra cost imposed on third parties when a negative externality is present.

6. _____: a benefit associated with the use of resources that is not reflected in prices. Also called *external benefit.*

7. _____: a person who seeks to enjoy the benefits of a public good without contributing to its costs.

8. _____: a cost associated with the use of resources that is not reflected in prices. Also called *external cost.*

9. _____: the use of government power to intervene in markets so as to reduce the risk of accidents and disease and to achieve other social goals such as equality of opportunity for all persons.

10. _____: goods whose benefits are rival in consumption and for which exclusion of those who refuse to pay is relatively easy.

11. _____: occurs when the marginal cost or marginal benefit of a good has been adjusted so that market sale of the item results in the efficient output.

CONCEPT REVIEW

Concepts 1 and 2: Externalities and government intervention in markets

1. The diagram below represents the market for the propellant used in aerosol sprays. Aerosol use has been responsible for the release of fluorocarbons into the atmosphere, causing a depletion of the earth's protective ozone layer. It is speculated that this will increase the incidence of cancer.

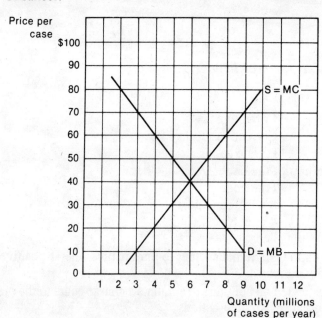

Price per case

Quantity (millions of cases per year)

a. On the figure above, find the market price and quantity. Price = $_____, quantity = _____ cases

b. The production and use of aerosol propellants with fluorocarbons result in _____ externalities.

c. Assume that the marginal external cost is $10. Show the marginal social cost curve in the figure above. The efficient levels of output and price that maximize society's net benefits are _____ cases and $_____, respectively. The market _____ (overproduces, underproduces) the propellant and charges a price that is too _____ (low, high).

d. Society would be better off with an/a _____ in output and an/a _____ in price. Government could intervene to achieve this outcome by using a corrective _____ (tax, subsidy) equal to the marginal _____ (social, external) cost of $_____. Show this graphically on the figure above.

2. An urban highway is built in a metropolitan area through a portion of the city previously having poor access to the central business district. The direct beneficiaries are the users of the highway, who include the residents in the proximity of the highway. But the presence of the
highway results in the development of commerce and industry near its major intersections,
which benefits the local residents whether or not they use the highway. Assuming that highways are produced by the private sector, the metropolitan market for highways is shown in the
figure below.

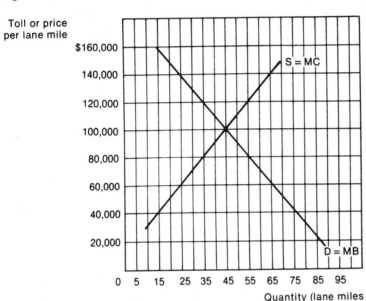

a. On the figure above, find the market toll and quantity of lane miles. Price or toll =
   $_____, quantity = _____ lane miles

b. The production and consumption of highways result in a _____ externality.

c. Assume that the marginal external benefit of the highway per resident is $20. Also assume
   that there are 1000 residents. Show the marginal social benefit curve on the figure above.
   The efficient levels of output and price is _____ lane miles and
   $_____, respectively. The market _____ (overproduces, un-
   derproduces) highways and charges a price that is too _____ (low, high).

d. The community would be better off with an/a _____ in lane miles and an/a
   _____ in tolls. Government could intervene in the market and use a corrective
   _____ (tax, subsidy) equal to the marginal _____ (social, external) benefit of
   $_____. Show this graphically on the figure above.

e. The _____ (tax could be levied on, subsidy could be given to) consumers equal to their individual marginal _____ (social, external) benefit of
   $_____.

305

Concept 3: *Public goods and government provision*

3. A community's siren system for early warning of tornadoes is made available by the public sector rather than by the private sector.

   a.

Characteristics of a Private Good	Characteristics of the Siren System
(1) _____	(1)_____
(2) _____	(2)_____
	(3)_____

   b. Why is the early warning system provided by the government?

   c. The efficient level or optimal provision of early warning sirens is at that level where _____ equals _____.

4. The following data represent the community's total social benefits (TSB) and total social costs (TSC) associated with an early warning system.

Sirens per Square Mile	TSC MSC ($ thousands)		TSB MSB ($ thousands)		Net Benefit ($ thousands)
0	0		0		____
1	3	____	30	____	____
2	9	____	54	____	____
3	18	____	72	____	____
4	30	____	84	____	____
5	45	____	90	____	____
6	63	____	90	____	____

   a. Complete the table and plot the marginal social cost and marginal social benefit curves on the figure below.

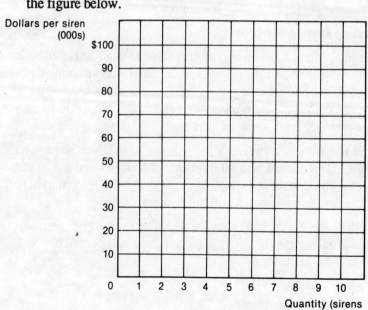

Dollars per siren (000s)

Quantity (sirens per square mile)

b. The efficient provision of early warning capability is _____ sirens. MSC = $_____, MSB = $_____. Show this graphically in the figure above.

c. If there are 500 residents in the community and all benefit from the warning system, a voluntary contribution of $_____ per person could be used to finance the system.

d. A voluntary contribution scheme will likely _____ (succeed, fail) because of the _____ problem. If a voluntary system will not work, how can the system be financed?

Advanced Application: Negative externalities and government intervention

5. The following equations are for a market in which a negative externality results from the production of the good.

$MB = a - bQ$ (market demand)

$MC = c + dQ$ (market supply)

$MEC = e$ (marginal external cost)

where   e is a positive constant

                    Q = output

                    P = price per unit

                    MC = marginal cost (private)

                    MB = marginal benefit = marginal social benefit

a. Find the market equilibrium price and quantity equations.

b. Find the equations for the socially efficient price and quantity.

c. Market price is too _____, and market quantity is too _____.

d. A tax per unit of the good equal to _____ will correct the misallocation of resources.

MASTERY TEST

Select the best answer.

1. A cost associated with the use of resources that is not reflected in price is known as a/an:
   a. positive externality.
   b. external benefit.
   c. negative externality.
   d. external cost.
   e. c and d.

2. A benefit associated with the use of resources that is not reflected in price is known as a/an:
   a. positive externality.
   b. public good.
   c. external cost.
   d. negative externality.

3. Which of the following must be added to marginal benefit in order to get marginal social benefit?
   a. Marginal cost
   b. Price
   c. Marginal social cost
   d. Marginal external benefit

4. The sum of the firm's marginal cost and the marginal external cost is called:
   a. total cost.
   b. total marginal cost.
   c. marginal social benefit.
   d. marginal social cost.
   e. opportunity cost.

5. The presence of negative externalities results in _____ output and a _____ price than is desirable for society.
   a. more, higher
   b. less, lower
   c. more, lower
   d. less, higher

6. The presence of positive externalities results in _____ output and a _____ price than is desirable for society.
   a. more, higher
   b. less, lower
   c. more, lower
   d. less, higher

7. Government can correct a negative externality by using _____, which result in a _____ market output and a _____ market price.
   a. subsidies to consumers, larger, lower
   b. corrective taxes, smaller, lower
   c. corrective subsidies to suppliers, larger, higher
   d. corrective taxes, smaller, higher

8. Government can correct a positive externality by using _____, which result in a _____ market output and a _____ market price.
   a. corrective subsidies to consumers, larger, lower
   b. corrective taxes, smaller, lower
   c. corrective subsidies to suppliers, larger, lower
   d. corrective subsidies to suppliers, larger, higher
   e. corrective taxes, smaller, higher

9. Externalities are caused by:
   a. the absence of property rights.
   b. poorly defined property rights, resulting in disputes.
   c. the lack of enforcement of existing property rights.
   d. All of the above.

10. A good whose benefits are rival in consumption and for which exclusion of those who refuse to pay is relatively easy is called a:
    a. normal good.
    b. rival good.
    c. public good.
    d. private good.

11. A good that provides benefits to all members of a community as soon as it is made available to any one member is called a:
    a. pure public good.
    b. rival good.
    c. normal good.
    d. private good.

12. Which of the following is not true of public goods?
    a. Public goods are not rival in consumption.
    b. Consumers cannot easily be excluded from the benefits of the good.
    c. Once the good is provided to one member of a community, it can be provided to each additional member at zero marginal cost.
    d. A system of voluntary financing of the public good can easily be established by those that benefit from the good.

13. The marginal social benefit of a public good is:
    a. the difference between the marginal benefit and marginal cost.
    b. the sum of the individual marginal benefits enjoyed by all consumers.
    c. the marginal social benefit less the marginal social cost of a private good.
    d. the market demand curve for the public good.

14. Voluntary cost sharing by the beneficiaries of a public good will not work because:
    a. income is insufficient to justify the good.
    b. of the constant price problem.
    c. of the free-rider problem.
    d. of rising opportunity costs.
    e. None of the above.

15. The market system produces _____ pure public goods.
    a. just the correct quantity of
    b. excess quantities of
    c. insufficient quantities of
    d. no

16. Market failure results from all but one of the following:
    a. the absence of property rights
    b. the lack of information
    c. inaccurate information
    d. profits that are too low

17. Social regulation refers to:
    a. specific antitrust statutes.
    b. corrective taxes and subsidies.
    c. government intervention in markets to achieve certain social goals, such as product and occupational safety.
    d. government's "big brother" attempt to interfere with the efficient functioning of the free enterprise system.

18. Which of the following is a reason why markets overallocate resources to the production of goods associated with negative externalities?
    a. Marginal social cost exceeds marginal benefit at the market level of output. A decrease in output by a unit reduces consumer benefits by less than the reduction in cost, producing a gain in net benefits.
    b. Marginal external cost is greater than marginal benefits, causing firms to overproduce.
    c. Marginal social benefit exceeds marginal cost at the market level of output. An increase in output by a unit increases benefits more than cost, producing a net gain.
    d. Markets with negative externalities overallocate resources to a good because only marginal external benefits are internalized.

19. In order to correct the misallocation of resources associated with the production of a good with positive externalities:

    a. a corrective tax should be levied equal to the marginal social cost.

    b. a corrective subsidy should be given equal to the marginal external cost.

    c. an excise tax should be levied equal to the marginal external benefit.

    d. a corrective subsidy should be given equal to the difference between marginal social benefit and marginal (private) benefit at the market level of output.

20. If all costs and benefits are reflected in market supply and demand curves:

    a. marginal external cost equals total cost.

    b. total costs equal total benefits.

    c. marginal external benefits and marginal external costs are equal to zero.

    d. marginal social costs equal marginal external benefits.

21. Markets fail to provide public goods because:

    a. public goods are rival, expensive, and entail sharply rising marginal cost.

    b. public goods are produced at zero economic profit, eliminating incentives for private production.

    c. once provided, the marginal cost of porduction is zero, implying that profit-maximizing firms will charge a zero price.

    d. public goods are nonrival and excludable goods that suffer from the free rider problem.

22. A chemical company discharges untreated wastes into a stream, imparing the quality of the stream. Which of the following best represents policy based upon the Coase Theorem?

    a. A corrective tax should be levied on the chemical producer equal to the marginal damage at the market level of output and discharge.

    b. The property right to the exclusive use of the stream must be assigned to recreational users of the stream.

    c. The property right to the exclusive use of the stream must be assigned to the chemical firm.

    d. The property right to the exclusive use of the stream can be assigned to either recreational users or the chemical company. In either case, the misallocation of resources will be eliminated.

THINK IT THROUGH

1. Explain the following statement. "The socially optimal or efficient level of pollution is not at a zero level."

2. Explain why the market will likely underallocate resources to the prevention of contagious diseases.

3. If a negative externality results from the lack of property rights or the lack of enforcement of those rights, what role can government play in reducing or eliminating externalities?

4. Explain how government can improve the efficiency of the economy's use of resources by providing information that either is not provided by the market or is provided in insufficient quantities or is misleading.

CHAPTER ANSWERS

The Chapter in Brief

1. Negative 2. Exceed 3. Higher 4. Much 5. Below 6. Less 7. Positive 8. Exceeds 9. Higher
10. Underproduces 11. Low 12. Few 13. More 14. Property rights 15. Benefits conferred
16. Corrective tax 17. External 18. Cut 19. Raise 20. Subsidy 21. Subsidy 22. More
23. Increase 24. Rise 25. Increase 26. Fall 27. Coase Theorem 28. are achieved regardless of
whether polluters or victims are assigned property rights 29. Not rival 30. Not subject 31. Zero
32. Not produce 33. Social 34. Free-rider problem 35. Social legislation

Key Terms Review

1. Marginal external benefit 2. Corrective tax 3. Corrective subsidy 4. Pure public good 5. Marginal external cost 6. Positive externality 7. Free rider 8. Negative externality 9. Social regulation
10. Private goods 11. Internalization of an externality

Concept Review

1.

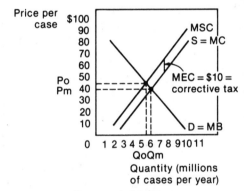

Pm = market price
Qm = market quantity
Po = socially optimal price
Qo = socially optimal quantity

   a. $40, 6 million b. Negative c. 5.5 million, $45, overproduces, low d. Decrease, increase, corrective tax, marginal external cost, $10

2.

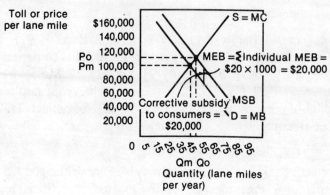

Toll or price
per lane mile

Pm = market price   Po = socially optimal price
Qm = market quantity   Qo = socially optimal quantity

a. $100,000; 45 b. Positive c. 50, $110,000; underproduces, low d. Increase, increase, corrective subsidy, marginal external benefit, $20,000 e. Subsidy could be given to, marginal external benefit, $20

3. a.

Characteristics of a Private Good	Characteristics of the Siren System
(1) Rival in consumption	(1) Nonrival in consumption
(2) Can exclude nonpayers	(2) Cannot exclude nonpayers
	(3) Zero marginal cost after provision to first individual

b. The siren system is provided by the public sector because a market cannot develop for a good that cannot be withheld from those that do not pay. Individuals have no incentive to purchase the good for a positive price because if it is purchased by one person, it is consumed by all others whether they pay or not.

c. Marginal social benefit, marginal social cost

4. a.

Sirens per Square Mile	MSC	MSB	Net Benefits
		($ thousands)	
0			0
1	3	30	27
2	6	24	43
3	9	18	54
4	12	12	54
5	15	6	45
6	18	0	27

314

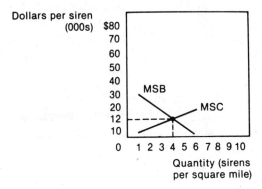

Dollars per siren
(000s)

Quantity (sirens
per square mile)

b. 4, $12,000, $12,000

c. $24

d. Fail, free rider. A mandatory tax can be used to force the free riders to share the marginal social cost of the warning system.

5. a. Setting the marginal benefit and marginal cost equations equal to each other and solving for quantity yields

$$Q = (a - c)/(d + b)$$

Substituting the equilibrium quantity equation in place of Q in the marginal benefit equation gives the market price

$$P = (ad + bc)/(d + b)$$

b. Adding the MEC to the marginal cost equation gives

$$MC = (c + e) + dQ$$

Setting this equation equal to the marginal benefit equation and solving for P and Q as above results in

$$Q = (a - c - e)/(d + b)$$
$$P = (ad + bc + be)/(d + b)$$

Since e is a positive constant, the presence of negative externalities decreases the socially optimal quantity and increases the socially optimal price.

c. Low, high

d. Marginal external cost or e

Mastery Test

1. e 2. a 3. d 4. d 5. c 6. b 7. d 8. c 9. d 10. d 11. a 12. d 13. b 14. c 15. d 16. d 17. c 18. a 19. d 20. c 21. c 22. d

Think it Through

1. A good entailing a negative externality (pollution) is overproduced by the market. A corrective tax equal to the marginal external cost will cause a reduction in the market quantity of the good to the socially desired level but will not necessarily result in zero pollution unless the tax

315

provides sufficient revenues for the cleanup of the pollution that continues to take place as a result of the production of the good at the socially desirable level. A producer in the long run might find that it is less costly to install pollution abatement facilities than it is to pay the tax. But this involves a comparison of the marginal benefits to the firm of pollution abatement with the marginal costs of cleaning up the pollution. There is no reason to believe that the firm's profit-maximizing level of pollution abatement will result in zero pollution.

2. The prevention of contagious diseases benefits the potential victims of the disease in that they continue to be healthy and productive citizens. Prevention also benefits society at large in that the economy and its institutions function more fully and efficiently with healthy and productive members of society than with individuals some of whom are out of the labor force or are disabled or less productive because of diseases. Individuals in the economy benefit from the economic activity and growth allowed in part by the prevention of diseases even if those individuals would have never contracted the disease. A market responds primarily to those who presently have the disease and require treatment, not to potential victims and other indirect beneficiaries. The marginal social benefits of disease prevention exceed the marginal benefits reflected in the market. The market will underproduce disease prevention.

3. Government could reduce the incidence of externalities by clearly defining and enforcing property rights where they exist and creating property rights where they do not exist. The commonly owned environment—the atmosphere, bodies of water, etc—is often polluted because no one individual has the right to prevent some other individual from polluting it. Class action suits by individuals without private property rights can enforce the collective property rights of society. Also, government can sell property rights to the highest bidder or allot them on the basis of many allocation schemes. Government can exercise the collective property right in the commonly owned property by passing legislation to impose costs on those that pollute. Government provides a system of courts to resolve property right disputes and enforce property rights.

4. The positions of both the marginal social benefit and marginal social cost curves depend in part on the accuracy and availability of information regarding, among other things, the quality, reliability, and safety of the good. The efficiency of consumer choice depends upon the availability of complete and accurate product information. Producers likewise require data for decisions but will produce only that information from which they can benefit. The market will not provide the necessary information to assess the extent of external costs or external benefits. By providing accurate, timely, and comprehensive information in excess of that provided by the market, government can improve the choices made by consumers, the decisions made by business, and the resource reallocation decisions of the government. Individual users of the government information benefit, but society as a whole benefits because of the more efficient use of scarce resources. Governments provide information on the climate, product safety, the purity and safety of drugs and food, contagious diseases, demographics, and the economy.

16 EXTERNALITIES AND THE ENVIRONMENT: POLICY ANALYSIS

CHAPTER CONCEPTS

After studying your text, attending class, and completing this chapter, you should be able to:

1. Discuss problems in estimating the costs and benefits of pollution control and choosing policies that result in the efficient level of environmental protection.
2. Describe actual and proposed policies designed to control pollution, and evaluate their impact on the environment and resource allocation.
3. Describe economic incentives to use natural resources and discuss policies that prevent overuse or depletion of these resources.

THE CHAPTER IN BRIEF

Fill in the blanks to summarize chapter content.

Pollution is an economic problem. It results in benefits to the polluter in the form of lower costs of production but imposes external costs on third parties. Pollution control creates benefits by reducing or eliminating the damage to resources that otherwise would occur. But scarce resources are required to clean up the pollution. Society's net benefit from environmental protection is maximized if pollution control is produced up to the level where the marginal social cost of controlling pollution (1)_____(is less than, just equals) the marginal social benefit to society. This would be the "efficient" level of pollution control. There is no reason to believe that this level of control (2)_____ (would not, would) eliminate pollution completely. In other words, an (3)_____ (efficient, inefficient) level of pollution is associated with an efficient level of pollution control.

Estimating the marginal benefits and costs of pollution control is (4)_____ (an, not an) easy task. Estimates of the marginal benefits must include the value of the benefits associated with the reduction in the incidence of pollution damage to people, material inputs, natural resources, and agricultural resources. If pollution causes death, a value must be placed on the reduction in death due to pollution control. If pollution affects the productivity or useability of resources, a value must be placed on the reduction in the incidence resource damage. In short, estimates of marginal benefits (5)_____(may not be, are) reliable, and it is likely that the public sector will choose a level of pollution control that is (6)_____(efficient, inefficient). The market will underproduce pollution control (or overproduce pollution), and government can improve upon the market's allocation of resources even if government is unable to precisely "maximize" net benefits.

Emission control policies include emission charges, regulation, and the use of property rights. An/A (7)_____ (emission charge, property right) is a charge per unit of pollution. The fee or charge can be set at a level where a profit-maximizing firm will be induced to clean up its emissions to some socially-desirable level. If a charge is high enough, it will be less costly to treat the emissions than to pollute and pay the charge. An effect of the emission charge is that it (8)_____ (allows, does not allow) firms flexibility in the methods used to clean up their discharge. A firm (9)_____ (does not have, has) an incentive to clean up pollution in the most efficient manner.

(10)_____ (Emission charges, Regulation) have/has been the dominant form of pollution control in the United States. The Environmental Protection Agency places limits on the amount of a pollutant that can be emitted. For instance, drinking water has a prescribed set of maximum chemical contaminant levels. If the emission limits are exceeded, a firm faces fines. The disadvantages of command-and-control regulation are that there are no incentives to employ the most efficient pollution abatement techniques. Regulations are often (11)_____ (flexible, inflexible) because they (12)_____ (allow several methods, prescribe a particular method) of compliance. In addition, firms have an incentive to just meet the allowed contaminant levels (13)_____ (but not, and often) to reduce emissions beyond that level. Therefore, if the marginal social benefits of pollution control vary regionally, inflexible national pollution standards are (14)_____ (inefficient, efficient).

Another way to control pollution would be for government to assign, lease, or sell pollution rights. The right to pollute could be limited to achieve the socially-preferred level of pollution. If pollution rights are sold, the level of demand for those rights determines their price. Some firms would pay the price necessary to pollute, whereas others would find it less costly to clean up their emissions. (15)_____ (Disadvantages, Advantages) of pollution rights include the ability of government to strictly control the level of pollution through the issuance of pollution rights. In addition, firms would have the flexibility to purchase the right to pollute or to seek the most cost efficient method of pollution abatement.

The EPA has recently instituted new programs in an effort to make their regulations less rigid. In many regions of the country, emissions offsets are employed. A new firm entering a region has to pay other firms already established in the region to reduce their emissions. In this way, the increase in pollution caused by the new firm is "offset" by a decrease in the emissions of existing firms. This is equivalent to (16)_____ (emission charges, the sale of existing property rights). The EPA also allows firms to exceed some contaminant levels if they emit other contaminants in amounts less than the maximum allowable limits. In fact, a firm can earn credits for emitting less than the allowable limits. These credits can be used later if the firm wants to exceed the limits or can be sold.

In the short run, the amount of proven reserves of depletable resources depend upon (17)_____ (the profitability of extracting them and making them available to the market; the finite stock of resources). An increase in its price will bring forth a greater quantity of the resource, and in the long run will result in additional exploration and search for new deposits of the resource, resulting in increased (18)_____(supply, demand). In addition, price increases give users of the resource an incentive to substitute less expensive resources and to develop technologies not requiring as much of the resource or allowing the use of other resources. Demand for a resource may actually fall in the long run, as was the case with oil.

Resources may be overexploited in the short run, imposing external costs on society. These external costs stem from a reduction in the future use of the resource. Common property resources are overused because (19)_____(regulations, property rights) have not been established for the use of the resource.

KEY TERMS REVIEW

Write the key term from the list below next to its definition.

Key Terms

Pollution	Depletable resource
Emission charges	Renewable resource
Emission standards	Common property resource
Pollution right	

Definitions

1. _____: prices established for the right to emit each unit of a pollutant.

2. _____: a government-issued certificate allowing a firm to emit a specified quantity of polluting waste.

3. _____: a resource (such as the ocean) whose use is not priced because property rights for payment of services have not been established.

4. _____: a natural resource that can be restocked over time, such as fish, timber, and wildlife.

5. _____: a resource for which there is a given amount of known reserves available at any point in time.

6. _____: limits established by government on the annual amounts and kinds of pollutants that can be emitted into the air or water by producers or users of certain products.

7. _____: waste that has been disposed of in the air, in water, or on land that reduces the value of those resources in alternative uses.

CONCEPT REVIEW

Concept 1: *Efficient level of environmental protection*

1. You are an administrator with the EPA and are responsible for determining the efficient level of pollution control (sulphur removal) from smokestack emissions of coal-fired electric power plants. These emissions result in acid rain and the deterioration of forests and lakes.

    a. What are some of the benefits associated with controlling smokestack emissions?

    b. The costs of controlling the emissions is the _____ cost of the resources used for pollution control in their next-best use. Explain.

c. Below are total social benefits and costs associated with reducing sulphur emissions.

Percent Reduction Sulphur Emissions	Total Social Benefits ($millions)	MSB	Total Social Costs ($millions)	MSC	Net Benefit
0%	0		0	_____	
10	180	_____	60	_____	_____
20	350	_____	140	_____	_____
30	510	_____	240	_____	_____
40	660	_____	360	_____	_____
50	800	_____	500	_____	_____
60	930	_____	660	_____	_____
70	1,050	_____	840	_____	_____
80	1,160	_____	1,040	_____	_____
90	1,260	_____	1,260	_____	_____
100	1,350	_____	1,500	_____	_____

(1) Complete the table.

(2) Plot the marginal social benefit and marginal social cost curves on the graph below.

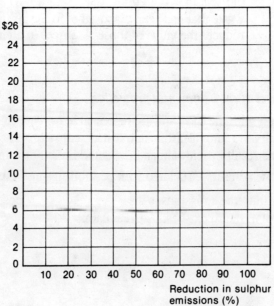

Dollars per percent change (milions of dollars)

$26
24
22
20
18
16
14
12
10
8
6
4
2
0

10 20 30 40 50 60 70 80 90 100

Reduction in sulphur emissions (%)

(3) The efficient level of pollution control is a _____ % reduction where
_____ equals _____ and _____ are maximized.
    MSB = $_____, MSC = $_____, Net Benefits = $_____.

(4) Identify the efficient level of pollution control on the graph above.

Concept 2: *Pollution policies*

2. Assume that for the example above each firm faces identical costs associated with removing a
given percentage of sulphur from smokestack emissions. Below are pollution control data for
a representative electric power company.

Sulphur Percent	Reduction Units	Total Cost ($ thousands)	MC per Unit Removed
0%	0	0	
10	50	25	_____
20	100	60	_____
30	150	105	_____
40	200	160	_____
50	250	225	_____
60	300	300	_____
70	350	385	_____
80	400	480	_____
90	450	585	_____
100	500	700	_____

a. Complete the table.

b. Plot the firm's marginal cost of pollution removal on the following graph.

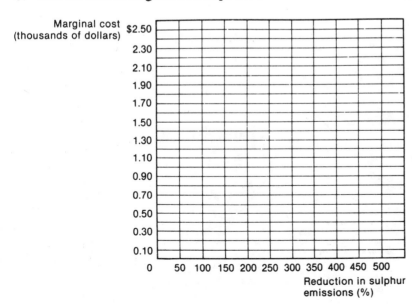

321

c. From question 1, it was found that the socially-desirable level of sulphur reduction was _____ %. For the power company above, this means reducing sulphur emissions by _____ units. An emission charge of $_____ would induce the power company to reduce emissions to the efficient level. Explain.

d. Show the emissions charge on the figure above and identify the efficient level of pollution (emission of sulphur).

e. If, because of new and more accurate estimates of the marginal social benefits of emission control, the EPA decided to reduce emissions further, it could _____ the emission charge.

3. List three advantages of using emissions charges as a means of controlling pollution.

a. _____

b. _____

c. _____

4. List three disadvantages associated with regulation as a means of controlling pollution.

a. _____

b. _____

c. _____

5. List two advantages associated with the assignment or sale of property rights as a means of controlling pollution.

a. _____

b. _____

Concept 3: *Depletable and renewable resources*

6. The market for oil, a depletable resource, is shown in the figure below.

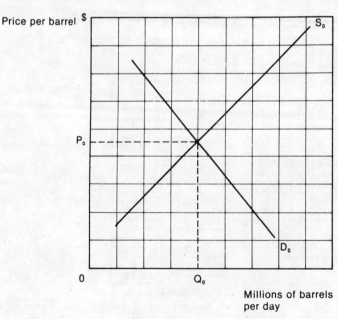

Price per barrel $

P_0

S_0

D_0

0   Q_0

Millions of barrels per day

322

a. At the current market price of oil, Po, the current quantity of oil demanded will eventually cause the supply of the depletable resource, oil, to _____. Show graphically. This causes the price of oil to _____.

b. The _____ in the price of oil will, in the long run, likely result in an/a _____ in supply, thus causing the market price to _____. Explain.

c. How will consumers of oil react in the long run to the increase in the price of oil today, and what are the implications for the market price and quantity?

7. The marginal benefits associated with catching fish from a common-property lake (one in which property rights do not exist) is shown below.

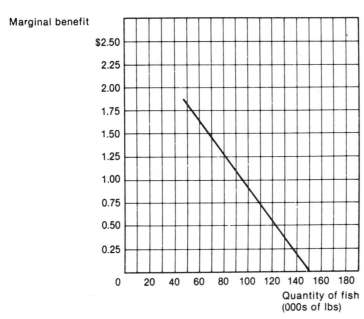

a. What quantity of fish will fishermen remove from the lake? _____ lbs. Why?

b. In order to maintain a given quantity of fish for future fishermen, a maximum catch of 80,000 lbs would leave a reproduction stock of fish just large enough to achieve future desired levels of fish production. The current catch of _____ lbs represents an _____ (overuse, underuse) of the renewable resource. Explain how property rights could be used to correct the problem.

c. Show on the graph above the effect of using property rights to correct the inefficient use of the lake.

323

MASTERY TEST

Select the best answer.

1. Pollution is an/a:
   a. public good.
   b. negative externality.
   c. positive externality.
   d. opportunity cost.

2. An emission creates pollution :
   a. all of the time.
   b. when the efficient level of pollution is reached.
   c. when the emission causes damage to resources.
   d. if it is emitted into the atmosphere.

3. The efficient level of pollution control is :
   a. that level associated with a zero level of pollution.
   b. that level produced by the market.
   c. that level where the marginal social benefits and marginal social costs of control are equal.
   d. at a level where total benefits equal total costs.
   e. None of the above.

4. Estimates of the benefits associated with a reduction in pollution are _____ to determine accurately and result in social choices regarding pollution control that are likely _____ social net benefits.
   a. easy, to maximize
   b. easy, not to maximize
   c. difficult, to minimize
   d. difficult, to maximize
   e. difficult, not to maximize

5. The market will _____ environmental protection.
   a. underproduce
   b. not produce
   c. overproduce
   d. produce the efficient quantity of

6. Which of the following would not be used in pollution control?

   a. Corrective subsidies

   b. Regulation

   c. Emission charges

   d. Property rights

7. Which of the following is considered an advantage of emission charges?

   a. The charge can be set at a level to induce a profit-maximizing firm to either clean up or restrict pollution to the desired level.

   b. The firm has an incentive to employ the most efficient technique of pollution cleanup.

   c. Charges allow flexibility by firms in various regions to deal with the pollution problem in the most appropriate way.

   d. All of the above.

8. The predominant method of pollution control in the United States is:

   a. regulation.

   b. emission charges.

   c. property rights sales.

   d. corrective taxes.

9. Regulation as a means of eliminating or reducing pollution is:

   a. efficient because it results in the maximum net benefits to society.

   b. inefficient because it is often inflexible, requiring a single method of compliance rather than allowing the firm to seek the cost efficient method of pollution abatement.

   c. effective because it creates incentives by firms to reduce pollution by more than the allowable limits.

   d. the only practical method of pollution control when the point source of pollution can be identified and the emission can be easily measured.

10. Common property resources are often polluted because:

   a. emission charges are set too low.

   b. regulation needs to be extended to include more than privately owned property.

   c. of the absence of property rights.

   d. of industrialization.

11. The efficient level of pollution control can be achieved by imposing an/a_____ on the polluter _____ the polluter's marginal cost of pollution cleanup at the socially-desired level of pollution reduction.

    a. regulation, increasing

    b. regulation, decreasing

    c. corrective subsidy, greater than

    d. emission charge, greater than

    e. emission charge, equal to

12. The EPA's emission offset is equivalent

    a. to an emission charge.

    b. to a subsidy.

    c. to a tax.

    d. in effect to a sale of property rights.

13. Under which EPA program can a firm earn credits for emitting less than the allowable limits of pollution? The credits can be used by the firm to exceed the limits in the future or can be sold to other firms.

    a. Emission charge

    b. Emission offset

    c. The "bubble"

    d. Leasing of property rights

14. The supply of proven reserves of a depletable resource depends

    a. upon the profitability of extracting the resource and making it available to the market.

    b. exclusively upon the technological ability to extract the resource.

    c. only on the finite supply of the resource.

    d. on the reserves presently being mined and the yet undiscovered reserves.

15. Other things constant, the supply of a depletable resource will in time _____, causing the price of the resource to _____, which in turn causes new exploration and the use of new extraction techniques and in the long run causes the supply of the resource to_____.

    a. increase, rise, increase

    b. increase, fall, decrease

    c. decrease, rise, decrease

    d. decrease, rise, increase

    e. increase, fall, increase

16. Which of the following property resources are likely to be overused?
    a. A private lake
    b. Your backyard
    c. A rancher's stock pond
    d. Ocean fisheries

17. Common property resources are overexploited because:
    a. of the absence of regulation.
    b. of the absence of corrective subsidies.
    c. of the absence of property rights.
    d. of competing regional interests.
    e. None of the above.

18. Given the data below, determine the efficient level of pollution reduction for a stream.

Percent of Pollution Reduction	Marginal Benefit	Marginal Cost
	($000s)	
20	$50	$ 5
40	40	15
60	30	30
80	20	50
100	10	80

    a. 20%
    b. 40%
    c. 60%
    d. 80%
    e. 100%

19. Which of the following is true of pollution?
    a. Pollution is a negative externality.
    b. Pollution exists because of the absence of assigned property rights or the lack of enforcement of those rights.
    c. The efficient level of pollution is not necessarily a zero level of pollution.
    d. All of the above

20. Given a firm's cost of treated discharge shown below, determine the appropriate emissions charge (or unit tax) necessary to induce the firm to treat at least 3000 gallons per day.

Marginal Cost of Treated Discharge	Discharge (gallons per day)
$10	1,000
20	2,000
35	3,000
55	4,000
85	5,000

   a. $25

   b. $1,000

   c. $35

   d. $105,000

   e. None of the above

21. Which of the following emission control policies is the most efficient and flexible policy?

   a. Regulation

   b. Emission charges

   c. Property rights

   d. Jawboning

THINK IT THROUGH

1. An environmentalist might argue that any emissions beyond that which can be safely absorbed by the natural environment reduces society's well-being. Do you agree? Explain.

2. Discuss the dominant approach to pollution control in the United States. What alternative approaches could be used? What are the advantages of these other methods of pollution control?

3. Can you think of any reason why it is necessary for federal and state governments to "manage" wildlife populations? Explain. What alternatives could be employed other than game limits?

ANALYZING THE NEWS

Using the skills derived from studying this chapter, analyze the economic facts that make up the following article and answer the questions below, using graphical analysis where possible.

1. Explain the advantages of allowing electric power utilities to trade "acid-rain" credits rather than requiring each utility to cut back emissions by equal amounts.

2. How might tradeable credits be used to more efficiently reduce carbon dioxide emissions?

ENVIRONMENT

Adam Smith Turns Green

Using market forces to clean air and water

Back in the days when environmentalism meant saving whales and wearing Earth Shoes, activists rarely met a regulation they didn't like. Was the local paper mill dumping chlorine into the river? Pass a law slashing allowable emissions and mandating the technology for achieving them. Were utilities spewing out sulfur dioxide, a cause of acid rain? Require each power plant to install scrubbers on its smokestacks. "Command-and-control" did make the nation's air and water cleaner, but it also made enemies in boardrooms and living rooms. Business lobbies hard against new regulations, and last fall almost every environmental referendum went down to defeat as voters equated green laws with a grab for the green in their wallets. Worse, traditional pollution control has begun to cost more and more even as it achieves less and less.

Enter an unusual coalition of free marketeers, politicians and environmentalists who believe there's a way to break the logjam. It goes by the name "market-based environmental incentives," and it means reforming markets so that it pays to clean up. It's "an attempt to put a green thumb on Adam Smith's invisible hand," says Sen. Tim Wirth of Colorado. Or as economists say, the goal is to make prices reflect the full social cost of goods, from a can of soda to a kilowatt of electricity. Today that is emphatically not the case. A homeowner who generates six bags of garbage pays the same fee for collection as someone who generates two; the amount of taxes someone pays for cleaning urban smog has nothing to do with whether she bicycles to work or steers her soot-belching station wagon down the freeway. Market-based environmentalism aims to correct these inequities.

The strategy took shape in "Project 88," a report presented to the incoming Bush administration by Wirth and the late Sen. John Heinz of Pennsylvania. Last year it became the basis for the new acid-rain provision of the Clean Air Act. Rather than making every power plant cut emissions of sulfur by the same amount, the act sets a national goal of 50 percent reduction. And it allows utilities to trade "acid-rain credits." For example, an old plant burning high-sulfur coal can, instead of laying out a fortune for scrubbers, pay a utility with newer equipment and low-sulfur coal to reduce its emissions by *more* than 50 percent. Result: the same sulfur reductions, but for $1 billion per year less.

Schemes like this make some environmentalists uneasy about allowing businesses to buy their way into compliance, but that's becoming a minority view. More than 100 bills in Congress propose a market approach to environmental problems. Last month Wirth unveiled Project 88-Round II, which details ways to use markets to fight global warming, waste and vanishing forests. Such policies "can do more for less," says Richard Morgenstern of the Environmental Protection Agency.

Cheaper fix: The biggest bang for the buck, yen or mark may come in global environmental threats, where the cost of solutions varies dramatically from country to country. For instance, Round II proposes tradable permits for carbon dioxide (CO_2), the chief greenhouse gas. Under an international accord, every country might start with a requirement to reduce CO_2 emissions by some number of tons, based on its population or gross national product. If Japan found it too expensive to, say, retool its already efficient factories so they required less oil, it could pay Poland to increase the efficiency of its plants. Since Cracow's factories are less efficient than Japan's, each ton of CO_2 reduced this way would cost the world economy much less than trying to squeeze more efficiency out of Tokyo, explains economist Robert Stavins of Harvard University, who directed Project 88. Similarly, if Ford found it too expensive to raise its fleet mileage, it could pay eastern European factories to do so: it's much cheaper to raise mileage from 10 miles per gallon to 30 than from 30 to 50.

Tradable permits may cut greenhouse gases better than the competing approach of taxing fossil fuels. "With a tax you never know how much of a decrease you'll get," says economist Dan Dudek of the Environmental Defense Fund, because no crystal ball tells policymakers how a price increase of, say, $5 per gallon of petrol will affect people's driving habits. In contrast, says Dudek, "permits let you accurately control the amount of carbon dioxide released." EDF was instrumental in selling President Bush on acid-rain permits.

Old newspapers: Garbage offers an inviting target for green economists. Under Seat-

Continued on next page

Source: "Adam Smith Turns Green: Using Market to Clean Air and Water," *Newsweek*, June 10, 1991, p. 60.

329

Continued from previous page

tle's "pay as you throw" policy, which charges more for every barrel of nonrecyclable trash, residents now generate an average of slightly more than one can per week, down from 3.5. Yet as more people separate glass, plastic and newspapers for recycling, markets have become so glutted that the price of these materials has plummeted, forcing some communities to *pay* to have "recyclables" carted to a landfill. To create demand for old newsprint, Congress is considering a national target for recycled content. The cheapest way to achieve the goal would be tradable permits. If mills supplying the hypothetical Sunbelt News were near forests but far from a source of recycled newsprint, the News could pay the Rustbelt Gazette, whose mill is up to the rafters in used papers, to increase its recycled content above 40 percent.

Sometimes taxes offer the simplest way to change behavior. Germany, for instance, is considering a tax on packaging that would reflect disposal costs. This kind of green tax could serve as a wedge for revamping the tax system in a popular way. Taxing such "bads" as hazardous wastes could generate $130 billion a year in the United States, calculates the Worldwatch Institute. That could be used to reduce taxes on "goods," such as labor and savings.

For all its appeal, the market is not a panacea. If one rich polluter pays everyone else to take on his share of toxics reduction, the air or water around his factory could become a poison hot spot, endangering the health of local residents. And a "smog bazaar" in Los Angeles, which allows polluters who cut emissions from one source to increase it from another, sparks criticism of "a market in cancer permits." Still, politicians as well as environmentalists are deciding that the thou-shalt-not school of pollution control has run its course.

SHARON BEGLEY *with* MARY HAGER
in Washington

CHAPTER ANSWERS

The Chapter in Brief

1. Just equals 2. Would 3. Efficient 4. Not an 5. May not be 6. Inefficient 7. Emission charge 8. Allows 9. Has 10. Regulation 11. Inflexible 12. Prescribe a particular method 13. But not 14. Inefficient 15. Advantages 16. The sale of existing property rights 17. The profitability of extracting them and making them available to the market 18. Supply 19. Property rights

Key Terms Review

1. Emission charges 2. Pollution right 3. Common property resource 4. Renewable resource 5. Depletable resource 6. Emission standards 7. Pollution

Concept Review

1. a. A reduction in sulphur emissions will reduce the incidence of acid rain, which will reduce the deterioration of lakes and forests. The benefits of controlling sulphur emissions are the commercial and recreational values of lakes and forests, which would have otherwise diminished as a result of pollution.

   b. Opportunity. Controlling pollution involves the use of scarce resources that have value in alternative uses.

   c. (1)

Sulphur Reduction	MSB	MSC	Net Benefits
			($ millions)
0%			$ 0
10	18	6	120
20	17	8	210
30	16	10	270
40	15	12	300
50	14	14	300
60	13	16	270
70	12	18	210
80	11	20	120
90	10	22	0
100	9	24	-150

(2)

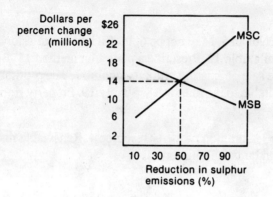

Dollars per
percent change
(millions)

Reduction in sulphur
emissions (%)

(3)   50, MSB, MSC, Net Benefits; $14 million, $14 million; $300 million

(4)   See figure above.

2. a.

Units	MC ($ thousands)
0	
50	0.5
100	0.7
150	0.9
200	1.1
250	1.3
300	1.5
350	1.7
400	1.9
450	2.1
500	2.3

b.

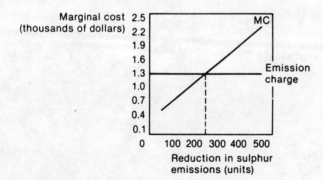

Marginal cost
(thousands of dollars)

Reduction in sulphur
emissions (units)

c. 50, 250; $1,300. As long as the charge exceeds the marginal cost of cleanup, a profit-maximizing firm will treat the effluent rather than pollute and pay the charge. If marginal cost exceeds the emission charge, the least-cost strategy would be to pollute and pay the charge. Therefore, a firm has an incentive to treat its discharge up to the point at which the emission charge equals the marginal cost of pollution treatment.

d. See figure above.

e. Increase

3. a. Emission charges can be set at a level to achieve the desired level of pollution reduction.

   b. Firms have the flexibility to employ techniques of pollution treatment that best fit their unique situation.

   c. Firms have an incentive to minimize costs of cleanup that improve the economy's resource allocation.

4. a. Regulations are often inflexible requiring a single method of compliance rather than allowing the firm to seek the most cost-efficient solution.

   b. Firms have no incentive to reduce pollution below the emission standards set by the EPA.

   c. Regulations that are uniform nationally do not allow for regional variations in the marginal social benefits of pollution control.

5. a. Issuance of property rights or government certificates granting the right to pollute can be sold or issued in an amount that will limit pollution to the socially-desired level.

   b. A market for these limited rights will develop in which some firms will find it more profitable to treat their effluent before discharge than to pay the market price for the right to pollute. Thus firms have an incentive to minimize costs associated with reducing emissions.

6. a. Decrease; increase

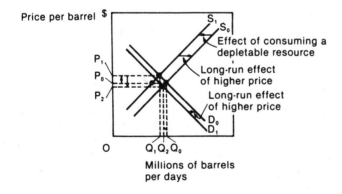

333

b. Increase, increase, fall. In the long run, there will be more exploration as a result of the higher prices, and new extraction technologies will likely be employed both of which increase the supply of oil. Other things being constant, this will reduce the price of oil.

c. Users of resources respond to rising prices by substituting relatively less costly resources and developing production techniques or products allowing the use of more plentiful and less costly resources. As in the case of oil, the higher short-run price of oil causes a movement up the demand curve in the short run, but it will also shift the demand curve leftward in the long run, causing long-run market price and quantity to fall.

7. a. 150,000 lbs. With no cost or price associated with the use of the resource, fishermen will catch fish up to the point where their total benefits are maximized, that is, where the marginal benefit curve intersects the quantity axis at a level of zero marginal benefits.

b. 150,000 lbs, overuse. Government certificates allowing the right to extract 80,000 lbs of fish annually could be sold. Assuming all benefits associated with fishing are private and there are no social goals involved other than preventing the overuse of the resource, the property rights scheme will result in the highest and best use of the resource (assuming competitive markets).

c.

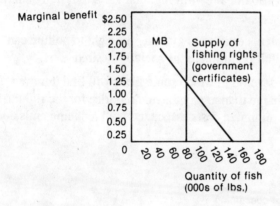

Self-Test for Mastery

1. b 2. c 3. c 4. e 5. a 6. a 7. d 8. a 9. b 10. c 11. e 12. d 13. c 14. a 15. d 16. d 17. c 18. c 19. d 20. c 21. c

Think it Through

1. Emissions are a by-product of production. The production of goods benefits society. But since emissions result in pollution, there is an external cost that is not reflected in the firm's costs of production. The firm will allocate too many resources to the production of the good. It is "efficient" to require the firm to reduce pollution only up to the level that maximizes social net benefits. Requiring the firm to reduce pollution to zero will likely mean that the opportunity costs of the pollution control resources will exceed the benefits to society from the reduction in pollution.

2. Regulation is the dominant method of pollution control in the United States. Emissions standards are established for various pollutants, and fines are imposed if the standards are violated. The regulations tend to be inflexible and do not allow firms to respond in the most efficient manner to emission reduction. Emission charges could be used giving firms the incentive to seek the most cost efficient method of pollution reduction. They are flexible and can vary by firm and region. Property rights could be established and sold, giving those in the market for pollution rights the incentive to seek the least-cost solutions to pollution reduction. The quantity of those rights can be set to achieve the desired level of pollution.

3. It is necessary to regulate or manage wildlife populations because of the fear that breeding stocks would eventually be depleted, reducing the commercial and recreational values associated with hunting and fishing for future generations. Private landowners can prevent excessive hunting—they have a legal remedy. Public lands and lakes are common property resources for which no individuals own property rights. In the absence of government involvement, public lands would be overhunted and public lakes would be overfished as individuals hunt and fish to the point where their marginal benefits equal zero. This assumes that no price or any other cost is associated with the use of the resource.

   The traditional approach to preventing overexploitation of wildlife populations is by regulation and establishing game limits. If the limits are exceeded, fines are imposed. Property rights are used to a limited extent. Certain hunting grounds may be opened only to a limited number of hunters. The rights to hunt are generally allocated on a lottery basis rather than sold in markets. User charges are used in the form of a license or stamp fee, but these are inflexible in the sense that they are not set to achieve specific game limits for each given species of game. If there are no social goals other than preventing the overexploitation of wildlife populations, a market for property rights or a hunting or fishing fee similar in concept to emission charges would achieve the desirable level of wildlife populations; furthermore, this would achieve it more efficiently than the current system of game limits and fines.

Analyzing the News

1. Requiring power utilities to cut back emissions by equal amounts is inefficient. Some utilities burn low-sulfur coal, whereas other utilities burn the more polluting high-sulfur coal. Requiring each utility to install the same sulfur-reducing scrubbing equipment imposes excessive costs on utilities that burn low-sulfur coal. With tradeable emissions credits, a utility using high-sulfur coal would have the option of installing scrubbers or purchasing credits (rights to pollute) from low-sulfur utilities that receive credits by emitting less pollutants into the atmosphere than the maximum levels prescribed in the emission standards. The advantage of this approach is that it is possible to reduce emissions to desired levels while also saving an estimated $1 billion per year in costs to utilities.

2. For the same reasons noted above, it would be inefficient to require each nation to reduce carbon dioxide emissions by the same amount or the same percentage. Such a policy would be inflexible and very costly. It would be far more difficult and costly for Japan to increase the efficiency of its already efficient economy in order to reduce fossil fuels consumption than it would be for Poland with its inefficient industrial structure. Tradeable permits, however, give each nation the option to increase efficiency and reduce fossil fuels consumption or purchase permits (rights to pollute) from nations that have earned credits by reducing carbon dioxide emissions more than required. It might be less expensive for Japan to pay Poland (to purchase credits from Poland) to increase the efficiency of Polish factories than for Japan to squeeze additional reductions in fossil fuels consumption from its factories.

17 THE ECONOMICS OF SPECIAL-INTEREST GROUPS: SUBSIDIZING AGRICULTURE AND INDUSTRIES

CHAPTER CONCEPTS

After studying your text, attending class, and completing this chapter, you should be able to:

1. Discuss special interest groups, their goals, and the impact of programs that benefit these interests on prices and resource allocation.
2. Analyze and evaluate the impact of government subsidies and tax breaks on resource use and prices.
3. Evaluate the impact of policies that subsidize farmers in the United States.

THE CHAPTER IN BRIEF

Fill in the blanks to summarize chapter content.

(1)_____ (Special interest groups, Lobbying associations), such as in agriculture, seek expenditures or special benefits from government that result in an increase in income. The costs of the benefits are dispersed over many millions of taxpayers and add little to a taxpayer's tax liability. Therefore, special interest legislation often encounters little resistance from the general public. Many individuals seek to use the power of government to increase their earnings above their opportunity costs. These people are (2)_____(income, rent) seekers. (3)_____ (Wages, Rents) are receipts in excess of opportunity costs that can be created by government by limiting the right to perform a given activity. Agricultural allotments and exclusive franchises are created by government policy and have the effect of (4)_____(decreasing farm incomes, creating rents).

Agriculture is a major special interest group in the United States. In 1933, the (5)_____(Agricultural Adjustment Act, Farm Price Support Act) was passed, controlling acreage in both production and prices. The primary goal of the Act was to prevent surpluses of agricultural commodities in order to keep prices and farmers' incomes from falling. More specifically, the goal was to keep the purchasing power of the farmers' income from falling. This is accomplished if the price of agricultural products rise at a rate fast enough to compensate for the (6)_____(cost increases associated with producing the commodities; rise in the prices of the goods and services consumed by farmers). This is known as (7)_____(parity, a price support). As of the mid-1980s, the parity price ratio was at an all time (8)_____(low of under 60%, high of just over 90%).

Government price supports and acreage control programs are intended to increase farm incomes. Government agricultural price supports increase farm incomes but result in (9)_____ (shortages, surpluses) if the price supports exceed market prices. Prices are supported through the loan support program through which a farmer can borrow from the government at a specified price per bushel. The agricultural commodity is used as collateral for the loan. The loan rate is generally set (10)_____(below, above) the market price per bushel. The farmer can choose to let the government keep the grain or repay the loan. The farmer will repay the loan only if the market price (11)_____(exceeds, is less than) the loan rate. Acreage control programs involve payments to farmers to (12)_____(expand, take land out of) production. The idea is to (13)_____(reduce, increase) supply and to keep market price, and hence farm incomes, at a higher level.

The government holds a large portion of the grain that it acquires off the market to prevent depressing prices and incomes. There are large storage costs and other costs associated with reducing these stocks of commodities. The (14)_____ (Target Price, Payment-in-Kind) program was an attempt to control farm production and to reduce government stocks of grain at the same time. Farmers that took acreage out of production were paid in kind with the government's stock of commodities.

Current methods of supporting farm incomes include (15)_____ (target prices, payment-in-kind) and direct subsidies. Target prices are government guaranteed prices. Farmers are generally required to restrict acreage in order to qualify for the Target Price program. If the guaranteed price exceeds the market price, farmers sell all of their output at the market price and the difference between the market and target price is made up by the government. Surpluses (16)_____ (develop, do not develop), but the acreage restrictions (17)_____ (do not necessarily, necessarily) limit or fix supply. The program, in effect, transfers income from taxpayers to farmers. Target prices result in (18)_____ (higher, lower) market prices than with traditional farm policies, but prices are not necessarily lower than would prevail in a competitive market.

Government policies can benefit special interest groups with direct subsidies and tax breaks. Subsidies increase the market price and quantity of the subsidized good if given to (19)_____ (consumers, producers), but they decrease market prices if given to (20)_____ (consumers, producers). The net price paid by consumers and received by producers is exactly the same, regardless if subsidies are given to producers or consumers. Both consumers and producers of the subsidized good benefit, as well as those that supply specialized inputs to the subsidized industry.

In addition to direct payments, subsidies can be in the form of (21)_____ (excise taxes, tax preferences). Certain activities, such as home ownership, are given preference in the tax code, which in effect "subsidizes" the activity through a lower tax liability. The losses in government tax revenues from the tax breaks are called (22)_____(tax expenditures, tax losses). Tax preferences benefit both buyers and sellers in the preferred markets, including the resource suppliers to those markets.

Some subsidies are "hidden" because they indirectly benefit certain groups. Examples of "hidden" subsidies include (23)_____ (agricultural loan supports, government loan guarantees) and government-provided insurance (flood insurance, for example). By transferring some of the risks associated with production in the private sector to the public sector, in effect the government is subsidizing business growth and development.

KEY TERMS REVIEW

Write the key term from the list below next to its definition.

Key Terms

Special interest group   Economic rents

Rent seeking   Parity

Parity price ratio   Target price

Acreage control programs   Tax credit

Tax preference   Tax expenditure

Definitions

1. _____: an organization that seeks to increase government expenditures or induce government to take other actions that benefit particular people.

2. _____: the ratio of an average of the prices of goods sold by farmers to an average of the prices of goods on which farmers spend their incomes.

3. _____: an exemption, deduction, or exclusion from income or other taxable items in computing tax liability.

4. _____: the idea that the prices of agricultural commodities must rise as fast as the prices of goods and services on which farmers spend their incomes.

5. _____: a reduction in the tax liability for a person or corporation making certain purchases or engaging in certain activities.

6. _____: the process by which people compete to obtain government favors that increase the economic rents they can earn.

7. _____: guarantees sellers a minimum price per unit of output.

8. _____: earnings that exceed the opportunity cost of an activity.

9. _____: provide cash payments to farmers who agree to take some of their land out of production for certain crops.

10. _____: the losses in revenue to the federal government as a result of tax breaks granted to individuals and corporations.

CONCEPT REVIEW

Concepts 1 and 3: *Special interest programs—Agriculture*

1. The diagram below represents a market for an agricultural commodity in the absence of government intervention.

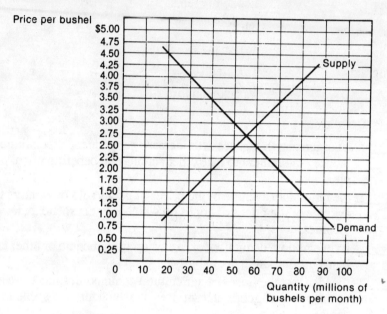

a. The current market price and quantity are $_____ and _____ bushels, respectively. Assume that the current market price results in a parity price ratio of 100%.

b. Because of improvements in production techniques, the supply of the commodity increases 10 million bushels at each price. Show this in the graph above and label the new supply curve, S1. After the change in supply, market price and quantity are $_____ and _____ bushels, respectively. Assuming all other prices are unchanged, the parity price ratio _____ (increases, decreases), which means that the farmers' purchasing power has _____ (increased, decreased).

c. Assume that farmers are able to win legislation ensuring a parity price ratio of 100%. This is accomplished through a commodity loan program that effectively establishes a price support. The supported price must equal $_____. At the supported price, quantity demanded equals _____ bushels and quantity supplied equals _____ bushels resulting in a _____ (shortage, surplus) of _____ bushels. Show graphically in the figure above.

d. The cost to the taxpayer of the _____ (shortage, surplus) is $_____. Shade in the area representing that cost in the figure above.

e. The price support program results in _____ prices to consumers and _____ taxes incurred or_____ government services received by society.

340

f. An acreage restriction program could also be used to achieve a price sufficient to yield a parity price ratio of 100%. How much would supply have to be reduced at each price? _____ bushels. This program results in either _____ taxes or _____ government services and _____ prices to consumers as well as _____ (an equality between quantity supplied and quantity demanded, surpluses).

2. The market below is for an agricultural commodity for which there is no government intervention.

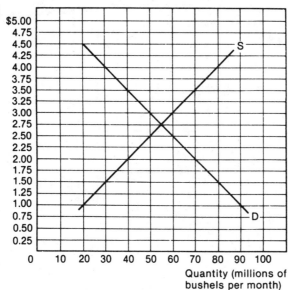

Price per bushel

Quantity (millions of bushels per month)

a. The current market price and quantity are $_____ and _____ bushels, respectively.

b. Because the market price is considered by farmers to be too low, farm lobbies are able to win special interest legislation guaranteeing a price per bushel—a target price which is above the prevailing market equilibrium price. To qualify for the program, farmers must restrict acreage. Suppose the acreage restriction phase of the program reduces quantity supplied at each price by 25 million bushels. Show the new supply curve in the figure above and label it, S1. Market price _____ to $_____ and market quantity _____ to _____ bushels.

c. At a target price of $4 per bushel, farmers will produce and make available to the market _____ bushels and will receive a market price per bushel of $_____ and a subsidy per bushel of $_____. Show in the figure above. Consumers will pay a price of $_____, and taxpayers will pay a total subsidy of $_____. Quantity demanded will _____ quantity supplied.

d. As compared to price supports or acreage restriction programs, the Target Price program results in a _____ price to the consumer. As compared to a competitive market

341

without government intervention, the Target Price program above results in prices that are
_____.

   e.   Target price programs, in effect, transfer income from _____ to
_____.

Concept 2:   *Effects of subsidies, tax breaks*

3. The diagram below represents a competitive market for a good.

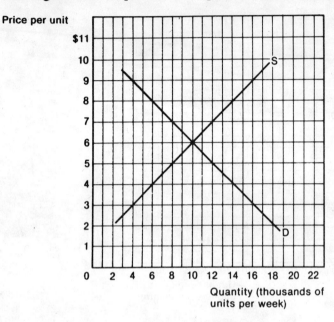

Price per unit

Quantity (thousands of units per week)

   a.   A subsidy of $1 per unit given to consumers results in a/an _____ in demand. Show in the diagram above.

   b.   Market price _____ to $_____ and market quantity _____ to _____ units. The net price (after deducting the subsidy) to the consumer at the new market quantity is $_____.

   c.   Given the initial demand curve, D, show the effect graphically in the diagram if the $1 subsidy is given to producers instead of consumers.

   d.   Market price _____ to $_____ and market quantity _____ to _____ units. The net price (after the subsidy is added) received by the producer is $_____.

   e.   Subsidies to consumers, as compared to subsidies to producers, result in _____ market prices. The net price paid by consumers and the net price received by producers are _____ for subsidies to consumers or for subsidies to producers.

4. List two indirect subsidies and give an example of each.

   a. _____

   b. _____

5. Give two examples of hidden subsidies.

   a. _____

   b. _____

MASTERY TEST

Select the best answer.

1. Special interest groups are composed of individuals that try to use the power of government to increase incomes above the opportunity cost of their activities. These individuals are:
   a. acting in society's best interest.
   b. called free riders.
   c. rent seekers.
   d. irrational.

2. An economic rent is a payment:
   a. in excess of the opportunity cost of an activity.
   b. made to lease building space.
   c. less than the cost of an activity.
   d. equal to the opportunity cost of an activity.

3. Which of the following acts sought to maintain farm income by implementing price supports and acreage restrictions?
   a. Payment-in-Kind program of 1933
   b. Food Security Wheat Reserve Act of 1933
   c. Agricultural Adjustment Act of 1933
   d. Rent Seekers Act of 1933

4. Which of the following is not a goal of U.S. farm policy?
   a. Maintaining farming as a viable business
   b. Maintaining an adequate supply of food
   c. Encouraging agricultural exports
   d. Reducing the size of family farms and increasing their numbers

5. The concept of parity:

    a. an equitable distribution of income among farmers.

    b. that farm commodity prices must keep in step with other prices in order to keep the farmers' purchasing power from falling.

    c. that a commodity price must be set above the market equilibrium price.

    d. None of the above.

6. As of the mid-1980s, the parity price ratio:

    a. is at an all time low of 20%.

    b. is at an all time high of 90%.

    c. has risen above the 80% level.

    d. is at an all time low of less than 60%.

    e. has fallen to just below 80%.

7. Price supports result in _____ and _____ prices to consumers.

    a. shortages, higher

    b. shortages, lower

    c. surpluses, higher

    d. surpluses, lower

8. Acreage restriction programs are similar to price support programs in that prices to consumers are _____ than unregulated market prices, but they are different in that quantity supplied _____ quantity demanded.

    a. lower, exceeds

    b. higher, exceeds

    c. lower, equals

    d. higher, equals

9. Which of the following programs pays farmers with government stocks of commodities to restrict acreage?

    a. Target price program

    b. Price support program

    c. Government commodity program

    d. Payment-in-kind program

    e. Acreage allotment program

10. Which of the following programs guarantees farmers a price per bushel but allows market supply and demand to determine the market price?
    a. Target price program
    b. Price support program
    c. Government commodity program
    d. Payment-in-kind program
    e. Acreage allotment program

11. Which of the following programs effectively transfers income from taxpayers to farmers without necessarily resulting in commodity prices lower than would prevail in a competitive market?
    a. Target price program
    b. Price support program
    c. Government commodity program
    d. Payment-in-kind program
    e. Acreage allotment program

12. Subsidies given to consumers result in an/a _____ market price and an/a _____ in market quantity.
    a. decrease, increase
    b. increase, decrease
    c. decrease, decrease
    d. increase, increase

13. Subsidies given to producers result in an/a _____ in market price and an/a _____ in market quantity.
    a. decrease, increase
    b. increase, increase
    c. decrease, decrease
    d. increase, increase

14. The net price paid by a consumer under a consumer subsidy program is _____ the net price paid by the consumer under a producer subsidy program.
    a. equal to
    b. greater than
    c. less than
    d. equal to or less than
    e. equal to or greater than

15. Which of the following is a deduction, exemption, or exclusion from income in computing taxes?
    a. Tax credit
    b. Tax liability
    c. Tax preference
    d. Tax expenditure

16. Which of the following is a reduction in tax liability resulting from engaging in some activity?
    a. Tax credit
    b. Tax liability
    c. Tax preference
    d. Tax expenditure

17. Which of the following is the loss in government tax revenue resulting from a tax break?
    a. Tax credit
    b. Tax liability
    c. Tax preference
    d. Tax expenditure

18. Government loan guarantees are an example of a/an:
    a. direct subsidy.
    b. indirect subsidy.
    c. lost subsidy.
    d. hidden subsidy.

19. Which of the following are objectives of United States agriculture policy?
    a. To ensure bountiful supplies
    b. To prevent shortages
    c. To prevent surpluses
    d. To maintain higher agricultural prices and farm incomes
    e. C and d

20. Under the loan support program:
    a. the government will purchase farm products when the market price exceeds the loan price.
    b. the farmer will sell all farm produce at the market price and receive subsidies from the government.
    c. when market price exceeds the loan price, farmers sell their output in the market and pay back the loan.
    d. farmers restrict acreage and sell their output to the government at supported prices.

21. Which of the following is not a characteristic or outcome of target prices?

   a. Surpluses do not develop.

   b. Income is transferred from taxpayers to farmers.

   c. Consumers pay lower prices for farm products than under traditional price support programs.

   d. Acreage restrictions necessarily limit supply.

22. Suppose government desires to increase the private production of a good by giving subsidies to either producers or consumers of the good. Which type of subsidy results in the lowest net price paid by the consumer and received by the producer?

   a. A subsidy given to producers.

   b. A subsidy given to consumers.

   c. It does not matter whether the subsidy is given to producers or consumers, the net price paid by consumers and received by producers is the same.

   d. The net price received by the producer is always lower than the net price paid by the consumer, so it is inconsequential whether the subsidy is given to producers or consumers.

23. Which of the following is an example of a hidden subsidy?

   a. Subsidy payments to producers

   b. Tax preferences

   c. Government-provided insurance

   d. Tax expenditures

THINK IT THROUGH

1. Discuss the advantages of a target price program as compared to a price support program.

2. You are on the staff of a U.S. congressman and have been asked to prepare a statement regarding the gains and losses associated with a subsidy program. Identify the typical benefits and costs as well as the gainers and losers.

3. Can you think of any reasons why a tax expenditure rather than a direct subsidy would be employed to promote a given activity?

CHAPTER ANSWERS

The Chapter in Brief

1. Special interest groups 2. Rent 3. Rents 4. Creating rents 5. Agricultural Adjustment Act 6. Rise in the prices of the goods and services consumed by farmers 7. Parity 8. Low of under 60% 9. Surpluses 10. Above 11. Exceeds 12. Take land out of 13. Reduce 14. Payment-in-Kind 15. Target prices 16. Do not develop 17. Do not necessarily 18. Lower 19. Consumers 20. Producers 21. Tax preferences 22. Tax expenditures 23. Government loan guarantees

Key Terms Review

1. Special interest group 2. Parity price ratio 3. Tax preference 4. Parity 5. Tax credit 6. Rent seeking 7. Target price 8. Economic rents 9. Acreage control programs 10. Tax expenditure

Concept Review

1. a. $2.75, 55 million

   b.

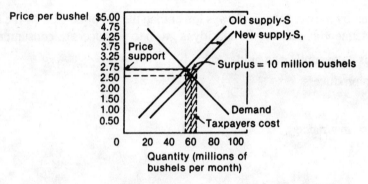

   $2.50, 60 million, decreases, decreased

   c. $2.75, 55 million, 65 million, surplus, 10 million

   d. Surplus, $27.5 million

   e. Higher, higher, fewer

   f. 10 million; higher, fewer, higher, an equality between quantity supplied and quantity demanded

2. a. $2.75, 55 million

b.

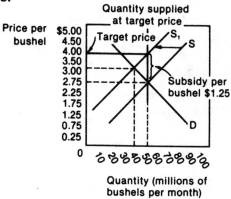

Increases, $3.38, decreases, 42.5 million

c.   55 million, $2.75, $1.25; $2.75, $68.75 million; equal

d.   Lower, not necessarily lower than would prevail in a competitive market

e.   Taxpayers, farmers

3. a.   Increase

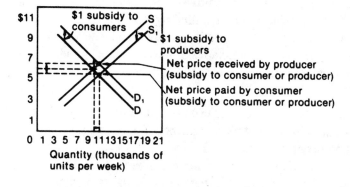

b. Increases, $6.50, increases, 11,000, $5.50

c. Shown in the graph above.

d. Decreases, $5.50, increases, 11,000, $6.50

e. Higher, the same

4. a. Tax credits: investment tax credits, child care tax credits

b. Tax preferences: interest exemption on home mortgage interest

5. a. Government loan guarantees

b. Government provided insurance, such as flood insurance

Mastery Test

1. c 2. a 3. c 4. d 5. b 6. d 7. c 8. d 9. d 10. a 11. a 12. d 13. a 14. a 15. c 16. a 17. d 18. d 19. e 20. c 21. d 22. c 23. c

Think it Through

1. A target price program does not result in surpluses, as is the case with price supports. Government does not have any costs associated with purchasing, storing, and disposing of surplus farm commodities. The commodity prices paid by consumers are likely to be less with the target price program and may even be as low as would prevail in an unregulated market. Nevertheless, with a target price program, taxes must be used to pay the farm subsidies. The program redistributes income from taxpayers to farmers.

2. The beneficiaries of a subsidy include the consumers of the good, the producers of the good, and the resource suppliers to the subsidized industry. If the subsidy is intended to correct a market misallocation of resources resulting from a positive externality, then society as a whole benefits as well. Because subsidy programs require tax funding, either taxpayers lose because of an increase in taxes or society loses through a reduction in government services. Income is effectively transferred from taxpayers to the beneficiaries of the subsidized good. If the beneficiaries of the subsidy have, on average, higher incomes than taxpayers, the distribution of income may become more unequal.

3. A direct subsidy is visible to voters, and beneficiaries usually can be readily identified. In contrast, an indirect subsidy is not as obvious to voters, and the benefits go to a general class of individuals or institutions engaging in certain activities. Furthermore, the tax expenditures resulting from these tax breaks are not appropriated on an annual basis, once enacted, there is no limit to the extent of the subsidy over time nor are there any criteria as to whether the tax expenditures have accomplished their goals. Also, tax expenditures do not show up in government budgets as expenditures—they represent lost tax revenues that are not clearly visible to the general public. In short, it is politically easier and more expedient to encourage activities through the tax system than risk the annual public debates associated with annual program appropriations in Congress.

18 PUBLIC CHOICE, GOVERNMENT SPENDING, AND TAXES

CHAPTER CONCEPTS

After studying your text, attending class, and completing this chapter, you should be able to:

1. Explain the process of public choice under majority rule.
2. Explain the principles used to evaluate taxes.
3. Explain how governments raise revenue and describe the major categories of expenditure for the federal, state, and local governments in the United States.

THE CHAPTER IN BRIEF

Fill in the blanks to summarize chapter content.

Public choices are made through voting. Under simple majority rule, as individuals pursue their most-preferred political outcome, a political equilibrium is reached at the median most-preferred outcome. This is known as the (1)_____ (plurality, median-voter) rule. A competitive market provision of goods allows consumers to purchase goods up to the point at which marginal benefits equal price. (2)_____ (Consumers cannot, Each consumer can) maximize utility. But with politically supplied goods, only the median voter maximizes satisfaction. Some citizens will receive more of the public good than they desire and some less.

Taxes are evaluated on the basis of efficiency and equity. Taxes can be levied on the basis of the taxpayer's ability to pay or the benefits received from the government good or service. A person with a higher income may pay more taxes than an individual with a lower income, and yet the tax can still be a (3)_____ (progressive, regressive) tax in which individuals with higher incomes pay a smaller percentage of their incomes in taxes than lower-income persons. A (4)_____ (progressive, regressive) tax, such as the personal income tax, requires individuals with higher incomes to pay a larger percentage of their incomes in taxes. A flat-rate tax is an example of a (5)_____ (regressive, proportional) tax in which persons with different incomes pay the same percentage of their income in taxes.

Economic decisions are based on (6)_____ (marginal, average) tax rates rather than (7)_____ (marginal, average) tax rates. Whether or not an individual engages in an activity or a change in some activity depends in part on the after-tax net gains. The decision to work an extra hour depends on the net take-home wage. What is important is not the worker's average tax per dollar earned, but the increase in tax associated with an additional hour of work. Taxes can result in efficiency losses from less employment, less productivity, and less saving and capital growth. This efficiency loss or (8)_____ (excess burden, tax loss) of a tax is the loss in net benefits from resource use caused by the distortion in choices resulting from taxation.

The (9)_____(democratic, federal government) system consists of various levels of government, each with its own powers to provide services and to regulate the private sector. The basic functions of government include (a) the establishment of rights to use productive resources and the regulation of private actions, (b) provision of goods and services, (c) redistribution of income, and (d) (10)_____ (stabilization of the economy, provision of armed forces). Government-provided goods and services can be categorized in two basic ways. Some publicly provided goods are made available free of charge to all members of society, and the cost is financed with taxes or through borrowing. National defense, public health, and (11)_____(national parks, welfare benefits) are some examples of this type of good. Some tax-financed government goods and services are made available only to some individuals meeting certain eligibility criteria. Examples include education, Social Security pensions, and (12)_____(national parks, welfare benefits).

At the federal level of government, as of 1989, income support was the (13)_____(largest, second largest) component of federal outlays. National defense is also a major federal government outlay, accounting for just over 25% of federal government expenditures. State and local governments spend just over (14)_____ (two thirds, half) of the amount spent by the federal government. At the state and local levels of government, (15)_____(welfare, education) accounts for more than one third of all expenditures, followed by income support, social insurance, and welfare as the second major type of expenditure. Road maintenance and transportation is also an important function at the state and local levels of government.

In 1989, federal government tax revenues (16)_____ (exceeded, fell short of) expenditures by $134 billion. This is referred to as a budget deficit. Deficits have to be financed by borrowing. The U.S. Treasury does this by issuing U.S. government securities. Major federal taxes in order of importance include the personal income tax, (17)_____ (the payroll tax, sales taxes), corporate profits taxes and excise taxes. State and local governments incurred a budget (18)_____(deficit, surplus) of $46.4 billion in 1989. Major state and local sources of revenue by order of importance include (19)_____(income, sales) taxes, property taxes, federal grants, (20)_____(income, sales) taxes, fees and charges, and payroll taxes.

KEY TERMS REVIEW

Write the key term from the list below next to its definition.

Key Terms

Taxes	Marginal tax rate
Federal system of government	Excess burden
	Public choices
Government transfers	Simple majority rule
Budget deficit	Most-preferred political
Budget surplus	outcome
Regressive tax	Political equilibrium
Progressive tax	Median voter
Proportional tax	Median voter rule
Average tax rate	Government failure

Definitions

1. _____: payments made directly to certain people or organizations for which no good or service is received in return at that time.

2. _____: that alternative for which the marginal benefit just equals the tax a voter would pay if he were able to purchase the good or service in a market at a price equal to his assigned tax per unit.

3. _____: a tax for which the percentage of income paid in taxes is the same no matter what the taxpayer's income.

4. _____: the loss in net benefits from resource use caused by the distortion in choices resulting from taxation.

5. _____: the extra tax paid on extra income or the extra dollar value of any other taxed item.

6. _____: the amount of taxes paid divided by the dollar value of the item taxed.

7. _____: choices made by voting.

8. _____: a tax for which the fraction of income used to pay it increases as income increases.

9. _____: a means for reaching public choices that enacts a proposal if it obtains affirmative votes from more than half the voters casting ballots in an election.

10. _____: a tax for which the fraction of income used to pay it decreases as income increases.

11. _____: an agreement on the quantity of a public good to supply through government, given the rule for making the public choice and given the taxes per unit of the public good for each voter.

12. _____: an excess of government revenues over government expenditures in a given year.

13. _____: given an odd number of voters, the voter whose most-preferred outcome is the median of all the most-preferred outcomes.

14. _____: the amount by which government expenditures exceed government revenues in a given year.

15. _____: states that when the marginal benefit of a pure public good declines for each voter as more of the good is made available, the political equilibrium under majority rule always corresponds to the median most-preferred outcome when there is an odd number of voters.

16. _____: numerous levels of government, each with its own powers, exist to provide services and regulate private affairs.

17. _____: exists when voters approve programs for which marginal costs exceed marginal benefits.

18. _____: compulsory payments associated with income, consumption, or holding of property that persons and corporations are required to make each year to governments.

CONCEPT REVIEW

Concept 1: *Public choice and voting*

1. Below are the marginal benefits associated with various quantities of a public good for five voters. Assume that the public choice rule is the majority vote and the tax cost per voter per year is $100.

Marginal Benefits ($)

Units of the Public Good	A	B	C	D	E
0					
1	200	140	80	125	110
2	180	130	70	100	105
3	160	120	60	75	100
4	140	110	50	50	95
5	120	100	40	25	90
6	100	90	30	0	85
7	80	80	20	-25	80

a. If each voter maximizes his net benefits, what is the most-preferred political outcome for each voter?

Voter	Units
A	____
B	____
C	____
D	____
E	____

b. At the following levels of public goods provision, indicate the vote for and against and whether the vote fails or passes.

Units	For	Against	Pass/Fail
0	____	____	____
1	____	____	____
2	____	____	____
3	____	____	____
4	____	____	____
5	____	____	____
6	____	____	____
7	____	____	____

c. Political equilibrium is achieved at what level of public goods provision? _____ units This quantity is the most-preferred political outcome of which voter?_____ This voter is called the _____ voter.

354

Concept 2: *Principles used to evaluate taxation*

2. Taxes are generally considered equitable if taxpayers pay taxes on the basis of their _____ or the_____ from the public good or service consumed.

3. Indicate for the taxes below whether they are progressive, regressive, or proportional taxes.

    a. _____ Federal personal income tax

    b. _____ Sales tax

    c. _____ Payroll tax (FICA)

    d. _____ Flat-rate tax

    e. _____ Cigarette excise tax

Concept 4: *Government revenues and expenditures*

4. List four functions of government and give an example of each.

    a. _____

    b. _____

    c. _____

    d. _____

5. Government goods and services can be classified as (1) goods that are made available to all citizens free of charge and (2) goods and services that are available only to certain citizens based on specific eligibility criteria. For each of the goods or services below, indicate whether the good or service is of the first or second category. Use (1) for the first category and (2) for the second category.

    a. _____ National defense   b._____ Medicaid

    c. _____ Roads   d._____ Fire protection

    e. _____ Food stamps   f._____ National parks

    g. _____ Police   h._____ Social security

    i. _____ Education

6. List the federal government's tax revenues in order of importance.

    a. _____

    b. _____

    c. _____

    d. _____

7. List the top three federal government expenditures in order of importance.

    a. _____

    b. _____

    c. _____

8. List state and local revenue sources in order of importance.

    a. _____

    b. _____

    c. _____

    d. _____

    e. _____

    f. _____

9. List major categories of state and local expenditures in order of importance.

    a. _____

    b. _____

    c. _____

MASTERY TEST

Select the best answer.

1. A voter's most-preferred political outcome is:
   a. when taxes are shared equally by all voters.
   b. when total benefits equal the total cost of the public good.
   c. at the level of public goods provision where the voter's marginal benefit just equals his tax share per unit of the public good.
   d. always satisfied more efficiently in the market.

2. If the public choice rule is the majority vote rule and voters know their respective tax shares and maximize net benefits, political equilibrium occurs:
   a. at a level of provision where the median voter maximizes net benefits.
   b. at the same level of provision as would be the case for a competitive market equilibrium.
   c. at a level of provision where all voters maximize net benefits.
   d. None of the above.

3. An advantage of having nonpublic goods produced by the market rather than by government is that:
   a. consumers can consume goods up to the point at which their net benefits are maximized.
   b. taxes will be lower.
   c. consumers can consume goods up to the point at which their marginal benefits equal the price of the good.
   d. a and c.
   e. None of the above.

4. _____ exists when voters approve programs for which marginal costs exceed marginal benefits.
   a. Anarchy
   b. Market failure
   c. The most-preferred political outcome
   d. Government failure

5. Two concepts of equity in taxation are the _____ and _____ concepts.
   a. egalitarian, utopian
   b. ability-to-pay, benefits received
   c. democratic, republican
   d. progressive, regressive

6. A tax for which the fraction of income used to pay it decreases as income increases is called a:
   a. progressive tax.
   b. regressive tax.
   c. proportional tax.
   d. flat-rate tax.

7. A tax for which the fraction of income used to pay it increases as income increases is called a:
   a. progressive tax.
   b. regressive tax.
   c. proportional tax.
   d. value-added tax.

8. A flat-rate tax is an example of :
   a. a progressive tax.
   b. a regressive tax.
   c. a proportional tax.
   d. the U.S. income tax.

9. The appropriate tax concept to be used in marginal analysis is the:
   a. total tax liability from the full extent of an activity.
   b. marginal tax rate.
   c. average tax rate.
   d. ability-to-pay concept.

10. Welfare payments fall under which of the following government functions?
    a. Establishment of rights to use resources and the regulation of private actions
    b. Provision of goods and services
    c. Redistribution of income
    d. Stabilization of the economy

11. Education expenditures fall under which of the following government functions?
    a. Establishment of rights to use resources and the regulation of private actions
    b. Provision of goods and services
    c. Redistribution of income
    d. Stabilization of income

12. Payments made by government to certain persons or organizations for which no good or service is currently received in return are called:
    a. government spending
    b. welfare benefits
    c. government off-budget expenditures
    d. government transfer payments

13. Which of the following was the largest federal government outlay in 1989?
    a. Income support
    b. Highways
    c. National parks
    d. National defense
    e. Education

14. Which of the following was the largest source of tax revenue for the federal government in 1989?
    a. Excise tax
    b. Corporate profits tax
    c. Sales tax
    d. Payroll tax
    e. Income tax

15. Which of the following was the largest category of spending at the state and local levels of government in 1989?

    a. Highways

    b. Education

    c. Welfare

    d. Police and fire protection

    e. Hospitals

16. Which of the following was the largest source of state and local government revenue in 1989?

    a. Sales tax

    b. Income tax

    c. Gross production tax

    d. Excise tax

    e. Property tax

17. The benefits-received principle of taxation applies to which of the following taxes?

    a. Sales taxes

    b. Income taxes

    c. Gasoline excise taxes

    d. Property taxes

    e. None of the above

18. A sales tax is viewed as a:

    a. benefits-received tax.

    b. fair tax according to the ability-to-pay criterion.

    c. progressive tax.

    d. regressive tax.

19. The excess burden of a tax:

    a. rises when tax rates increase.

    b. exists because taxes alter economic choices from what they would have been in the absence of the tax.

    c. falls as tax rates decrease.

    d. a and b

    e. b and c

20. Identify sources of state and local government revenue by order of importance.
    a. Sales tax, property tax, federal grants, income tax, fees and charges, and payroll tax
    b. Income tax, payroll tax, sales tax, federal grants, property tax, and fees and charges
    c. Property tax, sales tax, income tax, fees and charges, federal grants, and payroll tax
    d. Property tax, income tax, sales tax, user fees, payroll tax, and federal grants
21. As income rises from $20,000 to $30,000 to $40,000, tax revenue from a certain tax rises from $400 to $500 to $600. The tax in question is a:
    a. proportional tax.
    b. benefits-received tax.
    c. progressive tax.
    d. regressive tax.

THINK IT THROUGH

1. Explain why it is possible under a majority vote system for voters to pass legislation on single issues where voter contentment with legislative outcomes can range from a broad consensus to a great deal of dissatisfaction.

2. Describe what is meant by efficiency and equity in taxation.

3. Compare and contrast the expenditures and revenue sources of the federal government with those of the state and local levels of government.

CHAPTER ANSWERS

The Chapter in Brief

1. Median voter 2. Each consumer can 3. Regressive 4. Progressive 5. Proportional 6. Marinal 7. Average 8. Excess burden 9. Federal government 10. Stabilization of the economy 11. National parks 12. Welfare benefits 13. Largest 14. Half 15. Education 16. Fell short of 17. The payroll tax 18. Surplus 19. Sales 20. Income

Key Terms Review

1. Government transfers 2. Most-preferred political outcome 3. Proportional tax 4. Excess burden 5. Marginal tax rate 6. Average tax rate 7. Public choices 8. Progressive taxes 9. Simple majority rule 10. Regressive tax 11. Political equilibrium 12. Budget surplus 13. Median voter 14. Budget deficit 15. Median voter rule 16. Federal system of government 17. Government failure 18. Taxes

Concept Review

1. a.

Voter	Units
A	6
B	5
C	0
D	2
E	3

b.

Units of Public good	For	Against	Pass/Fail
0	1	4	Fail
1	4	1	Pass
2	4	1	Pass
3	3	2	Pass
4	2	3	Fail
5	2	3	Fail
6	1	4	Fail
7	0	5	Fail

   c. 3 units, voter E, median

2. Ability-to-pay, benefits received

3. a. Progressive b. Regressive c. Regressive d. Proportional e. Regressive

4. a. The establishment of rights to use resources and the regulation of private actions

   b. Provision of goods and services

   c. Redistribution of income

   d. Stabilization of the economy

5. a. 1 b. 2 c. 1 d. 1 e. 2 f. 1 g. 1 h. 2 i. 2

6. a. Personal income tax b. Payroll taxes c. Corporate profits taxes d. Excise taxes

7. a. Income support b. National defense c. Interest payments

8. a. Sales taxes b. Property taxes c. Federal grants d. Income taxes e. Fees and charges f. Payroll taxes

9. a. Education b. Income support, social insurance, and welfare c. Road maintenance and transportation

Mastery Test

1. c 2. a 3. d 4. d 5. b 6. b 7. a 8. c 9. b 10. c 11. b 12. d 13. a 14. e 15. b 16. a 17. c 18. d 19. d 20. a 21. d

Think it Through

1. If the marginal benefits from a public good for most taxpayers are similar with little variability and the tax share per taxpayer is the same, the majority vote rule will result in a political equilibrium in which many or most voters have most-preferred political outcomes that are very close to the median voter outcome. Only the median voter achieves the most-preferred political outcome, but the extent of dissatisfaction with the vote is much less than if there is considerable dispersion of marginal benefits. If a larger percentage of voters have most-preferred political outcomes that depart widely from the median voter outcome, there will be far more dissatisfaction with the vote.

2. Taxes can create an excess burden when there are tax-caused changes in individual and business behavior resulting from changes in net wages, net interest rates, and other prices or incomes. Efficiency can be improved if the tax is used to correct a negative externality. An efficient tax is one that raises tax revenue without causing an excess burden. The two basic concepts of equity in taxation are the ability-to-pay and benefits received concepts. The benefits received principle cannot be used where the benefits cannot be closely correlated with an individual's activity. The ability-to-pay criterion states that a fair tax is one for which an individual's tax liability is correlated with his or her ability to pay. Thus, higher income persons should pay more in taxes than those with lower incomes. This criterion does not indicate whether proportional, progressive, or regressive taxes are preferable, because ability-to-pay can be measured in absolute dollars or as a percentage of income.

3. The federal government provides national defense, Social Security, income security, interest payments on the public debt, and Medicare as well as other goods and services. These are financed with personal income taxes, payroll taxes, corporate profits taxes, and excise taxes. State and local governments provide education, income support, social insurance, welfare, road maintenance and transportation, police and fire protection, and other goods and services. State and local levels of government finance their activities with sales taxes, property taxes, federal grants, income taxes, fees and charges, and payroll taxes. The largest federal expenditure as a percentage of total spending is for income support, whereas the largest state and local expenditure is for education. Sales taxes are the major revenue source at the state and local levels of government, but personal income taxes provide the most revenue to the federal government.

PART V

INPUT MARKETS AND INCOMES: MICROECONOMIC ANALYSIS

PART EXERCISE

Inside Information: *Information on Labor Markets, Income Distribution, and Government Transfer Programs*

In the first three chapters of Part V, you will learn about labor markets and the determination of wage rates. For your particular state and region, detail the earnings characteristics of the population by industry employment, age, race, sex, etc. using *Employment and Earnings*. Use current and past issues of *Employment and Earnings* and determine if wages have changed in your area. Provide a plausible explanation for the change using the analysis presented in chapters 19, 20, and 21.

19   INPUT MARKETS AND THE DEMAND FOR RESOURCES

CHAPTER CONCEPTS

After studying your text, attending class, and completing this chapter, you should be able to:

1. Explain the concept of a perfectly competitive input market.
2. Show how much of a particular input, like labor, a profit-maximizing firm chooses to buy over a certain period in a competitive market.
3. Show how a firm's demand for an input depends on the productivity of the input and on the price the firm receives from selling the product of the input.
4. Show how the market price of an input depends on its supply and demand.

THE CHAPTER IN BRIEF

Fill in the blanks to summarize chapter content.

A competitive input market is one in which there is (1)_____ (lack of free, free) entry and exit of sellers of inputs, where the owners of resources (2)_____ (can, cannot) shift their resources to different locations in response to differences in input prices, and where buyers and sellers of resources (3)_____ (have, have no) control over resource prices. In competitive input markets, the forces of supply and demand determine market input prices and quantities employed.

The demand for an input is a derived demand—derived from the demand for the product produced by the input. The demand curve for an input is the (4)_____(marginal revenue product, marginal product) curve. Marginal revenue product is the input's marginal product times (5)_____ (average cost, marginal revenue). Marginal product is the extra production that results from the use of one additional unit of an input. For the case of a perfectly competitive product market, marginal revenue (6)_____ (is less than, equals) price. Therefore, for competitive input markets, marginal revenue product (7)_____ (is less than, equals) product price times the input's marginal product. Marginal revenue product is the contribution by an extra unit of an input to the firm's total revenue.

A profit-maximizing firm will employ an input up to the point at which the additional benefit from doing so (the marginal revenue product) (8)_____ (is greater than, equals) the additional costs (or marginal input costs). For the case of labor, a firm will employ labor up to the point at which the marginal revenue product of labor equals the wage, assuming a competitive input market. A firm's demand curve for labor is the marginal revenue product curve with the wage rate plotted on the vertical axis. Each point on the curve represents a profit-maximizing quantity of labor demanded at that wage rate.

An input demand curve will shift if the demand for the firm's output changes, if the prices of substitute or complementary inputs change, or if changes in technology affect the marginal product of the input. The demand for an input will increase (the demand curve will shift to the right) if the price of the product produced by the input (9)_____ (increases, decreases), if technological improvement (10)_____ (increases, decreases) the input's marginal product, if the price of a substitute input (11)_____ (increases, decreases), or if the price of a complementary input (12)_____ (increases, decreases). The opposite changes will cause the demand for an input to decrease and the input demand curve to shift to the left.

For the case of a monopoly product market, marginal revenue is (13)_____ (equal to, less than) price at each level of output, causing the monopolist's marginal revenue product curve for an input to lie (14)_____ (outside, inside) the market input demand for competitive firms. As a result, at a given wage the monopolist will maximize profit by hiring (15)_____ (more, fewer) units of the input than would be the case for competitive firms.

The market demand curve for an input is a summation of the individual firm-level demand curves for the input. It is downward sloping, as is the case for the firm's input demand curve. The supply curve for an input is upward sloping because higher input prices are necessary to cover (16)_____ (rising, falling) marginal costs associated with supplying the input. The market supply of and demand for an input determine the market price and quantity of the input. For example, if the demand for an input increases or supply decreases or some combination of the two, market input prices will (17)_____ (increase, decrease).

Economic rent exists when the market price of an input (18)_____ (equals, exceeds) the minimum price that sellers of the input will take. It represents a surplus over the opportunity costs associated with producing and providing an input and can be taxed away (19)_____ (reducing, without reducing) the quantity of inputs offered at the market price. Key facts regarding input markets include: (a) the prices of inputs are determined by the forces of supply and demand, (b) the price of an input equals its marginal revenue product for the case of competitive input markets, (c) the demand for an input is a derived demand, (d) productivity is a major determinant of input prices, and (e) for the case of competitive input markets, attempts by employers to pay less than the going market input price will fail.

KEY TERMS REVIEW

Write the key term from the list below next to its definition.

Key Terms

Input market	Marginal input cost
Competitive input market	Change in input demand
Derived demand	Market demand for an input
Marginal revenue product	Market supply of an input

Definitions

1. _____: a relationship between the price of an input and the quantity supplied for employment in all industries and other uses.

2. _____: the change in total revenue that results when one more unit of that input is hired.

3. _____: the sum of the quantities demanded by all industries and other employers using that input at any given price.

4. _____: the demand for an input that is derived from the demand for the product that the input is used to produce.

5. _____: a shift of an entire input demand curve caused by a change in one of the determinants of input demand other than price.

6. _____: a market in which neither individual buyers nor individual sellers can influence the prices of input services.

7. _____: the extra cost associated with hiring one more unit of an input.

8. _____: a market used to trade the services of productive resources for income payments.

CONCEPT REVIEW

Concept 1: *Perfectly competitive input markets*

1. List the characteristics of a perfectly competitive input market.

   a. _____

   b. _____

   c. _____

Concept 2: *Demand for an input by a profit-maximizing competitive firm*

2. Company X is a profit-maximizing firm selling in a competitive product market and hiring in a competitive input market. Company X uses semi-skilled labor to produce dampers used in office building ventilation systems. Below are data regarding labor productivity for the firm. Assume that the current market price per damper is $500.

Workers	Total Product (dampers/week)	Marginal Product	Marginal Revenue Product
0	0		
10	15	_____	$_____
20	28	_____	_____
30	39	_____	_____
40	48	_____	_____
50	55	_____	_____
60	60	_____	_____

a. Complete the table and plot the marginal revenue product curve in the diagram below.

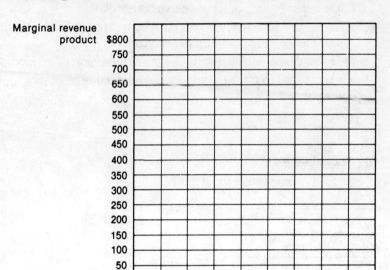

b. Assume that the prevailing weekly salary per semi-skilled worker is $550. Company X would employ _____ workers. The profit-maximizing level of employment occurs where _____ equals _____.

c. Suppose the market wage fell from $550 per week to $450 per week. Company X would employ _____ workers. If the market wage increased to $650, Company X would employ _____ workers.

d. Plot the quantities of labor demanded by Company X at the three wages considered in parts b and c in the figure below. For Company X, the input demand curve for semi-skilled labor is the _____ curve.

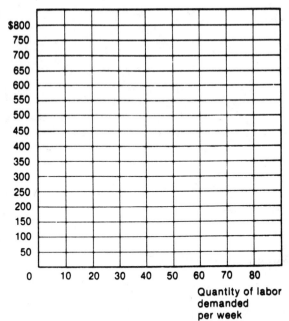

Wage per week

Concept 3: *Determinants of a competitive firm's input demand*

3. List three factors that will shift a firm's input demand curve.

   a. _____

   b. _____

   c. _____

4. Given the data in question 2 above, show what happens to the firm's marginal revenue product schedule and curve and its input demand curve for labor if the price per damper falls to $400.

Workers	Marginal Revenue Product
0	
10	$_____
20	_____
30	_____
40	_____
50	_____
60	_____

   a. Complete the table.

   b. On the first figure shown, plot the marginal revenue product curve associated with a price per damper of $400.

   c. On the second figure shown, plot the new demand for labor curve.

   d. The input demand curve shifts to the _____ (left, right).

e. At a wage of $550 per week, would Company X continue to hire the same number of workers given the reduction in the price of dampers? Explain.

f. The demand for an input is a _____ demand.

Concept 2: *The demand for an input by a profit-maximizing monopolist*

5. The product and employment data below are for an entire market.

Q	Ql	Pc	Pm	MRm	MPL	MRPc	MRPm
0	0	$2	$2.00				
1	5	2	1.80	$____	____	$____	$____
2	11	2	1.60	____	____	____	____
3	18	2	1.40	____	____	____	____
4	26	2	1.20	____	____	____	____
5	35	2	1.00	____	____	____	____

Q = thousands of units of output per week

Ql = workers

Pc = competitive firm's product price

Pm = monopolist's product price

MRm = monopolist's marginal revenue

MPL = marginal product of labor

MRPc = competitive firm's marginal revenue product

MRPm = monopolist's marginal revenue product

a. Complete the table.

b. Plot the competitive market input demand curve on the figure below.

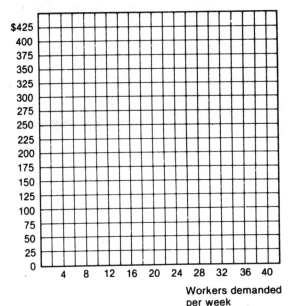

Wage per week per worker (vertical axis, $425 to 0 in increments of 25)

Workers demanded per week (horizontal axis, 4 to 40)

c. Plot the monopolist's input demand curve on the above figure.

d. At a wage of $250 per week, competitive firms will employ a total of _____ workers. At the same wage a monopolist will hire between _____ and _____ workers. Show this in the figure above. A monopolist hires _____ workers than a competitive firm.

Concept 4: *Market input prices and quantities*

6. The competitive market for skilled workers is shown below. The companies hiring skilled labor are selling output in competitive markets.

Hourly Wage	Quantity of Labor Demanded	Quantity of Labor Supplied
	(millions of labor hours per day)	
$10.00	30	105
9.75	35	95
9.50	40	85
9.25	45	75
9.00	50	65
8.75	55	55
8.50	60	45
8.25	65	35
8.00	70	25

a. In the diagram below, plot the demand and supply curves for labor and identify the market wage and level of employment. Wage = $_____, labor supplied _____ hours.

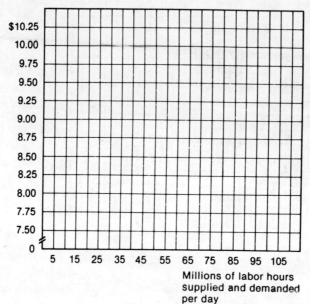

Wage per hour

b. On the figure above, show the effect of an increase in the market demand for labor. Market wage rates _____ and employment _____.

c. On the figure above, show the effect of an increase in the market supply of labor. Market wage rates _____ and employment _____.

d. For those workers willing to work for a wage no less than $8.25 per hour but who receive the market wage of $_____, economic rent per labor hour equals $_____. A maximum tax per hour of $_____ could be levied on worker income without affecting the quantity of labor supplied.

e. An increase in labor productivity will shift the _____ curve to the _____ (right, left) and will cause the market wage to _____ and market employment to _____.

f. A decrease in the market prices of the goods produced by the employers of skilled labor will shift the _____ curve to the _____ (right, left) and will cause the market wage to _____ and market employment to _____.

372

MASTERY TEST

Select the best answer.

1. Which of the following is not a characteristic of a competitive input market?
    a. There is an absence of close substitute resources.
    b. Both buyers and sellers of inputs are price takers.
    c. There is freedom of entry into and exit from input markets.
    d. Resources are mobile in that they can be used in other employments and in other locations.

2. The demand for an input is a/an _____ demand.
    a. normal
    b. individual
    c. derived
    d. market

3. Which of the following concepts represents the extra revenue a firm receives from the services of an additional unit of an input?
    a. Total revenue
    b. Marginal revenue
    c. Marginal product of an input
    d. Marginal revenue product of an input

4. The cost of employing an additional unit of an input is called:
    a. input cost.
    b. income.
    c. marginal revenue product.
    d. marginal cost.
    e. marginal input cost.

5. For the case of a perfectly competitive input market, the marginal input cost equals:
    a. the total cost of the input.
    b. the price of the input.
    c. the average cost of the input.
    d. marginal cost.

6. For the case of a perfectly competitive product market, the marginal revenue product equals:
    a. revenue times marginal product.
    b. price times total product.
    c. marginal revenue times average product.
    d. price times marginal product.

7. If at a firm's current level of employment the marginal revenue product of the last worker employed exceeds the marginal cost of labor, the firm should:

    a. decrease employment.

    b. maintain the existing level of employment.

    c. increase employment.

    d. produce less output and hire fewer workers.

8. A profit-maximizing competitive firm will hire labor in a competitive labor market up to the point at which the _____ equals the _____.

    a. average revenue product, product price

    b. total product, wage

    c. marginal revenue product, wage

    d. marginal input cost, wage

9. A firm's demand curve for an input is its:

    a. marginal cost curve.

    b. market demand curve.

    c. marginal product curve.

    d. marginal revenue product curve.

    e. None of the above.

10. An increase in the demand for the product produced by an input:

    a. will increase the supply of the input.

    b. will decrease the supply of the input.

    c. will increase the demand for the input.

    d. will decrease the demand for the input.

11. If labor and capital are substitute resources in production, an increase in the price of capital will:

    a. increase the demand for labor.

    b. increase the supply of labor.

    c. decrease the demand for labor.

    d. decrease the supply of labor.

12. Technological innovation that increases the marginal product of labor will:

    a. increase the demand for labor.

    b. increase the supply of labor.

    c. decrease the demand for labor.

    d. decrease the supply of labor.

13. A monopolist's marginal revenue product curve :

    a. is the monopolist's demand for an input.

    b. equals marginal revenue times marginal product.

    c. lies inside a competitive industry's demand curve for an input.

    d. is equated to the marginal cost of labor in order to maximize profits from the employment of a variable input.

    e. All of the above.

14. The market supply of an input is upward sloping because:

    a. a supply curve must be upward sloping.

    b. input suppliers face rising marginal costs as they make more of an input available to the market.

    c. price and quantity supplied are inversely related.

    d. price and quantity demanded are inversely related.

15. Economic rent is:

    a. a payment to landlords.

    b. the difference between what a resource supplier earns in the market and the minimum amount of income required by the resource supplier to maintain the same quantity of the input supplied.

    c. the maximum wage required by labor less the market wage.

    d. the minimum wage required by labor less the market wage.

16. What portion of an input supplier's income can be taxed away without affecting the quantity of inputs made available to the market?

    a. 0%

    b. 100%

    c. A portion equal to economic rent

    d. A portion equal to the input supplier's opportunity cost

    e. None of the above

17. An increase in the market demand for an input _____ market input price and _____ employment of the input.

    a. increases, increases

    b. decreases, decreases

    c. increases, decreases

    d. decreases, increases

18. An increase in the market supply of an input _____ market input price and _____ employment of an input.
    a. increases, increases
    b. decreases, decreases
    c. increases, decreases
    d. decreases, increases

19. If education increases the productivity of labor, the market labor _____ curve will shift _____ and cause the market wage to _____.
    a. supply, leftward, increase
    b. demand, leftward, increase
    c. supply, rightward, decrease
    d. demand, rightward, increase
    e. demand, leftward, decrease

20. Assume a competitive firm hires labor in a competitive labor market at a prevailing market wage of $12.00 per hour. Given the following data for the firm's marginal revenue product, determine the profit-maximizing level of employment.

Hours of labor	Marginal Revenue Product
500	$16.00
1,000	14.00
1,500	12.00
2,000	10.00
2,500	8.00

    a. 500
    b. 1,000
    c. 1,500
    c. 2,000
    e. 2,500

21. For the data given in number 20 above, how many workers will be hired if labor productivity (marginal product) increases by 50%?
    a. 500
    b. 1,000
    c. 1,500
    d. 2,000
    e. 2,500

22. For the data given in number 20 above, how many workers will be hired if the price of the firm's product increases by 20%?

    a. 500

    b. 1,000

    c. 1,500

    d. 2,000

    e. 2,500

23. As compared to a perfectly competitive firm, a monopolist:

    a. has a more elastic demand for labor.

    b. must lower price to increase output, resulting in a more elastic demand for labor.

    c. must raise price to the profit-maximizing price, resulting in a less elastic demand curve for labor.

    d. must lower price to increase output, resulting in a less elastic labor demand curve.

24. Suppose wage rates in Tulsa for a given type of labor are higher than wage rates for the same type of labor in Oklahoma City. Assuming that the labor market is perfectly competitive, what will happen to this interarea wage differential?

    a. Workers will leave Tulsa for Oklahoma City, increasing the supply of labor in Oklahoma City and decreasing the supply in Tulsa. Wage rates will continue to diverge.

    b. Workers will leave Oklahoma City for Tulsa, increasing the supply of labor in Tulsa and decreasing the supply of labor in Oklahoma City. These changes will continue until wage rates are the same in the two areas.

    c. Lower wages in Oklahoma City will increase the demand for labor, attracting industry and causing wage rates to be bid up to a level equal to wage rates in Tulsa.

    d. Industry leaves the high-wage area and moves to the low-wage area, causing a decrease in the demand for labor in Tulsa and an increase in Oklahoma City. Wage rates tend to equalize.

THINK IT THROUGH

1. Discuss intuitively how competitive input markets equalize wages of a given type of labor.

2. In 1986, the world price of oil fell dramatically. Discuss the likely impacts on input markets in the energy-producing regions of the United States.

3. Explain why movie or sports stars could have a much larger share of their income taxed than is currently the case without reducing the quantities of their services supplied.

4. Discuss the five key facts about input markets.

CHAPTER ANSWERS

The Chapter in Brief

1. Free 2. Can 3. Have no 4. Marginal revenue product 5. Marginal revenue 6. Equals 7. Equals 8. Equals 9. Increases 10. Increases 11. Increases 12. Decreases 13. Less than 14. Inside 15. Fewer 16. Rising 17. Increase 18. Exceeds 19. Without reducing

Key Terms Review

1. Market supply of an input 2. Marginal revenue product 3. Market demand for an input 4. Derived demand 5. Change in input demand 6. Competitive input market 7. Marginal input cost 8. Input market

Concept Review

1. a. Buyers and sellers of inputs are price takers .

   b. There is free entry into and exit of sellers from input markets.

   c. Economic resources can be transferred to different employments and to different locations.

2. a.

Marginal Product	Marginal Revenue Product
1.5	$750
1.3	650
1.1	550
.9	450
.7	350
.5	250

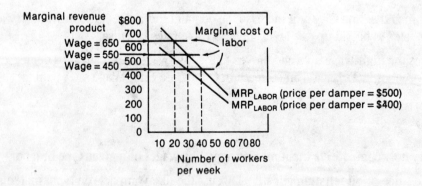

   b. 30; marginal revenue product of labor, wage per week per employee

   c. 40; 20

   d. Marginal revenue product

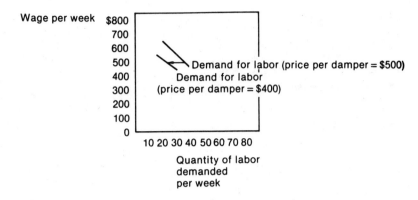

Wage per week

Quantity of labor demanded per week

3. a. A change in the demand for the output produced by the input

b. Changes in the productivity of an input

c. Technological changes affecting the marginal product of an input

4. a. Marginal Revenue Product

$600

520

440

360

280

200

b. Answer on the first figure above.

c. Answer on the second figure above.

d. Left

e. No. A decline in the price of dampers reduces the marginal revenue product relative to the marginal cost of labor. A profit-maximizing firm, by reducing employment, lowers labor costs more than revenues, thus increasing profit.

f. Derived

5. a.

MRm	MPL	MRPc	MRPm
$1.80	200	$400	$360
1.40	167	334	234
1.00	143	286	143
.60	125	250	75
.20	111	222	22

b.

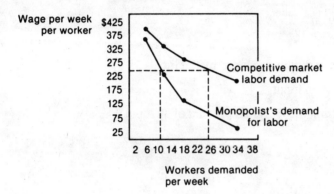

c. Answer in figure above.

d. 26; 5, 11; fewer

6. a. $8.75, 55 million

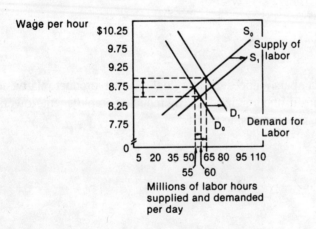

b. Rise, increases

c. Fall, increases

d. $8.75, $.50; $.50

e. Labor demand, right, rise, increase

f. Labor demand, left, fall, decrease

Mastery Test

1. a 2. c 3. d 4. e 5. b 6. d 7. c 8. c 9. d 10. c 11. a 12. a 13. e 14. b 15. b 16. c 17. a 18. d 19. d 20. c 21. e 22. d 23. d 24. b

Think it Through

1. Assuming free entry into and exit from a given labor market and the mobility of labor, if wages in region A exceeded wages for identical labor in region B, some workers would leave the low-wage region and move to the high-wage region in pursuit of higher wages. This would cause a reduction in the supply of labor in region B and an increase in the supply of labor in region A. Assuming given labor demand curves for the two regions, market wages in region A will fall while market wages in region B will rise. These changes will continue until there are no further gains by labor from moving from one region to the other. This occurs where the wage rates in the two regions for the given type of labor are equalized.

2. The large decline in oil prices reduced the marginal revenue products of labor and other inputs used by the oil industry. As the marginal revenue product of an input falls relative to the marginal cost of the input, profit-maximizing firms reduce employment. The oil industry reduced employment and cut production, causing regional recessions in those areas of the nation where the oil industry represents a significant portion of the regional economy.

3. Some top executives, sports and movie stars, and others receive such enormous annual incomes that the payments they receive for their services far exceed the minimum amounts required by these individuals to make their services available. It was recently reported that Michael Jackson's annual income was $97 million. Do you think that he would have withdrawn his services if he had earned only $87 million? The difference between the incomes received and the minimum incomes required by individuals to make their services available is called economic rent. Economic rent can be taxed away in its entirety without reducing the quantity of input services made available.

4. Simple conclusions emerge regarding competitive input markets. The prices of inputs used in production are determined by supply and demand. The price of an input equals the input's marginal revenue product—an input is paid an income equal to its contribution to the firm's revenues. The demand for an input is derived from the demand for the output produced by the input. Influences affecting product demand curves therefore influence input demand curves. An input's productivity is an important determinant affecting input prices. In competitive input markets, firms are input price takers—attempts to pay an input price below the market price and marginal revenue product will fail.

20 LABOR MARKETS, LABOR PRODUCTIVITY, AND PERSONNEL MANAGEMENT

CHAPTER CONCEPTS

After studying your text, attending class, and completing this chapter, you should be able to:

1. Analyze the choice to work and show how a person's labor supply curve depends on his or her preferences and other influences, such as nonlabor sources of income.
2. Show how the market supply of labor services is influenced by population and other demographic variables.
3. Explain why different wages are paid for different jobs, occupations, or skills.
4. Show how personnel management techniques can be used to motivate workers and increase the marginal revenue product of labor.

THE CHAPTER IN BRIEF

Fill in the blanks to summarize chapter content.

An individual's decision to work an additional hour depends on the additional gains versus additional losses from doing so. The (1)_____(marginal benefits, marginal costs) of an additional hour of work include the extra monetary and nonmonetary satisfaction received. The additional cost of an hour of work is the (2)_____ (wage, value of a forgone hour of leisure). The opportunity cost of leisure time increases as the individual works more hours. As a result, higher wages or other nonmonetary benefits are (3)_____ (necessary, unnecessary) to compensate the worker for the rising opportunity cost of leisure time. The individual's labor supply curve is upward sloping if an increase in wages, or an increase in the marginal (4)_____ (benefits, costs) relative to the marginal cost of work, induces the individual to work additional hours.

There are both substitution and income effects associated with a change in the wage. An increase in the wage makes an hour of work more valuable in terms of the goods and services that can be purchased with the higher income earned. This causes the opportunity cost of an hour of leisure to increase. An individual will substitute an hour of work for an hour of leisure. The substitution effect results in (5)_____(less, more) hours worked as wages rise. The income effect has just the opposite impact on hours worked. An increase in wages means that the worker can consume the same quantities of goods and services with (6)_____ (fewer, more) hours worked. If the substitution effect outweighs the income effect, the supply curve of labor is (7)_____ (upward sloping, backward bending). If the income effect outweighs the substitution effect, the labor supply curve is (8)_____ (backward bending, upward sloping). If the income and substitution effects just offset each other, the labor supply curve is (9)_____ (positively sloped, vertical).

Market wages depend upon the supply of and demand for labor. The supply of labor is influenced by population and the rate of participation in the labor force. Birth and death rates, immigration, and emigration all influence the supply of labor. Labor productivity is a key determinant of the demand for labor. Increases in a nation's labor productivity (10)_____ (increase, decrease) labor incomes.

Differences in wages among workers and jobs can be explained by productivity or quality differences. Differences in quality are influenced by natural abilities or other characteristics of the individual and by the extent of training or education. Differences in wages can also be attributed to working conditions. Some jobs have negative (11)_____ (externalities, nonpecuniary wages) in that nonmonetary aspects of the job make it less desirable than another job paying exactly the same wage. In order to induce people to accept employment in less desirable occupations, a compensating wage differential must be paid to the worker to make the total compensation from the job (12)_____ (equal to, greater than) to other jobs paying a lower wage but having higher nonmonetary benefits. Some jobs have nonpecuniary benefits that are greater than those for other jobs. These jobs pay a lower wage in order to equalize the total compensation among jobs.

An objective of (13)_____ (production, personnel) management is to adjust the monetary and nonmonetary characteristics of a job in order to increase the marginal revenue product of labor. But first, personnel managers must hire and train workers. The signals from the job seeker's resume and interview offer an (14)_____ (efficient, low-cost; inefficient, high-cost) method of screening. Once hired, the worker has to be trained. This is often a costly process, and firms tend to give firm-specific training. Where possible firms promote from within in order to avoid some of these training costs. A firm must monitor the actions of its workers to ensure that the owner's desires are met. Owners want to maximize profits, but when workers seek to maximize personal objectives that do not coincide with the owner's goal of profit maximization, workers shirk on the job. They engage in activities that increase their satisfaction, (15)_____ (but that increases, and lower) production costs and (16)_____ (increase, lower) worker productivity. One way to reduce shirking is to design and implement compensation systems tying together the interests of workers, managers, and owners. Profit sharing and stock options are two examples.

KEY TERMS REVIEW

Write the key term from the list below next to its definition.

Key Terms

Nonwage money income

Marginal cost of work

Marginal benefit of work

Labor supply curve

Substitution effect of a
  wage change

Income effect of a wage
  change

Human capital

Nonpecuniary wages

Compensating wage differential

Staffing

Signals

Screening

Internal labor market

Shirking

Backward-bending labor supply
  curve

384

Definitions

1. _____: represents the skills and qualifications of workers that stem from education and training.

2. _____: the nonmonetary aspects of a job that must be added to or subtracted from money wages to obtain total compensation per hour of work.

3. _____: implies that the substitution effect on a worker's labor services outweighs the income effect only at relatively low wages.

4. _____: a difference in money wages necessary to make total compensation for similar jobs equal when nonpecuniary wages are not equal to zero.

5. _____: the change in hours worked stemming from the change in income caused by the wage change.

6. _____: indicators displayed by job applicants and used by employers to predict the future satisfaction and productivity of a worker.

7. _____: the change in hours worked resulting only from a change in the opportunity cost of an hour of leisure.

8. _____: the process of recruiting and hiring workers to perform the various tasks required to produce goods and services.

9. _____: shows a relationship between a worker's hourly wages and labor hours supplied for work over a given period.

10. _____: a process in which an employer limits the number of applicants for a job to those it believes are the most likely to succeed in the company.

11. _____: the extra income received from extra work, including any nonmonetary satisfaction obtained from a job.

12. _____: behavior by workers that prevents a firm from achieving the maximum possible marginal product of labor over a given period.

13. _____: the value of extra leisure time given up to work.

14. _____: exists within a firm when it fills positions by hiring its own employees, rather than new employees, to fill all but the lowest-level positions.

15. _____: includes pensions, welfare payments and subsidies, interest, dividends, allowances, and any other type of income that is available independent of work.

CONCEPT REVIEW

Concept 1: *An individual's choice to work and labor supply curve*

1. Fred's marginal benefits and marginal costs associated with additional hours of work are shown below. Assume Fred's marginal benefit from a hour of labor is the market wage and that after 8 hours of sleep, Fred has 16 hours per day to allocate between work and leisure.

Hours per Day	Marginal Benefit	Marginal Cost
0		
1	$9	$1.50
2	9	3.00
3	9	4.50
4	9	6.00
5	9	7.50
6	9	9.00
7	9	10.50
8	9	12.00
9	9	13.50
10	9	15.00

a. Plot the marginal costs and marginal benefits on the figure below.

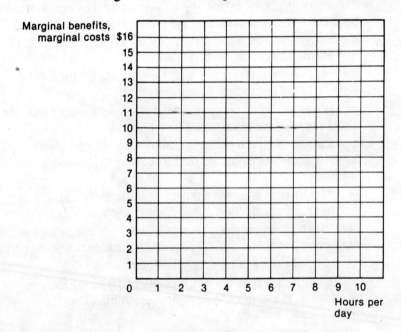

b. Fred maximizes net benefits from work by working _____ hours and consuming _____ hours of leisure. Show this in the figure above.

c. If the market wage increases to $12 per hour, Fred maximizes net benefits by working _____ hours and consuming _____ hours of leisure. Show this in the figure above.

d. If the market wage falls to $6 per hour, Fred maximizes net benefits by working _____ hours and consuming _____ hours of leisure. Show this in the figure above.

e. Plot Fred's labor supply curve in the figure below using market wages of $6, $9, and $12.

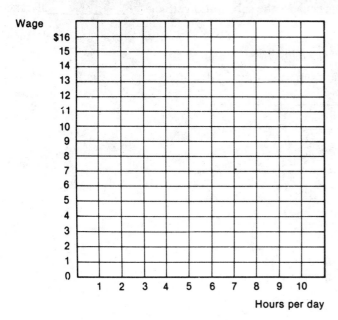

f. Fred's labor supply curve is his _____ curve.

2. Answer the following questions on the basis of the figure below.

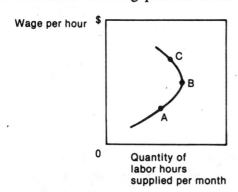

a. At point A, there is _____ relationship between the hourly wage and the quantity of labor supplied. This is because the substitution effect _____ the income effect of a wage change.

b. At point B, there is _____ relationship between the hourly wage and the quantity of labor supplied. This is because the substitution effect _____ the income effect of a wage change.

c. At point C, there is _____ relationship between the hourly wage and the quantity of labor supplied. This is because the substitution effect _____ the income effect of a wage change.

Concept 2: *Determinants of market wages*

3. What factors influence the market supply of labor? Give an example of each.

   a. _____

   b. _____

4. Below is a market for sales clerks.

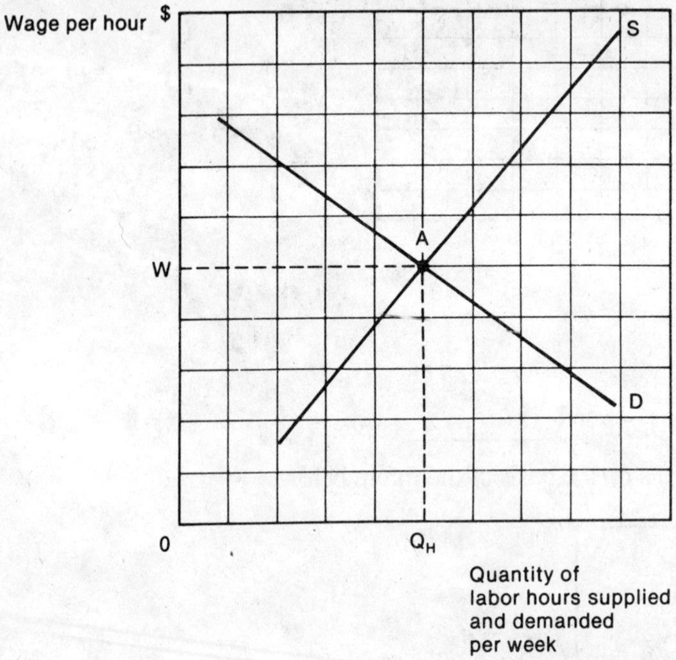

Wage per hour $

W

0   Q_H

Quantity of
labor hours supplied
and demanded
per week

   a. Assume that because of an increase in the birth rate some years ago, there is currently a large increase in the number of teenagers entering the labor force. The _____ curve for sales clerks shifts _____. Market wages _____, and employment _____. Show this graphically in the figure above.

   b. Assume that because of new technology, the marginal products of sales clerks increase. The _____ curve for sales clerks shifts _____. Given the initial market equilibrium at point A, wages _____ and employment _____. Show this graphically in the figure above. Worker productivity and wage rates are _____ related.

Advanced Application: *An individual's choice to work*

5. Suppose Fred's marginal cost and marginal benefit can be expressed as follows:

$$MB = Wo$$

$$MC = a + bH$$

where Wo represents the given market wage and H is the number of hours worked

a. Derive an expression for the number of hours worked that maximizes net benefits.

b. What happens to the net benefit-maximizing level of hours worked given changes in a, b, and W? Interpret.

c. If a wage tax, t, is levied on the hourly wage, what happens to the benefit-maximizing level of hours worked? (Assume that t is greater than zero but less than 1.)

MASTERY TEST

Select the best answer.

1. Which of the following is a definition for the marginal cost of work?
   a. The value of the time and toil involved in a job
   b. The wage
   c. The value of extra leisure time given up to work
   d. The additional production costs associated with the use of an additional unit of labor

2. The extra income received from extra work, including any nonmonetary satisfaction obtained from a job, is called:
   a. total pecuniary benefits.
   b. the marginal benefit of work.
   c. external benefits.
   d. the wage rate.
   e. nonpecuniary satisfaction.

3. In order to maximize the net benefits from work, an individual should work additional hours up to the point where:
   a. the total costs of labor equal the total benefits of labor.
   b. the wage equals marginal revenue.
   c. marginal revenue is greater than marginal labor cost.
   d. the marginal cost of work equals the marginal benefit of work.

4. An individual's labor supply curve:
   a. is upward sloping if the substitution effect outweighs the income effect of a wage change.
   b. represents combinations of wage rates and quantities of labor hours supplied.
   c. is an equilibrium relationship in that each coordinate point on the curve is a net benefit-maximizing quantity of hours supplied at that wage rate.
   d. may have sections that are upward sloping, downward sloping and even vertical.
   e. All of the above.

5. If the market wage rises such that an individual's wage exceeds the marginal cost of work and assuming that the substitution effect is dominant, the individual will maximize net benefits from work by:
   a. working additional hours.
   b. working fewer hours.
   c. consuming more leisure.
   d. consuming the same quantity of leisure.

6. The backward-bending portion of a labor supply curve occurs:
   a. when wages equal the firm's marginal product.
   b. where the substitution effect outweighs the income effect.
   c. only rarely and at low levels of income.
   d. where the income effect outweighs the substitution effect.

7. Which of the following is a determinant of the market supply curve for labor?
   a. Population growth
   b. Rate of labor force participation
   c. Birth rate
   d. Extent of immigration
   e. All of the above

8. Investment in capital _____ labor productivity, resulting in a _____ shift in the market _____ curve for labor.
   a. decreases, leftward, supply
   b. decreases, rightward, demand
   c. increases, rightward, demand
   d. increases, leftward, demand

9. The "baby boom" caused the market _____ curve for labor to shift _____, resulting in a/an _____ in market wages, others things held constant.
   a. supply, rightward, decrease
   b. demand, leftward, increase
   c. supply, leftward, increase
   d. demand, rightward, decrease

10. Training and education:
    a. are investments in human capital.
    b. increase the productivity of labor.
    c. increase a nation's living standards because of the increase in labor productivity.
    d. are one explanation for wage differences between different jobs and workers.
    e. All of the above.

11. Which of the following is an example of nonpecuniary wages?
    a. Hourly wage rate
    b. Air-conditioned workplace
    c. Health and retirement benefits
    d. Stock options

12. Which of the following is an example of nonpecuniary job benefits?
    a. Flexible work hours
    b. Opportunities for advancement
    c. Nonhazardous job
    d. Pleasant job or local amenities
    e. All of the above

13. If two jobs, job A and job B, are identical with the exception that job B is associated with nonpecuniary job benefits, job A will pay _____ job B.
    a. a higher wage than
    b. a lower wage than
    c. the same wage as
    d. None of the above

14. Firms often have a preference for promoting existing employees to fill new or vacant positions. Which of the following terms represents this concept?
    a. Staffing
    b. Signals
    c. Screening
    d. Internal labor market

15. Shirking by management and labor results when:

    a.   lazy employees are hired.

    b.   the interests of owners, management, and workers coincide.

    c.   goods and services are produced by government but never when private firms produce output.

    d.   the interests of owners, management, and workers do not coincide.

16. Shirking on the job:

    a.   is a problem unless a compensation system is devised in which managers and workers are induced to pursue the owner's goals for the firm.

    b.   is an insignificant problem because monitoring eliminates it.

    c.   is most efficiently reduced with monitoring.

    d.   is most efficiently reduced by compensation systems such as stock options and profit sharing, particularly if monitoring is costly.

    e.   A and d.

17. Assume that the marginal cost of work is value of the forgone leisure and the individual works and consumes leisure a total of 16 hours a day. Given the following data for an individual , determine the marginal cost of the 13th hour worked.

Leisure Hours	Marginal Benefits
1	$20
2	16
3	12
4	8
5	4

    a. $25

    b. $12

    c. $20

    d. $100

    e. $8

18. For the individual described in question 17 above, how many hours of labor per day will be supplied at a market wage of $8?

    a.   4

    b.   8

    c.   12

    d.   16

19. Assume that the individual described in question 17 above is informed that she has a limited time to live, causing her to value leisure time twice as highly as before. Given a market wage of $8, how many hours per day will she work?

a. 11

b. 9

c. 7

d. 0

e. 5

20. If an individual reduces hours worked as wage rates increase:

a. this individual is said to be irrational.

b. the substitution effect of a change in the wage rate outweighs the income effect.

c. the substitution effect of a change in the wage rate is outweighed by the income effect.

d. the substitution effect of a change in the wage rate is equal to the income effect, but the labor supply curve is backward bending.

21. If the market supply curve for labor is upsloping, this is an indication:

a. that for most people, the income effect of a change in the wage rate outweighs the substitution effect.

b. that for most people, the income effect of a change in the wage rate is outweighed by the substitution effect.

c. that for most people, the income effect of a change in the wage rate equals the substitution effect.

d. that the labor market is perfectly competitive.

THINK IT THROUGH

1. Why does the opportunity cost of leisure rise as an individual works additional hours per day?

2. If two occupations located in the same city and requiring the same skills, education, and experience pay different wage rates, there must be discrimination. True or false? Explain.

3. If two individuals working in the same occupation receive different wage rates, there must be discrimination. True or false? Explain.

4. If workers and managers have goals other than the owner's goal of profit maximization, explain how shirking arises and its implications for the firm and for the economy's allocation of resources. How can owners deal with the shirking problem?

CHAPTER ANSWERS

The Chapter in Brief

1. Marginal benefits 2. Value of a forgone hour of leisure 3. Necessary 4. Benefits 5. More 6. Fewer 7. Upward sloping 8. Backward bending 9. Vertical 10. Increase 11. Nonpecuniary wages 12. Equal to 13. Personnel 14. Efficient, low-cost 15. But that increases 16. Lower

Key Terms Review

1. Human capital 2. Nonpecuniary wages 3. Backward-Bending labor supply curve 4. Compensating wage differential 5. Income effect of a wage change 6. Signals 7. Substitution effect of a wage change 8. Staffing 9. Labor supply curve 10. Screening 11. Marginal benefit of work 12. Shirking 13. Marginal cost of work 14. Internal labor market 15. Nonwage money income

Concept Review

1. a.

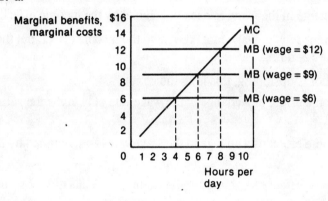

   b. 10, 6 c. 8, 8 d. 4, 12

   e.

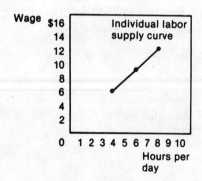

   f. Marginal cost of work

394

2. a. Positive, outweighs b. No, just offsets the c. Inverse, is less than

3. a. Population. The "baby boom" affects the number of workers entering the labor force and results in a rightward shift in labor supply curves.
   b. Rates of labor force participation. Even with a constant population, if more people are entering the labor force and seeking employment, labor supply curves will shift rightward.

4. a.

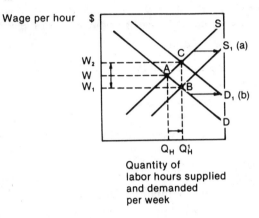

Quantity of
labor hours supplied
and demanded
per week

Market supply, rightward; decrease, increases

   b. Market demand, rightward; increase, increases; positively

5. a. Net benefits from work are maximized where the marginal cost of work equals the marginal benefit of work. Setting MB equal to MC and solving for H yields the net benefit-maximizing level of hours worked.

$$H = (W1 - a)/b$$

   b. A change in a shifts the marginal cost of work curve, whereas a change in b changes the slope of the curve. An increase in a or b decreases hours worked. Anything that causes Fred's marginal cost of work to increase relative to the prevailing wage will cause Fred to work less and vice versa. For instance, if Fred receives news that he has a terminal illness, the value of extra leisure time given up to work would increase. The marginal cost curve would shift upward, and Fred would work less. An increase in the market wage will increase Fred's hours worked and vice versa.

   c. Fred's willingness to work an additional hour is based on the wage received and available for expenditure. Taxes reduce spendable wages. It is necessary to reduce the before-tax wage by the amount of the tax.

$$Wa = \text{After-tax wage} = (1 - t)W1$$

Inserting Wa in the expression above for the net benefit-maximizing hours worked gives

$$H = [(1 - t)W1 - a]/b$$

Since t is a positive fraction, Fred's hours worked after taxes are imposed are less than the hours worked before the imposition of a wage tax. The marginal benefits of work fall relative to the marginal cost of work, and Fred reduces hours worked.

Self-Test for Mastery

1. c 2. b 3. d 4. e 5. a 6. d 7. e 8. c 9. a 10. e 11. b 12. e 13. a 14. d 15. d 16. e 17. b 18. c 19. a 20. c 21. b

Think it Through

1. Assuming an individual sleeps 8 hours per day, there are 16 hours to be allocated between work and leisure. An additional hour worked means that an additional hour of leisure is sacrificed. Because of diminishing marginal utility (or benefits), the value of an hour of leisure rises as less leisure time is available. Therefore the opportunity cost of an hour worked rises as more hours are worked and fewer hours are available for leisure.

2. There may be discrimination, but the difference in wage could be due to compensating wage differentials paid to compensate the worker for undesirable aspects of the job or because of the presence of nonpecuniary job benefits that allow employers to pay a lower wage. In both cases, total compensation received by the worker is the same even though wages differ. The individual working in the job with nonpecuniary job benefits receives a portion of his total compensation from the pleasant or desirable nonmonetary benefits of the job.

3. There may be discrimination, but a wage differential between two workers in the same occupation could also be due to differences in the productivity or quality of the two workers. It could also be due to regional differences in labor markets, including regional differences in product prices that may affect marginal revenue products. Regional amenities (weather, sports, fine arts, education, etc.) vary, thus affecting the nonpecuniary benefits associated with a given occupation located in different regions.

4. Assume that individuals maximize utility whether they are owners, workers, or managers. Owners maximize utility in part by maximizing the return to their invested resources—by maximizing profits. Workers and managers maximize utility by engaging in activities that give satisfaction. This may include earning income, consuming goods and services, exercising power, achieving job security, achieving prestige, and so on. If a firm's compensation system is not designed to encourage both workers and managers to seek the owner's goal of profit maximization, workers and managers will shirk on the job. They will, within the constraints of the job, engage in activities that enhance their welfare but do not necessarily maximize the firm's profits. Managers may decorate their offices with expensive furniture and art and hire attractive but possibly inefficient employees. Workers will likely not maximize their effort per hour worked in earning a wage income and assuring themselves of job security and promotion opportunities. The marginal products of managers and workers alike will not be at their potential. The firm's costs of production will be higher, and owners will not receive maximum profit. The economy is less efficient in that resources are underemployed because maximum output is not being achieved from a given complement of resources. The economy is inside its production possibilities curve.

   A firm can use stock options or an employment contract to encourage a manager to increase profits. If the manager's compensation is tied to the firm's profits, the manager will make more decisions consistent with the interests of the owner. Workers also can be motivated to seek the owner's profit goals with profit-sharing wage contracts.

21 IMPERFECTLY COMPETITIVE INPUT MARKETS: LABOR UNIONS, MONOPSONY, AND BILATERAL MONOPOLY

CHAPTER CONCEPTS

After studying your text, attending class, and completing this chapter, you should be able to:

1. Show how labor union practices can influence wages and affect the productivity of workers.
2. Describe the hiring practices of a monopsony firm and show how such a firm sets input prices.
3. Show how conflicts in input markets arise when monopoly and monopsony are simultaneously present.

THE CHAPTER IN BRIEF

Fill in the blanks to summarize chapter content.

Labor unions engage in collective bargaining to win higher wages and better working conditions and to achieve other goals. In (1)_____ (imperfectly competitive, competitive) product markets, labor unions can only succeed in getting higher wages if the entire industry is unionized. A union must erect barriers to entry to jobs for which it has been able to raise wages. It must also be able to prevent workers from making side agreements with employers.

The earliest unions in the United States were (2)_____ (craft, industrial) unions. The modern union movement began in 1886 with the (3)_____ (Congress of Industrial Organizations, CIO; American Federation of Labor, AFL), which included craft unions composed of skilled workers. In 1935, the (4)_____ (Congress of Industrial Organizations, CIO; American Federation of Labor, AFL) organized industrial unions. A/An (5)_____ (craft, industrial) union organizes all types of labor within an industry, regardless of skill level. In 1955, the AFL and CIO merged. Federal legislation prohibits closed shops and featherbedding, but allows states to pass right-to-work laws. The federal government can intervene and issue an injunction to delay a strike for a period of time. The labor movement has (6)_____ (declined since it peaked, expanded since it bottomed out) in the 1950s. Today, (7)_____ (more than 35%, less than 15%) of the U.S. labor force belongs to unions.

Unions try to increase wages by (8)_____ (expanding, restricting) the supply of labor or imposing an above-market equilibrium wage through the collective bargaining process. Unions (9)_____ (can also; cannot, however,) raise wages by promoting demand for the products they produce. If collective bargaining ends in stalemate, arbitrators will be used to mediate the issues. Evidence indicates that the average wage differential between unionized and nonunionized industries is between (10)_____ (25% and 33%, 10% and 20%) with the differential being much larger for certain industries or occupations. Evidence also indicates that a unionized work force is (11)_____ (more, less) stable, reliable, and productive than a nonunionized work force.

A pure (12)_____ (monopoly, monopsony) exists when there is a single buyer of an input that has few if any alternative employment opportunities. A monopsonist can set wage rates and other input prices. Because the monopsonist is the sole employer of the market supply of an input, it must pay higher input prices to induce input suppliers to make additional inputs available. But the higher input prices have to be paid not only to the new employees but to all existing employees as well. The monopsonist's marginal input cost (13)_____ (equals, exceeds) the wage rate (or average input cost). A profit-maximizing monopsonist will hire inputs up to the point at which the (14)_____ (marginal cost of an input, wage) equals the input's marginal revenue product. A monopsonist pays a wage (15)_____ (equal to, below) the marginal input cost of labor and the worker's marginal revenue product. The (16)_____ (competitive labor market, monopsonist) hires fewer workers and pays a lower wage than employers in a (17)_____ (competitive, monopsonistic) labor market.

A (18)_____ (bilateral monopoly, pure monopsony) exists when the demand side of an input market is represented by a monopsonist and the supply side is represented by a monopoly seller. Through the collective bargaining process a monopoly seller of an input such as a labor union can win a wage above the wage desired by the monopsonist, resulting in (19)_____ (less, higher) employment and higher wages that are closer to or equal to the worker's marginal revenue product.

KEY TERMS REVIEW

Write the key term from the list below next to its definition.

Key Terms

Labor union	Pure monopsony
Monopsony	Monopsony power
Collective bargaining	Marginal input cost
Craft union	Average input cost
Industrial union	Bilateral monopoly
Closed shop	

Definitions

1. _____: exists when only one buyer and one seller trade input (or output) services in a market.

2. _____: a union that represents all workers in a particular industry, regardless of their craft or skills.

3. _____: exists when a single firm buys the entire market supply of an input that has few, if any, alternative employment opportunities.

4. _____: an organization of workers in a particular skilled job, such as plumbers, electricians, carpenters, or musicians.

5. _____: the ability of a single buyer to influence the price of an input service it purchases.

6. _____: the process of negotiating for wages and improvements in working conditions between a labor union and employers.

7. _____: the change in total input cost associated with a change in input services hired.

8. _____: a single buyer with no rivals in an input market.

9. _____: the price of an input.

10. _____: an organization formed to represent the interests of workers in bargaining with employers for contracts concerning wages, fringe benefits, and working conditions.

11. _____: a union arrangement with an employer that permits hiring only of union members.

CONCEPT REVIEW

Concept 1: *Labor union practices*

1. Match the union legislation listed below to the following descriptions.
   Norris-LaGuardia Act (1932)
   Wagner Act (1935)
   Fair Labor Standards Act (1938)
   Taft-Hartley Act (1947)

   a. _____ allowed states to establish right-to-work laws

   b. _____ outlawed featherbedding

   c. _____ outlawed child labor

   d. _____ limited the power of federal courts to intervene in labor disputes

   e. _____ prohibited closed shops

   f. _____ was established to protect workers against unfair labor practices

   g. _____ gave courts the right to issue injunctions to delay strikes

   h. _____ guaranteed workers the right to form unions

2. The diagram below represents a competitive labor market with Wc and Lc representing the market wage rate and the level of employment, respectively.

   a. Show on the figure above the effect of a union-imposed wage rate of Wu. Employment is _____ (higher, lower) than for the case of a competitive labor market.

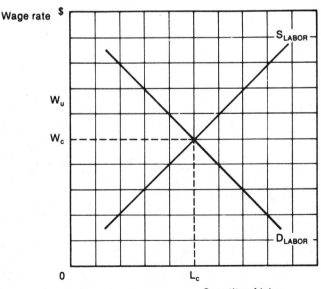

Wage rate $

S_{LABOR}

W_u

W_c

D_{LABOR}

0   L_c

Quantity of labor
supplied and demanded
per week

b. Show on the figure above the effect of an union policy of limiting the quantity of labor supplied in order to increase wages to Wu. Employment is _____ (higher, lower) than for the case of a competitive labor market.

c. The union-desired wage of Wu could alternatively be achieved by promoting or advertising the product produced by the union's members. Show on the figure above the effect of this approach. Employment is _____ (higher, lower) than for the case of a competitive labor market.

Concept 2: *Hiring practices of a monopsonist*

3. A large textile firm has a plant located in a small rural town and is virtually the town's only employer. Residents of the town are too far away from other communities to commute to a job. Therefore they have no alternative employment opportunities. Below are data for the town's labor supply and the textile firm's marginal revenue product schedule.

Wages per Day	Labor Hours Supplied per Day	Total Cost of Labor	Marginal Input Cost of Labor	Marginal Revenue Product
$50	600	$_____		
55	700	_____	$ _____	$175
60	800	_____	_____	155
65	900	_____	_____	135
70	1,000	_____	_____	115
75	1,100	_____	_____	95
80	1,200	_____	_____	75

a. Complete the table above and plot the marginal input cost of labor, labor supply, and marginal revenue product curves in the figure below.

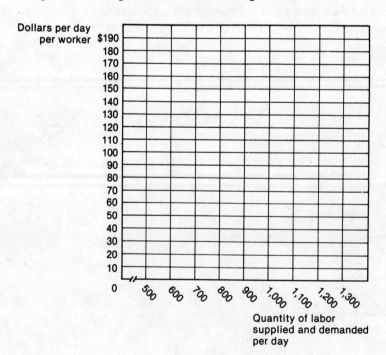

b. A profit-maximizing monopsonist will equate _____ and _____ and hire _____ workers and pay a wage equal to $_____.

c. The monopsonist's wage _____ the worker's marginal revenue product.

d. Assume that the labor market above is a competitive labor market having the same demand for labor as the textile firm. As compared to a perfectly competitive labor market, a monopsonist pays a _____ wage and hires _____ workers. Show this in the figure above.

Concept 3: *Simultaneous presence of monopoly and monopsony in input markets*

4. Assume that a monopsonist such as the one in the preceding problem is confronted by a union representing all workers in the town. The monopsony labor market is shown below.

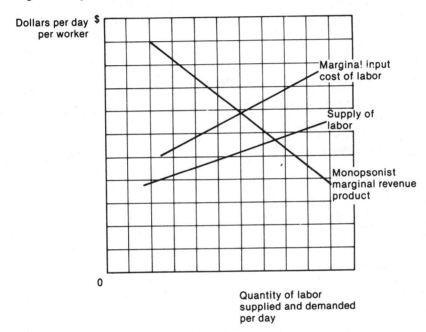

a. Suppose now that a monopoly union is able to win a union-desired wage of Wu, which is above the wage preferred by the monopsonist, Wm. On the figure above identify the monopsony wage and employment and label them Wm and Lm, respectively. Show the effect on employment of a union wage, Wu, greater than Wm.

b. For the case of bilateral monopoly, the wage will equal labor's marginal revenue product if the union wage is equal to or greater than the wage at which the _____ curve intersects the _____ curve.

MASTERY TEST

Select the best answer.

1. An organization formed to represent the interests of workers is called a/an:
    a. trade association.
    b. monopsony.
    c. labor union.
    d. industrial organization.

2. A goal or objective of unions is to:
    a. improve job safety.
    b. increase wages.
    c. achieve job security.
    d. All of the above.

3. If a union is successful in raising wages for some firms in a perfectly competitive industry:
    a. the firms will exit the industry in the long run.
    b. the firms will not be covering normal profits.
    c. the gains in wages by workers will be short lived.
    d. All of the above.

4. Which of the following acts outlawed child labor?
    a. Norris-LaGuardia Act of 1932
    b. Wagner Act of 1935
    c. Fair Labor Standards Act of 1938
    d. Taft-Hartley Act of 1947

5. Which of the following acts prohibited closed shops?
    a. Norris-LaGuardia Act of 1932
    b. Wagner Act of 1935
    c. Fair Labor Standards Act of 1938
    d. Taft-Hartley Act of 1947

6. Labor was guaranteed the right to form unions by the:
    a. Norris-LaGuardia Act of 1932.
    b. Wagner Act of 1935.
    c. Fair Labor Standards Act of 1938.
    d. Taft-Hartley Act of 1947.

7. Which of the following organizations is a federation of unions representing skilled labor as well as all types of labor in given industries?

   a. American Federation of Labor

   b. United Mine Workers

   c. United Rubber Workers

   d. Congress of Industrial Unions

   e. AFL-CIO

8. Union membership peaked in the _____, but is currently less than _____% of the labor force.

   a. 1920s, 20%

   b. 1930s, 40%

   c. 1940s, 18.1%

   d. 1950s, 15%

   e. 1960s, 24.2%

9. Which of the following is not usually practiced by unions as a means to raise wages?

   a. Investing in capital to increase worker productivity

   b. Restricting the supply of labor

   c. Imposing a union wage through the collective bargaining process

   d. Advertising or promoting the product produced with union labor

10. If unions increase wages by restricting the supply of labor or by getting a higher wage through negotiation:

   a. labor is unquestionably better off.

   b. industry employment actually increases.

   c. industry employment decreases.

   d. total wages received by labor as a group must increase.

11. A union may support a restrictive tariff on the import of foreign products because:

   a. domestic product prices are likely to increase.

   b. the marginal revenue product of labor in the protected industries will increase.

   c. wages paid in the protected industries will rise.

   d. All of the above.

12. Empirical evidence indicates that unions have raised average wages in unionized as compared to nonunionized industries by:

    a. 5% to 50%.

    b. 10% to 20%.

    c. 25% to 33%.

    d. 16.1% to 24%.

    e. 13%.

13. Evidence indicates that union work forces are _____ reliable and stable than nonunionized work forces and collective bargaining may _____ labor productivity.

    a. less, decrease

    b. more, decrease

    c. less, increase

    d. more, increase

14. A single firm that buys the entire market supply of an input is called a(n):

    a. monopolist.

    b. oligopoly.

    c. multinational firm.

    d. labor federation.

    e. pure monopsonist.

15. A monopsonist pays a wage that is _____ than the marginal cost of labor and is _____ than the worker's marginal revenue product.

    a. less, less

    b. greater, less

    c. greater, greater

    d. less, greater

16. As compared to a competitive input market, a monopsonist pays a _____ wage and employs _____ workers.

    a. lower, more

    b. higher, fewer

    c. lower, fewer

    d. higher, more

17. A monopsonist employs an input up to the point at which the _____ equals the _____.
    a. wage, supply curve
    b. marginal cost, marginal product
    c. wage, marginal cost
    d. marginal input cost, marginal revenue product of the input
    e. None of the above

18. The marginal input cost curve of a monopsonist:
    a. lies above the market input supply curve.
    b. is more steeply sloped than the market input supply curve.
    c. differs from the input supply curve because the monopsonist must not only pay higher input prices to attract additional inputs, but must also pay these higher prices to the suppliers of inputs currently employed.
    d. together with the marginal revenue product curve determines the profit-maximizing level of employment.
    e. All of the above.

19. Which of the following best defines a market in which only one buyer and one seller trade input services?
    a. Monopoly
    b. Monopsony
    c. Bilateral monopsony
    d. Bilateral monopoly

20. With bilateral monopoly, if unions can _____ wages, employment will _____ and the wage will come closer to or even equal the worker's _____.
    a. increase, decrease, marginal input cost
    b. increase, increase, marginal product
    c. increase, increase, marginal revenue product
    d. increase, decrease, marginal revenue product

21. If wage rates initially are equal for two competitive labor markets, market A and market B, what will happen to the wage and level of employment in market B if market A is unionized by a craft union?
    a. Cannot be determined from the information given
    b. Wage rates will rise and employment will fall
    c. Wages rates and employment remained unchanged
    d. Wage rates fall and employment increases

22. It is argued that union wage gains come at the expense of jobs. For which of the following cases does this hold true?

   a. Bilateral monopoly

   b. Craft unions

   c. Industrial unions

   d. Unions that advertise and promote the product produced by their members

   e. b and c

23. Given the following data for a monopsonist, determine the profit-maximizing level of employment and wage.

Labor Hours	Wage Per Hour	Marginal Revenue Product
100	$2	$14
200	4	12
300	6	10
400	8	8

   a. 300 hours, $6

   b. 200 hours, $4

   c. 100 hours, $2

   d. 400 hours, $8

24. Given the data for the monopsonist described in question 23 above, what would the competitive wage and level of employment be if the competitive market demand curve for labor was the same as the monopsonist's demand for labor?

   a. 100 hours, $2

   b. 200 hours, $4

   c. 300 hours, $6

   d. 400 hours, $8

25. If the monopsonist described above in question 23 is confronted by a powerful industrial union, resulting in collective bargaining and an agreed upon wage of $8, which of the following is true?

   a. The level of employment increases.

   b. The wage equals marginal revenue product.

   c. The wage and level of employment are the same as would occur in a competitive labor market where the competitive market demand for labor was the same as the monopsonist's demand for labor.

   d. All of the above.

THINK IT THROUGH

1. Explain why union attempts to raise wages in competitive firms will fail unless the entire competitive industry is unionized.

2. Compare and contrast the case of a monopsonist selling in a competitive product market with the case of a monopsonist that is also a monopolist in its product market.

3. Is it possible for the power of a monopoly union to just offset the power of a monopsonist such that wage and employment levels are the same as they would be in a competitive labor market? Explain.

4. Discuss the social gains and losses associated with unionism.

ANALYZING THE NEWS

Using the skills derived from studying this chapter, analyze the economic facts that make up the following article and answer the question below, using graphical analysis where possible.

1. Explain how "free agency" contributes to higher average baseball salaries.

2. If "free agency" reduces, but does not eliminate the monopsony power of baseball franchises, are baseball players underpaid or overpaid?

Salaries leap in baseball

'91 players average $880,000

By Hal Bodley
USA TODAY

CLEARWATER, Fla. — Major league baseball's average opening-day salary for 1991 will be approximately $880,000.

The increase is the largest in a single year, up 47.3% from the $597,537 average last season.

There are two reasons for the increase:

▶ Players, fearing a long work stoppage in 1990 during union negotiations with owners, arranged multiyear deals so lesser amounts were paid that season.

▶ Record-breaking free-agent signings during the off-season.

Consider:

For the first time, six teams will have a payroll in excess of $30 million. Last year, Kansas City was No. 1 at $23,617,090 — an average of $688,003.

Baseball's total payroll for 1990 was $433,179,757, and will easily climb above $600 million this year on opening day.

Though many of the multiyear contracts signed this off-season average between $4 million and $5 million, no player will hit the $4 million plateau this year.

The Los Angeles Dodgers'

Out of sight
The 1991 average player salary is up 47% from '90.

$597,537

$29,303

'70   '80   '90

Source: Major League Baseball Players Association

'91 SALARIES, 8E

By Keith Carter, USA TODAY

Darryl Strawberry, who left the New York Mets as a free agent, will be the highest-paid 1991 player at $3.8 million. He is one of 30 players who will earn $3 million or more.

There are 91 players making between $2 million and $3 million, and 100 between $1 million and $2 million.

Of the 650 players who will be on opening-day rosters (25 a club), 221 will earn $1 million or more — 34%.

The minimum salary is $100,000.

Baseball will not have its first $4 million player until 1992 when at least six, led by Dwight Gooden's $4,916,667, reach that level.

CHAPTER ANSWERS

The Chapter in Brief

1. Competitive 2. Craft 3. American Federation of Labor, AFL 4. Congress of Industrial Organizations, CIO 5. Industrial 6. Declined since it peaked 7. less than 15% 8. Restricting 9. Can also 10. 10% and 20% 11. More 12. Monopsony 13. Exceeds 14. Marginal cost of an input 15. Below 16. Monopsonist 17. Competitive 18. Bilateral monopoly 19. Higher

Key Terms Review

1. Bilateral monopoly 2. Industrial union 3. Pure monopsony 4. Craft union 5. Monopsony power 6. Collective bargaining 7. Marginal input cost 8. Monopsony 9. Average input cost 10. Labor union 11. Closed shop

Concept Review

1. a. Taft-Hartley Act b. Taft-Hartley Act c. Fair Labor Standards Act d. Norris-LaGuardia Act e. Taft-Hartley Act f. Wagner Act g. Taft-Hartley Act h. Wagner Act

2.

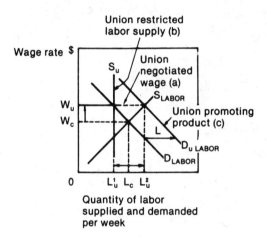

a. lower b. lower c. higher

3. a.

Total Cost of Labor	Marginal Input Cost of Labor
$30,000	$
38,500	85
48,000	95
58,500	105
70,000	115
82,500	125
96,000	135

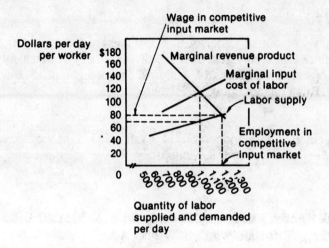

b. Marginal input cost of labor, marginal revenue product of labor, 1,000, $70

c. Is less than

d. Lower, fewer

4. a.

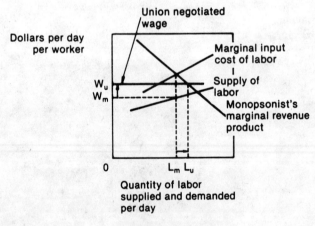

b. Labor supply curve, marginal revenue product curve

Mastery Test

1. c 2. d 3. d 4. c 5. d 6. b 7. e 8. d 9. a 10. c 11. d 12. b 13. d 14. e 15. a 16. c 17. d 18. e 19. d 20. c 21. d 22. e 23. a 24. d 25. d

Think it Through

1. In competitive long-run equilibrium, the firm is just earning normal profits and zero economic profits. If a union is successful in raising wages in a few of the industry's firms but not the entire industry, these firms will continue to sell at the prevailing market price but will have higher costs of production. The owners will not earn sufficient normal profits to keep them in the industry. In time, they will exit the industry and their employees will be unemployed or no longer working at the union wage. If all firms in the industry face a higher union wage, each firm's average cost and marginal cost curves rise. The minimum average cost of production is at a higher level, and in long-run equilibrium the product price will rise to equal the minimum average cost of production.

2. A monopsonist selling in a competitive product market has a marginal revenue product curve for an input that is found by multiplying product price times the input's marginal product. A monopsonist that is also a monopolist in its product market derives its marginal revenue product curve by multiplying marginal revenue by marginal product. Since marginal revenue is less than product price at a given level of output, the monopoly monopsonist will have a marginal revenue product curve that lies inside the competitive monopsonist's marginal revenue product curve. A competitive monopsonist pays a lower wage and employs fewer workers than a competitive input market. But a monopoly monopsonist pays a lower wage and employs even fewer workers than a competitive monopsonist.

3. Interestingly, it is possible to achieve the competitive market wage and level of employment in the case of a bilateral monopoly if the collective bargaining process results in a negotiated wage above the monopsonist wage such that the negotiated wage is at a level that equates the supply of and demand for labor (where the labor supply curve intersects the marginal revenue product curve). This assumes that competitive employers have the same aggregate marginal revenue product as the monopsonist. Wages and employment are at their competitive levels, and the wage equals the worker's marginal revenue product.

4. Unions add to a firm's cost of production and reduce profits received by the owners of the firm. Consumers purchase the products produced by union members at higher prices. But unions are responsible for increasing average wages in unionized industries and for improving working conditions. Wages in nonunionized industries are probably lower because unionization results in fewer jobs. The unemployed seek employment opportunities in the non-unionized labor markets, thus depressing market wages. Evidence indicates, however, that union work forces are more reliable and stable and that collective bargaining increases worker productivity.

Analyzing the News

1. Baseball franchises were able to exercise greater monopsony power prior to the era of free agency. Being the sole buyer of the services of baseball players and preventing players from selling their services to the highest bidder, franchises were able to pay an average salary considerably below the player's average marginal revenue product. Free agency had the effect of lessening the monopsonistic power of the franchises, causing the marginal input cost and supply of labor curves to become less steeply sloped. This had the effect of narrowing the difference between average salaries and the player's marginal revenue products and resulted in significantly higher salaries.

2. As noted above, free agency has lessened the extent of monopsonistic power, but has not eliminated it. Average salaries, while seeming ridiculously high, are still nevertheless lower than the player's average contribution to the franchises' revenues. Players, therefore, appear to still be underpaid.

22 INTEREST, RENTS, AND PROFIT

CHAPTER CONCEPTS

After studying your text, attending class, and completing this chapter, you should be able to:

1. Explain the concepts of capital and investment and show how the interest rate represents a crucial price influencing investment in new capital.
2. Analyze investment decisions and show how the interest rate affects those decisions.
3. Outline the influences on the supply of and demand for loanable funds that affect the equilibrium interest rate for various types of loans in a competitive market.
4. Explain how land rents are determined in competitive markets.
5. Understand how profit opportunities arise in an economy and how entrepreneurs seize those opportunities for personal gain.

THE CHAPTER IN BRIEF

Fill in the blanks to summarize chapter content.

In addition to wages, other types of income include rents, interest, and profit. (1)_____ (Interest, Rent, Profit) is a payment for the use of borrowed funds. (2)_____ (Interest is, Rents are, Profits are) paid to acquire land. (3)_____ (Interest arises, Rents arise, Profits arise) from the production and sale of output and accrues to the owners of businesses.

Businesses invest in (4)_____ (stocks, physical capital) either to replace worn-out capital or to expand capacity. Individuals invest in (5)_____ (financial assets, human capital) to increase their productivity and value in the market place. (6)_____ (Saving, Borrowing) is the income not consumed during the year that is available for capital investment. Investment in capital will take place up to the point at which the marginal revenue product from additional capital is (7)_____ (greater than, just equal to) the marginal input cost of capital. Expressed in percentage terms, investment will take place up to the point at which the (8)_____ (marginal return on investment, marginal revenue product of an investment) is just equal to the market rate of interest.

The loanable funds market determines the market rate of interest which, in turn, determines the profit-maximizing level of investment. A/An (9)_____ (decrease, increase) in the demand for loanable funds increases the market interest rate above the marginal return on investment and results in a/an (10)_____ (decrease, increase) in investment and vice versa. The expected marginal return on an investment is the present value of the stream of expected returns over the life of the investment project expressed as a percentage return. Future returns must be discounted to obtain their current or present value because dollars received in the future (11)_____ (are not worth as much as, are worth more than) the same amount of dollars received today. Dollars today could be invested at the prevailing market rate of interest, resulting in more future dollars. The (12)_____ (present value, cost) of an investment project is the sum of the discounted future returns over the life of the project. An increase in the interest rate (13)_____ (increases, reduces) the present value, whereas a decrease in the interest rate (14)_____ (increases, reduces) the present value. Firms will find it profitable to invest if the present value of an investment project (15)_____ (exceeds, is just equal to) its present cost. In perfectly competitive capital markets, the price of a capital asset is (16)_____ (less than, equal to) the present value of the asset.

The demand for and supply of loanable funds determine the market rate of interest and thus influence the present value of an investment project, affecting its profitability or desirability. The demand for loanable funds is (17)_____ (downward sloping, upward sloping) and can shift in response to changes in business expectations regarding future sales as well as imrovements in technology that affect the marginal revenue product of new capital. Households and government likewise demand loanable funds, but for different reasons. The market supply of loanable funds is (18)_____ (downward sloping, upward sloping) because people require more than a dollar of future consumption for each dollar saved (or not consumed). The additional compensation is in the form of higher interest rates. Also higher interest rates increase the opportunity cost to firms of holding idle funds or using those funds internally. As businesses minimize their holdings of idle balances and internal funds in response to higher interest rates, more funds are made available to the loanable funds market.

While the general level of interest rates is determined by the supply of and demand for loanable funds, specific rates of interest are affected by such factors as the risk associated with an investment or a loan, the length of a loan or maturity of a bond, the amount of collateral pledged to a lender, and the tax treatment of the asset. Higher risk requires (19)_____ (lower, higher) interest rates to compensate risk-averse individuals; otherwise they will invest in less risky projects. A lender may charge a (20)_____ (lower, higher) interest rate on a personal loan that is not collateralized as compensation for a greater exposure to risk of default. A tax-exempt bond with a low interest rate can still compete with taxed financial assets having higher yields for a portion of the available pool of savings because the after-tax yields are the same for both assets.

Rents are determined by the supply of and demand for usable land. Demand for land is determined by the (21)_____ (marginal revenue product, marginal cost) of land. The supply of land, however, is fixed—the market supply curve is perfectly (22)_____ (elastic, inelastic). Market rents are determined entirely by the market demand for land. Anything that changes the price of a good produced with land or alters the marginal productivity of land, such as climate, location, and access to water, utilities, or highways, will affect the (23)_____ (marginal revenue product, marginal cost) of land and cause the market rent to change. In central cities, land is fixed in supply and the highest bidders for the central parcels will put the land to its highest-valued use—such as with high-rise office buildings. Land at the periphery of an urban area is too far from the central city to be used as office space. The bidders for outlying parcels will be farmers, ranchers, and residential developers. The land will be allocated to the highest bidder based on the use that has the (24)_____ (highest, lowest) marginal revenue product. Because rent is a payment in excess of that which is necessary to bring forth the current quantity of land supplied (the current quantity of land is fixed regardless of rent), landlords could be taxed the full amount of their rent received (25)_____ (reducing, without altering) the quantity of land made available.

Profit is the return or reward to the owner. (26)_____ (Economic, Normal) profit is a payment equal to the opportunity cost of the owner's self-owned resources. Normal profits are necessary in order to keep the owner from exiting the industry—from taking his self-owned resources elsewhere. Economic profit and losses allocate resources among industries as some industries expand and some decline. (27)_____ (Economic, Normal) profit results from innovations and anticipation of consumer demands, risk taking, and the exercise of monopoly power.

KEY TERMS REVIEW

Write the key term from the list below next to its definition.

Key Terms

Rent

Capital

Investment

Depreciation

Saving

Marginal return on investment

Discounted present value

Risk

Risk averse

Definitions

1. _____: the amount of income not consumed in a given year.
2. _____: the percentage rate of return on investment of additional sums used to purchase more capital.
3. _____: the rate at which machines and structures wear out.
4. _____: the current value of funds to be received in future periods.
5. _____: the process of replenishing or adding to capital stock.
6. _____: measures the variation of actual outcomes from expected outcomes.
7. _____: an input created by people for the purpose of producing goods and services. It consists of tools, machinery, vehicles, structures, raw material, inventories, and human skills.
8. _____: describes an investor who, if given equal expected returns, would choose an investment with lower risk.
9. _____: the price that is paid for the use of land.

CONCEPT REVIEW

Concepts 2 and 3: *Investment decisions and the interest rate*

1. The Awax Paint Company is considering whether or not to install a new metering device for 1 year. The cost of the system is $95,000. The expected return from the metering device at the end of the year is $15,000 plus a resale value of $90,000 for the used metering device.

   a. The marginal return to the investment is expected to be _____ %. If the market rate of interest is 8%, Awax _____ (will, will not) install the new metering system.

   b. If the market rate of interest rises to 13%, Awax _____ (will, will not) install the device.

2. If Awax's metering device had a useful life of 5 years and did not have any resale value at the end of this period, determine the present value of the measuring system from the data given below.

	Expected Return	PV (10%)	PV (5%)
Year 1	$15,000	_____	_____
2	35,000	_____	_____
3	30,000	_____	_____
4	25,000	_____	_____
5	10,000	_____	_____

Total PV (10%) = $_____   Total PV (5%) = $_____

a. Complete the table.

b. At a present cost of $95,000 and a market rate of interest of 10%, Awax _____ (will, will not) install the device because the present value of the system _____ the present cost.

c. If the market rate of interest falls to 5%, Awax _____ (will, will not) install the device because the present value of the system _____ the present cost.

d. The present value of a capital asset and the interest rate are _____ related.

e. A decrease in the interest rate _____ the present value of proposed investment projects and results in a/an _____ in the volume of investment.

3. The diagram below represents the market for loanable funds and a given firm's marginal return on investment.

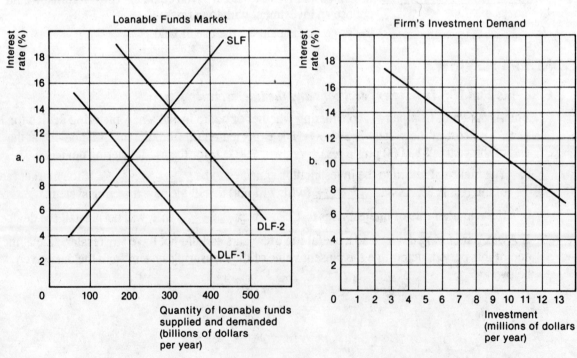

a. In part a of the diagram above, find the market rate of interest assuming the demand for loanable funds is given by Dlf-1. In part b of the diagram, find the firm's profit maximizing quantity of annual investment. Show this in the figure above. Interest rate = _____%, annual investment = $_____

b. A firm will invest up to the point at which _____ equals _____.

c. Assume that the market demand for loanable funds increases to Dlf-2. Find the new interest rate and the firm's annual level of investment. Show on the above figure. Interest rate = _____%, annual investment = $_____

d. An increase in the supply of loanable funds given the demand for loanable funds _____ the market rate of interest, causing a firm's current marginal return on investment to _____ the interest rate and resulting in a/an _____ in investment.

Concept 4: *Rent determination in competitive markets*

4. A large parcel of land exists at the periphery of an urban area, but is still used by farmers to grow crops. The data below represent the quantity of land supplied and demanded by farmers at this site.

Rent per Acre	Acres Supplied (per year)	Marginal Revenue Product (MRP)	Acres Employed
$100	1,000	$100	1,400
200	1,000	200	1,200
300	1,000	300	1,000
400	1,000	400	800
500	1,000	500	600
600	1,000 ·	600	400
700	1,000	700	200

a. Plot the far   r's marginal revenue product schedule and supply curve on the figure below.

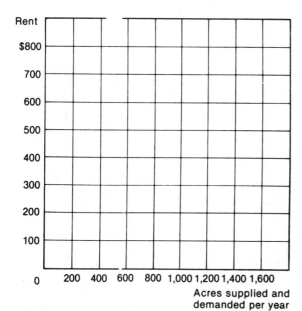

Rent

$800
700
600
500
400
300
200
100

0   200 400 600 800 1,000 1,200 1,400 1,600

Acres supplied and
demanded per year

417

b. The rent per acre at this site is $_____. Because the supply of land is perfectly _____, rent is determined entirely by _____. If there are no other bidders for the acreage, its highest-valued use is _____.

c. Suppose highways are extended to the site greatly improving access to the central city. Assume that at every acreage size employed a residential developer's marginal revenue product is double that of the farmer's marginal revenue product. Show the developer's marginal revenue product curve on the figure above. The market rent per acre _____ to $_____, and it highest-valued use changes from _____ to _____.

d. Rent is a payment _____ of the payment necessary to bring forth a resource. For the case above, the developer pays a total rent of $_____. What percentage of this amount could be taxed without affecting the quantity of land supplied or its highest-valued use? _____ %

MASTERY TEST

Select the best answer.

1. A payment for the use of funds lent by one person for the use of others is called:

   a. rent.

   b. interest.

   c. profit.

   d. wage.

2. A payment for the services of land is called:

   a. rent.

   b. interest.

   c. profit.

   d. wage.

3. _____ is/are a return to entrepreneurs for risks associated with the introduction of new products or techniques.

   a. Rents

   b. Interest

   c. Profits

   d. Wages

4. A profit-maximizing firm will add capital up to the point at which the _____ equals the _____.

   a. marginal revenue product, marginal input cost of capital

   b. marginal return on investment, interest rate

   c. present value of a capital asset, present cost

   d. All of the above

5. Which of the following concepts best explains the slope of the marginal return on investment curve?
   a. Profit maximization
   b. Law of diminishing marginal returns
   c. Law of increasing returns
   d. Equimarginal principle
   e. Diminishing marginal revenue

6. Present value can be defined as:
   a. the total return associated with a project.
   b. the end-of-the-period return discounted to its future value.
   c. the sum of the discounted future returns associated with a capital asset.
   d. the cost of the project.
   e. the sum of the discounted future profits associated with a capital asset.

7. The interest rate and the present value of a capital asset are:
   a. independent of each other.
   b. positively related.
   c. inversely related.
   d. unrelated.
   e. unimportant in investment decisions.

8. An increase in the market demand for loanable funds _____ the market rate of interest causing the interest rate to _____ the current marginal return on investment and resulting in an/a _____ in investment.
   a. decreases, fall below, increase
   b. increases, equal, decrease
   c. decreases, fall below, decrease
   d. increases, rise above, decrease

9. An increase in the market supply of loanable funds _____ the market rate of interest, causing the interest rate to _____ the current marginal return on investment and resulting in an/a _____ in investment.
   a. decreases, fall below, increase
   b. increases, equal, decrease
   c. decreases, fall below, decrease
   d. increases, rise above, decrease

10. Of the following factors influencing interest rates, which one does not result in higher interest rates?
    a. Higher risk
    b. Less collateral pledged against a loan
    c. Longer-term loan or bond
    d. Tax-exempt status

11. The supply of land:
    a. reflects the law of supply.
    b. is perfectly elastic.
    c. is upward sloping.
    d. is perfectly inelastic.
    e. is downward sloping.

12. A firm's demand for land:
    a. is downward sloping.
    b. is the firm's marginal revenue product curve for land.
    c. shifts if the price of the product produced with the land changes.
    d. determines the rent.
    e. All of the above.

13. Rent is determined:
    a. by the landlord.
    b. by shifts in supply of and demand for land.
    c. entirely by the demand for land.
    d. entirely by the supply of land.

14. The highest-valued use to which land is put is dependent upon the:
    a. marginal cost curves of the bidding firms.
    b. marginal revenue curves of the bidding firms.
    c. use desired by the supplier of land.
    d. marginal revenue product curves of the bidding firms.

15. A tax on land rents:
    a. will reduce the quantity of land supplied.
    b. will result in an increase in rents.
    c. will be passed forward to consumers.
    d. will not affect the quantity of land supplied, nor will it increase rents.

16. Which of the following is defined as the opportunity cost of owner-supplied resources?
    a. Total cost
    b. Profit
    c. Normal profit
    d. Economic profit

17. The profit reported by business:
    a. is greater than economic profit.
    b. includes normal profit.
    c. accounts for some of the opportunity costs of owner-supplied resources.
    d. All of the above.

18. Which of the following is not a source of economic profit?
    a. Innovations and anticipation of consumer demands
    b. Risk taking
    c. Exercise of monopoly power
    d. The owner's stock of self-owned resources

19. Assume that an investment project has a 2-period life earning $1,000 at the end of period 1 and another $1,000 at the end of period 2. Assume that there is no salvage value or residual value at the end of the project life. If the current market rate of interest is 10%, determine the present value of the project?
    a. $1,527.77
    b. $1,735.54
    c. $1,862.12
    d. $2,000.00

20. For the investment project described in question 19, what happens to the present value of the project if the market rate of interest rises to 20%?
    a. Present value rises to $1,735.54
    b. Present value stays at $2,000
    c. Present value falls to $1,527.77
    d. Present value falls to $1,862.12

21. Given an interest rate of 20% and the 2-period investment project described above, which of the following present project costs would induce a profit-maximizing firm to undertake the investment?

    a. $2,000

    b. $1,800

    c. $1,600

    d. $1,400

    e. C and d

22. The following data are for a residential developer's marginal revenue product curve for land. If this developer was the highest bidder for a fixed parcel of land of 300 acres, what is the rent per acre per year?

Acres	Marginal Revenue Product ($ per acre per year)
100	$1,000
200	900
300	800
400	700
500	600

    a. $200

    b. $500

    c. $1,000

    d. $700

    e. $800

23. Given the data for the developer in question 22, the supplier of this parcel of land will receive an annual economic rent of :

    a. $24,000

    b. $240,000

    c. $320,000

    d. $20,000

THINK IT THROUGH

1. Discuss intuitively how the principles of investment discussed in this chapter can be used in deciding whether or not to pursue a university degree.

2. Suppose that consumers are heavily indebted and have reached a point at which they must reduce their demand for loanable funds. Discuss the implications for the loanable funds market and for the level of business investment in physical capital.

3. If the market supply of and demand for loanable funds determine the market rate of interest, then why are there many different rates of interest at any one time?

4. Taxes levied on land are considered more efficient than taxes levied on improvements on the land (such as structures). Can you think of any reasons why?

CHAPTER ANSWERS

The Chapter in Brief

1. Interest 2. Rents are 3. Profits arise 4. physical capital 5. Human capital 6. Saving 7. Just equal to 8. Marginal return on investment 9. Increase 10. Decrease 11. Not worth as much 12. Present value 13. Reduces 14. Increases 15. Exceeds 16. Equal to 17. Downward sloping 18. Upward sloping 19. Higher 20. Higher 21. Marginal revenue product 22. Inelastic 23. Marginal revenue product 24. Highest 25. Without altering 26. Normal 27. Economic

Key Terms Review

1. Saving 2. Marginal return on investment 3. Depreciation 4. Discounted present value 5. Investment 6. Risk 7. Capital 8. Risk averse 9. Rent

Concept Review

1. a.10.53%, will b. Will not

2. a.

PV (10%)	PV (5%)
$13,636.36	$ 14,285.71
28,925.62	31,746.03
22,539.44	25,915.12
17,075.34	20,567.56
6,209.25	7,835.26
$88,386.01	$100,349.68

   b. Will not; is less than

   c. Will; is greater than

   d. Inversely e. Increases, increase

3. a.

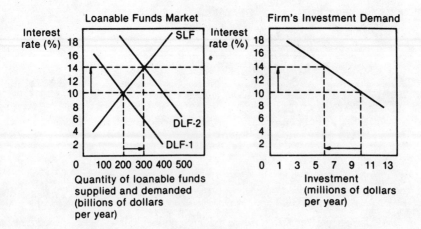

   10%, $10 million

b. Marginal return on investment, the market rate of interest

c. 14%, $6 million

d. Decrease, exceed, increase

4. a.

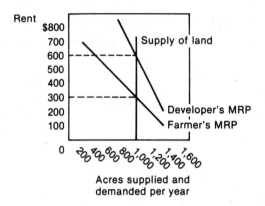

Rent

Supply of land

Developer's MRP

Farmer's MRP

Acres supplied and demanded per year

b. $300; inelastic, the demand for land; in agricultural production

c. Increases, $600, agriculture, residential development

d. In excess of, $600,000; 100%

Mastery Test

1. b 2. a 3. c 4. d 5. b 6. c 7. c 8. d 9. a 10. d 11. d 12. e 13. c 14. d 15. d 16. c 17. d 18. d 19. b 20. c 21. d 22. e 23. b

Think it Through

1. An investment in a college degree generates a stream of benefits over time and involves the explicit outlays of tuition, room, and board but also includes as a cost the forgone income that could have been earned if the individual had worked rather than attended college. Future benefits of a college degree include both pecuniary and nonpecuniary benefits. A net benefit-maximizing individual will compare the present value (or the sum of the discounted future returns) resulting from a college degree to the present costs, which include the forgone income mentioned above. If the present value of a degree is less than the present cost, the individual will not invest in a degree. If the present value is greater than the present cost, the individual will invest in a degree. For instance, assuming only pecuniary benefits are considered, a very highly paid executive will not likely take a 4-year leave of absence to earn a degree. The present value of a bachelor's degree is not likely to outweigh the current sacrifice of income.

2. If consumers reduce their demand for loanable funds, market rates of interest decrease. As interest rates decrease, firms find that projects that were previously unprofitable at higher interest rates are now profitable because interest rates have fallen below the marginal return on investment for many projects. Alternatively, falling interest rates increase the present value of an investment project relative to its present cost. Firms will increase investment, and the aggregate

level of investment in the economy may rise or fall depending upon the relative sizes of the consumer and firm effects.

3. The *average* level of interest rates is determined by the demand for and supply of loanable funds. Because different loans and financial assets have different characteristics, they command different rates of interest at any point in time. Interest rates are higher on financial assets that are riskier, involve a longer term to maturity, are less collateralized, and do not receive favorable tax treatment. Nevertheless, when the average rate of interest changes, these specific rates of interest are likewise changing in the same direction but with different lags and rates of change.

4. Efficient taxes are able to raise tax revenues without distorting resource allocation—without altering the allocation of resources that would prevail in the absence of the tax. Because land is fixed in supply and the payment to acquire land is economic rent, land could be taxed without altering the present quantity of land supplied or the use to which it is put. Landlords cannot escape the tax by taking their land elsewhere. Nor can the owner of the land pass the tax to the renter in the form of higher rents. If this was tried, the renter would find that the rent exceeded his marginal revenue product for the land and would leave. But the land owner needs the land employed in its most productive use in order to earn the highest rents to cover the tax.

Taxes on structures distort economic choices and resource allocation. Taxes on improvements result in an allocation of resources that differs from what would prevail in the market without taxes. Some improvements and structures are mobile. A tax can be avoided by moving the improvements to an area with a lower tax or no tax. In the long run, structures may be allowed to deteriorate, thus reducing the productivity of the land upon which the structure is located.

23   THE DISTRIBUTION OF INCOME AND THE ECONOMICS OF POVERTY

CHAPTER CONCEPTS

After studying your text, attending class, and completing this chapter, you should be able to:

1. Discuss the facts about income distribution in the United States.
2. Document the extent of poverty in the United States.
3. Discuss government assistance programs to the poor and the impact of these programs on incentives and well-being of recipients.
4. Explain the causes of income inequality and evaluate the impact of policies designed to reduce poverty and alter income distribution.

THE CHAPTER IN BRIEF

Fill in the blanks to summarize chapter content.

Income in the United States is not distributed equally. As a percentage of total money income, the lowest 20% of families in 1987 received (1)_____ (less than 5%, 15%) of the nation's income, whereas the richest 20% of families received almost (2)_____ (more than 43%, 33%) of total money income. The degree of inequality as reflected in the distribution of income has (3)_____ (decreased, remained relatively unchanged) from 1947 to 1987. The (4)_____ (welfare, Lorenz) curve is a useful tool for showing the degree of income inequality. The line of income equality results if a given percentage of families receive (5)_____ (that same, a greater) percentage of the nation's money income. For the United States the line is bowed outward, meaning that the distribution of income is skewed to the higher-income families. Policies designed to reduce the inequality will shift the Lorenz curve (6)_____ (away from, inward toward) the line of income equality.

As of 1988, about (7)_____ (6%, 13%) of the U.S. population were counted as poor—having incomes below the poverty income threshold. (8)_____ (The poverty threshold is, Welfare benefits are) determined by estimating the minimally acceptable food budget for a family of a certain size and multiplying by three. By this measure of poverty, the incidence of poverty fell dramatically from 1959 to the end of the 1970s (9)_____ (and continued to decline, but increased) in the early 1980s. Estimates of poverty do not take into account forms of government assistance other than cash assistance. If noncash government benefits were included, it is estimated that the poverty rate would fall to about (10)_____ (2%, 10%).

The incidence of poverty is (11)_____ (higher, lower) among blacks and Hispanics, female-headed households, and children than for the population as a whole. The (12)_____ (Hispanic minorities, elderly) have experienced the largest gains in reducing poverty, largely because of more generous private and public pensions (such as Social Security).

Programs designed to assist the poor are called welfare programs. Recipients must qualify for the programs based on a means test. Government assists the poor with cash and in-kind assistance. (13)_____ (Cash, In-kind) assistance programs include the AFDC and SSI programs. AFDC benefits vary widely by state and are at a level considerably below the poverty line. Examples of (14)_____ (cash, in-kind) assistance include Medicaid, food stamps, and housing assistance. In 1987, AFDC and SSI benefits were over $20 billion and in-kind assistance totaled $54 billion.

A disadvantage of the assistance programs mentioned above is that there are considerable work disincentives. As the welfare recipient works and earns income, welfare benefits drop such that it is not uncommon for a welfare mother, for instance, to lose 80 cents in cash and in-kind benefits for every dollar earned. The losses in production from these disincentives are one form of inefficiency associated with assistance programs. Another form of inefficiency results from the (15)_____ (resource underemployment, distortion of choices) caused by in-kind transfers. If a poor family prefers less food than it could purchase with the food stamps, the stamps are less highly valued than an equivalent amount of cash. If the family received cash instead, it would purchase the desired amount of food and other goods and attain a higher level of utility. However, this apparently is not a big problem because food stamp benefits are low and most families would probably consume more food than allowed by their food stamps. Medicaid is offered to the poor at a zero price. This results in (16)_____ (overconsumption, underconsumption) of medical services, which probably raises the prices of health care services to all consumers.

There are equity-efficiency tradeoffs in the welfare system. Increasing welfare benefits require additional tax revenues. If tax rates are increased, incentives to work, save, and invest are reduced. Improving the equity of the distribution of income results in some efficiency (17)_____ (gains, losses). Apparently, the United States has chosen over the years to minimize the efficiency losses and has shifted the Lorenz curve inward toward greater income equality (18)_____ (by a considerable, by only a very modest) amount. The (19)_____ (antipoverty, negative) income tax proposal has been suggested as a way to reduce poverty without creating efficiency losses as large as is presently the case. Politically, it is not likely to be seriously considered because it involves transferring income to the nonpoor and would require high tax rates.

Because poverty results from the lack of marketable skills or the inability to work, government can do a number of things to increase worker productivity and opportunities to work. The government could provide educational opportunities or subsidies. Economic growth could be promoted as well as worker training. Where discrimination exists it can be reduced or eliminated. Evidence indicates that some of the wage or income differentials observed are probably the result of discrimination, (20)_____ (but a significant share, and only a very small percentage) of the differentials can be attributed to factors other than discrimination, such as education or work experience.

KEY TERMS REVIEW

Write the key term from the list below next to its definition.

Key Terms

Lorenz curve
Poverty income threshold
Welfare programs

Means test
Negative income tax
Discrimination in
    labor markets

Definitions

1. _____: occurs when minority-group workers with skills, experience, and training comparable to those of workers in other groups are paid lower wages and have less opportunity for employment and advancement.

2. _____: government programs to assist the poor in the United States who are unable to work.

3. _____: the income level below which a person or family is classified as being poor.

4. _____: provides for government payments to people whose income falls below certain levels.

5. _____: establishes the fact that people in the groups eligible for welfare payments have incomes and property below the amounts that are minimally acceptable.

6. _____: a plotting of data showing the percentage of income enjoyed by each percentage of households ranked according to their incomes.

CONCEPT REVIEW

Concepts 1 and 2: *Distribution of income, poverty and the poverty threshold income*

1. Given the data below on the distribution of family income, answer the questions below.

	Percentage of Families	*Percentage of Total Income*
Highest	20%	43%
4th	20%	24%
3rd	20%	17%
2nd	20%	11%
Lowest	20%	5%

a. On the figure below, plot the Lorenz curve for the data above.

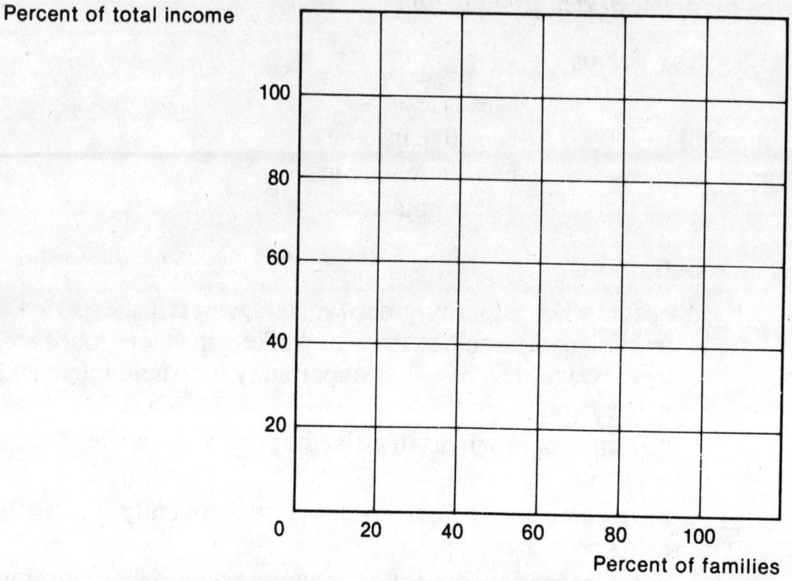

Percent of total income

b. On the figure above, identify the line of income equality.

c. On figure above, show the effect on the current distribution of family income of policies that reduce income inequality.

2. Which groups of individuals in the United States in 1988 had the highest incidence of poverty?

Group	Percentage of the Group Classified as Poor
a._____	_____ %
b._____	_____
c._____	_____
d._____	_____

3. If the federal government determines that the minimally acceptable food expenditure is $3 per person per day, determine the poverty threshold income for a:

a. Family of 2. $_____

b. Family of 3. $_____

c. Family of 4. $_____

d. Given the following distribution of four-person families, determine the poverty rate. (The poverty rate is the percentage of four-person families having incomes below the poverty-threshold income.)

Income	Families of Four
$51,000 and above	2 million
Below $51,000	27 million
Below $27,640	19 million
Below $13,140	3 million
Below $ 6,280	1 million

Poverty rate = _____ %

Concept 3: *Programs to aid the poor*

4. Match the cash and in-kind assistance programs listed below to the statements below.

AFDC   Medicaid   Housing assistance
SSI   Food stamps

a. _____ This program is federally funded and involves cash payments to the blind, aged, and disabled.

b. _____ This program is the most expensive of all federal programs that aid the poor.

c. _____ Only one person in four who are eligible for this program receives benefits.

d. _____ A program designed to aid families with dependent children.

e. _____ A program in which maximum benefits vary greatly by state. In 1990, these benefits were $118 per month in Mississippi but $846 in Alaska.

f. _____ This program provides the poor with stamps that can be redeemed for food.

g. _____ This program provides subsidized payments and rents to assist the poor in renting private housing.

h. _____ This program involves a service rendered for which the poor pay a zero price.

5. In the long run, government must pursue certain fundamental policies if poverty is to be reduced or eliminated. What are they?

a. _____

b. _____

c. _____

d. _____

MASTERY TEST

Select the best answer.

1. What percentage of the U.S population was classified as poor in 1988?
   a. 5%
   b. 9%
   c. 13%
   d. 18%
   e. 22%

2. In 1987, the highest 20% of the families in the income distribution received what percentage of total income?
   a. 20%
   b. Over 43%
   c. 67%
   d. 53%
   e. Less than 38%

3. In 1987, the lowest 20% of the families in the income distribution received what percentage of total income?
   a. 14%
   b. 21%
   c. Over 8%
   d. Under 5%
   e. 12%

4. The distribution of income in the United States from 1947 to 1987:
   a. has become more unequal.
   b. has become significantly more equal.
   c. has been stable.
   d. has coincided with the line of income equality.

5. Which of the following is a plotting of data showing the percentage of income enjoyed by each percentage of households ranked according to their incomes?
   a. Income curve
   b. Distribution curve
   c. Phillips curve
   d. Lorenz curve

6. If a nation's Lorenz curve lies below the line of income equality:
    a. proportionately more of the nation's income is received by the highest 20% of families than the lowest 20%.
    b. the income received by each 20% of families is 20% of the total income.
    c. proportionately more of the nation's income is received by the lowest 20% of families than the highest 20%.
    d. income is equally distributed.

7. Poverty in the United States is defined as:
    a. unwholesome living conditions.
    b. a level of income below the median income for all families.
    c. a level of income below the minimally acceptable annual food budget of a family of a given size times three.
    d. an income below 20% of the average family income.

8. The percentage of the U.S. population living in households having incomes below the poverty threshold level has _____ from 1959 to 1988.
    a. decreased
    b. increased
    c. remained remarkably stable
    d. increased for 2 decades and fallen for 5 years

9. Which of the following groups does not have a high incidence of poverty—a rate of poverty above the rate for the population as a whole?
    a. The elderly
    b. Female-headed households
    c. Blacks
    d. Hispanics
    e. Children

10. Which of the following groups has experienced the largest drop since 1959 in the percentage of its members who are poor?
    a. The elderly
    b. Female-headed households
    c. Blacks
    d. Hispanics
    e. Children

11. Which of the following assistance programs to the poor is not an in-kind assistance program?

    a. Food stamps

    b. Medicaid

    c. Housing

    d. AFDC

12. The most costly program to aid the poor is:

    a. the food stamp program.

    b. medicaid.

    c. federal housing assistance.

    d. SSI.

13. A Census Bureau study found that if income was defined as including money income and in-kind transfers, the percentage of the population having incomes below the poverty threshold level would be about:

    a. 0%.

    b. 5%.

    c. 8%.

    d. 10%.

    e. 14%.

14. Which of the following best illustrates the work disincentives present in the current welfare system?

    a. The vicious circle of welfare teaches children to be lazy.

    b. For each additional dollar earned, a welfare recipient may lose as much as 80 cents in welfare assistance.

    c. Even though the poor are able-bodied, they choose to not work in order to rip off the welfare system.

    d. An average welfare recipient faces a tax rate of 15%.

15. Policies that increase welfare benefits and require tax rate increases to fund the expanded programs:

    a. increase both equity and efficiency.

    b. decrease both equity and efficiency.

    c. increase efficiency, but decrease equity.

    d. increase equity, but decrease efficiency.

16. The negative income tax proposal:

    a. provides for a minimum-guaranteed income.

    b. involves high tax rates.

    c. transfers income to nonpoor families.

    d. is very costly.

    e. All of the above.

17. Which of the following policies should be undertaken by government in order to reduce or eliminate poverty?

    a. Programs that support equality of opportunity

    b. Programs the promote economic growth

    c. Programs that encourage or provide education

    d. Programs that encourage or provide training

    e. All of the above

18. Which of the following acts outlawed discrimination on the basis of race, religion, sex, or national origin?

    a. The Anti-discrimination Statute of 1955

    b. The Equal Rights Amendment of 1982

    c. The Civil Liberties Union Act of 1978

    d. The Civil Rights Act of 1964

19. If the bottom 40% of families realized an increase in their share of national income and the top 40% of families experienced a decrease in share, the Lorenz curve:

    a. remains a downsloping curve that is convex to the origin.

    b. does not move, but remains a linear, 45 degree ray from the origin.

    c. moves away from the line of equality.

    d. moves toward the line of equality.

20. Assume that the average poor family of three has a minimally adequate monthly food budget of $300. What is the annual poverty threshold income for this family?

    a. $10,800

    b. $900

    c. $9,800

    d. $12,200

21. Which of the following statements is (are) true regarding the incidence of poverty in the United States?

    a. The incidence of poverty is higher among children than for the nation as a whole.

    b. Compared to the nation as a whole, the elderly have experienced a marked decrease in the incidence of poverty.

    c. The incidence of poverty is higher among female-headed households than male-headed households.

    d. A and c

    e. All of the above

22. Which of the following is correct regarding government transfer programs in the United States?

    a. Most government transfers are cash transfers to households such as Aid to Families with Dependent Children and Supplemental Security Income.

    b. Most government transfers to households are in-kind transfers such as Supplemental Security Income and food stamps.

    c. For 1987, cash transfers to households such as Aid to Families with Dependent Children and Supplemental Security Income were over twice as large as in-kind transfers.

    d. For 1987, cash transfers to households such as Aid to Families with Dependent Children and Supplemental Security Income were less than half as large as in-kind transfers.

23. If a welfare mother faces an implicit marginal tax rate of 80%:

    a. tax rates are too high and should be reduced.

    b. she must send the government 80 cents for each additional dollar earned.

    c. she loses 80 cents in cash and in-kind benefits for each additional dollar earned.

    d. she may be discouraged from working additional hours per week.

    e. c and d

THINK IT THROUGH

1. Discuss how poverty is measured. Can you think of any limitations of the current method of defining poverty?

2. Discuss the nature of the efficiency-equity tradeoff associated with efforts to redistribute income.

3. Briefly discuss current programs to aid the poor and discuss the effectiveness of the programs in terms of the level of poverty and the distribution of income.

4. If poverty results from the lack of marketable skills, inability to work, or the lack of opportunity to work or attain skills, discuss the types of policies that government must pursue if it is to successfully reduce poverty.

CHAPTER ANSWERS

The Chapter in Brief

1. less than 5% 2. more than 43% 3. Remained relatively unchanged 4. Lorenz 5. That same 6. Inward toward 7. 13% 8. Poverty threshold is 9. But increased 10. 10% 11. Higher 12. Elderly 13. Cash 14. In-kind 15. Distortion of choices 16. Overconsumption 17. Losses 18. By only a very modest 19. Negative 20. But a significant share

Key Terms Review

1. Discrimination in labor markets 2. Welfare programs 3. Poverty income threshold 4. Negative income tax 5. Means test 6. Lorenz curve

Concept Review

1.

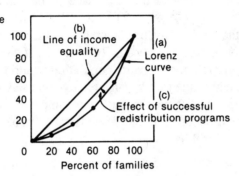

2. a. Female-headed households with dependent children; 33.6%

   b. Blacks; 31.6%

   c. Hispanics; 26.8%

   d. Children; just over 20%

3. a. $6,570 b. $9,855 c. $13,140 d. 7.69%

4. a. SSI

   b. Medicaid

   c. Housing assistance

   d. AFDC

   e. AFDC

   f. Food stamps

   g. Housing assistance

   h. Medicaid

5. a. Promote equal opportunity

   b. Promote economic growth

   c. Provide or subsidize education

   d. Provide, encourage, or subsidize training

Mastery Test

1. c 2. b 3. d 4. c 5. d 6. a 7. c 8. a 9. a 10. a 11. d 12. b 13. d 14. b 15. d 16. e 17. e 18. d 19. d 20. a 21. e 22. d 23. e

Think it Through

1. The poverty rate of a given group or population in the United States is the percentage of the group or population having incomes below the poverty income threshold. The poverty income threshold is determined by estimating the minimally acceptable food expenditure per day per person and multiplying that amount by three. Therefore the poverty income threshold for a family depends on the size of the family. One limitation of this measure of poverty is that it does not include in-kind goods or services received by households. If these benefits were included, it is estimated that the poverty rate for the entire population would fall to 10%. Another limitation is that the measure is an absolute rather than a relative measure of poverty. Over time more families might have incomes above the poverty income threshold but still retain their relative place in the distribution of income. In other words, they are likely to feel just as poor even though their absolute income level has risen.

2. Programs designed to reduce poverty and redistribute income, if successful, will improve equity (assuming that society feels that some redistribution is socially desirable). However, programs require resources that must be withdrawn from the private sector of the economy. If tax rates are ultimately increased to fund these programs, economic efficiency is reduced. Since most taxes are not neutral in their impact, distortions will occur in decisions regarding work, saving, and investment. The economy is operating inside its production possibilities curve. But this is the tradeoff—the opportunity cost of improving fairness in the economy is a lower level of production. The very fact that redistribution programs and tax laws have been in place for decades is evidence that society believes that some redistribution should take place.

3. The current approach to aiding the poor is through cash and in-kind transfers. Cash assistance includes Aid to Families with Dependent Children (AFDC) and Supplemental Security Income (SSI). In-kind programs include Medicaid, which is the most expensive program for the poor, housing assistance, and food stamps. The nation's poverty rate fell in the 1960s and until the end of the 1970s. In the early 1980s, the poverty rate increased substantially and has fallen to the present but still remains above the all-time lows of the late 1970s. From the answer to question 1 above, note that improvements in absolute income levels do not guarantee that a family's relative position in the distribution of income will improve. In fact, the Lorenz curve has shifted inward only a slight amount since the advent of these poverty programs. In the 1980s, the distribution of income has likely become less rather than more equal.

4. The government needs to treat the disease in addition to the symptoms. Poverty is the result of the lack of purchasing power. But the lack of purchasing power is related to the absence of marketable skills, the lack of opportunity to attain those skills or find employment, and both overt and subtle forms of discrimination. Evidence suggests that a considerable portion of the wage differentials among workers can be attributed to differences in skills, education, or experience.

438

But there is an unexplained component of these differentials that may be due to discrimination. Government programs that assure equal opportunity, not only to education and training, but also to the workplace and that increase workers' marginal products, such as programs designed to encourage the consumption of additional training and education, will in the long run be more effective in combatting poverty than short-term cash or in-kind transfers.

PART VI

INTERNATIONAL ECONOMIC ISSUES

PART EXERCISE

Inside Information: *Where to Go to Get Information on United States International Trade and Economic Conditions in Foreign Nations*

In Part X, you will learn about international trade issues. Use *United States Trade* and detail the volume and type of exports and imports for the year. What happened to net exports during the year? Assume that the change in net exports resulted from changes in foreign exchange markets. Based on what you have learned about foreign exchange markets, provide a plausible explanation for the change in net exports.

24 INTERNATIONAL TRADE, PRODUCTIVITY, AND THE ECONOMICS OF LESS DEVELOPED COUNTRIES

CHAPTER CONCEPTS

After studying your text, attending class, and completing this chapter, you should be able to:

1. Discuss recent trends in U.S. international trade.
2. Understand the underlying basis for international trade, the principle of comparative advantage and the gains in well-being possible from free trade with foreign nations.
3. Show how productivity changes in specific industries can affect their comparative advantage in international trade.
4. Discuss protectionism and analyze the impact on the economy of tariffs, import quotas, and other trade restrictions.
5. Discuss some of the unique economic problems of less developed countries and the causes of low per capita income and slow economic growth in those nations.

THE CHAPTER IN BRIEF

Fill in the blanks to summarize chapter content.

The United States exported over $300 billion in merchandise goods in 1988. (1) _____ (Agricultural products, Capital goods) accounted for the largest export category, 35.2%, while automotive products, (2) _____ (agricultural products, capital goods), and industrial materials and supplies were 10.2%, 11.9%, and 25.5% of total merchandise exports, respectively. Merchandise imports were $446.5 billion in 1988. The largest category of merchandise imports was capital goods, 22.8% of total merchandise imports, followed by automobiles and related products, industrial materials, and petroleum products. In contrast to the merchandise trade (3) _____ (deficit, surplus) incurred in 1988, the United States exported (4) _____ (fewer, more) services than were imported by almost $15 billion.

The United States is the largest international trader in the world. In the late 1980s, the United States exported a little more than (5) _____ (10%, 17.8%) of world exports, but accounted for a peak of (6) _____ (10% 17.8%) of world imports in 1985. In the late 1980s, U.S. exports have increased while U.S. imports have decreased. Canada and Japan are the two largest trading partners of the United States, accounting for 33.7% of U.S. exports and 38.8% of U.S. imports. In 1988, the United States ran a trade surplus with (7) _____ (Canada, Japan) of almost $2 billion, but had a trade deficit with (8) _____ (Canada, Japan) just short of $7 billion.

Nations engage in international trade because it is mutually beneficial for all trading nations to do so; otherwise they would not trade. Some nations may have a/an (9)_____ (comparative, absolute) advantage in producing goods, meaning that with a given complement of resources, one nation can produce more of an item than another nation with the same quantity of resources. But the presence of an absolute advantage in the production of an item does not indicate whether a nation should specialize in and export that good or whether the good should be imported. A country should specialize in and export those goods for which it has an/a (10)_____ (absolute, comparative) advantage and import those goods for which other countries have a comparative advantage. A nation has a comparative advantage in the production of a good relative to another nation if it produces the good at (11)_____ (lower, higher) opportunity cost than its trading partner.

Nations that trade on the basis of comparative advantage (12)_____ (gain at the expense of their rivals, mutually gain from trade). On an international scale, resources are used more efficiently as nations produce output based upon comparative advantages. World output, income, and living standards are (13)_____ (higher, lower) as a result of specialization and trade than would be the case in the absence of trade. All trading partners gain, although not equally. The distribution of the gains from trade is determined by the (14)_____ (foreign exchange rate, terms of trade)—the rate at which goods can be traded or exchanged for one another on international markets. A nation will be induced to trade goods for which it has a comparative advantage for import goods if it can obtain the imported goods at prices below the domestic opportunity cost of production. The real terms of trade are determined by (15)_____ (government, world demand and supply). For trade incentives to exist, the terms of trade must be (16)_____ (below, above) the opportunity cost of producing each additional unit of the good a nation desires to import. When countries specialize in and export those goods for which they have a comparative advantage and import goods for which other nations have a comparative advantage, the consumption possibilities curve of each nation lies (17)_____ (outside, inside) the production possibilities curve.

Changes in productivity can affect a nation's competitiveness in international markets. If a nation experiences slower technological growth or lower levels of investment in human and physical capital relative to those of its trading partners, in time it may lose its (18)_____ (absolute, comparative) advantage in those industries where international competitiveness requires improvements in productivity. The nation that invests more heavily in things that enhance productivity will eventually (19)_____ (gain, lose) a comparative advantage relative to the lagging nation and will capture a share of the international market that it previously did not have. Slow productivity growth (growth in output per labor hour) in the United States in the 1980s has been cited as a reason for the decline in the competitiveness of some U.S. export industries. The primary cause of the low productivity growth is believed to be the low rate of annual (20)_____ (government, investment) spending as a percentage of domestic production relative to other nations, particularly Japan. Increased government regulation and (21)_____ (falling wages, higher energy prices) have also been cited as factors contributing to the productivity decline of the 1970s.

As comparative advantage changes, nations losing the comparative advantage in a good no longer export that good. Industry sales and output fall, causing some workers with specialized skills to become unemployed and other suppliers of specialized inputs to experience a decline in income. Both the owners of the declining industry and its input suppliers are harmed. But this has to be balanced against the widespread gains to society when a nation produces on the basis of comparative advantage. Changes in comparative advantage are painful in the short run, but nations are better off in the long run by specializing in and exporting those goods for which they have a comparative advantage and trading for those goods for which they do not.

Several arguments, however, have been advanced for protecting domestic industries. It is argued that some industries may need to be protected from international competition to maintain production capacity (22)_____ (vital to national security, necessary to be self-sufficient). Protecting (23)_____ (large and established industries, new and emerging "infant" industries) from the rigors of international competition is considered a way of allowing an industry to grow in a sheltered environment until it attains sufficient economies of scale to compete internationally. Industries experiencing changes in comparative advantage can be spared some of the short run costs to specialized input suppliers and owners by receiving some protection from foreign rivals. Some industries are protected from what is viewed as unfair competition by foreign governments that subsidize their export industries. Arguments against free trade derive from changes in the (24)_____ (distribution of income that occur, efficiency with which goods are produced) as some industries fail and lose their comparative advantage.

Two methods of import protection are import tariffs and import quotas. A (25)_____ (quota, tariff) is a tax on an imported good. The intention is to reduce imports and increase the sales of domestic products. A tariff (26)_____ (raises, lowers) the price of the imported good to the consumer, (27)_____ (increases, reduces) the net price to the foreign producer, and generates tax revenue for the government. A/An (28)_____ (tariff, import quota) is a limit on the quantity of foreign goods that can be sold in a nation's domestic market. Like the tariff, an import quota (29)_____ (increases, reduces) the quantity of imported goods sold and (30)_____ (raises, lowers) the price to the consumer, but unlike a tariff, the import quota also (31)_____ (lowers, raises) the price received by the foreign producer. If the demand for the imported good is inelastic, the foreign producer (32)_____(is always worse off, may be better off) operating with a quota. Further, quotas raise no revenue for government. But protectionism invites retaliation from trading partners. If a nation's trading partners also impose import tariffs and quotas, all of the trading nations (33)_____ (lose, gain) because the level of international trade is lower and consumers in each country are paying higher prices than necessary.

(34)_____ [Newly industrialized countries, Less developed countries (LDCs)] have very low real per capita GNPs. This is because of (a) (35)_____ (high, low) rates of saving and capital accumulation, (b) poorly skilled and educated workers, (c) lagging technological know-how, (d) (36)_____ (high, low) population growth and unemployment, and (e) political instability and government policies that discourage production. These nations are dependent on foreign trade to acquire capital and technology necessary for increases in their standard of living. But unless they export enough to acquire the foreign exchange to purchase the imported goods, these nations will not be able to advance significantly without the help of gifts or loans from foreign nations.

KEY TERMS REVIEW

Write the key term from the list below next to its definition.

Key Terms

Specialization
Mutual gains from
    international trade
Absolute advantage
Comparative advantage
Real terms of trade

Consumption possibilities
    curve
Tariff
Import quota
Real per capita output
Less developed country (LDC)

Definitions

1. _____: shows combinations of two goods a nation can consume given its resources, technology, and international trade.

2. _____: the actual market exchange rate of one good for another in international trade.

3. _____: a tax on imported goods.

4. _____: a nation has a comparative advantage over a trading partner in the production of an item if it produces that item at lower opportunity cost per unit than its partner does.

5. _____: a limit on the quantity of foreign goods that can be sold in a nation's domestic markets.

6. _____: a nation has an absolute advantage over other nations in the production of an item if it can produce more of the item over a certain period with a given amount of resources than the other nations can.

7. _____: a measure of output per person in a nation; calculated by dividing real GNP by population.

8. _____: on average, citizens in all trading nations gain from exchanging goods in international markets.

9. _____: a country whose real GNP per capita is generally much less than $1000 per year.

10. _____: use of labor and other resources in a nation to produce the goods and services for which those resources are best adapted.

CONCEPT REVIEW

Concept 2: *Absolute vs. comparative advantage, terms of trade, gains from trade*

1. The domestic production possibilities of two nations, nation A and nation B, for two goods, cases of wine and boxes of cheese, are shown below.

Production Possibilities

	Nation A	Nation B
Wine (cases)	1 million	600,000
Cheese (boxes)	500,000	400,000

446

a. Plot the production possibilities curve for each nation in a and b in the figure below.

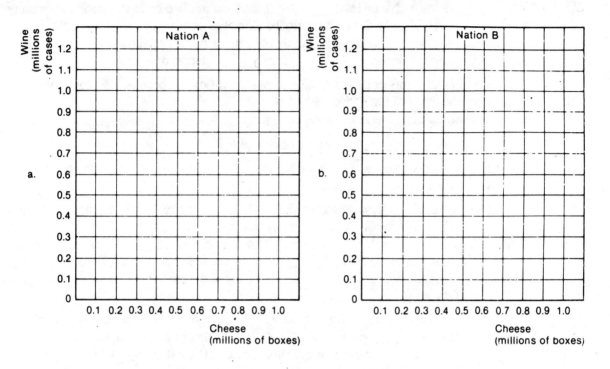

b. Assuming each nation has the same quantity of resources, 1000 workers, and both nation's produce only wine, the number of cases of wine per worker in nation A of _____ cases _____ the number of cases of wine per worker of _____ cases in nation B. Similarly, if both nations produce only cheese, the number of boxes of cheese per worker in nation A of _____ boxes _____ the number of boxes of cheese per worker in nation B of _____ boxes. Nation A has a/an _____ advantage in the production of both wine and cheese. Nation A's production possibilities curve _____ nation B's production possibilities curve.

c. In nation A, the opportunity cost of producing a case of wine is _____ boxes of cheese and the opportunity cost of producing a box of cheese is _____ cases of wine. The slope of nation A's production possibilities curve is _____, which means that the opportunity cost of producing an additional box of cheese is _____ cases of wine.

d. In nation B, the opportunity cost of producing a case of wine is _____ boxes of cheese and the opportunity cost of producing a box of cheese is _____ cases of wine. The slope of nation B's production possibilities curve is _____, which means that the opportunity cost of producing an additional box of cheese is _____ cases of wine.

2. Regarding the problem above, nation A has a comparative advantage in the production of _____, whereas nation B has a comparative advantage in the production of _____. Nation A should specialize in and export _____ and should import _____. Nation B should specialize in and export _____ and should import _____. For nation A to be induced to trade for _____, it must give up less _____ than that

implied by its domestic opportunity cost of _____. For nation B to be induced to trade for _____, it must give up less _____ than that implied by its domestic opportunity cost of _____. Trade will be mutually beneficial to both nations if 1 box of cheese trades for between _____ and _____ cases of wine. Alternatively, trade will result if 1 case of wine trades for between _____ and _____ boxes of cheese.

3. a. Assume that the terms of trade for cheese are set at 1 box of cheese = 12/7 cases of wine. What are the terms of trade for a case of wine?

   1 box of cheese = 1 and 5/7 (or 12/7) cases of wine

   1 case of wine = _____ boxes of cheese

   b. Given the terms of trade, in a and b in the figure above plot the consumption possibilities curve for each nation.

   c. If nation A specializes in wine and keeps 800,000 cases for its domestic consumption and trades 200,000 cases to nation B, how many boxes of cheese can it get in return? _____ boxes Given nation A's domestic opportunity cost of cheese of _____ cases of wine, it can domestically produce only _____ boxes of cheese by sacrificing 200,000 cases of wine. Trade results in a gain of _____ boxes of cheese over what was possible in the absence of trade.

   d. If nation B trades cheese for 200,000 cases of nation A's wine, how much cheese will it have to trade? _____ boxes of cheese. Given B's domestic opportunity cost of wine of _____ boxes of cheese, it can domestically produce 200,000 cases of wine only by sacrificing _____ boxes of cheese, but it only has to give up _____ boxes of cheese through international trade to acquire the same quantity of wine. Trade results in a gain of _____ boxes of cheese over what was possible in the absence of trade.

Concept 4: *Protectionism, tariffs, and quotas*

4. List four arguments in favor of protectionism.

   a. _____

   b. _____

   c. _____

   d. _____

5. In a and b in the figure below are shown the domestic and import markets for shoes.

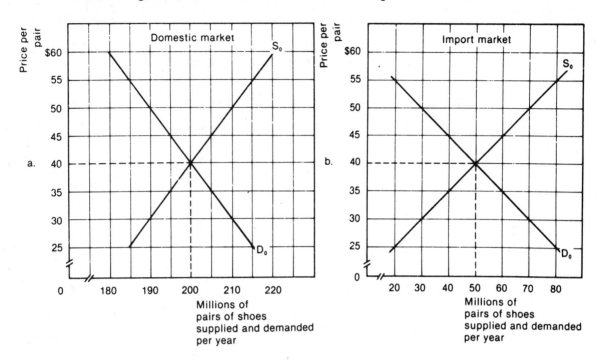

a. Suppose that domestic shoe manufacturers and their input suppliers are able to win an
    import tariff of $10 per pair of imported shoes. Show the new import supply curve in b
    above. The $10 tariff causes the price to the consumer to _____ to $_____ and the
    net price to foreign shoe manufacturers to _____ to $_____. Sales of imported
    shoes _____ to _____ million pairs. The tariff has raised tax revenue of
    $_____. Show these effects in b.

b. In a, assume that the decline in import sales causes an increase in domestic shoe demand
    by an equal amount at each price level. The domestic demand for shoes shifts _____
    by _____ million pairs of shoes. Domestic shoe prices _____ to $_____ and
    sales _____ to _____ million pairs.

c. In effect, the tariff redistributes income from _____ and _____ to the
    owners and input suppliers of the protected domestic shoe industry.

d. If an import quota had been used instead to achieve the lower level of import sales that you
    found in part a above, the price of imported shoes paid by the consumer and received by
    the foreign producer _____ to $_____. The domestic market price of shoes
    _____ to $_____, and sales _____ to _____ million pairs of shoes. In
    this case, the government receives _____ tax revenue and the foreign producer may
    experience a/an _____ in total revenue if the demand for imported shoes is
    sufficiently inelastic. Show the case of an import quota in b in the figure above.

449

MASTERY TEST

Select the best answer.

1. If a nation has a/an _____ in the production of an item, it can produce more of the item with a given quantity of resources than can other nations.
   a. special advantage
   b. comparative advantage
   c. absolute advantage
   d. mutual gain

2. A nation's comparative advantage is determined by:
   a. the total cost of production.
   b. the quantity of resources required to produce a unit of output.
   c. the opportunity cost of producing an item relative to a trading partner's opportunity cost of producing the same item.
   d. specialization in the production of all goods.

3. If nations trade on the basis of comparative advantage, a nation should specialize in and _____ those goods for which it has a comparative advantage and should _____ those goods for which other nations have a comparative advantage.
   a. export, import
   b. import, export
   c. export, export
   d. import, import

4. If nations trade on the basis of comparative advantage:
   a. a nation can gain only at the expense of trading partners.
   b. exporting nations gain and importing nations lose.
   c. importing nations gain and exporting nations lose.
   d. all trading partners mutually gain.

5. A nation will be induced to trade for imported goods if the nation can give up _____ goods through international trade for the imported item than implied by its domestic _____ cost of production.
   a. more, total
   b. more, opportunity
   c. fewer, variable
   d. fewer, opportunity

6. Which of the following refers to the rate at which goods are exchanged for one another in international markets?

    a. Exchange rate

    b. Terms of trade

    c. Specialization

    d. Opportunity cost

    e. None of the above

7. If nations trade on the basis of _____ advantage, the consumption possibilities curve lies _____ the production possibilities curve.

    a. absolute, inside

    b. a unique, parallel to

    c. comparative, parallel to

    d. comparative, outside

8. When a nation's productivity growth lags behind that of its trading partners, in time it may:

    a. lose its comparative advantage in some industries.

    b. gain a comparative advantage as a result of the lag in productivity growth.

    c. diversify with "infant" industries.

    d. experience a reduction in the opportunity cost of producing the good.

9. Lagging productivity growth of a nation relative to its trading partners:

    a. results in a loss of comparative advantage in some industries.

    b. results in an increase in the opportunity cost of producing some goods relative to that of foreign rivals.

    c. results in a loss of income to the owners and specialized input suppliers in the industries experiencing lagging productivity growth.

    d. All of the above.

10. Which of the following have been cited as reasons for the slow productivity growth in the United States in the 1970s?

    a. Average annual net investment of 6% of domestic production

    b. Increased government regulation to improve working conditions and the environment

    c. Rising energy prices

    d. All of the above

    e. None of the above

11. Which of the following is not an argument in favor of protectionism?
    a. National security
    b. Reducing structural unemployment
    c. Protecting infant industries
    d. Protecting U.S. industries against subsidized foreign producers
    e. Goal of self-sufficiency

12. Which of the following is a tax on an imported good?
    a. Income tax
    b. Import quota
    c. Rationing tax
    d. Tariff

13. A tariff does which of the following?
    a. Increases the price of the imported good to the consumer
    b. Decreases the net price received by the foreign producer
    c. Increases the price of the domestic good
    d. Redistributes income from domestic consumers and foreign producers to the protected industry
    e. All of the above

14. Which of the following places a limit on the quantity of a foreign good that can be imported into a domestic market?
    a. Import capacity limit
    b. Import quota
    c. Export quota
    d. Tariff

15. An import quota does which of the following?
    a. Increases the price of the imported good to the consumer
    b. Increases the price received by the foreign producer
    c. Increases the price of the domestic good
    d. Redistributes income from domestic consumers to the protected domestic exporter
    e. All of the above

16. Which of the following is a country whose real GNP per capita is generally less than $1000 per year?
    a. A newly industrialized country
    b. A less developed country
    c. An industrialized country
    d. A socialist state

17. Which of the following is a reason for low per capita output in a country?
    a. Low rates of saving and investment
    b. Poorly skilled and educated workers
    c. High population growth and unemployment
    d. Lagging technology
    e. All of the above

Answer the following questions based upon the data below.

Production Possibilities

	Good X	Good Y
Country A	100	50
Country B	200	150

18. Which of the following statements is true?
    a. Country A has an absolute advantage in the production of both goods X and Y.
    b. Country B has an absolute advantage in the production of good X, but not good Y.
    c. Country B has an absolute advantage in the production of good Y, but not good X.
    d. Country A has a comparative advantage in the production of good Y.
    e. None of the above

19. Which of the following statements is true?
    a. Country A has a comparative advantage in the production of good X.
    b. Country B has a comparative advantage in the production of good Y.
    c. Country B should specialize in and export good X.
    d. Country A should specialize in and export good Y.
    e. A and b

20. If countries A and B trade on the basis of comparative advantage, which of the following terms of trade would result in mutually-gainful trades?

    a. $1X = (3/2) Y$

    b. $1Y = (3/2) X$

    c. $1X = (1) Y$

    d. $1Y = (2/3) X$

21. Assume that country B specializes in the production of good Y. Country B keeps 100Y for domestic consumption and trades 50Y for good X. If the terms of trade are $1X = (2/3) Y$, what are the gains to nation B from trade?

    a.   8 1/3X

    b.   15Y

    c.   75X

    d.   66 2/3X

22. Given the information in question 21, what are the gains to nation A from exporting good X to country B?

    a.   25X

    b.   12 1/2Y

    c.   25Y

    d.   37 1/2Y

THINK IT THROUGH

1. "In international trade, one nation's trade surplus (exports in excess of imports) must be another nation's trade deficit (imports in excess of exports). Therefore the mercantilists must have been correct in stating that a nation should encourage exports and discourage imports." Evaluate this statement.

2. The United States has lost its international competitiveness in some basic industries, particularly those that produce standardized goods with large economies of scale. Can you think of any reasons why?

3. If a nation employs protectionist measures such as tariffs or quotas and trading partners retaliate in kind, discuss some likely consequences.

CHAPTER ANSWERS

The Chapter in Brief

1. Capital goods 2. Agricultural products 3. Deficit 4. Fewer 5. 10% 6. 17.8% 7. Canada
8. Japan 9. Absolute 10. Comparative 11. Lower 12. Mutually gain from trade 13. Higher
14. Terms of trade 15. World demand and supply 16. Below 17. Outside 18. Comparative
19. Gain 20. Investment 21. Higher energy prices 22. Vital to national security 23. New and
emerging "infant" industries 24. Distribution of income that occur 25. Tariff 26. Raises
27. Reduces 28. Import quota 29. Reduces 30. Raises 31. Raises 32. May be better off 33. Lose
34. Less developed countries (LDCs) 35. Low 36. High

Key Terms Review

1. Consumption possibilities curve 2. Real terms of trade 3. Tariff 4. Comparative advantage
5. Import quota 6. Absolute advantage 7. Real per capita output 8. Mutual gains from
international trade 9. Less developed countries (LDCs) 10. Specialization

Concept Review

1. a.

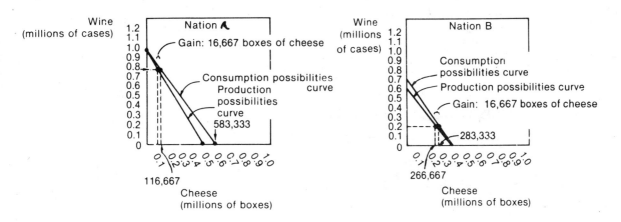

b. 1,000, exceeds, 600; 500, exceeds, 400; absolute; lies farther from the origin than

c. 1/2, 2; -2, 2

d. 2/3, 1.5; -1.5, 1.5

2. Wine, cheese; wine, cheese; cheese, wine; cheese, wine, 2 cases of wine; wine, cheese, 2/3 boxes of cheese; 1.5, 2; 1/2, 2/3

3. a. 7/12 box of cheese

   b. Shown on figure above

   c. 116,667; 2, 100,000; 16,667

   d. 116,667; 2/3, 133,333; 116,667; 16,667

4. a. National security

   b. Protect infant industries

   c. Reduce structural unemployment

   d. Protect U.S. industries against subsidized foreign producers

5. a.

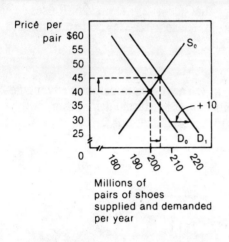
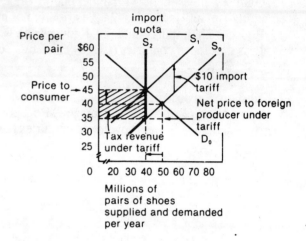

   Rise, $45, fall, $35; fall, 40; $400 million

   b. Rightward, 10; increase, $45, rise, 205

   c. Consumers, foreign producers

   d. Increase, $45; increases, $45, rise, 205; no, increase

Mastery Test

1. c 2. c 3. a 4. d 5. d 6. b 7. d 8. a 9. d 10. d 11. e 12. d 13. e 14. b 15. e 16. b 17. e 18. e 19. e
20. b 21. a 22. b

Think It Through

1. A nation's wealth is not defined in terms of the foreign currency (or gold during the mercantilist era) earned from trade surpluses, but by the total goods consumed by the nation in part as a result of international trade. A nation may run a trade deficit yet still consume more goods than if the nation engaged in no international trade. It is true that a trade deficit means a lower level of domestic aggregate demand and level of real GNP, but that level of real GNP may be higher than it would have been if the nation did not produce and trade on the basis of comparative advantage.

2. The United States has experienced lagging productivity growth in several of its heavy industries—those that produce standardized goods and whose firms realize substantial economies of scale. Other nations have had more rapid productivity growth in some of these industries, taking away the comparative advantage once enjoyed by the U.S. industries. New techniques of production were being introduced abroad at a time during which many U.S. plants were aging

456

and becoming obsolete. U.S. firms were not investing enough in new plant and equipment and technology to maintain their relatively lower opportunity cost of production. Several foreign nations that have captured the comparative advantage from the United States have done so by investing a greater percentage of their domestic production in physical capital and technology. They also have an advantage in having a relatively less costly labor force.

3. If all trading nations are engaging in protectionist measures, all lose in that the volume of international trade will be lower, the level of world output and living standards will be lower, and household real incomes will be lower because the prices of imported and domestic goods will be higher than in the absence of trade restrictions.

25

THE ECONOMICS OF FOREIGN EXCHANGE AND THE BALANCE OF INTERNATIONAL TRADE

CHAPTER CONCEPTS

After studying your text, attending class, and completing this chapter, you should be able to:

1. Understand how international transactions between the United States and the rest of the world involve the exchange of dollars for units of foreign currency.
2. Use supply and demand analysis to show how exchange rates of one currency into another are established in foreign exchange markets and explain the causes of currency appreciation and depreciation. Discuss the evolution of the current international monetary system and understand how a balance of trade deficit in the United States in a given year implies an increase in net foreign acquisition of U.S. financial and other assets in that year.

THE CHAPTER IN BRIEF

Fill in the blanks to summarize chapter content.

International trade requires the exchange of currencies. The (1)_____ (foreign exchange rate is, terms of trade are) the price of one nation's monetary unit in terms of the monetary unit of another nation. The (2)_____ (stock market, foreign exchange market) is a market in which currencies are exchanged. Here the forces of supply and demand determine the rate at which any two currencies are exchanged. For example, a U.S. importer wants to purchase foreign goods with dollars but foreign exporters want to be paid in their own currencies. An exchange of currency must take place. For a fee, the importer can use dollars to purchase a bank draft denominated in foreign currency from a U.S. bank. This constitutes (3)_____ (a demand for, an increase in the supply of) the foreign currency.

Equilibrium in the foreign exchange market occurs where the supply of and demand for a currency are equal—where the supply and demand curves for a currency intersect. If the price of a currency (expressed in terms of units of another currency) is higher than the equilibrium exchange rate, a (4)_____ (shortage, surplus) of the currency will cause a decline in the exchange rate. If the exchange rate is below the equilibrium exchange rate, a (5)_____ (shortage, surplus) of the currency results in an increase in the exchange rate. Influences that shift the demand or supply curves will alter the exchange rate between two currencies. Several factors can affect the equilibrium exchange rate of the U.S. dollar: (a) foreign demand for U.S. exports, (b) U.S. demand for imports, (c) real interest rates in the United States relative to those in foreign nations, (d) profitability of direct investment in U.S. businesses and real estate relative to profitability of similar investments in foreign nations, (e) expectations of an increase in the price of the dollar in terms of foreign currency, and (f) the price level (6)_____ (established by the Bretton Woods agreement; in the United States) relative to the price levels in foreign nations.

If real interest rates in the United States rise relative to interest rates in Great Britain, for instance, the British will increase their (7)_____ (supply of, demand for) U.S. dollars in the foreign exchange markets in order to purchase higher-yielding U.S. financial assets. As the demand for dollars rises relative to the supply of dollars, the exchange rate of the dollar (8)_____ (falls, rises). The dollar will be exchanged for more British pounds than previously. Conversely, the British pound will be exchanged for (9)_____ (more, fewer) U.S. dollars. The dollar (10)_____ (depreciates, appreciates) and the pound (11)_____ (depreciates, appreciates). British goods valued in dollars fall in price, and U.S. goods valued in British pounds increase in price. As a result, U.S. goods exported to Great Britain become (12)_____ (more, less) price competitive with British domestic output. Likewise, in the United States, British imported goods become (13)_____ (more, less) expensive relative to U.S. domestic output.

The (14)_____ (nominal, real) exchange rate is the price of a unit of one nation's currency in terms of a unit of a foreign currency. The (15)_____ (nominal, real) exchange rate is the sacrifice of goods and services produced in their own countries that foreign buyers must make when they use their own currency to purchase a unit or the currency of another nation. If the real interest rate increases, the real exchange rate of the dollar (16)_____ (decreases, increases), reducing the attractiveness of U.S. exports to foreigners. Net exports fall, causing aggregate demand to decrease. Aggregate supply, however, increases because of the decline in the cost of imported inputs. According to the aggregate supply and demand model presented in a previous chapter, real GNP and the price level will fall. Just the opposite is expected if the real exchange rate (17)_____ (falls, rises). Empirical evidence indicates that it may take as long as 2 years before changes in real exchange rate significantly influence import prices.

The foreign exchange market described above is a free market often referred to as a (18)_____ (fixed, floating or flexible) exchange rate market. Prior to the 1930s, however, exchange rates were fixed within narrow limits. This was accomplished by the gold standard, under which currencies were convertible into (19)_____ (gold, the U.S. dollar) at fixed rates. This meant that each currency had (20)_____ (several exchange rates, a unique exchange rate) relative to every other currency. Exchange rates remained fixed as long as the gold price of each currency remained (21)_____ (flexible, unchanged). Nations concerned with domestic macroeconomic problems would often devalue their currency rather than allow an outflow of gold that would reduce the nation's money stock. Devaluation alters exchange rates, however. This system was replaced in 1944 by the (22)_____ (managed float, Bretton Woods system) in which the values of foreign currencies were tied to the U.S. dollar rather than to gold. The United States abandoned its role as the guarantor of exchange rate stability when it chose to suspend convertibility of the dollar into gold in (23)_____ (1971, 1961). In 1973, the United States and other nations abandoned the fixed exchange rate system in favor of the (24)_____ (modified gold standard, flexible exchange rate system). Today the foreign exchange market is characterized as a managed float rather than a freely floating or flexible exchange rate system. The Federal Reserve System and foreign central banks intervene in the market to effect desirable changes in exchange rates.

The balance of payments for a nation shows the net exchange of the nation's currency for foreign currencies from all transactions between that nation and foreign nations in a given year. In the United States the balance of payments consists of the current account and the capital account. The (25)_____ (capital, current) account shows the effect of the volume of goods and services traded on international markets, including changes in investment income and other miscellaneous transactions. The balance (26)_____ (on the current account, of trade) represents the difference between the value of merchandise exports and imports. The balance (27)_____ (on the current account, of trade) is more comprehensive in that it measures U.S. net exports for the year, including transactions involving services, investment income, and transfers. As recently as 1981, the United States had a surplus in its current account balance but had a large merchandise trade deficit.

In 1988, the current account registered a (28)_____ (deficit, surplus) of over $126.5 billion. This means U.S. citizens supplied $126.5 billion more to foreigners than foreigners supplied in foreign currencies to Americans. A net outflow has must offset (financed). When the current account is in deficit, the United States must sell assets or borrow to finance the deficit. These transactions are shown in the (29)_____ (capital, current) account. As foreigners purchase U.S. financial and real assets at a rate greater than U.S. citizens purchase those assets abroad, the net inflow of dollars just offsets the current account deficit.

KEY TERMS REVIEW

Write the key term from the list below next to its definition.

Key Terms

Foreign exchange rate
Foreign exchange market
Foreign exchange
Currency appreciation
Currency depreciation
Purchasing power parity
Gold standard
Balance on current account
  of the balance of
  payments

Bretton Woods system
International Monetary
Fund (IMF)
Special drawing right (SDR)
International balance of
  payments
Balance of trade
Managed float
Real exchange rate
Nominal exchange rate

Definition

1. _____: the price of a unit of one nation's currency in terms of a unit of a foreign currency.

2. _____: the price of one nation's monetary unit in terms of the monetary unit of another nation.

3. _____: the sacrifice of goods and services produced in their own countries that foreign buyers must make when they use their own currency to purchase a unit of the currency of another nation.

4. _____: a market in which buyers and sellers of bank deposits denominated in the monetary units of many nations exchange their funds.

5. _____: an international monetary system that required that currencies be converted into gold at a fixed price.

6. _____: the money of one nation held by citizens of another nation either as currency or as deposits in banks.

7. _____: describes the current international monetary system, under which central banks affect supply of and demand for currencies in ways that influence equilibrium in foreign exchange markets.

8. _____: occurs when there is an increase in the number of units of one nation's currency that must be given up to purchase each unit of another nation's currency.

9. _____: established under the Bretton Woods agreement; set rules for the international monetary system to make loans to nations that lack international reserves of dollars.

10. _____: occurs when there is a decrease in the number of units of one nation's currency that must be given up to purchase each unit of another nation's currency.

11. _____: an international monetary system developed in 1944 and based on fixed exchange rates, with the value of foreign currencies tied to the U.S. dollar.

12. _____: a principle that states that the exchange rate between any two currencies tends to adjust to reflect changes in the price levels in the two nations.

13. _____: a paper substitute for gold that is created by the International Monetary Fund and is distributed to member nations to use as international reserves.

14. _____: a statement showing the net exchange rate of a nation's currency for foreign currencies from all transactions between that nation and foreign nations in a given year.

15. _____: the difference between the value of merchandise exported by a nation's firms and the nation's imports of foreign-produced goods.

16. _____: measures U.S. net exports for the year, including transactions involving services, investment income, and transfers.

CONCEPT REVIEW

Concept 2: *Foreign exchange rates, foreign exchange markets, and international balance of payments*

1. The figure below represents a foreign exchange market for the U.S. dollar and the Canadian dollar.

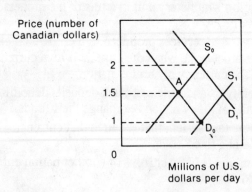

Price (number of Canadian dollars)

Millions of U.S. dollars per day

a. Given demand curve Do and supply curve So, the equilibrium exchange rate between the Canadian and U.S. dollar is 1 U.S. dollar = _____ Canadian dollars or alternatively, 1 Canadian dollar = _____ U.S. dollars.

b. A U.S. good valued at $1000 in U.S. dollars would cost _____ Canadian dollars. A Canadian good valued at 100 Canadian dollars would cost _____ U.S. dollars.

2. List six factors that influence the exchange rate of the dollar.

   a. _____

   b. _____

   c. _____

   d. _____

   e. _____

   f. _____

3. Referring to the figure above, suppose real interest rates in the United States rise relative to interest rates abroad, causing the demand for dollars to increase to D1.

   a. What are the new exchange rates?
      (1) 1 U.S. dollar = _____ Canadian dollars
      (2) 1 Canadian dollar = _____ U.S. dollars

   b. The U.S. dollar has _____, and the Canadian dollar has _____.

   c. A U.S. good valued at 1000 U.S. dollars now costs _____ Canadian dollars. A Canadian good valued at 100 Canadian dollars now costs _____ U.S. dollars.

   d. U.S. goods become _____ price competitive in Canada, and Canadian goods become _____ price competitive in the United States.

4. Referring to the figure above, given the initial demand curve, Do, assume that U.S. firms increase their imports from Canada, causing the supply of U.S. dollars to shift to S1.

   a. What are the new exchange rates?
      (1) 1 U.S. dollar = _____ Canadian dollars
      (2) 1 Canadian dollar = _____ U.S. dollar

   b. The U.S. dollar has _____, and the Canadian dollar has _____.

   c. A U.S. good valued at 1000 U.S. dollars now costs _____ Canadian dollars. A Canadian good valued at 100 Canadian dollars now costs _____ U.S. dollars.

   d. U.S. goods become _____ price competitive in Canada, and Canadian goods become _____ price competitive in the United States.

5. Identify which of the following represent a *capital account* and which represent a *current account* transaction in the balance of payments and state whether the transaction results in an *inflow* or *outflow* of U.S. dollars.

   a. U.S. exports of services increase.

   b. Foreigners purchase U.S. Treasury bills.

   c. Automobile imports into the United States increase.

   d. Transfers to foreigners increase.

   e. U.S. firms purchase factories abroad.

   f. Rich oil sheiks purchase Texas ranch land.

   g. Hitachi receives income from its U.S. plants.

   h. Foreigners increase imports of U.S. merchandise goods.

   i. U.S. citizens purchase stock in foreign enterprises.

	Capital or Current Account?	Inflow or Outflow?
a.	_____	_____
b.	_____	_____
c.	_____	_____
d.	_____	_____
e.	_____	_____
f.	_____	_____
g.	_____	_____
h.	_____	_____
i.	_____	_____

MASTERY TEST

Select the best answer.

1. A market in which buyers and sellers of bank deposits denominated in the monetary units of many nations exchange their funds is known as the:

   a. loanable funds market.

   b. money market.

   c. capital market.

   d. foreign exchange market.

2. If the price of a dollar in terms of units of a foreign currency is above the equilibrium exchange rate, a _____ exists, which will put _____ pressure on the equilibrium exchange rate of the dollar.

   a. shortage, downward

   b. shortage, upward

   c. surplus, downward

   d. surplus, upward

3. If a $10,000 U.S.-made automobile is sold in France and the exchange rate between the dollar and the franc is $1 = 8 francs, the U.S. automobile sold in France will cost _____ francs.

   a. 20,000

   b. 40,000

   c. 60,000

   d. 80,000

   e. 100,000

4. The exchange rate between the dollar and the franc is $1 = 8 francs, and the price of a bottle of imported French wine is $5. If the exchange rate changes to $1 = 4 francs, the dollar price of the French wine _____ to $_____.

   a. falls, $2.50

   b. rises, $10

   c. rises, $20

   d. does not change

5. An increase in foreign demand for U.S. exports will _____ demand for the dollar, causing the dollar to _____.

   a. decrease, appreciate

   b. increase, depreciate

   c. increase, appreciate

   d. decrease, depreciate

6. An increase in U.S. demand for imports will _____ the _____ U.S. dollars, causing the dollar to _____.

   a. increase, demand for, appreciate

   b. increase, supply of, appreciate

   c. decrease, supply of, depreciate

   d. decrease, demand for, appreciate

   e. increase, supply of, depreciate

7. If real interest rates in the United States rise relative to interest rates abroad, the _____ dollars will _____, causing the dollar to _____.

   a. demand for, increase, appreciate

   b. demand for, increase, depreciate

   c. supply of, decrease, depreciate

   d. supply of, increase, appreciate

8. If the rate of inflation in the United States rises relative to the rate of inflation in foreign nations, U.S. exports _____ and imports _____, causing the demand for dollars to _____ and the supply of dollars to _____.

    a. increase, decrease, rise, fall

    b. decrease, increase, fall, rise

    c. increase, increase, fall, fall

    d. decrease, decrease, rise, rise

9. The price of a unit of one nation's currency in terms of a unit of a foreign currency is called:

    a. the nominal exchange rate.

    b. the real exchange rate.

    c. foreign exchange.

    d. purchasing power parity.

    e. None of the above.

10. Empirical evidence suggests that:

    a. import prices respond very quickly to changes in exchange rates.

    b. net exports respond within a year to changes in the exchange rate of the dollar.

    c. import prices are slow to respond to changes in exchange rates, taking up to 2 years to be affected.

    d. there is an immediate link between exchange rates and import prices.

11. The Bretton Woods agreement:

    a. represented a new international monetary system.

    b. tied the value of foreign currencies not to gold but to the dollar.

    c. was established in 1944.

    d. also established the International Monetary Fund.

    e. All of the above.

12. The present international monetary system is best described as a:

    a. fixed exchange rate system.

    b. purchasing power parity system.

    c. flexible exchange rate system.

    d. managed float.

13. Which of the following summarizes the transactions involving the international exchange of goods and services, investment income, and other miscellaneous transactions?

    a. Balance of trade

    b. Statistical discrepancy

    c. Current account

    d. Capital account

14. Which of the following is the difference between the value of merchandise exported and merchandise imported?

    a. Balance of trade

    b. Balance on the current account

    c. Budget balance

    d. Balance of payments.

15. Which of the following measures net exports for the year, including transactions involving services, investment income, and transfers?

    a. Balance of trade

    b. Balance on the current account

    c. Budget balance

    d. Balance of payments

16. When the current account is in deficit, the capital account must:

    a. be balanced.

    b. be zero.

    c. not add to the deficit.

    d. have an equal and offsetting surplus.

Answer the following three questions based upon the data below.

(Millions of dollars per day)

French Francs (per dollar)	Quantity of Dollars Demanded	Quantity of Dollars Supplied
9	10	50
7	20	40
5	30	30
3	40	20
1	50	10

17. Which of the following is the equilibrium exchange rate between the dollar and the franc?

    a. 1 franc = 1 dollar

    b. 1 franc = 20 cents

    c. 1 franc = 14 cents

    d. 1 dollar = 5 francs

    e. B and d

18. If the quantity of dollars supplied increases by 20 million dollars at each exchange rate, what happens to the equilibrium exchange rate?

    a.   The dollar appreciates to 1 franc = 7 dollars

    b.   The dollar depreciates to 1 dollar = 3 francs

    c.   The franc depreciates to 1 franc = 33 1/3 cents

    d.   The exchange rate remains unchanged at 1 dollar = 7 francs

19. An increase in the demand for American goods by the French _____ the demand for dollars by 10 million dollars at each exchange rate and causes the international value of the dollar to _____ to _____.

    a.   increases, appreciate, 1 dollar = 7 francs

    b.   increases, depreciate, 1 dollar = 3 francs

    c.   decreases, appreciate, 1 dollar = 5 francs

    d.   decreases, depreciate, 1 dollar = 3 francs

20. If the rate of inflation increases more in France than in the United States, the franc will likely:

    a.   appreciate.

    b.   depreciate.

    c.   remain unchanged.

    d.   depreciate until the dollar becomes stronger.

21. Assume that the balance of payments current account is in deficit. Which of the following will likely occur if domestic interest rates rise relative to foreign interest rates?

    a.   The demand for dollars by foreigners will increase.

    b.   The dollar will appreciate.

    c.   Net exports will fall.

    d.   The current account deficit will increase.

    e.   All of the above

THINK IT THROUGH

1. How can the Fed, through domestic monetary policy, cause the U.S. dollar to depreciate?

2. How can the Fed, through direct intervention in foreign exchange markets, cause the U.S. dollar to depreciate?

CHAPTER ANSWERS

The Chapter in Brief

1. Foreign exchange rate is 2. Foreign exchange market 3. A demand for 4. Surplus
5. Shortage 6. In the United States 7. Demand for 8. Rises 9. Fewer 10. Appreciates
11. Depreciates 12. Less 13. Less 14. nominal 15. real 16. increases 17. falls 18. Floating or
flexible 19. Gold 20. A unique exchange rate 21. Unchanged 22. Bretton Woods system 23.
1971 24. Flexible exchange rate system 25. Current 26. Of trade 27. On the current
account 28. Deficit 29. Capital

Key Terms Review

1. Nominal exchange rate 2. Foreign exchange rate 3. Real exchange rate 4. Foreign exchange
market 5. Gold standard 6. Foreign exchange 7. Managed float 8. Currency appreciation
9. International Monetary Fund (IMF) 10. Currency depreciation 11. Bretton Woods system
12. Purchasing power parity 13. Special drawing right (SDR) 14. International balance of payments
15. Balance of trade 16. Balance on the current account of the balance of payments

Concept Review

1. a.   1.5, 2/3

   b.   1,500, $66.67

2. a.   Foreign demand for U.S. exports

   b.   U.S. demand for imports

   c.   Real interest rates in the United States relative to those in foreign nations

   d.   Profitability of direct investment in U.S. businesses and real estate relative to profitability
        of similar investments in foreign nations

   e.   Expectations of an increase in the price of the dollar in terms of foreign currency

   f.   The price level in the United States relative to the price levels in foreign nations

3. a.   2, 1/2

   b.   Appreciated, depreciated

   c.   2,000; 50

   d.   Less, more

4. a.   1, 1

   b.   Depreciated, appreciated

   c.   1,000; 100

   d.   More, less

5. a.   Current, inflow

   b.   Capital, inflow

   c.   Current, outflow

   d.   Current, outflow

   e.   Capital, outflow

f. Capital, inflow

g. Current, outflow

h. Current, inflow

i. Capital, outflow

Mastery Test

1. d 2. c 3. d 4. b 5. c 6. e 7. a 8. b 9. a 10. c 11. e 12. d 13. c 14. a 15. b 16. d 17. e 18. b 19. a 20. b 21. e

Think It Through

1. If the Fed pursues an expansionary monetary policy that reduces the real rate of interest in the United States relative to interest rates abroad, Americans will increase their demand for foreign currencies by supplying more dollars to the international foreign exchange markets in order to purchase higher-yielding foreign financial assets. The increase in the supply of dollars relative to demand will cause the dollar to depreciate. The expansionary monetary policy will also increase the nation's income, causing imports to increase. In order to increase imports, Americans must supply dollars to acquire foreign exchange to purchase the foreign goods. This too will cause the dollar to depreciate. If the expansionary monetary policy is also inflationary such that the rate of inflation in the United States rises relative to foreign rates of inflation, U.S. exports will fall and imports will rise. This will cause foreign demand for the dollar to fall and the supply of dollars to increase, also resulting in depreciation of the dollar.

2. If the Fed wished to depreciate the dollar, it could purchase foreign currencies with its dollar holdings, causing the demand for foreign currencies to rise and the supply of dollars to increase. This in turn would cause the dollar to depreciate relative to the foreign currencies purchased by the Fed.

470

26 SOCIALISM AND THE CENTRALLY PLANNED ECONOMY

CHAPTER CONCEPTS

After studying your text, attending class, and completing this chapter, you should be able to:

1. Discuss the ideas of Karl Marx and the ideological underpinnings of socialism.
2. Discuss the way a centrally planned economy operates and how the Soviet economy has functioned as a command economy.
3. Discuss the process of reform of the economy of the Soviet Union, the shortcomings to the process of "perestroika," and the difficulties any centrally planned economy will encounter in moving to a system of free markets.

THE CHAPTER IN BRIEF

Fill in the blanks to complete the chapter summary.

(1)_____ (Capitalism, Socialism) is associated with private ownership of resources, freedom of enterprise, and an economy in which markets allocate resources. (2)_____ (Capitalism, Socialism), in contrast, is associated with government ownership of productive resources and central planning. Prices and resource allocation are determined by central planners rather than by markets.

According to Karl Marx, only (3)_____ (labor, capital) produces value. Even capital is the past product of labor. Marx argued that capitalists hire labor at subsistence wages, generating a (4)_____ (marginal revenue product, surplus value)—the wages paid to labor are less than the value of the worker's production. Capitalists therefore exploit workers and will continue to do so until the working class revolts and establishes a socialist state. Most workers, however, earn incomes well above a subsistence level in market economies. Marx did not foresee the enormous gains made in (5)_____ (profits, labor productivity) as a result of technology and capital formation. Over time, the (6)_____ (supply of, demand for) labor has outpaced the (7)_____ (supply of, demand for) labor, resulting in increases in real wages. The working class has not revolted in a manner envisioned by Marx because of gains in real living standards and social policy designed to alleviate some of the failures of market systems.

The Soviet Union is a (8)_____ (market, command) economy in which resources are allocated by central planners who set production goals. The (9)_____ (Gosplan, Politburo) is the central planning board for the Soviet Union and drafts 5-year plans listing production goals for the economy. The government sets prices to ensure the satisfaction of the output goals. Prices of many goods have been kept artificially low as a way of subsidizing consumption. But when prices are set below the level that equates supply and demand, (10)_____ (surpluses, shortages) become a problem. Shortages can be eliminated with a (11)_____ (lump sum, turnover) tax if it is equal to the difference between the price that would equate supply and demand and the lower subsidized price. Shortages are reduced, but only from a reduction in quantity demanded. Quantity supplied remains fixed at the planners' production target.

In recent years, the Soviet Union has tried to improve economic efficiency. Under (12)_____ (glasnost, perestroika), enterprises choose their output mixes, can trade goods with other enterprises, and can use profits earned to invest or reward workers and managers. The Law of State Enterprises of 1987 and the Law on Cooperatives of 1987 are two major parts of perestroika. The Law on Cooperatives legalized certain private and cooperative enterprises and was revised in 1988 to allow cooperatives to pursue a great variety of business activities, including the right to engage in banking and foreign trade. The Law of State Enterprises defines the rights and duties of business enterprises.

As of January 1, 1988, the Soviet economy began to institute reforms such as putting (13)_____ (10%, 60%) of Soviet enterprises on a self-financing basis. These firms are required to earn a profit or they will be shut down. Managers (14)_____ (will be, will not be) able to decide what is to be produced and how to produce it. In fact, many prices will be determined by markets rather than by central planning. Even prior to these reforms, farmers were allowed to sell produce in markets from private plots. These plots are considerably more productive than collective farms in producing food, accounting for as much as (15)_____ (25%, 75%) of Soviet agricultural output. Economic incentives are also used to motivate Soviet labor and existed prior to the reforms instituted at the beginning of 1988. In 1987, private enterprise was legalized in 29 areas, primarily in crafts and services. These changes will be beneficial to the Soviet economy. Managers will no longer have incentives to just meet output targets or exceed those targets, but will now have incentives to minimize costs in order to generate profits. This will result in a (16)_____ (less, more) efficient use of resources. As of 1990, Soviet citizens have the right to own small businesses, although significant restrictions remain regarding the private ownership of natural and capital resources.

Despite these reforms, the Soviet Union has experienced slow growth since the mid-1960s. It is estimated that Soviet real GNP even declined in 1989 and 1990. The Soviet Union remains a command economy that prevents perestroika reforms from markedly improving economic incentives. The price system still does not guide the flow of resources to ensure the production of goods in strong demand.

Other socialist systems vary in the degree to which central planning and markets are relied upon to allocate resources. Yugoslavia, Poland, and Hungary have had reform programs in place for a number of years. In 1956, (17)_____ (Hungary, Poland) privatized agriculture, while (18)_____ (Poland, Hungary) decentralized managerial decisions beginning in 1968. Nevertheless, these economies continued to rely on central planning. Economic liberalization of Eastern Europe is expected to continue in the aftermath of the political liberalization of the late 1980s. By 1990, Poland was moving quickly to a market economy. Poland began removing government subsidies and price controls, closing inefficient enterprises, and began to allow prices to be determined by supply and demand. The Polish currency was made legally convertible to dollars and other foreign currencies. Czechoslovakia is also trying to introduce market pricing systems. Even Romania is allowing farmers to lease additional land and to sell their crops at market prices rather that at government prices.

In evaluating capitalism and socialism, important considerations include: (a) the extent to which the pursuit of self-interest and market exchange of goods and services produce results that coincide with a general consensus regarding national goals, (b) the way an economic system distributes well-being among members of a society, (c) the achievement of technological efficiency, (d) freedom of choice and responsiveness to consumer demands, and (e) economic growth and fluctuations.

KEY TERMS REVIEW

Write the key term from the list below next to its definition.

Key Terms

Economic system
Socialism
Labor theory of value
Surplus value
Command economy
Centrally planned economy

Gosplan
Materials balance
Consumer sovereignty
Turnover tax

Definitions

1. _____: an economy in which politically appointed committees plan production and manage the economy to achieve political goals.

2. _____: the central planning board for the Soviet Union.

3. _____: an economy in which resource allocation decisions are determined largely by the central planning authorities who set production goals.

4. _____: exists when the supply of each intermediate product equals its demand as an input in some other productive process.

5. _____: defined by Karl Marx as the difference between a worker's subsistence wage and the value of the worker's production over a period.

6. _____: the responsiveness of the market economy to changes in consumer demand.

7. _____: maintains that only labor can produce something worth paying for.

8. _____: a sales tax used to raise revenue for the government; often used in planned economies to eliminate shortages in consumer markets.

9. _____: an economic system that is usually associated with government ownership of resources and central planning to determine prices and resource use.

10. _____: an accepted way of organizing production, establishing rights to ownership and use of productive resources, and governing economic transactions in a society.

CONCEPT REVIEW

Concept 2: *Production targets, shortages, the turnover tax, and black markets*

A competitive market for a good is shown in the figure below.

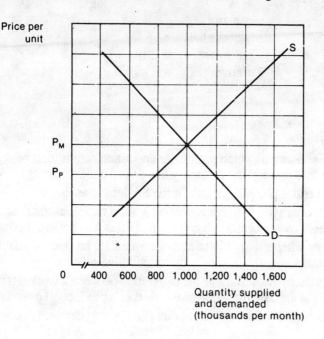

a. Assume that this market economy now becomes a command economy in which central planners set production targets. Show the effect of a production target of 800,000 units where planners establish a price of Pp per unit. At the controlled price of Pp, there exists a _____ of _____ units.

b. If the official government price is raised to the previous market level of Pm, there exists a _____ of _____ units.

c. In order to eliminate the _____ and still maintain the production target of 800,000 units, a turnover tax equal to the difference between _____ and the _____ could be used. However, if a turnover tax is used in this manner, consumers in the command economy pay _____ prices and consume _____ output than they did previously in the market economy.

d. Black markets will likely develop because some consumers will be willing to pay _____ prices than a government price like Pp in order to have additional units of the good. Even if a turnover tax eliminates shortages, black markets will likely still exist because the marginal cost of supplying an additional unit of a good will likely be _____ than the government price that eliminates shortages.

MASTERY TEST

Select the best answer.

1. An economic system that is usually associated with government ownership of resources and central planning is known as:
   a. capitalism.
   b. fascism.
   c. socialism.
   d. a market system.

2. Which of the following individuals argued that only workers create value?
   a. Adam Smith
   b. George Bush
   c. Karl Marx
   d. Karl Menninger

3. Marx argued that capitalists exploit workers by paying them a _____ in order to create _____.
   a. subsistence wage, surplus value
   b. wage equal to their marginal product, profits
   c. portion of their profits, good will
   d. wage less than their profit per worker, maximum growth for their enterprises

4. What main factor did Marx not foresee in making his prediction that workers would not rise above a subsistence standard of living?
   a. Population growth
   b. Growth in household consumption
   c. Growth in labor productivity
   d. Advances in technology
   e. C and d

5. The Soviet Union is an example of a:
   a. market economy.
   b. mixed-market system.
   c. democratic socialist state.
   d. command economy.

6. Which of the following is the Soviet Union's central planning board?
    a. Ministry of Industry
    b. Soviet Monetary Alliance
    c. *Perestroika*
    d. Gosplan

7. As of January 1, 1988, economic reforms were initiated in the Soviet Union. Which of the following is an economic reform?
    a. Requiring some soviet enterprises to earn a profit
    b. Allowing managers of some enterprises to decide what to produce and how to produce it
    c. Allowing many prices to be determined by markets
    d. All of the above

8. A turnover tax is:
    a. used to reduce surpluses.
    b. used to finance the soviet economic reforms.
    c. used to reduce shortages.
    d. the difference between the cost of a good and the price that equates supply and demand.

9. One advantage of a planned economy is that:
    a. it is more efficient.
    b. it responds more rapidly to changes in consumers' desires.
    c. it has achieved the highest living standards in the world.
    d. it can avoid fluctuations in aggregate demand and thus avoid the costs associated with business cycles.

10. Which of the following is true regarding private enterprise in the Soviet Union?
    a. The Soviet economic reforms have privatized collective farms.
    b. Private farm plots account for as much as 25% of the Soviet Union's total agricultural output.
    c. In 1987, private business was legalized in 29 areas.
    d. Most individuals engaged in private enterprise are in crafts or services.
    e. B, c, and d

11. In which of the following nations is a majority of enterprises state owned but worker managed?
    a. People's Republic of China
    b. France
    c. Yugoslavia
    d. Argentina

12. In which of the following nations is government ownership of or financial interest in large industrial enterprises common?

    a. United Kingdom

    b. France

    c. Italy

    d. All of the above

    e. A and c

13. In assessing the merits of capitalism vs. socialism, which of the following considerations are important?

    a. The extent to which the pursuit of self-interest and market exchange of goods and services produce results that coincide with a general political consensus regarding national goals

    b. The way an economic system distributes well-being among members of a society

    c. The achievement of technological efficiency

    d. Freedom of choice and responsiveness to consumer demands

    e. All of the above

14. Shortages in the Soviet Union are primarily the result of:

    a. output quotas that are too small.

    b. prices that are set at levels below those that equate supply and demand.

    c. inefficient bureaucracy.

    d. prices that are set at levels above those that equate supply and demand.

15. Under perestroika, enterprises have been allowed to:

    a. choose their output mixes.

    b. trade with other enterprises.

    c. use profits to invest or reward managers and workers.

    d. All of the above

16. Which of the following laws was revised in 1988 to allow cooperatives to pursue a greater variety of business activities, including the right to engage in banking and foreign trade?

    a. Law on Cooperatives

    b. Law of State Enterprises

    c. Glasnost

    d. Perestroika

17. Which of the following statements is not true regarding the Soviet Union?

    a. The Soviet Union has experienced slow growth since the mid-1960s.

    b. Soviet real GNP declined in 1989 and 1990.

    c. The Soviet Union remains a command economy that prevents perestroika reforms from markedly improving economic incentives.

    d. The price system still does not guide the flow of resources to ensure the production of goods in strong demand.

    e. Prices are determined by market forces.

18. By 1990, which of the following countries was moving most rapidly to a market economy?

    a. Hungary

    b. Albania

    c. Poland

    d. Yugoslavia

    e. Czechoslovakia

THINK IT THROUGH

1. Identify and briefly discuss some of the main differences between capitalism and socialism.

2. Several nations have returned state-owned enterprises to the private sector, whereas other socialist nations have instituted major market-based reforms. Can you think of any reasons why?

ANALYZING THE NEWS

Using the skills derived from studying this chapter, analyze the economic facts that make up the following article and answer the questions below, using graphical analysis where possible.

1. How could a plant run under a Communist form of leadership fail to run efficiently?

2. As Poland and other Eastern European nations make the transition from government-controlled to market-controlled economies what adjustment will plant managers and employees have to make?

Troubled tractor plant puts Polish government to the test

By Joseph A. Reaves
Chicago Tribune

WARSAW—This could be the week that was for one of Poland's biggest industrial giants.

The sprawling Ursus tractor factory on Warsaw's western outskirts is bankrupt. Officials say they can't meet their payroll Tuesday and can't pay an $870,000 power bill due Saturday.

Unless something drastic happens, the factory will be forced to shut down. More than 9,000 men and women will be thrown out of work overnight. And President Lech Walesa will face his most serious challenge since coming to power seven months ago.

Ursus is more than merely Poland's lone tractor producer and one of its largest industrial plants. It is a political symbol.

Throughout the 1980s, Ursus workers were at the forefront of anti-communist demonstrations. Ursus stood firm when other factories were cowed by the strong-arm tactics of Poland's communist police.

Three weeks after he was sworn in as president, Walesa paid homage to the workers at Ursus by making a surprise visit to the plant. He praised the workers for their support and vowed to make their lives better.

But decades of communist mismanagement and inefficiency undermined Walesa's pledge. The plant is producing only a few tractors a month. It is $106 million in debt. And Walesa now has to decide whether to bail out a loyal, but losing, enterprise, or to let Ursus collapse on its own demerits.

It is a decision Walesa and his government are likely to face repeatedly in the coming months.

Industry minister Andrzej Zawislak said last week that Ursus was just the tip of the iceberg. Some 1,600 of Poland's 4,500 state-owned factories are unprofitable, or soon will be, he said.

On the whole, state enterprise, which contributes 80 percent of income to the budget, is on the verge of bankruptcy, Zawislak said.

In any country, the demise of a company like Ursus, with 9,000-plus workers, would be worrisome. But, in Poland the impact would be devastating.

Poland is 19 months into a U.S.-backed economic reform program that has been both effective and agonizing. Some 1.6 million people—9 percent of all workers—have lost their jobs in a country where unemployment was officially unknown two years ago.

Figures released last week by the government statistics bureau showed that, for the first time in 11 years, losses exceeded profits in state enterprises in the first half of 1991. Industrial production dropped 9.3 percent in the same period. And real wages were down 17.3 percent.

Ursus is a mirror of those failings, which Prime Minister Jan Krzysztof Bielecki blames on communist-inspired incompetence.

"We are dealing here with an example of economic incompetence, not to say sabotage, on a scale perhaps unheard of in this country," Bielecki said last week after a three-hour crisis meeting with the Ursus management.

"If we go on operating this way, the whole point of the economic reforms is jeopardized."

Hours after Bielecki's visit, four deputy ministers and two general directors of the Industry Ministry were fired. Then, on Monday, the minister of industry, Zawislak, resigned.

In a television interview last week, Zawislak said that Ursus was on the verge of collapse because its managers failed to change with the times.

"The concept of the tractor industry developed in the 1970s to match the central economy was continued," the minister said. "The result is that it collapsed because it had to."

Ursus produced 29,000 tractors last year, but ran deeply in the red. Former director Henryk Szczygiel, who was fired several weeks ago, claimed the plant needed to sell 42,000 tractors just to break even.

A new management team, headed by acting director Jan Buczkowski, met late last week with government representatives and proposed a bailout scheme, details of which were kept secret. The leader of the Solidarity trade union at the factory said Prime Minister Bielecki assured him the government "will find a solution."

"The problem right now is we have no source of cash," Buczkowski said. "There's no money for wages, and I myself will not collect my July pay for the first time in my 30 years of work."

Three small Ursus satellite plants across the country were shut down earlier this week because they couldn't pay their power bills. Workers at those plants received only a fraction of their pay in June and may go without any salary in July, company officials said.

Those closures, and the threatened collapse of the main plant, have tested the patience of even the most loyal Ursus workers. There are growing signs of frustration with the government they helped bring to power.

"For three years we have been talking about the things that are happening in our plant and the threats that are facing it," said Janusz Sciskalski, chairman of Solidarity at the main Ursus plant, who hinted last week his workers were being "sabotaged" by the government.

"If no efforts are being made to counteract all this and warnings are being played down, I guess we have good reason to speak of sabotage."

Another prominent labor leader was even more outspoken.

Zdzislaw Odczimek, head of the powerful Workers Council at the main factory, predicted widespread protests unless the government came up with the money to bail out Ursus on payday this Tuesday.

"If we aren't paid, then on Aug. 13 the work force ... will be marching on the Belvedere [the presidential palace], and I'll be at their head," he said.

Source: "Troubled Tractor Plant Puts Polish Government to the Test," *The Chicago Tribune*, July 30, 1991, Section 3, pp. 1-2.

CHAPTER ANSWERS

The Chapter in Brief

1. Capitalism 2. Socialism 3. Labor 4. Surplus value 5. Labor productivity 6. Demand for 7. Supply of 8. Command 9. Gosplan 10. Shortages 11. Turnover 12. Perestroika 13. 60% 14. Will be 15. 25% 16. More 17. Poland 18. Hungary

Key Terms Review

1. Centrally planned economy 2. Gosplan 3. Command economy 4. Materials balance 5. Surplus value 6. Consumer sovereignty 7. Labor theory of value 8. Turnover tax 9. Socialism 10. Economic system

Concept Review

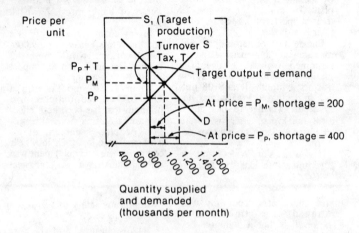

a. Shortage, 400,000

b. Shortage, 200,000

c. Shortage, the subsidized price, price that would equate supply and demand; higher, less

d. Higher, less

Mastery Test

1. c 2. c 3. a 4. e 5. d 6. d 7. d 8. c 9. d 10. e 11. c 12. d 13. e 14. b 15. e 16. a 17. e 18. c

Think It Through

1. Capitalism relies on self-interest, private ownership, and markets to allocate resources. Socialism is distrustful of self-interest (the profit motive) and in the extreme case of a command economy, resources are allocated with extensive central planning. Capitalism rewards input suppliers on the basis of the quantity and productivity of inputs supplied. This is not necessarily so if markets are imperfectly competitive. A socialist state earns a profit from state-owned resources and redistributes it to workers in the form of wages and services. Modern mixed economies try to achieve equity in the distribution of income through transfer payments. In a competitive market economy, firms have an incentive to keep costs as low as possible, resulting in technological efficiency. Managers in socialist states often confront a much different set

of costs and incentives, which reward managers not for minimizing costs, but for meeting production targets. In capitalist economies with competitive markets, consumers are sovereign. There is free choice in consumption, the employment of inputs, and the production of output. In a socialist state, individual freedoms are much less important than the achievement of political goals. A capitalist system is subject to recurrent ups and downs in real GNP and the rate of unemployment. The incidence of business cycles can be lessened considerably in command economies because aggregate demand is strictly controlled. If there are ups and downs in production, they are likely the result of supply-side shocks rather than fluctuations in aggregate demand.

2. Competitive economies that rely on markets to allocate resources realize a higher level of technological efficiency than economies that rely on central planning. In a market system, self-interest coordinates decisions such that resources are allocated to their most productive employments. Workers are free to offer their labor services to the highest bidder. Entrepreneurs bring resources together to produce goods desired by consumers in hopes of earning a profit. Economic survival in a competitive economy requires technological efficiency. Firms that are unable to produce at minimum possible unit costs will exit the market in the long run. Even in the case of modern mixed economies having many imperfectly competitive markets, the level of efficiency is much higher than in command economies. Most socialist nations are recognizing the power of incentives. As noted in the text, the Soviet Union is embarking on major market-based reforms that require the pursuit of self-interest in order to succeed.

Analyzing the News

1. Under the Communist system, production levels were targeted by the government. As long as these targets were met there was no incentive on the part of plant managers to produce more—even if demand conditions called for increased production. More significant perhaps is the fact that plants were not run as profit-maximizing entities. There were virtually no incentives on the part of managers to be innovative or efficient. Workers in such plants also faced severe disincentives to be as productive as possible. As long as they met their quota, it was not necessary to worry about quality.

2. For these nations the introduction of markets and competition will create short-run transitional problems. For managers, competition will mean they must now worry about productivity, costs amd employee morale. For workers, if they shirk on the job they will find it more likely that other workers will be hired to replace them. The transition to a market economy will take time and will not be easy, as this Polish plant and its government have discovered.